UNSUNG

Unsung

A HISTORY OF WOMEN
IN AMERICAN MUSIC

Century Edition

Christine Ammer

AMADEUS PRESS
Portland, Oregon

This second edition of *Unsung: A History of Women in American Music* is revised and expanded from the first edition, copyright © 1980 by Christine Ammer, published by Greenwood Press, Westport, Connecticut.

Century edition published in 2001 by Amadeus Press
(an imprint of Timber Press, Inc.)
The Haseltine Building
133 S.W. Second Avenue, Suite 450
Portland, Oregon 97204
U.S.A.

Printed in Hong Kong

Library of Congress Cataloging-in-Publication data

Ammer, Christine.
    Unsung : a history of women in American music / Christine
Ammer.—Century ed., 2nd ed.
      p.   cm.
    Includes bibliographical references (p.   ) and index.
    ISBN 1-57467-058-1 — ISBN 1-57467-061-1 (pbk.)
    1. Women musicians—United States. 2. Women composers—United
States. 3. Musicians—United States. 4. Composers—United States.
I. Title.

ML82 .A45 2000
780'.82'0973—dc21

                                      00-042017

To all women musicians,
then and now

CONTENTS

2

PREFACE TO THE
CENTURY EDITION

*F*OR THIS ENLARGED and revised second edition, I have tried to bring the text up to date, based on my own research and that of others in the field during the past two decades. I have inserted new material throughout the book, rewritten and restructured portions of the text, and added two new chapters. Dozens of composers and performers have been added, including women involved in ragtime and jazz from the late 1800s to the present. Singers remain omitted, as in the first edition. They compete only with other women in their own voice parts, and hence are immune to the gender discrimination faced by women composers, instrumentalists, and conductors. This book does include a few brief discussions of men musicians, as did the first edition, in order to set the scene for the accomplishments of women.

An important development since the publication of the first edition has been the increasing interest of students and scholars in researching and writing the history of women in music. There have been substantial new biographies of individual women composers, dissertations on and musical analysis of their compositions, and collected recorded music and scores. And there has been increasing public interest in their music. Since 1983, three women have been awarded the Pulitzer Prize for their compositions, whereas previously only men had won it. Colleges, universities, and conservatories have increasingly instituted courses on women in music and usually engage women scholars to teach them.

The picture for performers also has changed. An increasing number of women are seen in first-rank orchestras, a handful of women conductors have gained national attention, and individual instrumentalists have won recognition. In 1999 the Avery Fisher Prize was given to a woman for the first time—in fact, to three women violinists.

Consequently it has been suggested that *Unsung* is no longer an appropriate title for this book, but given the perspective of two centuries, from 1800 to 2000, the achievements of women musicians are still largely overlooked. The standard texts for courses in music history still omit all but a very few women. Men still outnumber women by two to one in the major orchestras. Men's compositions outnumber women's enormously in catalogs of recordings. Men music faculty members both outnumber and outrank women. The Metropolitan Opera as of 2000 has not produced a single opera by a woman composer since it first did in its 1902–3 season. As for the general public, just imagine the proportion of individuals who have heard of Beethoven to those who have heard of Amy Beach or Ellen Taaffe Zwilich. So *Unsung* it remains, in the hope that this description will not always be true.

Although this book focuses especially on the lives and work of outstanding individuals, it does not pretend to include all the women who have been active in American music since 1800. Such an exhaustive survey remains to be done. Moreover, in contemporary music it may not even cover all those who will be regarded, with adequate hindsight, to have been the most important of our time.

For the century edition I extend heartfelt gratitude to Adrienne Fried Block, City University of New York; film composer Jeanine Cowen; J. Michele Edwards, Macalester College; Joan Ferst, Cleveland Women's Orchestra; Ellie Hisama, Brooklyn College Conservatory of Music; Ralph Locke, Eastman School of Music; Jeff Ostergren, American Symphony Orchestra League; Karin Pendle, University of Cincinnati College-Conservatory of Music; Sharon Guertin Shafer, Trinity College, Washington, D.C.; Catherine Parsons Smith, University of Nevada, Reno; Paul M. Tai, New World Records; and Judith Tick, Northeastern University. Special thanks also to musicologist Liane Curtis and trumpeters Susan Fleet and Susan Slaughter who have been outstandingly active on behalf of women musicians, and to the composers, conductors, and instrumentalists who openly shared their experiences with me. This book has been vastly improved through their assistance and advice; its errors and shortcomings are solely my own.

PREFACE TO THE
FIRST EDITION

*I*N THE MID-1970s America's bicentennial prompted celebrations of national achievement in many areas of endeavor, including music. At least two ambitious surveys of American music were undertaken by commercial record companies, yet the only woman composer represented on any of several dozen records issued was Mrs. H. H. A. Beach. The implication was that there had been no other women composers.

In 1975 I was asked to introduce to a concert audience the Quintessence, a wind quintet made up wholly of women. To prepare my introduction I looked for background information about women instrumentalists and discovered, after a few days of research, that almost no such information was readily available. Again, the implication was that there had been no women instrumentalists. But here, at least, there was a perceived discrepancy: The school orchestras in which our children play invariably include as many or more girls than boys, whereas the symphony orchestras we see consist predominantly of men.

Several years of research showed that women indeed have been writing and performing music for as long as men have. But, owing to the social climate of earlier times, their work went unnoticed, unpublished, unperformed, and was quickly forgotten. This book is a history of the role played by women in American music, as performers, composers, and teachers, during the past 200 years. The musicians included are instrumentalists, conductors, and composers; singers have been omitted because, for a variety of reasons, considerable information about them is widely available.

I am deeply grateful to the many persons who have answered questions and made suggestions, criticisms, and corrections and, in particular, to those who have assisted the vast amount of research that went into this book. Among those who merit special thanks for helping are Roberta Bitgood, American Guild of Organists; Willa Brigham, Henniker, New Hampshire; Constance T. Ellis, Augusta, Maine; Neva Garner Greenwood, Falls Church, Virginia; Calderon Howe, New Orleans; Anne Hull, Westport, Connecticut; Walter S.

Jenkins, Tulane University; Virginia Koontz, Sacramento; Ruth Lomon, Lexington, Massachusetts; Katherine D. Moore, Knoxville, Tennessee; Patricia Morehead, Toronto; Barbara J. Owen, Organ Historical Society; Harrison Potter, South Hadley, Massachusetts; William Strickland, Westport, Connecticut; Milos Velimirovic, University of Virginia; Frances Wiggin, Maine Federation of Music Clubs; the staffs of the music divisions of the Boston Public Library and New York Public Library; Esta J. Astor, Maine Historical Society; R. Jayne Craven, Public Library of Cincinnati and Hamilton County; Rosalinda I. Hack, Chicago Public Library; Marjorie McDonald, National Federation of Music Clubs; Wayne D. Shirley, Library of Congress; Judith Wentzell, Portland (Maine) Public Library; James B. Wright, University of New Mexico Library; scholars Adrienne Fried Block, Laurine Elkins Marlow, Carol Neuls-Bates, and Judith Tick, who have done valuable research on women in music; and composers Beth Anderson, Karen Phillips, Julia Smith, and Nancy Van de Vate, who have been extraordinarily active on behalf of their fellows.

1

THE FIRST FLOWERING —
AT THE ORGAN

Then if there must be a Singing, one alone must sing, not all (or if all), the men only, and not the women. And their reason is: Because it is not permitted to a woman to speake in the Church, how then shall they sing? Much less is it permitted to them to prophecy in the Church. And singing the Psalms is a kind of Prophecying.

Reverend John Cotton, 1647 tract in defense of psalm singing[1]

*T*HESE WERE THE ARGUMENTS of those early Puritans who felt that true Christians should sing to the Lord only within their own hearts. Unlike them, the Reverend John Cotton believed that singing is both harmless and beautiful, and that the entire congregation, male and female, should worship the Lord in song. Presumably some others agreed with him. But for the most part the early American colonists, if they did not actually oppose music, paid scant attention to it. Music was all right in its place, but its place was miniscule indeed. To the sober and practical settler, it was a luxury, a "frill," a view still held at the start of the twenty-first century by some public school educators who would eliminate it from the curriculum. This sentiment was expressed in a letter from Leonard Hoar, who later became president of Harvard College, written to his nephew Josiah Flynt from London in 1661. Hoar wrote that he would not bring his nephew a fiddle because music was a waste of time; he would, however, bring instruments for Josiah's sisters, "for whom 'tis more proper and they also have more leisure to looke after it."[2]

The same strictures did not always apply to vocal music, for the colonists did sing. It is not known today exactly what they brought with them from England in the way of secular music, but congregational singing was and is a part of many Protestant church services, and there is a clear record of the psalters (psalm books) that they used. Indeed, among the first books ever printed in British North America was the Bay Psalm Book, a translation of the psalms made by Puritan ministers in 1640 and published in many subsequent editions.

In the typical congregation, however, there rarely were enough books to go around, and even if there had been, few if any of the members could read

13

music. Consequently, by the later 1600s most churches in America used the practice of lining out; that is, the minister or deacon or clerk would read aloud each line of a psalm before it was sung by the congregation. The dozen or so melodies that were used for all the psalms were familiar. However, they had been learned long ago and transmitted by rote, so that in time distortions inevitably crept in.

By the 1720s it was well recognized by those who had any training or ear for music that most congregational singing was abysmally bad. In 1721 the Reverend Thomas Walter described psalm singing as "a mere disorderly noise . . . sounding like five hundred different tunes roared out at the same time, and so little in time that they were often one or two words apart."[3] Walter was among a few concerned individuals who began trying to remedy the situation. They published instruction books for reading the notes, and some instructors set themselves up as "singing masters" and began to conduct "singing schools" where they taught the "rudiments of Vocal Musick."

The singing masters traveled from town to town, using a room in someone's home or in a tavern or the local school for a classroom. Practically all pursued another trade, their music representing but a sideline. The typical singing school met two to three evenings per week for three months or so, after which the singing master moved on to another town. The master taught the fundamentals of vocal performance, especially tone production, note reading, and ensemble singing.[4]

There was no question but that singing schools were coeducational. Indeed, their enormous popularity was due chiefly to the fact that they gave young people a legitimate excuse to meet together during the evening, ostensibly—and also actually—to learn to read music and sing from the tune books. They thus provided a rare opportunity for social intercourse and courtship that could hardly have occurred without the presence of both sexes.

The singing school originated in the New England colonies but rapidly spread up and down the length of the Atlantic coast, and it soon gave rise to the first school of native American composition. From the 1720s to the 1770s numerous new collections of church music had appeared, but they were largely compilations of English hymns and anthems. The singing schools fostered a growing demand for new tunes and new tune books, and in time many of the singing masters themselves obliged by composing songs for this purpose. Between about 1750 and 1825 literally thousands of pieces were written, by William Billings, Daniel Read, Andrew Law, and countless lesser-known men. Many of these tunes are spirited, original, and beautiful, and although for a time they were considered crude and unsophisticated, they are earning new admiration today.

The best products of singing-school training entered the ranks of organized church choirs, to provide sturdy leadership for faltering congregational singing. At least, this was true for the male pupils. Not many girls and women were permitted to sing in the eighteenth-century church choir, and in those Episcopal churches where singing was part of the liturgy they were excluded entirely.

Solos by women singers were not unknown, but they had no place in church. Operas, chiefly in the form of the popular English ballad opera (of which the most famous is and was John Gay's *Beggar's Opera*), were being performed in New York, Charleston, and other American centers during the second half of the eighteenth century, but they were viewed more as theatrical performances than as music. A number of English singers became well known through such performances, and by the late eighteenth century a few, such as Mrs. Oldmixon, Miss Broadhurst, and Miss Brett—all Englishwomen—were considered fine musicians.

Ballad operas were not the only musical import during the late 1700s. Portions of the oratorios of Handel and Haydn and works by Grétry, Stamitz, and Mozart began to be heard increasingly. Concerts of instrumental and vocal music, presented sporadically from the 1730s on, became more frequent, and during the last decade of the eighteenth century a large-scale immigration of professional European musicians took place. One of the most talented of the new arrivals was J. C. Gottlieb Graupner, a German oboist who had played in Haydn's orchestra in London. He came to Prince Edward Island in the early 1790s, went in 1796 to Charleston, where he married, and finally settled in Boston in 1797 or 1798. His wife, Catherine, was a talented and highly experienced singer, who as Mrs. Hellyer (or Hillier) had made a successful career in English ballad opera. Catherine Graupner soon appeared on the concert platform beside her husband. A program presented by Graupner on May 15, 1798, in Salem included two solos by his wife with instrumental accompaniment, as well as a song by a Miss Solomon, a duet by Mrs. Graupner and Mr. Collins, and a quartet by three gentlemen and Mrs. Graupner. In subsequent years Catherine Graupner became one of Boston's leading soloists, and upon her death in 1821 the principal Boston music journal, the *Euterpiad*, said that "for many years she was the only female vocalist in this metropolis."

The inadequacies of existing choirs and choral groups became all too apparent when they attempted the newly imported choruses of Handel and Haydn, or anthems by Purcell, Blow, and Arne. The music was simply too ambitious for even the most gifted of the singing-school graduates. As a result, musical societies began to be formed for the express purpose of learning and performing more difficult and larger works, such as Handel's *Messiah* and Haydn's *The Creation*. Free from the restrictions imposed by religious worship, these groups could, in theory, include women. In fact, however, they did so only by express invitation rather than routinely.

Among the earliest organizations was the St. Cecilia Society of Charleston, South Carolina, founded in 1762; it had 120 members who were permitted to invite ladies.[5] The Stoughton (Massachusetts) Musical Society was founded on

November 7, 1786, by residents of Stoughton, Canton, and Sharon, neighboring towns just south of Boston. It proved to be somewhat less exclusive than most: Women were invited to take part in the singing of choruses, although they were not actually considered members, a rule that remained unchanged for a century. Likewise, the Handel Society of Dartmouth College, founded a few years later, met weekly to prepare the best musical works attainable. Members were chosen after an examination and counted their admission an honor; ladies were admitted only as "honorary members."

By far the most influential of the numerous societies formed during the first half of the nineteenth century was Boston's Handel and Haydn Society, which today claims to be the oldest still in existence. It was formally organized on April 20, 1815, with a constitution signed by thirty-one gentlemen, after a series of meetings held in Graupner's Hall. The chorus of the society was made up of members of the choirs of nine Boston churches, presumably the cream of the crop. Although women were not then—and long were not—admitted as members, the tradition of permitting them to sing began with the first concert. On December 25, 1815, a chorus of ninety men and ten women performed the first part of *The Creation* and selections from Handel's works. By 1817 the chorus had been enlarged to 150, of whom twenty were women.

Allegedly there were sound reasons for excluding women singers. Since women were not supposed to lead, in melody or elsewhere, the men sang the melody, usually in the tenor, as well as taking the alto (or counter) part, while the harmony assigned to the women was necessarily sung an octave higher. Consequently, as one contemporary critic described it, "Our ears were assailed with females singing thirds and fifths above the melody or treble. This custom ought to be abolished, being inconsistent with the true principles of choral harmony. Soprano voices should invariably confine themselves to the melody."[6]

Although several early church music compilers had given the melody to the soprano,[7] the older custom deplored by the critic persisted widely. His advice was not heeded by the Handel and Haydn Society for some years, and lesser, more provincial choruses probably were even slower to come round. In 1827, when Lowell Mason conducted the society in portions of Mozart's Requiem Mass, the ranks of the women singers were reinforced and they finally got the treble part; moreover, a few women altos were allowed to join the two or three countertenors who normally sang the alto part. By 1830 the society had about 100 male singers and twenty-five "female assistants"; the latter were not members and took part by express invitation only. The overall balance of parts produced by this proportion takes little effort of imagination: The bass voices undoubtedly drowned out the sopranos. The famous nineteenth-century critic John Sullivan Dwight commented a few years later, with admirable restraint, that the parts were "poorly balanced."[8]

In view of this obvious prejudice against women musicians, it is all the more remarkable that in 1818 and again in 1820 the Handel and Haydn Society should offer the position of organist to a woman, one Miss Sophia Hewitt. In her late teens at the time, she declined the first invitation but accepted the second, and, for the next decade, she worked for the society as organist and accompanist. She was the only woman they ever employed in this capacity, before or since. Moreover, at times during this period she also served as organist at two of Boston's principal churches, Chauncy Place Church and Catholic Cathedral, the only woman to fill such an important position.

Although the role of women in vocal music had been clearly defined by the colonists, their position with regard to instrumental music was more ambiguous. Instruments had been abhorred by the early Puritans, who would not permit any instrument in church. Nevertheless, by 1713 an organ was imported from England, and the following year it was installed in Boston's King's Chapel.[9] It was one of the first organs in North America, though earlier ones may have been in New York's Old Trinity Church and Philadelphia's Gloria Dei Church.[10] Whether due to high cost or lingering prejudice, relatively few other churches acquired organs, and in 1800 most church choirs still were accompanied, if at all, by flute, bassoon, and "bass viol" (cello). In 1815 only four Boston churches had organs, though that number was doubled by the following year.[11]

As for home instruments, according to Dwight's estimate[12] fewer than fifty of Boston's 6000 families owned a piano. Keyboard instruments—harpsichords and later pianos—had long been considered genteel enough for ladies to play. Indeed, by extension they came to be regarded as somewhat effeminate. Thus the ad placed in the *Columbian Centinel* in 1799 by Mrs. P. A. von Hagen, a Dutch organist who had recently moved to Boston from New York, respectfully informed the ladies of Boston that she was prepared to teach them the harpsichord and piano forte, as well as voice and organ.[13] Presumably gentlemen would have no interest in such pursuits, or if they did, they would not consider being taught by a lady. But such instrumental playing was almost exclusively confined to the home. During the eighteenth century, just about the only participation by women in public concerts was as singers, and even that was relatively rare. The Handel and Haydn Society did not engage a soprano or alto soloist for some years.[14] Thus a piano performance such as that by Miss M. A. Wrighten in Boston on October 3, 1795, of Kotzwara's *Battle of Prague* was a distinct novelty.[15]

Presumably Sophia Hewitt had unusual qualifications to be offered a position by such a prestigious organization as the Handel and Haydn Society. However, the facts concerning her life are sparse, and even the exact date of her birth has been lost.[16]

A great deal more is known of her father's history, and from it something of Sophia's early life may be pieced together. James Hewitt, born in 1770 in Dartmoor, England, entered the Royal Navy while in his teens but took a dislike to it and became a musician. He soon became leader (principal violinist) of the orchestra at the court of King George III, and allegedly King George IV presented him with an Amati cello. In 1790 he married a Miss Lamb, but both his wife and an infant daughter died a year later; in 1792 he was persuaded to come to New York and lead the orchestra of the Old American Company, a theatrical group organized by John Henry (of Hallam and Henry).

Very soon after his arrival in New York, Hewitt announced his first concert, which according to current custom was to be a "benefit" for himself and four other newly landed musicians. The program for this event, held on September 21, 1792, attests to Hewitt's sophisticated tastes; included were a Haydn overture, a quartet by Pleyel, and a symphony and flute quartet by Stamitz. Among the "novelty" items offered was *Overture in 9 movements, Expressive of a Battle,* composed by Hewitt himself.

During the next few years, Hewitt was extremely active in New York as a violinist, composer, concert manager, and publisher (he bought the New York branch of Benjamin Carr's Philadelphia music publishing firm in 1798). He composed the music for what is believed to be the very first American ballad opera, an anti-Federalist piece named *Tammany,* with a libretto by Ann Julia Hatton, sister of the English actress Mrs. Siddons and wife of a New York maker of musical instruments. *Tammany* was first produced on March 3, 1794, and the composer, who presumably also led the orchestra in the premiere, was hissed, booed, and even physically attacked by pro-Federalist members of the audience. The work was hailed by the anti-Federalists, however, and whatever his true political sentiments may have been, Hewitt became famous, or infamous, for this opera.

He also found time for courtship, and in 1795, at New York's Trinity Church, he married Eliza King, the daughter of a British army officer. The second Mrs. Hewitt was an educated woman. She had studied in Paris, where she had resided during the French Revolution, and had come to America with her father, who had an estate to settle. She was not a musician, at least not professionally. There is no record of her joining in her husband's musical performances, a collaboration that might have been expected, since Hewitt had an unusually open attitude toward women musicians. Shortly after coming to America, he had collaborated on a book of songs for piano or harpsichord with Mary Ann Pownall (1751–1796), an English actress, singer, and composer who came to America in 1792 with the Hallam and Henry Company. The book was advertised in a number of newspapers in 1793, and the following year Pownall and Hewitt produced another book, *Six Songs for the Harpsichord.*

When the children of Hewitt's second marriage began to come along, it was Hewitt who undertook their musical education. The Hewitts had four sons and two daughters, all of whom eventually became involved with music. Sophia Henriette Hewitt was the oldest, born in 1799 or 1800.[17] A child prodigy, she first performed in public at the age of seven: She played a piano sonata in a concert put on by her father at New York's City Hotel on April 14, 1807.

She played again in February and April of the following year, and she continued to appear in public on various occasions until she was twelve. Reportedly she was always warmly received.

Despite his many activities in New York, Hewitt decided to move to Boston, probably in 1812. He had visited that city earlier, having led an orchestra there on September 26, 1808, to begin the season. This probably was the orchestra established sometime in 1807 or 1808 and conducted by Gottlieb Graupner, who, as John Sullivan Dwight put it, "formed the nucleus of the first meagre combination which could be called in any sense an orchestra."[18] In any event, in 1809 Catherine Graupner sang the premiere of a song by James Hewitt, "How Cold and Piercing Blows the Wind." It is probable that Hewitt and the Graupners were acquainted. In 1810 Hewitt played in a Boston concert on June 26, in another in August, and on October 2 he "celebrated his return to Boston" with yet another concert, in which his daughter Sophia performed a piano sonata by Pleyel.

By this time Graupner, whose activities included music publishing and a music store on Franklin Street, had organized his sixteen-man instrumental group, the Philharmonic Society, in which he himself played double bass and conducted. Formed early that year, the society began as a quasi-social group that met weekly to perform Haydn's symphonies. Hewitt, however, was not invited to play with them. Indeed, at least one writer presumes a growing rivalry between him and the Graupners, and believes that considerable coldness developed.[19] Perhaps Hewitt presented a threat to Graupner's established rule over Boston's concert life. Or, more probably, audiences were dividing their time among a greater variety of events, and to the extent that Hewitt added to the competition he was unwelcome.

By 1812 Hewitt had two regular jobs in Boston: He was organist at Trinity Church, and he was in charge of music at the Federal Street Theatre. In 1814 Sophia again appeared in public, playing Steibelt's piano concerto, *The Storm*. Of this performance *Repertory* reported: "It is far beyond our ability to do her ample justice. . . . the spontaneous bursts of applause which followed are the best tribute of praise. We never witnessed a performance on the Piano Forte which could compare with it."[20]

Sometime during the next few years Sophia is thought to have moved back to New York, where she taught music at Mrs. Brenton's Boarding School. She also sang occasionally at the New York Oratorios and often performed at the concerts of the Euterpian Society. She had studied organ with George K. Jackson, and in New York she took harp and piano lessons with Mr. Ferrand and Mr. Moran.[21]

On August 28, 1817, Sophia was back in Boston, where she performed the piano part of a trio by Henri Joseph Taskin and *German Hymn* by Pleyel with variations for piano and flute, as well as singing a song composed by her father, "Rest Thee, Babe," and several glees, a popular form of part song. In December she appeared with the Handel and Haydn Society in New York, and the following year the society offered her the position of organist for the first time, but she refused.

The society had had considerable turnover in organists. Its first organist, Samuel Stockwell, died in the course of the second season. Jackson, Sophia's teacher, would have been a logical replacement, but he asked too high a fee when invited to play for a *Messiah* performance, and so Samuel Priestly Taylor was invited to come up from New York. In 1817 Taylor agreed to come to Boston for a fortnight to play the organ at the final four rehearsals and three concerts for the sum of $200 plus expenses, which also was a steep price. In the end Samuel Cooper became organist for the remainder of the season, at the end of which Jackson's services were again sought. Reportedly Jackson demanded full control of the society if he was to deal with it in any capacity, which meant he would have to be named president. Instead the society offered the job to Sophia Hewitt and, when she declined, reappointed Taylor.

That Sophia should have been considered an acceptable substitute for either Jackson or Taylor was high praise indeed. Jackson (1745–1822), born in Oxford, England, had been a choirboy at the Chapel Royal, sang at the Handel commemoration in London (1784), and received the degree of Doctor of Music from St. Andrews College (Scotland) in 1791. Five years later he came to America, landing in Norfolk and gradually working his way up the Atlantic coast. He settled in New York as a teacher but in September 1812 he moved to Boston. Within weeks he was made organist at the Brattle Street Church. A crusty character, the 300-pound organist was banished to western Massachusetts during the War of 1812 because, never having become an American citizen, he was officially an enemy alien and therefore not allowed to remain near Boston Harbor. In 1815 he returned to Boston and was organist successively at King's Chapel, Trinity Church, and St. Paul's, quarreling with each before moving on to the next post. Nevertheless, during these years he was regarded as Boston's outstanding musician and teacher, having written a treatise on theory and published several collections of choral music, as well as compositions of his own.[22]

Taylor, a much younger man (born in 1778), had also begun his musical career as a choirboy in England but was already playing the organ by the age of twelve. He came to America in 1806 and the following year was appointed organist of Christ Church in New York. He subsequently directed concerts at St. Paul's, called Oratorios, and is credited as being the first to introduce Anglican chant to New York. Taylor accepted the Handel and Haydn Society's appointment in 1818, but in January 1820 he resigned; however, he considerately offered to remain until a replacement had been found.

By that time Sophia had appeared a number of times in Boston with the Philharmonic Society, which regularly assisted at the Handel and Haydn performances, as well as in recitals and other events. Her father was living in New

York during 1818 and 1819,[23] and possibly other members of the family joined him there during those years. Sophia made at least three appearances in New York in 1818. But by spring of 1820 she was again living in Boston, as seen from the following advertisement in the April 1 and April 8 issues of the *Euterpiad*:[24] "Miss Hewitt begs leave to inform her friends that she teaches the Piano Forte, Harp, and Singing—Her terms may be known by applying at Mrs. Rowson's, Hollis Street, or at the Franklin Music Warehouse, No. 6 Milk Street." On April 13, 1820, Sophia performed a piano concerto in a concert for the benefit of a Mr. Granger, probably the violinist of the Philharmonic Society, which was presented under the direction and patronage of that society. At the same concert the society's leader and Sophia's future husband, Paul Louis Ostinelli, performed a piece for solo violin.[25]

Ostinelli was, according to one writer, a graduate of the Paris Conservatory. The same writer says the violinist made his Boston debut in 1818, but at least a year earlier he was already playing second violin in a thirteen-man orchestra led by Graupner at a Handel and Haydn concert. On September 7, 1818, Ostinelli gave a concert—this may have been his debut as a soloist—and at a second concert given the following week a composition of his own was performed. This second concert also featured the first performance in Boston of a work by Beethoven (the particular work is not named); by coincidence, the second performance of Beethoven's work, on February 27, 1819, featured his Piano Sonata in A-flat, op. 26, by Sophia Hewitt. Allegedly she never played Beethoven in public again.[26]

By June 1820 Sophia had been joined in Boston by at least one other Hewitt and had moved. A series of advertisements in the *Euterpiad* announced her new address at 32 Federal Street "where she will be happy to instruct a Class of Scholars either on the Harp or Piano Forte."[27] On September 9 Sophia was accompanist for a recital by Mrs. French, who was at least as notable a soprano as Jackson was an organist. On September 26 Sophia was formally engaged as organist to the Handel and Haydn Society. About the time of her appointment, one critic noted that she was "the leading professional pianist of Boston. . . . Her ability as an organist may be estimated from the fact that [at] the rehearsals and concerts of the [Apollo] Society she played the most elaborate accompaniments from copies which had been sorely neglected by the proof reader."[28] There is some question as to how much Sophia was paid. Harold Earle Johnson, author of a history of the society, said her predecessor, Samuel Taylor, was paid $87.50 per quarter but the society paid Sophia only $62.50 and later reduced this sum to $50 per quarter. However, this reduction allegedly was due to rising costs and reduced attendance at concerts, and the orchestra's fees were correspondingly reduced.[29]

If these salary cuts actually were made, it must have been during the first year of Sophia's employment. The earliest receipts of the Handel and Haydn Society still in existence date from 1819, but the first for an organist is dated

November 6, 1821, signed by Sophia Hewitt, for receiving $50 for one quarter's salary as organist (July 23 to October 23, 1821). Trinity Church, an early leader in Boston's music, paid its organist $100 per year in 1800 and raised this to $200 about 1810, and "through a succession of distinguished ministrations on the organ by James Hewitt [c. 1812–1816] and the thrice-eminent Dr. Jackson [c. 1817] the salary remained the same."[30] It seems unlikely that the Handel and Haydn Society's offering would have been very different. Its orchestra members were paid $40 each for the entire season—some receipts signed by Louis Ostinelli attest to this figure—so it appears quite reasonable that the organist, who had to play at weekly rehearsals as well as at special rehearsals and concerts, would be paid $200 per year. In any event, that is what Sophia was paid from July 1821 to October 30, 1830. At some time during this period Sophia also was organist at Chauncy Place Church and the Catholic Cathedral, but there is no record of when, or of how much she was paid.

Obviously she did not consider herself fully occupied, for in the *Euterpiad* during the November, December, and January following the start of her engagement with the Handel and Haydn Society she announced her willingness to teach piano, organ, harp, and singing. Since organs were even scarcer in Boston than pianos, it is likely that either the society or one of the churches let her use its organ for this purpose.

Sophia's activities during 1821 are not evident other than in salary receipts from the Handel and Haydn Society. The next year, however, was to be one of her busiest. On April 27, 1822, the *Euterpiad* announced a public benefit concert for Miss Hewitt, consisting of instrumental and vocal music presented "with the assistance of the Gentlemen of the Orchestra and many Amateurs of distinction." The editor goes on to say that she "takes rank, in her line, with the first of the profession, and as a Pianiste is confessedly among the most attractive to a general audience." Even discounting the florid turn of phrase then current and the fact that Sophia was a steady advertiser in this journal, the writer's admiration seems sincere. The next issue of the journal carried her biography—one in a series of biographies of distinguished contemporary musicians—in which her keyboard artistry is described: "Her Playing is plain sensible and that of a Gentlewoman; she neither takes by storm, nor by surprise, but she gradually wins upon the understanding, while the ear, though it never fills the senses with ecstacy, drinks in full satisfaction."[31]

The benefit concert took place the following week to a full house, and on May 25 the *Euterpiad* carried the expected good review, expressed with becoming restraint: "The efforts of Miss Hewitt to produce an evening's entertainment worthy of the liberal patronage she experienced on the evening of the 14th were highly satisfactory." In the same issue Sophia ran an advertisement thanking her friends and the public for their patronage, and the members of the "Societies"—suggesting her involvement with more than just the Handel and Haydn Society—and the orchestra for their liberal assistance.[32]

At least one gentleman of the orchestra must have been especially helpful and was rewarded a few months later. On a Sunday in August 1822 Sophia and Louis Ostinelli were married.[33] Sophia had taken to heart critic and biographer John Rowe Parker's description of her virtues: "the present instance [meaning Sophia] proves sufficiently that the public exercise of a talent is not incompatible with the grace, the ornament, and all the virtues of domestic life."[34]

At this time the newlyweds were the stars of the younger musical world. Sophia was held in the highest regard. Ostinelli was leader of both the theater orchestra and the Philharmonic Society and gave lessons in violin, Spanish guitar, lyre, and singing at their home at 32 Federal Street, as well as offering to accompany on the violin any of Sophia's pupils who should require it. The couple was in demand for recitals and soon began to travel about New England. In October they went to Portland, Maine, to perform in the church of the Reverend Dr. Nichols, the old First Parish Church of Portland, in which an organ had been installed the preceding spring. Sophia was to play the organ, and Ostinelli to lead the orchestra and introduce the solos on the violin, while members of Portland's Beethoven Society, which had been founded in 1819, and other "Amateurs" were to assist.[35] Most likely Ostinelli had considerable conducting experience from his work as leader with the Handel and Haydn Society; although the society's original by-laws, later revised, said the president must also conduct, both chorus and orchestra tended to follow the time indicated by the leader.

The following year Sophia was the first to perform on a new English organ purchased for $550 by the South Parish Church of Augusta (Maine). The records here say that she had married "but a few months before" and that the Ostinellis were still on their wedding tour.[36] However, if they did undertake an extended tour of New England, it is not indicated in the receipts of the Handel and Haydn Society, which show no interruption of Sophia's salary. On the other hand, she may have been excused from some rehearsals during a wedding trip without losing any pay, and in fact the signature and handwriting on one receipt, dated May 1, 1823, and acknowledging payment for January 23 to April 23 of that year, differ somewhat from the others, so perhaps someone else collected her salary for her. Interestingly enough, except for two later receipts signed by Sophia (as Sophia Ostinelli), the remainder, through 1830, are signed by her husband. Obviously this was customary at the time, since married women had no legal rights, could not own property, and had no money of their own. The receipts for a number of married vocal soloists were also signed by their husbands.

On September 25, 1823, Ostinelli played in another concert in Portland, Maine, performing two pieces for violin. At this time Ostinelli was considered without equal in America and would perform only "fine music." Once, when asked to play for dancing, Ostinelli cut the strings of his violin rather than perform.[37] How New Englanders reacted to such a dramatic gesture is unknown, but the anecdote certainly underlines the fact that Ostinelli was a serious musician, of a different breed from the country fiddlers who played dance music.

The next few years show a gap in musical reviews of the Ostinellis, but in 1826 the *Salem Register* tells of a last concert by Mrs. Mangeon, a well-known singer who, like many another before and since, gave a number of "last" performances toward the end of her career. On this occasion she was assisted by Mrs. Ostinelli, singer Miss Eberle, and several gentlemen. Mrs. Ostinelli played a concertante on the piano and provided piano accompaniment throughout.[38]

In 1827 Sophia's father died. James Hewitt had been estranged from his wife for some years, during which he had moved about—family records report-edly mention his involvement in several southern theater companies. He was seriously ill for the last months of his life and wrote several heartrending letters to his second son, James Lang Hewitt (1807–1853), a music publisher in Boston. He died in either New York or Boston, the former seeming more likely.[39] He left a large number of original compositions—keyboard pieces, waltzes, battle pieces, rondos, teaching pieces, and, especially, marches.

By this time the Ostinellis had a child, their first and, so far as is known, their only one. Their daughter Eliza was born in Boston, perhaps as early as 1824 but possibly later—no record of her birth survives. Again the Handel and Haydn Society did not interrupt Sophia's salary; presumably she contin-ued to perform during at least part of her pregnancy and following her con-finement. No portrait or written description of Sophia survives, but some years later a former neighbor recalled the family during this period and describes Ostinelli: "He was of middle stature or a little under, rather stout, with broad shoulders, and carried his head a trifle one side, the result of professional habit, and moved with an elastic step. His features were good and the expression of his countenance lively."[40]

On April 20, 1828, Sophia gave another benefit concert in which the Handel and Haydn Society assisted. The audience was large and enthusiastic, and the performance was judged to be "of the first order."[41] Sophia's reputa-tion seemed firmly entrenched. Nevertheless, by the late 1820s American musical tastes were becoming more sophisticated. Not only were the standards for performance rising, but formal musical training, especially when acquired in Europe, came to be greatly admired. In this respect Sophia's training, if not her execution, was found wanting. It was not "scientific," which was the cur-rent term of highest praise for a musician. At least, some members of the Han-del and Haydn Society found her lacking in this regard, as did the highly influ-ential Lowell Mason.[42] As a result, according to the society's records, their treasurer, a Mr. Coffin, who was reelected August 2, 1830, "used his influ-ence" to have Mrs. Ostinelli replaced by a German organist named Charles Zeuner.

This move aroused the great indignation of Sophia's friends, who, in a letter signed by thirty-eight members, remonstrated against it on the ground that she had filled the position "with ability and success for eleven years" and hence ought not to be dispossessed by "a German professor of music . . . whose qualifications . . . however scientific . . . cannot, we presume, be placed in competition with one who has presided so long and faithfully, and with so much satisfaction to a majority of the Society."

The protest was to no avail. The society's board declined to reconsider by a vote of seven to five, and Zeuner was formally engaged on September 24, 1830. However, the board gave Sophia a double ticket, admitting two, to the society's concerts and rehearsals and offered her the free use of Boylston Hall, which was rented by the season, for a concert at the end of the season.[43]

Heinrich Christoph Zeuner, who later changed his name to Charles, certainly did have more "scientific" training than Sophia. Born in 1795 in Eislcbcn, Saxony, he not only could play the organ well but was said to "understand orchestral effects" and be skilled in both the theory and practice of instrumental and vocal music. In Boston, where he arrived in 1824, he was regarded as one of the best educated musicians in America. Perhaps in part to underline the wisdom of the society's decision, Zeuner composed an organ concerto, for organ and full orchestra, which was performed at the Handel and Haydn Society concert of November 20, 1830.[44] Nevertheless, the society did not consider his scientific training worth more hard cash than Sophia's, or perhaps, as one present-day member of the society has suggested, Yankee instinct correctly told them they could get a foreigner for less. In any case, they paid Zeuner exactly the same salary as Sophia, $50 per quarter.[45]

Sophia did not avail herself of the board's offer of Boylston Hall, at least not immediately. About this time she may have returned to Maine, for one writer says she succeeded Charles Nolcini as organist of Portland's First Parish Church and in turn was replaced by Sarah H. Gilman in 1832.[46] However, the Boston city directory lists her in 1830 and again in 1831 as having a musical academy, first on Norfolk Avenue and later at 3 Morton Place. There is no subsequent Boston address for Sophia.

During the next few years Sophia continued to appear in Boston regularly. On February 12, 1831, she performed in a benefit for James Kendall, and on April 21, 1832, a benefit for her was held in which the Tremont Theatre Orchestra took part. (Ostinelli was then its leader.) The summer of 1832 she toured the Canadian Maritime provinces with flutist William Hanna, and in September she was back in Boston, teaching piano, harp, and voice, even though the directory lists no residence for her at that time. On May 12, 1833, she gave still another benefit in Boston, at which the Handel and Haydn Society sang selections from Haydn's *The Creation* and Beethoven's *Mount of Olives*.[47]

Little is known about her remaining years, but she appears to have been separated from Ostinelli from some time in the 1830s. In July 1833 the

Eastern Argus of Portland, Maine, she announced her return to that city and her willingness to give piano and voice lessons at her residence at B. C. Attwood's, Congress Street.[48] This ad continued to run through December. Whether she then returned to the Boston area or remained in Maine is not known, but on August 5, 1834, she appeared in Boston in a benefit for Mr. Walton, the last concert of hers on record. One writer maintains that Sophia moved to Portland because of marital difficulties, became organist at the First Parish Church there, and also taught to support herself and her daughter.[49] Indeed, the penultimate record of Sophia dates from May 1845, when the First Parish Church paid Mme Ostinelli $31.25 as organist, a quarterly payment perhaps. The only other record of Sophia is of her death, which occurred in Portland in 1846, when she was forty-six.

One reason for this paucity of information is that most of the official records of Portland were destroyed in a great fire in 1866. Hence there is no record of a will for Sophia, nor do the surviving local newspapers contain an obituary. No compositions of hers survived either, although it is safe to assume she produced some. All organists of her time had to have the compositional skill to realize the actual chords and embellishments in music for which only a figured bass was supplied. During her early years with the Handel and Haydn Society, it published several books of vocal music with keyboard accompaniment, but if Sophia had any hand in these, she was not given credit. Most likely she also composed teaching pieces for her pupils.

Louis Ostinelli continued to be active in Boston until 1843. He was leader of the Tremont Theatre Orchestra, the city's outstanding ensemble, and was called on to play with many other artists, off and on from the late 1820s until 1842. He also served as orchestral leader for a number of other groups, including the Billings and Holden Society (1836–1837, 1840), the Boston Academy of Music (1841–1842), and the Handel and Haydn Society (1842–1843).

The Ostinellis' daughter, Eliza, became a singer. Some Boston gentlemen pledged enough money to give her the requisite European education, and on November 26, 1843, escorted by her father, Eliza sailed for Naples. In Italy she studied under several well-known teachers, and in 1847, a year after her mother's death, she married an Italian cellist, Count Alessandro Biscaccianti. Her American debut took place on December 8, 1847, at New York's Astor Place Opera House, as Amina in *La Sonnambula.* In May 1848 she sang in Boston with the Handel and Haydn Society in two concerts, and she soon became an established favorite, appearing with a number of groups from 1848 to 1850.[50] Henry Wadsworth Longfellow described her as "a fine little woman of genius, with her large eyes and coquettish ways."[51] In 1849 and again in 1851 Eliza appeared as soloist with the Boston Musical Fund Society, performing arias by Verdi, Bellini, and Donizetti. In 1852 she was in San Francisco, where she received glowing reviews and is said to have raised the staggering total of $1 million for various charities. The following year she was in Lima, Peru, and presumably she spent the next few years touring. In 1859 she returned to Boston and gave a concert at which her husband assisted on the cello. Again she was enthusiastically received. During this visit, she was quoted as saying that, contrary to widespread belief, her father was not dead but was enjoying good health and residing in Italy.[52] Thereafter, however, Eliza's fortunes declined.[53] She returned to Europe, and in 1896 she died impoverished at the age of seventy-two at the Rossini Foundation Home for Musicians in Paris.[54]

So far as opening a new field for women organists was concerned, Sophia Hewitt Ostinelli cannot be said to have had much influence. Although the number of women organists increased nearly as rapidly as the number of nineteenth-century American churches that acquired organs, they did not win fame or fortune. The large, rich city churches continued to hire men, and concert organists were few and far between. In 1885 one writer said, "Lady organ players are becoming noted in England," and cited two women who had performed at a recent exhibition in London.[55] The implication is that they were still a rarity.

Some years earlier, however, one woman organist, Lillian S. Frohock, achieved some renown in the concert hall, in Boston and elsewhere. From July 1864 to November 1866 she gave regular organ recitals at Boston's Music Hall, playing works by Bach, Haydn, Mozart, Schubert, Schumann, Mendelssohn, and Chopin, and alternating with such renowned organists as Benjamin J. Lang, W. Eugene Thayer, and John Knowles Paine. She reportedly gave a successful concert in Brooklyn, New York, in 1869.[56] At some point she went to study in Germany, then the mecca of well-trained musicians, and the *Musical Record* notes her return in 1878.[57] And a decade later, a writer reminisces that Frohock had been a remarkable organist. She played every Saturday afternoon at the Music Hall and was organist at the Arlington Street Church.[58] Another writer of the 1860s tells of two "lady organists" who earned as much as $500 per year playing two Sabbath services in addition to teaching during the week to support themselves and their families.[59]

But in 1901 a major article about women organists and choir directors stated that, of the many hundreds of women who officiated as church organists throughout the United States, very few had ventured into the concert hall. Moreover, the important city churches persisted in hiring only men. The conservatories were training women organists, but they did not find prominent employment.[60]

Leonard Ellinwood's excellent 1953 book on American church music, with its large appendix of biographies of church musicians, names only three women, two of them organists.[61] One is Caroline Lattin Beardsley (1860–1944), who began as a church organist at the age of twelve and in 1883 became organist and choir director of the Second (United) Congregational Church in

Bridgeport, Connecticut. From 1909 on she held this post simultaneously with another at the B'nai Israel Temple in Bridgeport. An expert sightreader, she was much in demand as an accompanist. During the 1920s she organized an annual Lenten recital series at the church to which she brought many distinguished organists.

The other woman organist is Mary Cherubim Schaefer (1886–1977), who was born in Wisconsin into a family of organ builders. She was given her first lessons by her brother Charles, and from ages thirteen to eighteen she was organist and choir director in her home parish of Slinger. In 1903 she joined the Sisters of St. Francis and studied with John Singenberger, whom the Milwaukee community had hired to teach music. For several years she was organist and choir director at St. Lawrence Church near Milwaukee, performing Gregorian chant and Renaissance motets and Masses. In 1908 Schaefer became head of the St. Joseph's Convent music department in Milwaukee, which under her leadership was expanded into the St. Joseph's Convent Conservatory of Music (later called Alverno College of Music). She remained director until 1935. Meanwhile she also studied at Marquette University and in 1922 earned her bachelor of music degree with highest honors. In 1935 she was assigned to St. Joseph's Convent in Campbellsport, Wisconsin, and was relieved of academic duties so she could devote herself entirely to composition. In all she composed three Masses, numerous motets and hymns for women's voices and organ, several sets of the *Alverno Hymnal,* and collections of organ music. She also wrote a number of books, including *Liturgical Choir Book,* published in 1939, and *The Organist's Companion,* in 1945.

Very few other women organists are mentioned in the literature. In 1878 Clara Conant played Schumann's Fugue on B-A-C-H in Worcester, Massachusetts, becoming the first woman organist to perform publicly in Mechanics Hall; she also had appeared in the Worcester Music Festival of 1873.[62] The *Musical Herald* of May 1886 reported a graduate organ recital at the New England Conservatory by Nellie P. Nichols, who "can claim rank as an accomplished organist."[63] The first decades of the twentieth century saw the success of a few more women organists. Carrie B. Wilson Adams (1859–1940), born in Ohio and a long-time resident of Indiana, was an organist, choral conductor, and composer who wrote many anthems, several cantatas, and some church operettas. Mary Chappell Fisher, a church and concert organist born in Auburn, New York, edited the organ department for a special women's issue of *Etude Music Magazine* in 1909—she did not single out one woman organist of note for coverage in the issue. And Patty Stair (1869–1926) of Cleveland was a church and concert organist and composer who was the first Ohio woman to become a fellow of the American Guild of Organists. She taught at the Cleveland Conservatory for twenty years. Her compositions include two light operas, an intermezzo for orchestra, and some fifty songs, anthems, and instrumental works for violin, piano, and organ. Her *Berceuse* was performed by violinist Maud Powell. Her many unpublished works were deposited in the Library of Congress in 1917.

In February 1925 *Etude* reported that the women organists of Boston had formed a Women Organ Players Club, the first of its kind. The magazine also noted, in the following issue (March 1925), that when the American Guild of Organists was founded, in 1896, it had only four women among its 145 members, but now, in 1925, of its 536 associates, 250 were women, and of 192 fellows, forty-eight were women. The first woman to become a fellow, by passing an examination, was Gertrude Elizabeth McKellar, in 1904. Nevertheless, not until the 1970s did the American Guild of Organists elect its first woman president.

A distinguished American woman organist of the later twentieth century was Catharine Crozier. Born in Oklahoma in 1914, she began to study violin, piano, and organ at an early age, making her first recital appearance as a pianist at the age of six. She was awarded a scholarship to the Eastman School of Music, where she studied organ with Harold Gleason, whom she later married, and then did graduate work with, among others, the French virtuoso Joseph Bonnet. In 1938 she was appointed to the Eastman faculty, and in 1953 she replaced Gleason as head of the organ department. Later, after his death, she published two revisions of his *Method of Organ Playing*, widely regarded as the bible of organ teaching.

Following her debut before the national convention of the American Guild of Organists in 1941, Crozier appeared in countless recitals, in concert with orchestras, and over radio and television stations throughout the United States, Canada, and Europe. From 1955 to 1969 she was organist of Knowles Memorial Chapel at Rollins College, in Florida. Later she moved to California, and in 1994 to Oregon. Throughout her long career Crozier continued to teach, both privately and at numerous American universities, and she served on the jury for numerous international organ competitions. In 1962 she was chosen, along with E. Power Biggs and Virgil Fox, the two most distinguished American men organists, to play the inaugural organ recital at Philharmonic Hall in New York's Lincoln Center. Two years later she played a solo recital there. In 1975 she performed a concerto with orchestra at the inauguration of the organ in Lincoln Center's Alice Tully Hall, and the next year she also returned to play a solo recital there. Of this last, the *New York Times* reviewer said that Crozier may be an "honored veteran among organ players" but "she can still run rings around much of her younger competition, not only in interpretive style but in sheer technique as well."[64] In 1979 she received the International Player of the Year award of the American Guild of Organists. In her mid-eighties, in semiretirement, she still gave organ concerts and taught master classes at various colleges, playing not only Bach but contemporary organ works. In 1998 she told an interviewer, "I spend a lot of time on every piece. I want to get it, let it go, and come back and see how it is."[65]

Another outstanding organist is Marilyn Mason, known worldwide as concert organist, lecturer, adjudicator, and teacher. Born in 1925 in Alva, Oklahoma, she first studied with her mother, Myrtle E. Mason. In 1944 she went to study with Palmer Christian, head of the organ department at the University of Michigan, which was to be her base for nearly all her life. After receiving her master's degree she went to France to study analysis with Nadia Boulanger and organ with Maurice Duruflé. She eventually became university organist and chair of the organ department at Michigan. Mason was the first woman organist to play in Westminster Abbey, in Latin America, and in Egypt. She served as a judge in nearly every major organ competition throughout the world. In addition, she commissioned and premiered some sixty works by contemporary organ composers. She also pursued her commitment to stylistic integrity through scholarly research into the construction and tonal design of historic organs in France, Germany, and Spain. She received many honors, among them an honorary doctorate from the University of Nebraska, and she was chosen Performer of the Year in 1989 by the American Guild of Organists.[66]

In the late twentieth century, Dorothy J. Papadakos was making an impressive name for herself. Born in 1960 in Coral Gables, Florida, she moved to New York in 1980 and, without yet having graduated from college, joined the staff of the Cathedral of John the Divine as Night Watch Organist. She completed her education at Barnard College and received a master's degree in organ performance from Juilliard in 1986. In addition to organ, she studied improvisation with organists Paul Halley and Gerre Hancock, and with Lyle Mays, keyboardist for the Pat Metheny Group. She gradually advanced through the ranks at the Cathedral of John the Divine, one of New York's largest churches, and in 1990 became its organist, the first woman to be appointed to this position.

Describing herself as a crossover organist rather than a purely classical type, Papadakos regards improvisation as her specialty and is interested in all styles—jazz, silent film, even playing with animals such as humpback whales and Amazon birds, along with traditional music. Her compositions include traditional liturgical music (settings of the Beatitudes, Magnificat, Missa Divinum), film scores (*O Night without Objects*, *The Science of Whales*), and jazz (*Christmas Traveler*). As a recitalist she tours widely and is known for her improvisation workshops. "The one advantage to being an American woman in this field," she said on November 1, 1999, "is that you do stick out. Especially if you're the renegade I am, trying to change the perception of what pipe organs can do and be."[67]

Of course, women are legion as church organists, although rarely in such important posts as Papadakos. They often combine organ playing with the job of choir director. Since only a tiny percentage of churches are wealthy enough to pay well, the job of church organist is close to the bottom of the professional pay scale. In practically all churches, moreover, the job is part time, thus paying even less. A national survey conducted by the American Guild of Organists in 1973 revealed that among church organists holding a degree in organ or sacred music, unmarried men earned some 60 percent more than unmarried women ($5,300 per year versus $3,300). According to Beverly Scheibert, writing in the August 1976 issue of the *Diapason,* women still were being excluded from the larger church positions, which are generally filled through word-of-mouth advertising. And lest one think that married status was somehow relevant, married men with no music degree were earning substantially more than women with years of costly training ($3,800 more per year on the average). The figures have increased—in 1999 the average organist with at least a master's degree and responsibility for directing the adult choir (if not the youth or children's choir, or all three) earned between $10,000 and $15,000 a year in all but the largest churches—but the disparity between rates for men and women still exists.

In 1909, an organist writing about the prejudice against women organists said—very optimistically, it now seems—that this bias was fast disappearing:

> Unfortunately for the women organists, the average audience accepts as necessarily good the indifferent work of many men organists, but the women must play doubly well to be appreciated, and then—most wonderful of compliments!—"She plays as well as the men do!" It is nearly time that the ears should judge of a musical performance. They are the only competent judges.[68]

2

THE "LADY VIOLINISTS" AND
OTHER STRING PLAYERS

*S*HALL LADIES play the violin? Ridiculous, said many. Unsuitable, ungraceful, unladylike. According to one writer of the late nineteenth century, "The picture of an angel fiddling a solo, be it ever so divinely, is an ideal incongruity, and invokes laughter."[1] How surprising, then, to read in 1877 in *Dwight's Journal of Music* from the highly respected critic John Sullivan Dwight that not only is the violin "the most gentlemanly of instruments" but also "it is equally the most womanly."[2] And at the same time, the critic of a major Boston paper reviewed a recital of Julius Eichberg's violin pupils at the Boston Conservatory and warned, "Well might the orchestral fiddlers cry out at the sight of Mr. Eichberg's twenty-four lady violinists at work on his concerto yesterday, 'We are ruined by cheap female labor!'"[3]

From the ridiculous to the sublime took less than half a century. In 1850 a woman violinist was a rarity in Europe as well as in America. By 1875 at least two women, Czech-born Wilma Normann-Neruda (later Lady Hallé) of England[4] and French-born Camilla Urso of the United States, were ranked with the great male virtuosos of their time—Henri Vieuxtemps, Olé Bull, and Joseph Joachim. In 1884 the *New York Sun* ran a piece called "Boston's Girl Fiddlers," which claimed that although the taste for violin playing among ladies had started only about five years earlier, at present 400 to 500 ladies were studying the violin and countless others had advanced enough to pursue the instrument on their own.[5] By the turn of the twentieth century, the American musicologist Henry Lahee said that the violin had become, in the past forty or fifty years, a fashionable instrument for ladies and "correspondingly popular as a profession for those [ladies] who are obliged to earn a living."[6] Moreover, in recitals in New York, Boston, Chicago, and other U.S. cities with an active musical life, it is apparent that women violinists, both as soloists and as accompanists, were fairly commonplace by 1900, and a number of them were well established as violin teachers.

How did this change come about? By the mid-nineteenth century Puritan prejudices against musical instruments had been largely overcome, to be sure, and not only in church. The principal home instrument, then as today, was a keyboard instrument, first the harpsichord and later the piano. When families could afford an instrument and the leisure required to play it, girls were taught music much as they were taught embroidery or French, as a social grace. The accepted instruments for girls were those that could be played in a demure seated position, that is, the keyboard instruments and the harp. Efforts to learn the violin, flute, or even the organ, which had pedals requiring an ungainly posture, were frowned on as unsuitable, even as late as 1874.[7] And in 1901 violinist George Lehmann reminisced, "Only a little more than a quarter of a century earlier . . . the mere thought of a refined young gentlewoman playing the violin, either in private or in public, was indeed intolerable."[8]

Public performance, of course, was scarcely encouraged. True, as early as 1824 a concert at St. Mathew's Church in New York featured Mrs. Fagan, a singer, accompanied by Mrs. Geaufreau, a harp player,[9] but it is safe to assume that neither of these ladies was considered quite respectable—though a harp, to be sure, was not so terrible.

Why the harp should have been considered appropriate for women, and even "feminine," is a bit of a mystery. One of the earliest solo performances by a woman on a non-keyboard instrument was that of harpist Mrs. Blessner, in Boston, on November 8, 1846. Her appearance created a sensation, and she was acclaimed by a very large audience.[10] To this day, though men harpists exist, orchestras reluctant to admit women players of any other instrument will often—even as a rule—employ a woman harpist. The hidebound Vienna Philharmonic Orchestra employed a freelance woman harpist for years, but not as an official orchestra member, and only considerable pressure in the 1990s resulted in the formal accession of a woman to its harp chair. The Fourteenth National Conference of the American Harp Society, held in Boston in 1977, had about 375 registered participants, among whom women outnumbered men five to one.[11] In the late 1990s the statistic still held; women harpists by far outnumbered men. The American Harp Society presently has more than 3000 members, the majority in the United States, and acknowledges that the harp world is predominantly female.

Further, though the harp clearly has its limitations as a solo instrument, among the most successful touring recitalists of her time was Maud Morgan (1864–1941), a New York harpist who made her debut in 1874 in a recital with Olé Bull and others. During the 1880s, she frequently performed together with her father, organist George W. Morgan (1823–1892). Moreover, though harpists at this time usually participated in popular concerts, Maud Morgan largely confined herself to serious music. In 1924 she celebrated her golden jubilee at Carnegie Hall in New York, marking fifty years of performance on the concert stage.

Morgan's legacy remained alive into the late twentieth century through two prominent women harpists: Heidi Lehwalder and Susan Allen. Harp virtuoso Lehwalder was the first recipient of the prestigious Avery Fisher Award in 1976.[12] Born in 1950 in Seattle, she was given a harp at the age of seven by her mother, a Seattle Symphony cellist who loved chamber music and was always looking for a good harpist. Heidi took to the instrument and was encouraged to try a solo career by both her family and Milton Katims, music director of the Seattle Symphony. She avoided playing in an orchestra except for three years during her teens, when she played with the Youth Symphony of Seattle; she knew that most orchestral harpists do not like to do solo work and there were relatively few solo harpists around. She herself made forty-seven solo appearances with the Seattle Symphony. She spent several summers at Rudolf Serkin's summer school and festival in Marlboro, Vermont, and in time became a member of its touring chamber ensemble, Music from Marlboro. Through it she became friends with two other members, flutist Paula Robison and her husband, violist Scott Nickrenz, and in 1972 the three musicians formed the Orpheus Trio, which was soon giving as many as forty concerts per season, and toured for eight years.

The Avery Fisher Award entitled Lehwalder to a concert with the New York Philharmonic. Of her performance, *New York Times* critic Peter Davis said she displayed more aggressive assertiveness than most harpists, and with her the delicacy and refinement customarily associated with harp music took second place to structural clarity, forceful musical gestures, and a willingness to take technical chances; he deemed her a "resourceful and sensitive musician as well as a thoroughly accomplished virtuoso." By 1999 Lehwalder had performed with more than sixty-five orchestras throughout the United States and was a frequent guest artist with the Chamber Music Society of Lincoln Center and at numerous music festivals. In addition, she is the founder and director of the Fredericksburg Festival of the Arts in Virginia and of Seattle's Belle Arte Concerts.

A contemporary of Lehwalder's, Susan Allen[13] is well known throughout North and South America, Australia, and Europe for her world premieres of new music for harp and electric harp. She has performed on television, radio, and at major music festivals, as well as in concert and recital. Born in 1951 in California, Allen graduated from the California Institute of the Arts and returned there to teach in 1983. She collaborated with such notable composers as John Cage, Morton Feldman, and Mel Powell, and championed the music of women composers (she recorded Concerto for solo harp and orchestra by Germaine Tailleferre with the New England Women's Symphony under Antonia Brico). In 1984 Allen presented one of the first recitals devoted exclusively to music for harp and electronics. She also worked in jazz and improvisation. She joined the cross-cultural ensemble Vighnesh, led by South Indian vocalist-composer Ganasaraswathy Rao, and has studied traditional Korean music on the kayagum with Okja Paik. In 1998 she gave a solo recital in New York of world premieres for harp; among them was Mel Powell's final work, *Seven Miniatures: Women Poets of China,* for voice and harp.

If piano and harp were the only generally acceptable instruments for women in the mid-nineteenth century, the appearance of women violinists must have been startling indeed. Yet the *Musical Gazette* of April 26, 1847, states without further comment, perhaps dismissing them as amateurs, that "Messrs. Covert and Dodge have given several concerts in Boston and vicinity assisted by two Misses Macomber, from Maine. One of these ladies plays the violin and the other the violoncello."[14] But only five years later, in 1852, a ten-year-old girl violinist inspired both New York and Boston critics to lavish praise on her performance of standard works by De Bériot and Grétry, Paganini and Viotti. Even at the age of ten Camilla Urso was no amateur. She had been performing before a paying public for several years, and during the remaining half-century of her career she was to inspire hundreds of other girls to take up the violin.

Who was this prodigy? Camilla Urso was born in Nantes on June 13, 1842, the oldest child and only daughter of a Sicilian flutist, Salvatore Urso, and a Portuguese singer.[15] Her father played in theater and opera orchestras, and on Sundays served as church organist. At the age of four Urso began to go with her father to the theater when he was performing, and at not quite six she began, after a year of insistent entreaty, her first violin lessons, with the theater orchestra's concertmaster, Félix Simon. The general reaction to the child's lessons was a blend of amusement and outrage. Nevertheless, she first appeared in public at a benefit concert for the widow of the orchestra's bassoonist, who had died suddenly, and she was, after initial guffaws, a resounding success.

Realizing that their daughter was unusually gifted and being urged by her teachers, Urso's parents moved the family to Paris and tried to enroll her at the Conservatory there. At first they could not even get a foot inside the door. The normal enrollment age was ten, and no girl had ever been admitted. Finally, after nine months of delay the family could ill afford—Camilla's father could not find work in Paris, and her mother had to take in sewing and washing—the Conservatory director, the opera composer Auber, agreed to hear her play. After this audition, the eight-year-old was admitted immediately.

Urso spent three years at the Conservatory in all, but from time to time she had to make concert tours in the provinces in order to earn money. By the time she left, at ten, she had been awarded the coveted first prize in violin and offered a three-year tour of the United States under the sponsorship of an American businessman named Faugas, who offered the child $20,000 a year. Accompanied by her father and her aunt Caroline, Urso sailed for New York, only to find that the concerts planned for her had been undersubscribed and the businessman allegedly forced into bankruptcy, though he may have been a swindler as well.

The Ursos found themselves stranded. Fortunately, Marietta Alboni, a renowned Italian contralto, was then in New York and, hearing of their plight, she kindly arranged a concert. The glowing reviews in the influential *New*

York Herald led to a Boston concert sponsored by piano manufacturer Jonas Chickering. Engagements followed in New York, Philadelphia, and again Boston.

In April 1853 Urso, not yet eleven years old, was invited to join the Germania Musical Society of Boston on a two-month tour that took them through Ohio and as far west as St. Louis. In June, Urso returned to New York and joined soprano Henrietta Sontag for an eighteen-concert tour that took them down the Ohio and Mississippi rivers to New Orleans. Her touring career throughout the United States continued until 1855, when she abruptly retired to private life, settling in Nashville, Tennessee. She did not play in public, except for a few charity concerts, for the next seven years. Charles Barnard, Urso's biographer, ventures no explanation for the retirement. No doubt there was public speculation that at thirteen the child prodigy had, as so often happens, burned herself out.

But in 1862, at the age of twenty, Camilla Urso returned to New York and resumed an active career. Dwight, who had extolled her first Boston appearances, again praised her warmly for her performance with the Boston Philharmonic under Carl Zerrahn in February 1863. "She played divinely," said Dwight, "but one wishes she would play better pieces."[16] She was playing the (then) standard violin works of Alard, Simon, Artot—composers deservedly forgotten today—as well as a Vieuxtemps concerto.

For the next two seasons Urso toured the United States and Canada, performing with all the major orchestras as well as giving recitals. In 1865 she returned to France for a year, and *Dwight's Journal of Music* quotes a review of her performance of the Mendelssohn Violin Concerto with Pasdeloup's renowned Paris orchestra that describes her as simply magnificent. The following season she repeated this work with the Harvard Music Association in Cambridge, leading Dwight to call her playing "a marvel of art."[17] It was this rendition that led the principal "members of the Music Profession of Boston"—among them conductors Carl Zerrahn and Benjamin J. Lang, composer John Knowles Paine, cellist Wulf Fries, and several dozen other men—to write her a signed testimonial that stated in part: "It is not enough to say it was a wonderful performance for a woman; it was a consummate rendering, which probably few men living could improve upon."[18]

Beginning about 1868, Urso began to spend her summers in France, and at some point around this time she married a Frenchman, Frédéric Luer, who became (or already had been) director of the touring Camilla Urso Concert Company. It was customary during this period for a small group of musicians to band together and tour from city to city and country to country, giving concerts. Usually such a group would form around one star performer, whose name was the principal drawing card, and, depending on the nature of the star's specialty—voice, piano, or violin—it would include one or more violinists and pianists and several singers, enough to perform operatic duets, if not quartets. If the star was a pianist, a second pianist might be engaged to accompany the singers or violinist. The rationale of this practice was to provide variety for the programs, since it was felt that few audiences, particularly in smaller towns and rural areas, would tolerate an entire evening of violin or piano solos, or even a solo singer.

Camilla Urso herself had decided views about what constituted a proper program and the artist's duty to educate the public. In an interview published in 1874, she is quoted as saying, "It would be rash, I am certain, to give programs composed purely of classical music to audiences untutored to it . . . but a few choice '*morceaux*' of the masters should be introduced in every program, and this policy, which I have followed for years, will prove a beneficial result to the cause of good music and elevate the taste." And elsewhere in the same issue, the magazine printed a program Urso had arranged for the coming season:

Kreutzer, Trio from *Night in Granada* (vocal)
Chopin, Polonaise, op. 53, no. 8 (pianist Auguste Sauret)
Fesca, "Winged Messengers" (song)
Mendelssohn, Violin Concerto (with piano reduction of the orchestra parts)
Flotow, Duet from *Stradella* (men's voices)
Beethoven, Violin Sonata (not specified)
Handel, "Rejoice Greatly" from *Messiah* (solo voice)
Leclair, Sarabande and Tambourin for violin solo
Mendelssohn, Song (not specified)
Verdi, Trio from *Ernani* (vocal)[19]

Of course, for concerts in major musical centers and for performances with large orchestras, Urso's own repertory included all the major works for violin that were then being played—the concertos of Mozart, Beethoven, Mendelssohn, Vieuxtemps, Bruch, and Rubinstein—as well as the special repertory displaying the violinist's technical facility—the bravura works of Paganini, Tartini's notoriously difficult "Devil's Trill" Sonata, and the like. Moreover, she often premiered the works of her contemporaries, such as the violin virtuoso Joseph Joachim.

Unlike most violinists of her day, Urso would play only from memory. In January 1869, appearing with the Harvard Musical Association orchestra (a group that performed regularly from 1865 to 1880 and is considered the forerunner of the Boston Symphony), she played only the first movement of Beethoven's Violin Concerto because she had not yet memorized the rest.[20] She then played the entire work at her Testimonial Concert later the same month and repeated it with the New York Philharmonic. Also in January she was made an honorary member of the Philadelphia Philharmonic Society, a signal honor since the orchestra did not, of course, include a single woman violinist.

Later in 1869 Urso went to San Francisco, where she put on a benefit pageant and raised a huge sum to help that city's Mercantile Library.

Urso was always very conscientious about her work. In 1874, an extremely busy year for her, it was reported that "every day she takes an hour for slow and patient practice in making long sustained notes, in order to obtain a strong pure tone. Then she plays scales and finger exercises of all kinds for two or more hours, and then such sonatas and other great works as she uses in her concerts. Everything is played slowly, carefully, and thoughtfully."[21] And fourteen years later, by now a veteran of thirty years on the concert stage, Urso still says, "I ought to practise even now six hours a day in order to retain my art. I never bring out a new concerto without devoting six months' study to it. First I learn the violin part and next the other parts. Then I have other parts brought in, so that the entire score is virtually filled in."[22]

That Urso found time for serious practice and study is a testament to her strong constitution, for her schedule was extremely hectic. Take, for example, the 1873–74 season, which she began as the featured star of the Worcester (Massachusetts) Music Festival in late September. In Worcester the only local performers in public concerts until about 1870 were men, but visiting women artists had been well received since the 1840s.[23] The festival, which dated from 1858, was long one of the most notable in the country. In 1873 it was conducted by Carl Zerrahn, who reigned there from 1866 to 1890.[24] About 1870 the festival began to feature star performers[25]—musicians of international reputation—and most of the great singers, pianists, and violinists of the latter nineteenth century performed there at one time or another, including harpist Maud Morgan.

In 1873, at her first appearance at Worcester—she returned in 1878— Urso performed the Mendelssohn Violin Concerto and Paganini's *Witches' Dance.*[26] In October and November her company, which at that time included several singers, pianist Auguste Sauret (brother of violinist Emile Sauret), and her husband, performed in Boston a number of times. *Dexter Smith's Musical, Literary, Dramatic and Art Paper* then listed the company's forthcoming schedule: December 16, Ithaca, New York; December 18, Hudson, New York; December 19, Rondout, New York; December 22, Pittsfield, Massachusetts; December 23, Westfield, Massachusetts; December 25, Middletown, New York; December 30, Meriden, Connecticut; January 1, Newport, Rhode Island.[27] Bearing in mind that the musicians were traveling in coal-powered railroad cars in midwinter, this could hardly have been a comfortable undertaking. The next major commitment of the season was a series of four Concerts Classiques, all in Boston, which presumably were confined to serious music. The first two took place as scheduled, on February 23 and March 9, but the last two had to be postponed for a time, because Urso had a serious accident in which her hand was injured. But by May 25 she apparently was able to play again.[28]

Subsequent seasons were at least as exhausting. In June 1879, for example, the *Musical Record* reported that in the season just ending the Camilla Urso Concert Company had appeared in more than 200 concerts in fifteen states, two territories, and Canada. It had traveled more than 15,000 miles, beginning in Massachusetts and going west as far as Denver. The gross receipts totaled more than $100,000, the maximum for a single concert being $2,789.50.[29] That fall Urso went to California, and from there embarked on a lengthy tour of Australia and New Zealand. In Sydney alone the company gave twenty-seven concerts at which Urso played 171 times (fifty-eight compositions by thirty-seven different composers).[30] She then returned to New York and performed in various East Coast cities. Thereafter she planned yet another long tour, this time a three-month junket through the South, together with singer Marie Nellini and the Mendelssohn Quintette Club, a men's chamber group from Boston.

From time to time Urso settled down briefly to teach, notably in Boston in 1884, where she attracted violin students from all over the United States and Canada while she continued to fill engagements in and around the city.[31] In 1890 she settled in New York City, at first intending to start her own violin school but then joining the faculty of Jeannette M. Thurber's National Conservatory of Music of America.[32]

At the fifth concert of the New York Philharmonic Society in 1893 Urso performed the premiere of a violin concerto by Edward Lassen, and the reviews indicate that her ability had not diminished with middle age. The highly respected critic H. E. Krehbiel said that the concerto was not a great work but that it was beautifully performed. "She belongs in the rank of the foremost of living artists," he said. "In her case the idea of sex, which so often obtrudes itself and modifies critical judgment, is never thought of . . . she does not play like either man or woman, but like a sound, noble, earnest and inspired musician."[33]

And what of Camilla Urso's own views concerning women violinists? As early as 1883 she said that women as a rule play in better tune than men, with greater expression and certainty than the average orchestral musician.[34] Nevertheless, she considered the rewards insufficient, for in an article published in 1891 she said, "My life is made up of hard work, and under the circumstances I should say to young girls who are thinking of becoming professional violinists, 'Don't.' Solo playing and teaching are all that are open to women violinists now-a-days."[35] Her implication is that a soloist's life, with constant tours, was very difficult, but the only alternative, and perhaps a financial necessity, was teaching. A steady orchestra job with a good organization, such as the Boston Symphony or New York Philharmonic, was infinitely preferable, because one was paid to play and need not travel constantly.

Even in 1891 the pay of a first-class violinist was good, and an orchestra position was a great opportunity. It placed the player before the public, which brought in more pupils at higher rates. The best first-violin players in Boston, for example, earned between $5,000 and $10,000 per year, in today's terms equivalent to at least $90,000 per year. No wonder, said one writer, that women were looking forward to this field, and no wonder that men preferred to keep it to themselves![36]

In May 1893 Urso was appointed to the Advisory Council of the Women's Branch, World Auxiliary on Music. She was invited to address the Woman's Musical Congress at the World's Columbian Exposition in Chicago in 1893, where she said outright that women should be admitted to theater orchestras—by far the biggest employers of musicians in the United States before the days of movies, radio, and television—in order to earn a living, and because they were not hired many good women violinists were out of work.[37] Five years later Urso again firmly said that women should play in orchestras on an equal footing with men.[38]

As it happened, Camilla Urso herself never managed to amass enough money to retire. Indeed, during the last years of her life she occasionally appeared in vaudeville shows, and she was harshly criticized for stooping so low. But some took her part. George Lehmann said she deserved the widest sympathy for accepting such opportunities to redeem her broken fortunes,[39] and another reviewer, having seen her during a one-week engagement in Cleveland in 1900, said, "She maintains the dignity of her art perfectly in this new departure, and is literally bringing good music to the masses."[40] She died in New York on January 20, 1902.

Inspiring as Urso's example may have been to American girls of the 1870s, it is doubtful that a single woman virtuoso—even if she was Camilla Urso—could have given rise to a whole wave of girl violinists. For one thing, teachers had to be willing to take on girl students, and there is no reason to suppose that American music teachers and schools were any more ready to do so than the Paris Conservatory was in 1850. But one person did believe girls should study the violin, and as it happened he was an extremely dynamic and dedicated violin teacher. He encouraged girls to perform, individually and in groups, and they flocked to him and his school from all over the United States.

This man was Julius Eichberg, born in 1824 in Düsseldorf, Germany, educated in Germany and at the Brussels Conservatory under Fétis and De Bériot, among others. He immigrated to the United States about 1856. By 1858 Eichberg had moved from New York to Boston, where his brother was established as a merchant, and in October of that year he became director of music at the Boston Museum, which held periodic concerts although sometimes of dubious quality. In 1860 *Dwight's Journal of Music* noted that it was a pity that Eichberg, who was very talented, had such a humdrum job, for he really deserved better.[41]

But Eichberg seems to have been content, for he stayed on at the Boston Museum until 1866 or so. During this time, he did a considerable amount of composing, both music for strings and a number of comic operettas. The first and most successful of these, *The Doctor of Alcantara*, was introduced at the

Boston Museum in 1862. It was followed by *The Rose of Tyrol* in 1863 and *The Two Cadis* in 1868. Productions of these operettas took Eichberg away from Boston from time to time, but in December 1867 he returned and was appointed concertmaster of the Boston Symphony under conductor Carl Zerrahn. This appointment was presumably of brief duration, for by 1868 Eichberg was director of the newly founded Boston Conservatory of Music, and shortly afterward he also succeeded Zerrahn as superintendent of musical instruction in the Boston public schools, two posts in which he exerted enormous influence on music education.

In June 1868, at the first "exhibition concert" of the Boston Conservatory, Eichberg and his daughter performed a Beethoven Serenade for violin and piano, and from that time on the recitals and concerts presented by Boston Conservatory students attracted wide audiences and, considering the fact that they were, after all, student recitals, received a great deal of attention from the press.

Eichberg was an enthusiastic teacher. He wrote a very popular violin method book and saw to it that his students participated in many concerts. He also appears to have exercised his "equal rights" policies almost immediately, for by 1871 his pupils included young Persis Bell, the first of what was to be a remarkable series of talented girl violinists. In that year, at the age of thirteen, Bell performed at the Worcester Music Festival, where allegedly "many preferred her even to Camilla Urso."[42] She continued to appear in Boston Conservatory recital programs until February 1875. Sometime during the next few years she married another violinist, Leandro Campanari, moved with him to Cincinnati, and in 1882 returned with him to Boston, but she appears to have abandoned her own career after marriage.

In the December 1874 recital of the Boston Conservatory, Eichberg's own Concertante, for four violins with piano accompaniment, was performed by twenty-four violin students, nineteen boys and five girls. This occasion marked the first appearance of three young women—Lillian Chandler, Lillian Shattuck, and Lettie Launder—who formed the nucleus of the first all-female string quartet, which not surprisingly called itself the Eichberg Quartette. On February 9, 1878, together with Abbie Shepardson, they gave the first string quartet performance that critic John Sullivan Dwight had ever heard from four young ladies, with Shattuck playing first violin, Shepardson second violin, Chandler viola, and Launder violoncello. Dwight said of them, "They were well matched; tone and bowing both were excellent; and Haydn's genial *Variations on the National Hymn of Austria* were on the whole quite satisfactorily interpreted."[43] The quartet gave several other concerts that spring, and in the fall of 1878, at the Worcester Festival, it performed the Andante and Presto from Mendelssohn's Quartet no. 4 and also Eichberg's Concertante, for four violins. This performance prompted the following remarks from the *Evening Gazette* reviewer:

A violin seems an awkward instrument for a woman, whose well formed chin was designed by nature for other purposes than to pinch down this instrument into position. Nevertheless, we cheerfully bear witness that four bright damsels in a row, all a-bowing with tuneful precision, is an interesting and even a pretty sight.[44]

Somewhat less coyly, the New York *Music Trade Review* reported, "Their playing was noticeable for its unity, precision, and fine quality of tone, careful phrasing, and intelligent conception."

More telling, perhaps, is the fact that the Eichberg Quartette was invited back, and it played in the Worcester Festival of 1880. Meanwhile the quartet had performed in New York, getting an excellent review in the *New York Times,* and in Philadelphia, where it also was favorably received. However, the Philadelphia correspondent for the *Musical Record,* writing under the pseudonym Scintillo, includes a cryptic comment: "We are glad to see one more avenue open to women. . . . Those who can solace themselves and others with music ought to be content, even though deprived of the *vote.*"[45]

Julius Eichberg was very much aware of his minority stand. In his article entitled "Lady Violinists" published in 1879, he said that one would think that this instrument, requiring little muscular strength but great adroitness and agility, would have attracted women from the beginning, but even as late as 1842 only a few ladies took it up. Shortly after that date he, Eichberg, had had as fellow students under De Bériot two young girls, Teresa and Maria Milanollo, who were fine violinists.[46] Their success, Eichberg went on, inspired others to take up the instrument, and at the time of his writing there were so many fine lady violinists that string orchestras would soon be recruited from this constantly increasing number.

In his article Eichberg sends a clear message in support of female musicians:

> While we take a pardonable pride in the many fine players of the male sex who sought our advice and studied with us for years, we should be remiss in failing to credit our female students with at least an equal degree of talent, industry and success. We gladly espouse the cause of women's right to play upon all the instruments of the orchestra and to bring all their fine faculties to bear upon the proper rendition of our great symphonic works.[47]

It is obvious that Eichberg gave his female pupils an extra measure of devoted attention, an early example of affirmative action, as it were. Some rewarded him well, pursuing active and successful careers. The Eichberg Quartet continued under that name (though dropping the terminal *te*) into the 1890s, with somewhat different personnel. In 1882 it returned to Boston after a year's study in Berlin under Joseph Joachim; by that time Launder had replaced Shepardson as second violin, Emma Grebe was playing viola, and Laura Webster cello. Their repertory now included the quartets of Mozart and Haydn, and they undertook a very successful tour that took them as far north as Nova Scotia and New Brunswick and also to the Deep South. By 1886 Launder had been replaced by another Eichberg pupil, Alice Gray Lathrop of Fredonia, New York. In 1891, the quartet, still intact, gave some highly successful concerts, playing Haydn and Beethoven in Boston, a city which then had the stiffest competition in the quartet arena, represented by the Kneisel and Adamowski quartets.

Eichberg died in 1893, but his legacy lived on. At the turn of the twentieth century Lillian Shattuck and Laura Webster both were established string teachers in Boston. Another Eichberg pupil, Edith Lynwood Winn, was not only a prominent violin teacher but became an outspoken champion of women musicians, frequently writing in national music journals.

Two of the best pupils of Eichberg's last years continued as soloists and chamber players. Olive Mead (1874–1946) had begun her studies at the age of seven with Eichberg and went on to study under Franz Kneisel. She performed as a soloist with major orchestras in the United States and Europe for about a decade. Late in 1903 she founded the Olive Mead Quartet, whose other members were Vera Fonaroff, Gladys North, and Lillian Littlehales. They performed regularly in New York City until 1917, giving two or three concerts a season. The other Eichberg pupil was Georgia Pray Lasselle, a cellist, who at first appeared largely with amateur groups like the Beethoven Club and Chromatic Club but eventually joined the American String Quartette, with which she performed until about 1910. And still another Eichberg pupil, Caroline Nichols, went on to form a highly successful all-women orchestra, the Fadettes, more fully described in Chapter 5.

Although none of Eichberg's pupils achieved the world renown of Camilla Urso, his work gave impetus to aspiring girl violinists across the country. At least four other American girls born in the 1860s went on to successful careers as solo violinists: Maud Powell, Geraldine Morgan, Nettie Carpenter, and Arma Senkrah. All studied in Europe, and one, Powell, achieved an eminence almost equal to that of Camilla Urso.[48]

Maud Powell was born in 1867 in Peru, Illinois.[49] She took piano lessons early and at age eight began studying the violin with G. W. Fickensher in Aurora and then William Lewis in Chicago, soon afterward appearing as an "infant prodigy." In 1881 she was taken to Leipzig to study under Henry Schradieck; Geraldine Morgan was in her class there. She next went to the Paris Conservatory, where she was the first of eighty-eight applicants to be admitted for only six openings, and studied under Charles Dancla, with Nettie Carpenter as a classmate. Heard by Joachim at some concerts in England, Powell was persuaded to complete her European studies with a year under his tutelage in Berlin, where she again encountered Geraldine Morgan. In 1885 she made her formal debut with the Berlin Philharmonic in Bruch's Violin

Concerto in G minor. In July of that year she made her American debut with the Theodore Thomas Orchestra in Chicago and then was engaged to play with the New York Philharmonic in November, followed in close succession by concerts in Brooklyn, Orange (New Jersey), and Philadelphia.[50]

In 1901 violinist George Lehmann wrote that Powell's success was not immediate,[51] but that would be difficult to verify from either the number of her engagements or the reviews she received. In March 1887, when she made her debut with the Boston Symphony in the Bruch concerto, a reviewer said, "She must have frightened the first violinists just behind her. . . . Such breadth of tone, such boldness of attack, and such clear double-stopping are seldom heard."[52] In that year Powell signed a three-year contract for an American-European tour managed by L. M. Ruben, beginning that October in New York. And in November 1890, beginning her fourth concert season under Ruben's management, another reviewer said she was without a peer of her own sex in her profession.[53]

Three months later, in February 1891, Powell performed the Violin Concerto in G minor written for her by Harry Rowe Shelley at the Brooklyn Academy of Music, and in April 1891 she appeared as soloist in Theodore Thomas's farewell concert in New York. Thomas, leaving New York for the Chicago Symphony, had been the first conductor in the United States to engage her, and she had made annual tours with his orchestra since her debut. In June 1891 it was announced that she was to perform in seventy-five concerts with Patrick S. Gilmore's band in the coming season. In 1892 she toured Germany and Austria as the one representative American violinist with the New York Arion Society, conducted by Frank van der Stücken, and the following year she was soloist—the only woman among the violin soloists—at the World's Columbian Exposition in Chicago. On that same occasion she also read a paper entitled "Woman and the Violin" for the Women's Musical Congress, and together with the composer she played Amy Beach's *Romance,* for violin and piano, which had been dedicated to her. In 1894 she organized the Maud Powell String Quartet with Joseph Kovarik, second violin, Franz Kaltenborn, viola, and Paul Miersch, cello, which went on a worldwide tour.

By 1898, however, the quartet had disbanded and Powell resumed her solo career, traveling throughout the United States. She once made a thirty-week tour as soloist with John Philip Sousa's band, often giving two concerts per day, leading one writer to say, "She has beyond doubt given more violin recitals in this country than any other native violinist."[54] She also made extensive tours abroad. In 1903 she toured in Europe with Sousa's band and its manager, H. Godfrey "Sunny" Turner. The son of an English journalist and former manager of London's Empire Theater, Turner and Powell became friends and were married in 1904. He then became her manager, and the couple settled in New York.[55] Later in the 1904–5 season she appeared as soloist with the Pittsburgh Orchestra, along with Fritz Kreisler.

In January 1907 George Lehmann said that Powell was the only American woman violinist who continued to improve year after year and who was of unquestionable international note, always adding to her repertory. That season she had introduced a new concerto by Sibelius, which, in Lehmann's opinion, could not be redeemed even by her fine performance.[56] Powell was always interested in presenting new works. During her long career, she performed the American premieres of concertos by Arensky, Bruch, Dvořák, Lalo, Saint-Saëns, Sibelius, and Tchaikovsky,[57] and introduced numerous works by American composers, among them Amy Beach, Marion Bauer, Henry Holden Huss, and others.

Powell's activity did not slow down with middle age or with marriage. In 1904, she became the first violinist ever to make phonograph recordings, and between 1904 and 1919 she made several dozen records for the Victor Talking Machine Company. In the 1905–6 season she made a tour of South Africa. In 1908 she formed the Maud Powell Trio with two English sisters, cellist May Mukle and pianist Anne Mukle Ford. It toured the American continent from coast to coast but survived only for one season. Until 1910 Powell made alternate European and American tours each year; thereafter, however, she remained in the United States. She played everywhere, not just in large cities but in small towns and at colleges and women's clubs. Though these engagements inevitably brought her smaller fees, she felt she had a mission in carrying music to those who did not ordinarily hear top-rank artists. In 1907 and again in 1910 she was soloist at the Worcester Festival. In 1911 she introduced a new concerto by Max Bruch at the Norfolk (Connecticut) Festival. She also gave at least one concert in New York per season from 1909 to 1918, and throughout World War I she entertained troops at military camps and hospitals. In addition to all these performances, she wrote articles and made excellent transcriptions for violin and piano. Other than these and some arrangements, the only music Powell composed was a cadenza for the first movement of the Brahms Violin Concerto, op. 77.

As early as 1893, in her speech for the World's Columbian Exposition, Powell predicted that more and more women would take advantage of the opportunities open to violinists. The concert stage, she said, was as open to them as to women singers, and the field of instruction was naturally theirs, since they usually were more sympathetic and conscientious than male teachers.[58] Fifteen years later she was invited to edit the violin section in a special issue of *Etude* devoted to women working in music—the first woman to do so for any monthly issue in the twenty-six years of the journal's history. She did such an outstanding job that her material was continued in the subsequent issue.[59]

The opportunities for the talented woman violinist were now unlimited, said Powell in 1909. Girls played in quartets, in orchestras, or earned their living by solo playing, though for the last she emphasized that not every talented violinist could expect to have a brilliant stage career. To prove her point, Powell cited the fact that the Buffalo Symphony Orchestra had had Nora Clench at its first-violin desk more than a decade earlier, that the Women's Symphony Orchestra of Los Angeles, with Cora Foy "in the concertmaster's chair," had existed for sixteen years, and that there were several "ladies' orchestras" conducted by women, as well as some all-women's string quartets. "The field of orchestral playing is open to women," she declared. "I see no reason why women should not be regularly employed if they wish to be. . . . If women really want orchestral work, they will get it. Prejudice of the American masculine mind is easily broken down. The 'Union' accepts women members."

Powell's knowledge of this blissful state of affairs was not firsthand—she herself never applied for an orchestra job and, as a soloist, was not even required to join the musicians' union. In fact, her statements were far from accurate. The reason for the large number of "ladies' orchestras," which are discussed more fully in Chapter 5, was that they represented practically the only opportunity for women instrumentalists to engage in orchestral and even ensemble playing. About a year before her death, however, Powell admitted "When I first began my career as a concert violinist . . . a strong prejudice then existed against women fiddlers, which even yet has not altogether been overcome. Yet I kept on. . . ."[60]

True to her wish that she play the violin up to the last minute of her life, Maud Powell died while on tour, January 8, 1920, at the age of fifty-one.[61] Her extensive library, including violin works with her practice and performance notes in the margins, was given to the Detroit Public Library. In her will she bequeathed her beloved Guadagnini violin to "the next great woman violinist." Turner presented it to Erica Morini a year later, almost to the day, on the occasion of Morini's debut in Carnegie Hall.[62]

Another prominent woman violinist of the era was Geraldine Morgan, a fellow student of Powell's in Leipzig in the fall of 1882. Meeting the two girls prompted the American composer Sidney Homer, who was in Leipzig at that time with his wife, contralto Louise Homer, to comment later, "This was the beginning of that wonderful succession of women fiddlers. All honor to these pioneers with their great courage and great art."[63]

The same age as Maud Powell, Morgan was born in New York, the daughter of John Paul Morgan, founder of the Oberlin Conservatory of Music and organist at Old Trinity Church. Morgan studied under Leopold Damrosch in New York and then went to study with Schradieck in Leipzig, accompanied by her mother, a composer and translator of songs.[64] From Leipzig Morgan went on to study with Joachim in Berlin. She remained there for eight years and became the first American to win the German crown's Mendelssohn Prize, in 1886. She made numerous successful tours in Europe and Great Britain and became famous especially for playing Bach's Double Concerto with Joachim at the Crystal Palace Concerts in London.

In 1892 Morgan returned to the United States and made her debut with the New York Symphony in Bruch's Concerto in G minor, using a Stradivari violin lent her by Joachim. In New York she became the founder and director of the Joseph Joachim School of Violin Playing, based at Carnegie Hall, which advertised itself as the only school in America authorized by Joachim himself to teach his method. She also founded the Morgan String Quartet, which gave two quartet recitals in New York in 1901. Like the Maud Powell Quartet, it included only one woman, Morgan herself, along with Eugene Boegner, Fritz Schaeffer, and her brother Paul Morgan. The same year she married Benjamin F. Roeder, and the couple had one son born in 1906. Morgan continued in solo performances after her marriage, appearing once or twice a year in New York until about 1910. She died of cancer in New York on May 20, 1918.

Two other remarkable New York–born violinists of this era, Nettie Carpenter and Arma Senkrah, had much briefer careers than either Powell or Morgan. Carpenter, born in 1865, also went to Europe at an early age. The *Musical Herald* of December 1882 reports that "she has been playing in London with much success; she is only twelve years of age." Carpenter went on to study at the Paris Conservatory, winning the first prize for violin there in 1884, and she proceeded on a circuit of highly successful European and American tours. She toured, at various times, with the Anton Rubinstein, Josef Hofmann, Marcella Sembrich, and Adelina Patti companies, among others, and she was a favorite of the virtuoso Pablo Sarasate, with whom she studied for a short time in Spain. In 1891 she married Leo Stern, an English cellist. Her public career came to an end with this marriage, which did not last long, and it never really resumed.

Arma Senkrah was born in 1864 in New York as Arma Levretta Harkness. Later she decided to spell her name backward on the theory that foreign-sounding names had more appeal to English-speaking audiences. The *Musical Herald* of March 1888 relates that when she asked the eminent pianist-conductor Hans von Bülow for his autograph, he wrote in her book, "Homage to Senkrah, from Snah von Wolüb." Taking exotic pseudonyms was not a female idiosyncrasy; the English violinist John Dunn, for example, took the name Ivan Donoiewski.

Her mother took Arma to Germany at the age of nine, and three years later, at twelve, she went to Paris, where she so impressed violin professor Jean-Delphin Alard that he had her admitted to the Conservatory even though the entrance examinations had ended and the classes were filled.[65] She studied there under Massart and Vieuxtemps and later at the Brussels Conservatory with Wieniawski. In 1882 she made her debut at the Crystal Palace in London, and in 1884 and 1885 she made several tours of Europe. In the fall of 1888 several American papers announced her marriage at Weimar to a German attorney named Hoffmann and her subsequent retirement to private life. She gave up her very promising career, and twelve years later, on September 4, 1900, she gave up her life as well, for at only thirty-five years of age she shot herself, allegedly because her husband was infatuated with an actress.[66]

Almost a generation younger than Senkrah was Leonora Jackson, born in Boston in 1879.[67] She studied under Joachim in Berlin and received the Mendelssohn Prize in 1897. For several years she toured Europe and then returned to New York, where her first appearance, at an open rehearsal of the New York Philharmonic on January 5, 1900, got only a lukewarm reception. Critic W. J. Henderson said, "She elected for some inscrutable reason to play the Brahms Concerto," and went on to vilify her bad judgment in choosing this difficult work, as well as that of the "totally inexpert women who gave her a musical education" and who presumably convinced her that she had "already scaled the Alps." But he grudgingly admitted that her bow arm was "the best I have ever seen among women," that her tone was big, and that her phrasing had some good points. Nevertheless, he concluded that she had "no business to play the Brahms Concerto for any one but a teacher."[68]

At least part of the reason for this bad review was the fact that Jackson's "imminent" return from Europe had been announced a number of times during the previous two years but had been repeatedly postponed because of lucrative European engagements. Thus several New York papers began to talk of her as "too high and mighty" to perform in her own country. Clearly this view was not universal, for Jackson proceeded to tour the United States with considerable success. In March 1900 Herbert E. Hall of the *Musical Record* said she received a most cordial welcome everywhere, and that since her New York appearance with the Philharmonic she had played with the Chicago Symphony, Cincinnati Orchestra, Pittsburgh Orchestra, again at Chicago, at Atlanta, for the Evanston (Illinois) Musical Club, Minneapolis Philharmonic Society, and St. Paul (Minnesota) Schubert Club, followed by an engagement at Springfield (Massachusetts) and eight appearances with the Boston Symphony Orchestra (at Fall River, Boston, Baltimore, New York, Brooklyn, Philadelphia, and Providence)—a schedule worthy of Camilla Urso! Further, said Hall, she had dates booked at Orange, Poughkeepsie, Nashville, Akron, Cleveland, Grand Rapids, Chicago, St. Louis, Cincinnati, Louisville, Ann Arbor, Detroit, "and so on west in the late spring." On the other hand, Theodore Thomas, with whose orchestra she had played the Brahms Concerto in January 1900, refused to reengage her, saying she simply was not good enough.[69] And Thomas had no prejudice against women violinists per se, having frequently employed both Urso and Powell.

The following year, 1901, Jackson gave more than 150 concerts, and in October 1902 it was said that she had given 184 concerts that season. Her next two seasons took her to Europe to study, part of the time in Berlin. August 1903 found her in Prague, studying with Otakar Sevčik. She returned to the United States and in 1907 married a Brooklyn realtor, Michael L. McLaughlin, and retired from concert life. They were later divorced, but on October 12,

1915, she married W. Duncan McKim, a widower considerably older than she, and settled in Washington, D.C. Thereafter she gave only occasional private recitals in her home to benefit worthy charities; she never taught. She died in 1969.

A number of other American women violinists from this era were somewhat less prominent but proficient enough to appear as soloists with major orchestras in Europe and America. Marie Nichols, born in Chicago in 1879 and trained in Europe, settled in Boston around 1900 and pursued a very successful career as both touring soloist and teacher. Dora Valeska Becker, born in Texas in 1872, studied in New York and then under Joachim in Berlin, making her debut with the Berlin Philharmonic in 1890. She made several successful American tours and introduced a number of important violin works to American audiences. Maine-born Elise Fellows White (1873–1933) studied and performed in the Boston area, and also in Vienna, and made extended concert tours of the United States and Canada until the beginning of World War I. She also composed songs, violin pieces, and choral works. Jeanne Franko, born in New Orleans, studied with Vieuxtemps and gave many concerts in the New York area in the 1880s and 1890s. In 1895 she formed a trio with Celia Schiller, piano, and Harold Kronold, cello. She married Hugo Kraemer and continued to teach and perform occasionally. She died in 1940 at the age of eighty-five, having outlived her two violinist brothers, Sam and Nahan, and her two sisters, Rachel and Thelma. Thelma was the mother of bandmaster Edwin Franko Goldman.

A quite different case is that of English-born violist and composer Rebecca Thacher Clarke (1886–1979).[70] Born near London to an American father and German mother, she studied at the Royal Academy of Music and at the Royal College of Music, where she was Sir Charles Villiers Stanford's first woman pupil in composition. Her musical education ended when her father threw her out and she was forced to earn her living as a violist. In 1912 she was one of six women chosen by Sir Henry J. Wood to augment the Queen's Hall Orchestra. In the next few years she also joined a successful all-women string quartet, headed by violinist Nora Clench. In 1916 she left London for an extended period of touring and giving concerts that would last through 1923. During this period she made a four-year American tour, in 1916–20, and a world tour, in 1922–23, with cellist May Mukle. She also participated at least four times in the Berkshire Festival of Chamber Music sponsored by Elizabeth Sprague Coolidge. During all this activity she produced her two finest compositions, Viola Sonata, in 1919, and Piano Trio, in 1921. Both these works were written for Berkshire Festival competitions, and the sonata tied for first place with Ernest Bloch's *Suite for Viola.* Coolidge herself broke the tie in favor of Bloch's work. In 1921 the Piano Trio was a runner-up. At last, in 1923 Coolidge awarded Clarke a $1000 commission, resulting in her Rhapsody for cello and piano. Although she frequently visited the United States, often for extended stays, Clarke returned to London in 1924 and remained based there until the outbreak of World War II. She joined the English Ensemble, an all-women piano quartet, which toured Europe in 1928 and traveled again in 1931 to Italy, Holland, and France.

In 1939, as war broke out, Clarke came to the United States, where she remained for the rest of her life. At first she lived with her brothers from 1939 to 1942, and then took a job as a governess in Connecticut. In 1944 she married pianist James Friskin and settled in New York. Thereafter she stopped composing, except for one song and some revisions of earlier works. In the early 1940s she made only a few public appearances, premiering her *Passacaglia on an Old English Tune* at Temple Emmanuel and giving a few performances of her Viola Sonata. She also taught violin, viola, theory, and composition, but privately. She remained in New York until her death at the age of ninety-three. Today she is remembered more as a composer than as a performer, even though her musical output was not large—fifty-two songs, eleven choral works, and twenty-two chamber works for various instruments. As testament to the issues surrounding a woman composer, in a 1918 recital featuring several of her compositions, she felt embarrassed at the repetition of her name and so the program listed her 1917 *Morpheus,* for viola and piano, as the work of one "Anthony Trent."

Also among outstanding violists of the twentieth century was Lillian Fuchs (1903–1995). The sister of notable violinist Joseph Fuchs, she studied violin with Franz Kneisel and composition with Percy Goetschius at the New York Institute of Musical Art (which became the Juilliard School). Soon after her debut in 1926 as a violinist, she switched to viola, which remained her principal instrument. For two decades she was a member of the Perolé String Quartet and became known for her expressive tone and excellent technique. She taught at the Manhattan School, Mannes College of Music, and Juilliard, and also composed several dozen works for solo viola. Among them were *12 Capricci* of 1950, *Sonata pastorale* of 1956, and *Fantasy Etudes* of 1961. In 1994 she received the National Service Award of Chamber Music America.

Women also were attracted to the cello, though never to the extent that they embraced the violin. The two principal cello teachers in America during the late nineteenth century were both based in Boston, Joseph Adamowski of the Adamowski Quartet and August Suck, cellist with the Boston Theatre and longtime member of the Boston Symphony. Suck claimed to be the first to teach the cello to girls in the United States, but in view of Julius Eichberg's record this claim seems a little belated. Eichberg-trained cellists include Lettie Launder and Laura Webster, both members of the Eichberg Quartet for a time, and Georgia Pray Lasselle. And in January 1889 *Etude* announced that Lucy Campbell of Boston, another Eichberg pupil, had been awarded a share of the Mendelssohn Prize at the Berlin Royal Conservatory, the first cellist of either sex ever so honored.

A decade or so later a Swiss cello virtuoso, Elsa Ruegger, came to the United States on a tour that took her to New York, Pittsburgh, Cincinnati, Detroit, Cleveland, and St. Louis. She played sonatas and concertos with various large orchestras, receiving universally good reviews. Another European cellist, May Mukle,[71] became a close friend of Maud Powell's and joined Powell's tour to South Africa in 1905. Born in 1880 in London, Mukle by the age of eleven could support herself with concert engagements. During her long career she performed throughout the world and was sometimes called "the female Casals." Powell persuaded her to come to the United States in 1908 and she was booked solid from January through May. The following season she and her pianist sister Anne Mukle Ford joined Powell in the Maud Powell Trio.

Other women cellists of some note were Beatrice Harrison and Naomi Hewitt, who were known in New York and Boston between about 1913 and 1935. And slightly later came Canadian-born Zara Nelsova, who toured for eighteen years with her sisters Anna and Ida as the Canadian Trio. She studied with Pablo Casals and moved permanently to the United States in 1953. In 1979 Nelsova gave a New York recital that showed she had, after four decades on the concert stage, lost none of her verve or artistry. One other cellist of international reputation was the young Englishwoman Jacqueline du Pré (1945–1985), who, after a brilliant beginning in the 1960s, contracted multiple sclerosis while in her late twenties and was forced to stop performing.

As chamber musicians, however, women string players have had somewhat wider success. A solo career requires an extraordinary talent and a certain charisma that will continue to attract audiences. Violin and cello recitals have never been as popular as piano recitals, and to appear as soloist with an orchestra sets up a series of further requirements, not the least of which is enough money to pay a whole orchestra (unless a soloist already has enough of a reputation to be invited to appear with an orchestra). Chamber music, on the other hand, can satisfy an audience's desire for a group of performers and at the same time lessens the demands placed on a single performer. However, the chamber literature requires greater musical sophistication from the audience.

In the course of the later nineteenth century women string and keyboard players did perform in chamber ensembles, and not only in the large eastern cities. As early as 1885 *Freund's Weekly* reported that a Mrs. Trowbridge of Detroit, together with her daughters Mary and Clara, all three violinists, gave several concerts in Ohio.[72] In April 1888 Baylor College, in Belton, Texas, had a new all-female string quartet directed by Professor G. H. Rowe, whose wife was the quartet's cellist, and this ensemble was said to be the first of its kind in Texas.[73]

It could be argued, perhaps, that these were amateur or at best only semi-professional groups. Nevertheless, by the late 1890s American conservatories and music schools—with five large ones in Chicago alone[74]—were turning out enough violinists to create a demand for performance opportunities, and indeed Chicago then had three resident professional all-male string quartets. By the turn of the century several all-women's chamber ensembles had succeeded the Eichberg Quartet. The Scharwenka Trio (Jennie Ladd Parmelee, violin; Ida Mead Holden, cello; Elma Horne, piano) performed in Boston. The American String Quartette included Georgia Pray as cellist and survived with varying personnel until about World War I. The Carolyn Belcher Quartet (Carolyn Belcher and Anna Eichhorn, violins; Sara Corbett, viola; Charlotte White, cello), also of Boston, and The New York Ladies Trio (Miss Pilat of Austria, violin; Flavie Van den Hende, cello; Hilda Newman, piano) performed around the same period. In the Midwest, the Mrs. Hahn String Quartet (Mrs. Adolf Hahn[75] and Mary Louise Wright, violins; Ada Parke, viola; Nina Parke, cello) gave its first concert in November 1900 in Home City, Ohio, and the Chicago Ladies Trio (Catherine Hall Thatcher, violin; Elizabeth Pickens, cello; Anna Weiss, piano) was based in that city.

Also prominent in New York from about 1910 to 1917 were the Edith Rubel Trio and the Gisela Weber Trio. In the 1920s New York had the Marianne Kneisel String Quartet (Marianne Kneisel and Elizabeth Worth, violins; Lillian Fuchs, viola; Phyllis Kraeuter, cello), organized by the daughter of Franz Kneisel, Boston Symphony concertmaster and founder of an important early string quartet (the Franz Kneisel Quartet, 1886–1917), and the Durrell String Quartet (Josephine Durrell and Edith Robound, violins; Anna Golden, viola; Mildred Ridley, cello).

From the time that Boston's all-male Beethoven Club, consisting of two violins, viola, bass, and flute, admitted cellist Georgia Pray in 1890,[76] women occasionally joined previously all-male chamber groups. Both Maud Powell and Olive Mead founded their own quartets in which each was the only woman, but in the late 1890s Chicago had the Studio Trio (Miss Marion Carpenter, violin; Mr. Day Williams, cello; Mrs. Annette H. Jones, piano) and Boston had the Currier String Quartet (Frank Currier and Marie Schumacher, violins; Bertram Currier, viola; Charlotte White, cello). In New York Adele Margulies, a pianist and prominent teacher, formed the Margulies Trio (with violinist Leopold Lichtenberg and cellist Victor Herbert, later replaced by Leo Schulz), which gave concerts every season from about 1889 to 1918, and in the 1920s there were the Musical Art Quartet, all men except for cellist Marie Roemaet-Rosanoff; the Boston Quintet, with cellist Alma LaPalme, a pupil of Charlotte White; and the Curtis Quartet, made up of faculty members from the Curtis Institute, all men in 1929 except for first violinist Lea Luboshutz (1885–1965). Luboshutz was a former pupil of Eugène Ysaÿe's and sometime soloist with leading orchestras. This trend of popularity for chamber ensembles was revived from about 1980 on.

During the first half of the mid-twentieth century, however, the gains that had been made by women concert violinists between 1870 and 1920 appeared to be largely lost. From 1910 to the late 1920s Canadian-born Kathleen Parlow (1890–1963), a pupil of Leopold Auer and considered a genius by the Russian master, toured the United States and Canada, but from 1929 on she devoted herself largely to teaching.[77] And there was Ruth Pierce Posselt, born in 1914 in Medford, Massachusetts, who appeared for some years as a child prodigy and then returned to the concert stage in the early 1930s. She won the Schubert Memorial Prize in 1932 and undertook a European tour that year, but despite enthusiastic reviews her appearances after this were relatively rare. She married Richard Burgin, who was concertmaster of the Boston Symphony from 1920 to 1962, and appeared with him at least once, in the orchestra of the Opera Company of Boston in 1979.

A contemporary of Posselt's was Carroll Glenn, who became known for her bold style of playing and big tone and for her championing of American composers. Born in 1919 in Chester, South Carolina, she began her studies at the age of four with her mother and at the age of eleven came to New York to study with Edouard Dethier at Juilliard, becoming the youngest student to be admitted there. By the age of twenty-one she had won the four major awards open to young American musicians at that time—the Naumburg, Schubert Memorial, National Federation of Music Clubs, and Town Hall. She went on to perform with the leading conductors of her time and the major orchestras of the world. She and her husband, pianist Eugene List, founded the Southern Vermont Music Festival. She also taught widely, at the Eastman School of Music, Manhattan School of Music, and elsewhere, as well as abroad. She died of a brain tumor in 1983, at the age of sixty-four.[78]

In the 1930s and 1940s, however, with the one exception of Erica Morini, virtually no women violinists of international renown were on the concert stage, and fewer and fewer appeared in prominent chamber groups. Although World War I had created some demand for women string players to replace men away at war, they all gave way to the returning men, and World War II did not seem to create a similar demand.[79]

Economics undoubtedly was a factor, but the matter of women's versus men's earnings has long been a murky one. In 1900, for example, violin teacher Edith Lynwood Winn maintained that female pianists and violinists received as much compensation for their services as men, and therefore men regarded women performers as economic rivals.[80] Only eight years later—too short a time for a total turnabout—pianist Olga Samaroff held that she could get as many or more engagements as a male performer simply because her fee was lower than a man's.[81] Some women musicians deny that economics has anything to do with their exclusion. Erica Morini, the only woman violinist of her generation to pursue a long-term successful career as a soloist, believed that most women "lack the concentration, the will power, and the willingness to sacrifice everything to art which is absolutely necessary if one is to become a fine artist." Although just as many women as men are born with a great talent for music, maintained Morini, most lack the single-minded drive and determination to bring their talent to fulfillment.[82]

Morini herself, born in Vienna in 1904, first studied the violin with her father and then with Otakar Sevčik at the Vienna Conservatory. She made her debut at Leipzig under Artur Nikisch's baton, and she later performed with Felix Weingartner and other famous conductors. She made her American debut at Carnegie Hall in January 1921—critics said this seventeen-year-old girl would take the place of Maud Powell, who had died almost exactly a year earlier. Indeed, in May 1921 Powell's husband Sunny Turner supposedly lent (some stories say "gave") Morini his wife's valuable Guadagnini violin for her American tour.[83] Thereafter Morini toured for several years in the United States, returned to Europe for a time, and then settled permanently in the United States. She married Felice Siracusano, but the couple had no children, Morini believing it impossible to combine a family with her career. In 1953, during a performance of the Brahms Violin Concerto with the New York Philharmonic, Morini's A-string snapped. She exchanged instruments with the concertmaster, John Corigliano, so fast that the movement continued almost without a break. Meanwhile an orchestra member repaired the string and returned it to Morini in time for her cadenza.[84] From the 1960s on she devoted herself more and more to teaching. In 1976, at age seventy-two, she gave a New York recital for the first time in ten years, and reviewers praised her excellent but unobtrusive technique and consistently beautiful tone; one called her recital one of the season's most musically satisfying events.[85] She died in 1995, at the age of ninety-one. By then her recordings were long out of print, but in 1998 Arbiter, a label focusing on previously unreleased recordings, brought out a number of Morini's concert performances. According to the *New York Times* review of new releases, "Morini's playing is powerful, focused, and personalized with the richly lyrical touch that was always her hallmark."[86]

Though the American Federation of Musicians vehemently denies any sex discrimination against its members, financial or otherwise, only since the late 1960s have women resurfaced in prominent professional chamber ensembles, including string quartets, trios, and chamber orchestras. By the mid-1970s the personnel of both Alexander Schneider's Brandenburg Ensemble and the Chamber Music Society of Lincoln Center was nearly half women. The all-female Vieuxtemps Quartet (Marnie Hall and Masako Yaganita, violins, Linda Lawrence, viola, and Evelyn Steinbock, cello) lasted from 1972 to 1976. Of the major American string quartets of the late 1970s, only the Composers Quartet (half and half), the Cleveland Quartet (one woman; later replaced by a man), and the Primavera Quartet (all women and winners of the 1977 Naumburg Chamber Music Award) were bucking the trend. In the mid-1970s at least four all-women's trios were formed: the New York Lyric Arts Trio (Mary Blankstein, violin; Wendy Brennan, cello; Gena Raps, piano); the Caecilian Trio (Sally O'Reilly, violin; Beverly Lauridsen, cello; Annie Petit, piano); the Walden Trio (Gwyndolyn Mansfield, flute; Maxine Neuman, cello; Joan Stein, piano); and the Jubal Trio (Lucy Shelton, soprano [replaced in 1990 by Christine Schadeberg]; Sue Ann Kahn, flute; Susan Jolles, harp), winner of the 1976 Naumburg Foundation Chamber Music Award. Of these only the Jubal Trio survived into the late 1990s. By the end of the twentieth century, however, women were predominant in at least three well-known string quartets, the Lark Quartet, Lydian Quartet, and Cassatt Quartet, as well as participating with men in other groups, such as the Borromeo Quartet and Coolidge Quartet.

The Lark Quartet (Diane Pascal and Jennifer Orchard, violins, Anna Kruger, viola, and Astrid Schween, cello) was formed in 1985 in New York, where its members reside. Late in 1999 Danielle Farina replaced Kruger as their violist. Winners of the prestigious Naumburg Award in 1990 and gold medalist at the 1991 Shostakovich International String Quartet competition in Russia, the group tries to balance traditional repertory with new commissions and previously unknown works. For example, in 1999 in a special series at Columbia University it played an entire program of twelve-tone music, half of which was virtually unknown: quartets by Nikolai Roslavets and Arthur Lourié, written in 1910 and 1915 respectively, as well as works of Anton Webern and Alexander von Zemlinsky. Composer Aaron Jay Kernis's Pulitzer Prize–winning String Quartet no. 2 was written for the Lark Quartet. The group also has set out to develop new audiences for chamber music through school appearances and college residencies and visiting professorships at various institutions. In the late 1990s it was the quartet-in-residence at Columbia University. In addition to touring throughout the United States, the quartet has traveled to China, Australia, Russia, Mexico, New Zealand, and many European countries.

The Lydian Quartet (Wilma Smith and Judith Eissenberg, violins, Mary Ruth Ray, viola, and Rhonda Rider, cello) was founded in 1980 to be artists-in-residence at Brandeis University in Waltham, Massachusetts. In 2000 the quartet is still there, although in 1987 Smith left to become concertmaster of the New Zealand Symphony and was replaced by Daniel Stepner. Initially audiences were somewhat upset that the Lydians were no longer all-female, but Stepner's excellent playing won over most of them. Winner of the Naumburg Award in 1984, the quartet performed thirty to forty concerts per year, and toured both in the United States and Europe. In addition to teaching, it ran the undergraduate performance program at Brandeis. Twice honored for adventurous programming by ASCAP (American Society of Composers, Authors and Publishers) and Chamber Music America, the quartet performed numerous premieres of works written for it by John Harbison, Lee Hyla, Steve Mackey, and others.

An example of a successful cellist specializing in chamber music is the Lydians' founding member Rhonda Rider, who also taught cello and chamber music at Boston Conservatory and was a member of the Boston Conservatory Chamber Players. Born in 1956 in Michigan, she graduated from the Oberlin Conservatory and Yale School of Music. She was principal cellist in the New Haven Symphony while studying at Yale and won the Concert Artist Guild Award in 1980, which gave her New York and Chicago debuts as a soloist. Rider occasionally played solo recitals but remained dedicated to chamber music, believing it gave her greater choice of repertory and performance venues. She also enjoyed teaching, serving as director of the Artist Diploma Program at Brandeis and of the university's summer music festival. In 1995 Rider joined a new piano trio, the Triple Helix, with violinist Bayla Keyes and pianist Lois Shapiro. Like the Lydian Quartet, the group is dedicated to the performance of contemporary music as well as the traditional repertory.

Another successful all-women quartet is the Cassatt Quartet, formed in 1985 and named for the celebrated American impressionist painter Mary Cassatt. Violinist Muneko Otani and violist Michiko Oshima were born in Japan and studied both there and in the United States; violinist Jennifer Leshnower and cellist Kelley Mikkelsen were born in the United States. Based in New York, the quartet has performed throughout North America, Europe, and the Far East and has received numerous awards. Their repertory ranges from the classical period to the present day, with a considerable commitment to contemporary composers such as Tina Davidson and Julia Wolfe. They also have served as artists-in-residence at numerous schools, among them the State University of New York at Buffalo and Syracuse and East Carolina universities.

Unlike these three quartets, the Borromeo Quartet, formed in 1989 by four musicians from the Curtis Institute, has two men, violinists Nicholas Kitchen and Ruggero Allifranchini, and two women, violist Hsin-Yun Huang and cellist Yeesun Kim. After studying individually at Curtis, the four became the first ensemble accepted by the New England Conservatory for its prestigious Artist Diploma program in 1990, and upon graduation in 1992 they were invited to join the faculty and serve as the conservatory's quartet-in-residence. Since then they have become widely known as an outstanding ensemble. (Early in 2000, William Fedkenheuer replaced Allifranchini, and Mai Motobuchi replaced Hsin-Yun Huang.) The Borromeo is not unique in its mixed-gender personnel. The Kronos Quartet, founded in 1973 and renowned as a leading voice for new music (as of 1999 some 400 works have been written or commissioned for it), has included a woman cellist, Joan Jeanrenaud, since 1978. (Late in 1999, she was replaced by another woman, Jennifer Culp.) And the once all-male Muir String Quartet, winner of the Naumburg Award in 1981, hired Boston Symphony Orchestra violinist Lucia Lin in 1998.

In the second half of the 1900s a new generation of women string players had emerged as soloists. Texas-born violist Karen Ann Phillips was performing widely in solo recitals as well as with major orchestras.[87] She was not permanently affiliated with a chamber group but often appeared as a guest artist with established groups. Born on October 29, 1942, in Dallas, Phillips attended schools there and in 1960 went to the Eastman School of Music, where she received a bachelor's degree in 1964. She then spent a term at Yale's Summer School of Music, a year at Philadelphia's Curtis Institute, and two years at Juilliard, from which she received a postgraduate diploma in 1967. From 1969 to 1971 she was an affiliate artist with the Los Angeles Music Center, and from 1971 to 1972 with the Worcester (Massachusetts) Arts Association; in these capacities she gave several hundred recitals, lectures, workshops, and demonstrations at schools, service clubs, church groups, and women's clubs.

Throughout the 1970s Phillips pursued an active career as a soloist, becoming known especially for her performances of contemporary music, much of it extremely difficult from a technical standpoint, and frequently giving premieres of new works for her instrument. A number of composers wrote pieces specifically for her, among them Morton Feldman, Netty Simons, Marga Richter, David Bedford, Claire Polin, and Elisabeth Lutyens. In a 1975 article entitled "Today's Viola"[88] Phillips described some difficulties of the new literature: Luciano Berio's *Sequenza VI* calls for random wide sliding of the fingers and quick alternation between the ordinary and the harmonic positions; Tonia Scherchen's *Lien* demands six different kinds of pizzicato; David Bedford's *Spillihpnerak* (Karen Phillips's name spelled backward) calls for a kind of bowing in which the hairs of the bow are loosened, the bow is reversed, and the body of the viola slips between the hairs and wood of the bow, so the hair can move across all four strings, producing four tones at the same time.

In addition to performing, Phillips herself composed songs for voice and piano, orchestral works, and chamber music. She also taught, made many recordings, and in 1975 began a weekly half-hour radio program on New York's municipal station. Entitled *Overture to Women,* it was devoted to women musicians and composers. Phillips believed women composers need extra support and publicity, and her radio program, for which she worked without pay, was a step in that direction.

Besides Phillips, others in the new generation of violinists rising to fame in the 1970s included Korean-born Kyung-Wha Chung, who shared the Leventritt Violin Prize with Pinchas Zukerman in 1967. Chung was carving out a career as a soloist. Romanian-born and Israeli-bred Miriam Fried became, in 1971, the first woman to win the prestigious Queen Elisabeth of Belgium Competition and was performing with major orchestras and in recitals all over North America and Europe.

Ani Kavafian, a member of the Chamber Music Society of Lincoln Center from 1979 on, was the 1977 winner of the Avery Fisher Career Grant, entitling her to a concert with the New York Philharmonic, a cash award of $1000, and six engagements with other American orchestras. A soloist with many of America's leading orchestras, she premiered Tod Machover's Concerto for hyper violin and orchestra and Henri Lazarof's Concerto for violin and string orchestra, as well as Michelle Ekezian's *Red Harvest: Concerto for Violin and Orchestra,* which was composed for her and performed with the Brooklyn Philharmonic in 1997. Kavafian was born in 1946 in Turkey to Armenian parents and came to the United States at the age of nine. She earned a master's degree from Juilliard, where she studied with Ivan Galamian. As a chamber musician she is a member of the Walden Horn Trio with pianist Anne-Marie McDermott and hornist Robert Routch, and she is part of the da Salo String Trio with violist Barbara Westphal and cellist Gustav Rivinius.

Ani Kavafian also often appeared in concert with her sister, Ida Kavafian. Born in Turkey in 1952, Ida, too, became a violinist and a violist. She made her debut as a recitalist in New York in 1978 and was warmly received. A winner of the Avery Fisher Career Grant in 1988, she had studied with Mischa Mischakoff and Oscar Shumsky. Among composers with whom she worked closely were Toru Takemitsu, who wrote a concerto for her, and jazz greats Chick Corea and Wynton Marsalis, with whom she toured and recorded. Since her founding membership in the contemporary music ensemble TASHI in the 1970s, she has also toured and recorded with the Guarneri Quartet and the Chamber Music Society of Lincoln Center, of which she became an artist member in 1989. In the 1990s she was for six years the violinist of the Beaux Arts Trio, among the most highly regarded piano trios in the world, which gave eighty to 100 concerts a year all over the world. In the late 1990s she cofounded a new group, Opus One, with pianist Anne-Marie McDermott, violist (and her husband) Steven Tenenbaum, and cellist Peter Wiley.

The last two decades of the twentieth century saw the rise and widespread acceptance of many more women string players: Stephanie Chase, Nadja Salerno-Sonnenberg, Pamela Frank, Sarah Chang, Hilary Hahn, Midori, violist Kim Kashkashian, cellist Sharon Robinson, and classical guitarist Sharon Isbin. Stephanie Chase became a successful violin soloist in the romantic and modern literature. In addition she developed a thriving career as a period instrument player, playing Mozart and Beethoven on an instrument of the kind used during their day. Born in Illinois in 1957, she began to play the violin at the age of two. Her first teacher was her mother, Fannie Chase, and later teachers included William Lincer and Arthur Grumiaux. At the age of nine she won the Chicago Symphony Orchestra's youth competition and began to appear nationwide in recitals and as soloist with an orchestra. Her recording of the Beethoven Violin Concerto on an 18th-century Tyrolean instrument was the Critic's Choice in 1993. The noted musicologist H. C. Robbins Landon said of it, "Stephanie Chase has a great sense of style, a matchless technique, and flawless intonation."[89]

In 1999 three young violinists—Salerno-Sonnenberg, Frank, and Chang —tied to win the coveted Avery Fisher Prize, the first time it was ever awarded to a woman. The prize is an award to support outstanding performing musicians and in 1999, to commemorate its twenty-fifth anniversary, the usual cash award was doubled to $50,000. It is separate from the Avery Fisher Career Grant, which awards $10,000 to each of up to five emerging artists annually; seventy-three such grants were awarded from 1974 to 2000, many of them to women, and Salerno-Sonnenberg, Frank, and Chang had all been recipients. The more select Avery Fisher Prize is awarded only when the eleven-member executive awards committee agrees upon a musician who merits it; it had last been given to pianist Garrick Ohlsson in 1994.

Nadja Salerno-Sonnenberg was born in Rome in 1961 and emigrated to the United States in 1969 to study at the Curtis Institute of Music. She later studied with Dorothy DeLay at Juilliard. A winner of the 1981 Naumburg International Violin Competition and the 1983 Avery Fisher Career Grant, she acquired an ardent following as well as considerable criticism for her highly charged music-making and dramatic performances. In addition to the standard violin repertory, in the late 1990s she also became known for crossing over to popular music, recording the Hollywood score for the motion picture *Humoresque* on a CD that includes Gershwin's "Embraceable You" and other songs, as well as working closely with contemporary composers such as William Bolcom.

Pamela Frank, daughter of acclaimed pianists Claude Frank and Lillian Kalir, frequently played chamber music both at home and in public. Frank, born in 1968, began her violin studies at age five with Shirley Givens and later studied with Szymon Goldberg and Jaime Laredo. Her formal debut came in 1985, and in 1988 she received the Avery Fisher Career Grant. In 1989 she graduated from the Curtis Institute of Music. During the next decade she appeared with many leading orchestras in Europe and North America and frequently performed in recital with her father and with pianist Peter Serkin. She played her first Carnegie Hall recital in 1995 and often performed in chamber groups. In 1998 she premiered a new violin concerto by Ellen Taaffe Zwilich.

Sarah Chang was born in Philadelphia in 1981 to Korean parents. She began studying at age four and within a year performed with orchestras in the Philadelphia area. Her auditions by age eight led to immediate engagements as soloist with the New York Philharmonic and Philadelphia Orchestra. In 1992 she became the youngest ever recipient of the Avery Fisher Career Grant. By age seventeen she had appeared with almost every major orchestra in the United States and Europe and had reached even wider audiences through numerous television appearances, such as a "Live from Lincoln Center" broadcast with the New York Philharmonic and an "Evening at Pops" appearance with the Boston Pops.

Just as Chang began on the concert stage as an acclaimed child prodigy, Hilary Hahn, too, was playing with major orchestras from a remarkably young age. Hahn, born in Baltimore in 1980, began playing the violin at the age of four in the Peabody Conservatory Suzuki program. From the age of five until she entered the Curtis Institute at the age of ten, she studied with Klara Berkovich. At Curtis she studied with Jascha Brodsky and continued to work with him until his death at age eighty-nine. Thereafter she regularly played for Jaime Laredo and studied chamber music with Felix Galimir and Gary Graffman. She made her debut at age eleven with the Baltimore Symphony Orchestra, and in the next few years worked as soloist with the New York Philharmonic, Pittsburgh and Detroit symphonies, and Philadelphia and Cleveland orchestras. She also appeared in recitals and performed chamber music at the distinguished Marlboro Music Festival, as well as touring in Europe and Australia. Her first recording, of unaccompanied Bach solo partitas and sonatas, prompted David Mermelstein to write, "From the outset she establishes herself as a formidable talent, displaying unusual confidence and poise in her bowing. . . . Amazingly she displays no fear in this daunting repertory."[90]

Another child prodigy, Midori, born in Japan in 1971, made her debut with the New York Philharmonic at the age of eleven. Thereafter she was acclaimed not only for her extraordinary playing at a young age but for her unusual aplomb. At one concert while performing a concerto she twice broke a string and had to borrow violins to continue, which she managed without interruption. She went on to perform with most of the world's leading orchestras in addition to presenting recitals and collaborating with others in chamber music. In 1992 she established a foundation that provides concerts and other educational activities in New York public schools for children who would not otherwise have an opportunity for involvement in the arts. She herself participated in many of the foundation's programs, and many other artists, ranging from young ensembles to well-known soloists, have been involved.

Violist Kim Kashkashian, born in Michigan of Armenian descent, graduated from the Peabody Conservatory, where she studied with Walter Trampler and Karen Tuttle. She subsequently appeared as soloist with major orchestras in New York, Berlin, Vienna, London, Munich, and Tokyo, as well as in recital all over the world and in chamber ensembles at the Marlboro Music Festival. As guest artist, she played with the Beaux Arts Trio, and Tokyo, Guarneri, and Emerson string quartets. She worked extensively with contemporary composers, such as Barbara Kolb, John Harbison, Sofia Gubaidulina, and Alfred Schnittke. She also taught at the Mannes College of Music and Indiana University. Later she moved to Germany where she became professor of viola at the Berlin Hochschule für Musik. In 2000 Kashkashian accepted a post at Boston's New England Conservatory of Music.

Cellist Sharon Robinson became known as both a soloist and chamber musician. Born into a musical family (her father played bass, her mother violin, and all her siblings are string players), she gave her first concert at age seven and has won numerous awards, including the Avery Fisher Recital Award and the Leventritt Award. Her close relationships with contemporary composers have led to numerous commissions for solo and chamber works, as well as concertos from Leon Kirchner, Arvo Pärt, Ellen Taaffe Zwilich, and others. In 1999 she appeared with her husband, violinist Jaime Laredo, and the Indianapolis Symphony in the world premiere of Ned Rorem's Double Concerto for Cello and Orchestra. In 1978 she was a cofounder of the Kalichstein-Laredo-Robinson Trio, which remains active after two decades.

The first woman to enter the top ranks of solo guitarists is Sharon Isbin.[91] Born in 1960 in Minnesota, she planned to be a scientist like her professor-father, but when she was nine years old her family went to Italy and there she took her first classical guitar lessons. Her teachers included Andrés Segovia and Oscar Ghiglia. She also studied Bach with Rosalyn Tureck and collaborated with her in preparing the first performance editions of the Bach lute suites for guitar. At the time of this writing, Isbin plays sixty concerts a year in the United States, travels to Europe annually, and heads the guitar departments at the Juilliard School, where she created the division, and at the Aspen Music Festival. She has played chamber music with Nadja Salerno-Sonnenberg and the Emerson String Quartet, among others. She also has commissioned new works for guitar from John Corigliano, Lukas Foss, Ned Rorem, David Diamond, Joseph Schwantner, and Joan Tower. Corigliano's 1993 *Troubadours* required her to use electronic reinforcement for the instrument, and in order not to distort the natural sound of the classical guitar she devised a unique wireless sound system for her performances.

Even though women string players at the start of the twenty-first century are finding many more openings and much more support than in the past, orchestras offer by far the largest number of opportunities for them. The road there, however, as Chapters 5 and 11 will show, has also been a rocky one.

3

SEATED AT THE KEYBOARD

Sit in a simple, graceful, unconstrained posture. Never turn up the eyes or swing about the body; the expression you mean to give will never be understood by those foolish motions. . . . However loud you wish to be, never thump. . . . Aim more at pleasing than at astonishing. . . . Never bore people with ugly music merely because it is the work of some famous composer, and do not let the pieces you perform . . . be too long.

Harper's Magazine, September 1851[1]

THIS ADVICE from *Harper's Magazine,* addressed to "Musical Misses," indicates without a doubt that playing the piano was considered a social grace of accomplished young ladies of the mid-nineteenth century. By 1852, women already had been playing keyboard instruments for a very long time. The frontispiece of the earliest and most important printed collection of English virginal (a kind of harpsichord) music, *Parthenia,* dating from 1612 and 1613, pictures a young woman at the keyboard, and in the eighteenth century, as harpsichord and clavichord were replaced by the piano, women moved quite naturally to it.

As with the voice and other instruments, though, public performance was another matter. In the Puritan mind it was too closely allied to theatrical productions and therefore was sinful. At the very least a musician appearing in public was no more respectable than an actor or actress. For children, however, who were not quite considered "people" in Puritan society, this stricture seemed not to apply to them. What was not appropriate for a lady, even a young one, might still be countenanced in a little girl. The earliest public keyboard performances by women in the United States were those of child prodigies, or of exceptionally gifted children, at least.

Sophia Hewitt made her debut in New York in 1807 at the age of seven, and she continued to play in public throughout her childhood. She was only eighteen and an experienced performer when the Handel and Haydn Society first offered her the job of organist. Another very young keyboard player of

the early 1800s in Boston was Mlle Eustaphiève (later Mme Peruzzi), the little daughter of the Russian consul who also played in Graupner's band.

Among the first documented keyboard performances by young women
was a subscription concert advertised in the Boston *Columbian Centinel* of
November 21, 1792, which included "A Sonata on the Piano Forte by a Young
Lady."[2] Then in 1795, also in Boston, came Miss M. A. Wrighten's performance of the much abused *Battle of Prague,* the most popular of the so-called battle pieces in which the music imitates the sounds of battle.[3] This was a year
after Elisabeth von Hagen had moved to Boston from New York and offered
to teach piano, harpsichord, organ, and voice to young ladies. Von Hagen also
composed keyboard music, producing an impressive set of variations called
The Country Maid. [4]

Other than Sophia Hewitt's appearances as both a soloist and an accompanist during her years in Boston, public performances by women pianists
were rare until about 1850. Several accounts survive of a concert at New York
City Hall on May 10, 1830, by the Musical Fund Society, at which Miss Sterling played Herz's *Grand Variations on "Ma Fanchette est charmante."* The
Mercantile Adviser, lavish to the point of bombast, said that "the keys of her
piano seemed gifted with vocal powers." Sterling continued to perform this
piece, along with Moscheles's *Fall of Paris,* another battle piece, during the
next five years.[5]

In the 1840s two other young women pianists attracted attention. One was
Josephine Bramson, whose farewell concert at Boston's Melodeon got a rave
review in the *Evening Transcript* of January 3, 1846. The other was a seventeen-
year-old Englishwoman, Jane Sloman, who had moved with her parents to New
York in 1839 and gave eight very successful concerts in Boston in November and
December 1841. She returned to Boston in 1842 and 1844 as well.[6]

Presumably other women pianists performed for the American public
between 1800 and 1850; however, none could be classed as a virtuoso performer of the kind that increasingly dominated the concert scene in Europe. By
1836 Clara Wieck (later Schumann) had been named Imperial Chamber Virtuoso by the Hapsburg court, and Marie Pleyel (1811–1875) had long since
created a sensation in Belgium, Austria, Germany, and Russia. Of comparable
caliber both in ability and popularity was the first American piano virtuoso,
Louis Moreau Gottschalk (1829–1869), who, after a few years in Europe,
made his first triumphant tour of the United States in the 1853–54 season. By
then the American public was ready to embrace a brilliant soloist, and if the
music performed tended to sacrifice more lasting qualities for flamboyancy
and technical bravura, it disturbed American audiences no more than it did the
Europeans who thronged to hear Liszt perform the works of Moscheles and
Herz and the like, along with only an occasional Beethoven sonata.[7]

The American public got its wish in 1862 with the arrival of an eight-
year-old Venezuelan girl, Teresa Carreño, who for the next half-century was to

thrill audiences all over the world. A grandniece of Simon Bolívar and the daughter of a minister of finance ousted by revolution, Teresa received her first piano lessons from her musical father.[8] She made her New York debut on November 25, 1862, at Irving Hall, sharing the program with violinist Theodore Thomas (better remembered for his fame as a conductor) and others. She played a rondo by Hummel together with a string quintet, and pieces by Thalberg and Gottschalk. Gottschalk, when he heard her play, said he would teach her whenever he came to New York, but his heavy touring schedule did not permit regular lessons. During the next two months, she gave five more concerts, and then made her Boston debut on January 2, 1863. It was followed by some twenty concerts in the Boston area, whereupon Carl Zerrahn invited her to play Mendelssohn's *Capriccio brillante* with the Boston Philharmonic Society orchestra. She accepted, although she had never seen the work, and learned it in three days. The critics were ecstatic in their praise—all except John Sullivan Dwight, who admitted that he was not partial to child prodigies but allowed that this one might prove interesting.

In March the Carreños went to Cuba, and in April Teresa made her Havana debut. She returned to the United States in the fall and soon thereafter played for President Abraham Lincoln at the White House, for an encore improvising on the president's favorite song, "Listen to the Mockingbird."[9] (She was to return to the White House fifty-five years later to play for President Woodrow Wilson.) On December 22, 1863, Teresa celebrated her tenth birthday in Boston by giving a concert with Benjamin J. Lang, noted pianist, organist, conductor, and teacher. She included two of her own compositions, *Impromptu* and *La Emilia Danza.*

For the next couple of years Carreño remained in the United States, but in March 1866 she and her family sailed for Liverpool, to pursue her career in Europe. In May she went to Paris and, now a ripe twelve-year-old, made her debut at the Salle Érard and became a protégé of the influential Madame Érard herself. Carreño met Rossini, who gave her letters of recommendation, and Liszt, who offered to teach her free of charge in Rome, an offer she did not accept.

Among other musicians Carreño met during this period were the composers Gounod, Auber, and Berlioz, the publisher M. Heugel, who began to publish some of the compositions she somehow found time to produce, and the singer Adelina Patti. In part through Patti's influence, Carreño at the age of fourteen began to study voice. For the summer of 1868 she returned to London, where Anton Rubinstein heard her play and offered to teach her. In later years she always said the deepest influences on her career had been Gottschalk, who had first introduced her to classical music; Liszt, who had told her to cultivate her own individuality and not follow blindly the paths of others;[10] and Rubinstein, who called her "his sunshine" and became, she felt, her true guide and mentor.[11]

Her tours as a teenager came under the management of the great impresario Maurice Strakosch. When the Franco-Prussian War broke out, Carreño was stranded in London, unable to return to France. Needing work, she turned to Strakosch's bitter rival, Colonel Mapleson, who booked her for an extensive tour of England as well as for the famous London Promenade Concerts, conducted by Sir Arthur Sullivan at that time. It was during this period, in 1872, that Carreño was called on to make an impromptu opera debut in Edinburgh. The singer who was to play Queen Marguerite in Meyerbeer's *Les Huguenots* fell ill, and Carreño quickly learned this difficult soprano part to replace her.

In the fall of 1872 Carreño began an extensive American tour as pianist with the singer Carlotta Patti (Adelina's sister), the aging tenor Mario, and violinist Emile Sauret. The company went to New York, Canada, Boston, and Charleston. And in 1873, at the age of nineteen, she married Sauret and settled in London, where their child, Emilita, was born on March 23, 1874. In June the young couple gave their first joint concert, and in fall they began another American tour, leaving the baby in London with a Mrs. Bischoff. This tour took the Saurets as far as the Pacific Coast and ended in New York. At its end the marriage was falling apart. Sauret returned to England alone, and Carreño, remaining in America, agreed to let Mrs. Bischoff, by now very attached to Emilita, adopt her child.

Too downhearted to begin another tour, Carreño went to Boston and looked up an old friend, the voice teacher Hermine Rudersdorff, who hired her as an accompanist and agreed to give her voice lessons. After a year, on February 25, 1876, Carreño made her formal operatic debut as Zerlina in Mozart's *Don Giovanni* at the New York Academy of Music. Several New York and Boston performances followed, and the reviews were favorable, but she now decided that her voice was not good enough after all and she would return to the piano.

The part of Don Giovanni in Carreño's operatic debut was sung by the Italian baritone Giovanni Tagliapietra, who soon afterward became her second husband. The couple settled in the New York suburb of New Rochelle and had three children: Lulu, 1878–1881; Teresita, born 1882; and Giovanni, born 1885. Between babies Carreño performed and toured. Although she would have been happy to retire at this point, her husband was a compulsive gambler, as well as a drinker and philanderer, and she had to function as the family's principal financial support.[12]

On tour in the spring of 1883, with conductor Leopold Damrosch, Carreño introduced Grieg's Piano Concerto, a work with which she was associated for the rest of her career and which she helped make popular in America. The following year she gave the premiere performance of Edward MacDowell's second *Suite Moderne* in a concert in Chicago.[13] MacDowell had come to Carreño for piano lessons in 1876, when he was only fourteen, and she became his lifelong friend, encouraging his compositions and performing them frequently all over the world. He later dedicated his Concerto in D minor to her.

Carreño herself also continued to compose. The *Teresita Waltz,* written shortly after her third daughter's birth, became one of her regular encore pieces, and the sheet music for it had a steady sale for many years in both the United States and Europe. She also wrote a serenade, waltzes, fantasies, ballades, and other piano pieces, and a hymn for the Bolívar Centennial of Venezuela in 1883.

Carreño's schedule during the 1880s was very full. She played at the Worcester Festival four times (1880, 1885, 1887, 1888), a record number of appearances for a single artist. She toured Canada and the United States a number of times, both with and without her husband. In 1885 she returned to Venezuela, where she was received as a national heroine. She was invited to return the following year, not only as a pianist but as the organizer and director of an Italian opera company. She left most of the organizational details of this assignment to her husband, who apparently lacked the talent for it, for when the Teresa Carreño Opera Company opened its season in Caracas, it was immediately beset with difficulties. The public became hostile to the company, the conductor and assistant conductor both walked out, and for some weeks Carreño herself took up the baton and conducted performances of *La Favorita, La Sonnambula,* and *Lucia di Lammermoor.* This was her first and last experience on the podium. It also signaled an irreparable rift in her second marriage.

Upon her return to the United States Carreño continued to perform widely, her popularity undiminished. The pyrotechnical displays of her earlier years were by now giving way to a more balanced musical approach. Thus one respected critic said of her, in January 1888, "Her touch is inclined to be a little too percussive but the eminently musical qualities of her style overbalance this. Earlier in her career she sacrificed much for mere effect, but she plays now more soberly and certainly more intellectually."[14]

Nevertheless, Carreño herself was not wholly satisfied. In 1889, with her second marriage ended, she decided to go to Germany and test her mettle there. Her German debut with the Berlin Philharmonic on November 18, 1889 was an instant success. Critics raved over her "unconventional" playing and her dramatic temperament. Hans von Bülow, the great German pianist who was turning more and more to conducting and usually had little use for women as musicians, said she was the most interesting player of the present day. There could be no higher praise.

For the next seven years Carreño made Germany her home base, from which she toured all over Europe. In May 1891 she concluded a three-month tour in which she had performed nearly every night, leading one writer to say, "Only an American woman could do such an enormous amount of work; . . . and everywhere is tremendously successful."[15] The Budapest papers called her the "female Rubinstein." Her passionate interpretations gave rise to a number of other sobriquets, chief among them "Valkyrie of the Keyboard" and "Lioness of the Piano."

The principal other pianist of Europe at this time was a Scottish-born pupil of Liszt's, Eugène d'Albert, and in 1891 the two virtuosos finally met for the first time. The following year they were married and settled in Dresden, and their first child, Eugenia, was born. D'Albert was a splendid pianist, but he believed himself to have an even greater vocation for composing. Carreño encouraged him, and she gave the premiere of his Second Piano Concerto, under his baton. Unfortunately, the critics praised her playing but not the concerto or its composer. Repeat performances of the work had the same result, and D'Albert, never easy to get along with, accused her of undermining him. In September 1894 their second daughter, Hertha, was born, but they were divorced soon afterward. Carreño installed her four children in a house on the Kurfürstendamm in Berlin, and to support them she kept on performing. During the next season, she gave some seventy concerts, traveling throughout Europe, and she returned to composing; she completed her String Quartet in B, which was warmly received. She continued with her strenuous schedule, touring during the concert season and spending summers with the children in the mountains. She also became more serious about teaching. She developed a fine set of technical exercises, which, however, were never published. A number of her articles appeared in music journals around this time, and she published one small book on how to use the pedals to achieve different tone colors.[16]

In January 1897 Carreño began a five-month concert tour of the United States, opening with the New York Philharmonic in Rubinstein's Concerto in D minor and moving on to Chicago, Boston, and Milwaukee. At forty-three Carreño was a mature artist. She still could thrill audiences with her fiery interpretations of Romantic music—Chopin, Liszt, and of course, Grieg—but she also could play Mozart and Beethoven properly. Indeed, von Bülow said she was the only woman pianist who could play Beethoven well; she could play intelligently but also had the requisite virtuoso technique and brilliance.[17]

In 1898 Carreño was back in Germany with her children. In that year, always a champion of contemporary American music, she gave the German premiere of Amy Beach's Violin Sonata in Leipzig with the first violinist of the Halir Quartet. In 1899 and 1900 she returned for two more big tours of the United States. On these she frequently combined her appearances with orchestras—in Chicago, Cincinnati, Pittsburgh, Cleveland, Boston—with separate solo recitals, so that she was often giving four or five performances in one city within a few days. She was still performing enormous programs. On November 27, 1900, for example, a program of hers in New York included works by Mozart, Beethoven, Chopin, and Schumann, among others. That same month she played Tchaikovsky's Concerto in B-flat minor with the New York Philharmonic, prompting the prominent New York critic W. J. Henderson to call her "the Cleopatra of the keyboard. She has more temperament than the other two pianists [Dohnhányi and Gabrilowitsch] put together," although, he went on to say, "she is not always discreet. But it is hard for flaming temperaments always to be discreet, as readers of biographies of musicians well know."[18]

Accordingly, on June 30, 1902, she scandalized the public yet again, not only embarking on her fourth marriage but choosing her erstwhile brother-in-law, Arturo Tagliapietra, brother of Giovanni who had died some years earlier. But this marriage proved to be a very happy one.

Now in her fifties and presumably no longer needing the income so badly, Carreño nevertheless continued to tour all over the world. In 1906–7 she undertook a lengthy journey to Australia, New Zealand, and across the United States. In 1909 she began another two-year tour of the United States, New Zealand, Australia, and South Africa. In January 1913 she was in London to perform MacDowell's *Celtic Sonata* in celebration of the fiftieth anniversary of her first public appearance. And in 1913–14 she was again in America.

Carreño continued to tour Europe throughout the first years of World War I and attracted huge audiences, but late in 1916 she gave up her home in Berlin and moved with Arturo to New York; both were U.S. citizens. She intended at last to cut down her concert schedule—in 1916 alone she had given seventy-two concerts in Europe, traveling from Romania to Spain—and devote herself more to teaching. But in the spring of 1917 she was on tour again, this time in Cuba. The tour was interrupted, however, when she became ill. In June she returned with her husband to New York, and within a few weeks she was dead. Some twenty years later, her ashes were returned to Venezuela, where a memorial concert was given in her honor.

Her funeral in New York was attended by many famous musicians, and she was widely eulogized. One obituary notice skillfully captured the essence of her life—she was first and foremost a pianist, the greatest of her sex, with a brilliant technique, always good taste, and Latin fire. As a person, she was characterized by great kindliness, charm, and common sense. In sum, Carreño was a great artist and a great woman.[19]

There is no way of knowing how good a pianist Carreño was by modern standards. She left no recordings. She did at one time make some music rolls for player pianos, but these she later disowned. She did, however, leave advice to other pianists. In one article, Carreño told young pianists to avoid commercial motives; they could never compete with player pianos in technique, so they must emphasize beauty of expression. To accomplish this, a relaxed body was essential above all. She recalled that Edward MacDowell, when he had first come to her as a boy, was very stiff, and she had tried to help him relax his arms and hands. Later, some of Carreño's former pupils recalled some of her specific advice. One remembered that Carreño always told her to press the tone out of the piano, not to hit the notes but to squeeze them. Use a relaxed hand and wrist, she said, and rely on the weight of the whole arm for power.[20] Another recalled her emphasis on controlled relaxation, not just "letting go," and her opposition to keyboard mannerisms.[21] This advice is as sound today as it was then.

Although Carreño was less outspoken than Camilla Urso regarding the opportunities for women performers, her enormous success undoubtedly had an effect on other young women. After the Civil War the appearance of women pianists in public became less of a rarity in the United States. The concerts of the Boston Philharmonic Society, given regularly from 1844 to 1863, frequently included women singers, and in 1860 they featured their first woman pianist, twenty-year-old Mary Fay, as soloist in the Mendelssohn G minor Concerto and two movements of Chopin's Concerto in E minor. Fay returned in 1862 to play in three more concerts with the society. The following year, on April 11, 1863, Eliza Josselyn made her debut at a Boston Philharmonic concert, playing the same Mendelssohn concerto and a Liszt transcription of *Rigoletto*.

The New York Philharmonic Society first employed a woman pianist, Mme Eugenie de Rhoade (or Roode), in 1856, and in 1857 Mme J. Graever performed with the society no fewer than three times. Thereafter, no woman instrumentalist appeared until after the Civil War, when Alide Topp played twice in 1867, Anna Mehlig twice and Mrs. Davison once in 1869, and Marie Krebs once in 1870.

Topp, Mehlig, and Krebs were German, and Krebs in particular achieved great renown in Europe. All three pianists were admired by conductor Theodore Thomas, who brought each along on tour at various times between 1870 and 1874. Also during this period, the Worcester Festival featured its first woman pianist, Flora Alger, in 1874. Another European, London-born Madeleine Schiller, was active around this time. After a brilliant debut at the Gewandhaus in Leipzig, she married Marcus Elmer Bennett of Boston and lived in the United States from 1873 on. She, too, frequently played under Theodore Thomas in New York through the 1870s and early 1880s.

By 1880, local concerts frequently included a woman pianist, and not just to accompany singers—accompanists were listed separately—but to perform in her own right. However, none achieved the stature of Teresa Carreño. It was not until the late 1870s that an American rival did appear on the scene, Julia Rivé-King. In fact, in 1881, when Carreño was on tour in Chicago, critics compared these two performers, and they concluded that Carreño was the greater genius but Rivé-King the better artist. A few years later the music critic John C. Freund wrote, "The other day Mme. Carreño, Mme. Rivé-King, and Miss Bloomfield, all three remarkable pianists of different schools, met and had a chat together."[22] It would be illuminating to know just what they said.

Rivé-King was definitely a different sort of artist from Carreño, and her career was confined largely to the United States. She seems to have been more of a musician's musician. In May 1875, when at age eighteen she made her first appearance with the New York Philharmonic Society in Liszt's Concerto in E-flat and Schumann's very difficult *Faschingsschwank aus Wien,* the orchestra and conductor Carl Bergmann joined the audience in giving her a standing ovation. By April of the following year the notoriously restrained (for that time) *Dwight's Journal of Music* acclaimed her as America's first pianist and compared her with both von Bülow and Rubinstein.[23] In the late 1870s Theodore Thomas was said to regard her as the finest American pianist. The span of her career was even longer than Carreño's—she made her official debut about 1873, in Europe, and in 1936 she was still teaching in Chicago.

Julia Rivé was born in Cincinnati in 1857.[24] Her father, Léon Rivé, was a painter. Her mother, the French-born Caroline Staub Rivé (1822–1882), was an eminent voice teacher who had studied with Manuel Garcia and composed some music herself. Julia first appeared in public accompanying her mother, and by the age of eight she was an accomplished pianist. Around 1870 she was taken to New York to study with William Mason and S. B. Mills, and in 1872 to Europe, where she studied with Carl Reinecke at Leipzig, Blassman at Dresden, and Liszt at Weimar. She made her debut in Leipzig under Reinecke's baton, playing Beethoven's Concerto no. 3 and Liszt's Rhapsody no. 2. The audience was astounded that she could manage these two very different works so well. A European concert tour was arranged for her but was abruptly canceled when she was called home by her father's death in a railway accident. This marked the end of her European career.

That winter Rivé appeared in Cincinnati, and in December 1874 she made her Chicago debut with the Apollo Club; a few months later came her New York debut. In fall 1875 she was back in the Midwest, giving ambitious recital programs such as the following one in Indianapolis on November 25, 1875: Beethoven, Sonata, op. 111; Schumann, *Etudes symphoniques;* Mendelssohn, *Rondo capriccioso;* Schubert, Sonata, op. 120; Chopin, Rondo in E-flat major; Liszt, transcription of the Allegretto from Beethoven's Symphony no. 8; Raff, *Grand Waltz de Concert.*[25]

In February she returned east to play Beethoven's "Emperor" Concerto with the New York Philharmonic, and in July she gave a series of highly successful recitals in Philadelphia. In August she was in Cincinnati, playing Bach, Mozart, Beethoven, Mendelssohn, Schumann, Wagner, Chopin, and Liszt. The following year, in April 1877, it was said that she had given 300 concerts that season, playing simply everywhere, from tiny towns to major cities. In one week in Chicago alone she played before a total of 6000 persons.[26] In June 1877 she married Frank H. King, her manager, in Milwaukee, where she opened the 1877–78 season in September with a "grand testimonial concert."

So far Julia Rivé-King's career does not sound too different from Carreño's—child prodigy, early study with a musical parent, later study with great masters, highly acclaimed debut, a hectic concert schedule scarcely interrupted by marriage, ambitious programs. But as a performer and, one must conclude, in personality, Julia Rivé-King was considerably different from Carreño. For one thing, she never catered to her audiences; no flashy curtain raisers or encores for her. She played as difficult programs for unsophisticated audiences as she played in big cities. She herself strongly preferred Beethoven to Liszt, though she never dropped the latter's works from her repertory. Somehow, said the midwestern correspondent for *Dwight's Journal of Music* in 1877, she had found the secret of being popular without lowering her standards. One clue to her success was her modesty and simplicity. She once wrote a friend, "I am still too young to have fathomed so great a master as Beethoven, but I love him above all others."[27]

Like Clara Schumann, and unlike most pianists of that era, Rivé-King memorized all the works she played, and her memory was considered prodigious. Her technique, apparently, was excellent, but she never sacrificed musicianship for the pyrotechnics of a brilliant performance. Her style, said one admirer, "combines native delicacy with true artistic fervor."[28]

Relatively early in her career Rivé-King discovered her bent for teaching. In 1878 she was already holding master classes for advanced pupils during the summer, and though she was well able to support her career with performance alone, she always took time to teach. She also turned to composition, of both original works and transcriptions of other pieces for piano. At a concert with the Harvard Musical Association in February 1879, she played the Chopin E minor Concerto and her own transcription of an organ prelude and fugue by Haberbier-Guilmant, of which one writer said, "For facility and brilliancy of execution, sure touch, powerful and yet delicate method, Mme King [ranks] among greatest artists." The same writer also admired her technical fluency but said she lacked soulful sentiment.[29]

She was, we may safely conclude, more of the eighteenth and twentieth centuries than of the nineteenth, at least in execution. Compared to the passionate Carreño, the "Valkyrie of the Piano," Rivé-King was an intellectual, a classicist. But as a composer she was a child of her time. At her April 17 farewell recital for the 1878–79 season in Boston, she played her transcription for piano of two movements of Mendelssohn's Violin Concerto—a composition that would only have been undertaken in her day—and John Sullivan Dwight loyally said it was a "musicianly and clever piece of work."[30] She also transcribed for piano Vieuxtemps's *Ballade et Polonaise de Concert, Grande fantasie,* based on Bizet's *Carmen,* and some Scarlatti sonatas. Her original compositions include *Polonaise héroique,* which she dedicated to Liszt, the tone poem *Bubbling Spring,* Impromptu in A-flat, and a number of salon pieces, including some for four hands.

Rivé-King continued to tour, playing recitals and with orchestras. In September 1880 she formed the Rivé-King Concert Company, together with several singers and a violinist, which toured widely for the 1880–81 season. Such tours were not without their hazards. In the spring of 1881 Rivé-King was injured in a collision on the Wabash line and sued the railroad for $700,000.

The suit was settled two years later, Rivé-King receiving $4250.[31] By then she had abandoned her company, which appears to have been active only that one season.

In fall of 1881 Rivé-King played the Saint-Saëns Concerto no. 2 in G minor at the Worcester Festival.[32] She had announced that she would, after traveling almost constantly for seven years, spend the 1881–82 season in New York, teaching a few advanced students and filling occasional concert engagements.[33] New York appears to have been her home until 1890, insofar as such an inveterate traveler could be said to have a home. The summer of 1882 found her in California and Oregon, and in spring 1883 she undertook the first of a number of extensive tours with Theodore Thomas and his orchestra, which Frank King had helped arrange. They appeared, over a period of two and a half months, in thirty cities, from Baltimore to San Francisco. The company consisted of sixty men, five singers, and Rivé-King. In the spring of 1884 she was on still another coast-to-coast tour with Thomas and was booked for concerts in Baltimore and other eastern cities for the fall. Sometime during the year Rivé-King collapsed and was forced to retire for a time to recover her health. She had played more than 200 concerts with Thomas alone, and an estimated total of 1800 concerts since her debut.

By the spring of 1885, however, Rivé-King had recovered and was on the road again, touring the South and West. *Freund's* of May 1885 reported that she was getting rave reviews everywhere, had performed brilliantly in Chicago, and had moved on to two recitals in Louisville, where the program included her own *Mazourka des graces.* The following year she undertook another long tour of the South and West. Apparently she took more time off in 1887—no long spring tour is reported—but she was active again in the 1887–88 season. Critic James Huneker, in an evaluation of pianists published in *Etude* in January 1888, described her: "A finished technic and a very large tone are her principal characteristics. A reserve . . . has led many critics to declare that her playing lacked fire and passion . . . she has both in plenty. . . . Madame King is a great pianiste."

In 1890 Rivé-King moved back to Chicago, though her traveling continued. In the spring of 1891 she was again touring the larger cities, but in the 1891–92 season she appeared as a regular soloist with the Chicago Orchestra. For some reason, perhaps illness, she was not one of the six women pianists engaged to play at the World's Columbian Exposition in Chicago in 1893. She performed at the Worcester Festival in 1894, playing the Tchaikovsky *Fantasy* for piano and orchestra, op. 56, and for an encore a rhapsody written especially for her by Saint-Saëns. She then gave a series of orchestral concerts and recitals throughout the East and West during the 1894–95 season, and toured with Anton Seidl's orchestra in 1896, 1897, and 1898, but reviews of her concerts are sparser from the late 1890s. Her reputation, however, had not diminished. In 1899 in an article on American virtuosos in *Etude,* J. S. Van Cleve called her the greatest woman pianist of American birth, ranked her with Carreño and Bloomfield-Zeisler, and said her repertory was unsurpassed except perhaps by von Bülow and Rubinstein.[34] By then she had played a total of about 4000 concerts, 500 of them with orchestra.

In February 1900 Frank King, ten years her senior, died. Plainspoken and seemingly uncultivated, he had in reality been a warm, kindhearted man, extremely knowledgeable about pianists, pianos, and piano music, and an excellent advisor to his wife. From that time on Rivé-King devoted herself largely to teaching, appearing only rarely in performance. She joined the piano department of Chicago's Bush Temple of Music early in the 1900s and remained there until a year before her death. In May of 1929 *Etude* reported that Rivé-King, "a great favorite of the last generation and one of the first American women pianists to win fame," had given a recital in Chicago on February 27, and despite her age of seventy-four she was still an admirable performer. In August 1932 she is mentioned again; she is described as the most brilliant American female pianist of the period 1885–1900 and one of the few remaining of Liszt's pupils, still actively teaching in Chicago. She died in 1937 at the age of eighty-two, having given two recitals as recently as the fall of 1936, and was buried, according to her wish, in her husband's grave in Cincinnati.

Despite her long career and her extensive tours throughout the United States, Rivé-King was rather quickly forgotten. Or perhaps her more measured, intellectual approach to the keyboard never won her as many admirers as flashier performers seemed to attract. Fannie Bloomfield-Zeisler, on the other hand, also a midwesterner by upbringing and just a few years younger than Rivé-King, was still remembered, at least in name, by a few older musicians in the 1970s. She, too, had a career that spanned a half-century, and it is said that in sum both she and Rivé-King were more successful than most American men pianists of their time.[35]

Fannie Blumenfeld was born in 1865 in Bielitz, Silesia (Austria), but her family moved to Chicago before she was two and changed their name to Bloomfield. She showed musical talent at a very early age and studied first with Bernhard Ziehn and Carl Wolfsohn, both respected Chicago teachers. In 1877 Madame Annette Essipoff,[36] the great Russian pianist, was on tour in Chicago and heard the child play, and she told her parents to send her to Vienna to study with Leschetizky.

The Bloomfields took her advice, and Fannie studied in Vienna for five years, from 1878 to 1883. In 1883 she made a successful debut there and then returned to the United States, making her American debut in Chicago late in 1883. In January she appeared with the Beethoven Society of Chicago, under Carl Wolfsohn, and John C. Freund said, "She has a marvelous technique, phrases beautifully, plays with fire and passion, and is altogether the most deserving young pianist . . . in many a long year."[37] The *Chicago Tribune* and other papers concurred. She went on to score similar successes in Milwaukee, St.

Louis, and Baltimore. The following season she played with the Boston Symphony under Wilhelm Gericke and then in New York, and was warmly praised by all the critics. The peppery A. L. of *Freund's,* however, said of her performance of Weber's *Concertstück* with the New York Symphony under Walter Damrosch that it was a pitiful waste of talent to perform this work at all.[38]

In October 1885 Fannie Bloomfield married Sigmund Zeisler (1860–1931), a Chicago lawyer, and appears to have taken some months off from touring. But the 1886–87 season found her on the road again. She gave a recital in Baltimore, where she was said to be "the finest pianist heard in Baltimore for some time." In December she appeared in New York, again with the Symphony Society under Damrosch, and she was active in the Midwest the following spring, performing a number of times in Chicago and other cities.

By this time Bloomfield-Zeisler was a seasoned concert artist. Her style of playing was more like Carreño's than Rivé-King's. James Huneker said of her in April 1887:

> Here was something rare in pianism, particularly from a woman. Breadth, color, fire, variety of tonal shading, and an intensity of attack that was positively *enthusing. . . .* Crudities of style and conception there were abundant traces of, but time is fast mellowing them, and her noble sonorous touch in cantabile playing is one of the most delightful things to listen to.[39]

Amy Fay, herself a fine pianist and established teacher, later said of Bloomfield-Zeisler's performance of Rubinstein's D minor Concerto, a hair-raisingly difficult piece, "She dashed it off like a mere bagatelle."[40]

In August 1888 Bloomfield-Zeisler and her husband sailed for Southampton, beginning a six-month European tour. She went to Bayreuth and to Vienna to visit Leschetizky[41] and Mme Essipoff, and the latter persuaded Bloomfield-Zeisler to appear with her in a joint performance in London. In March 1889 she returned to America and resumed her active career, performing with a number of major orchestras. In July 1890 she appeared in Detroit at the fourteenth annual convention of the Music Teachers National Association (MTNA), the only notable woman on their entire three-day program. Accompanied by her husband, she presented an essay on the piano and a talk on women and music. In her talk, according to a later report, "she admitted the limitations of femininity but maintained that in music their work was marked by powerful masculine force." [42] (That was one way of getting around the age-old argument that women are the weaker sex in every respect.) Further, she acknowledged that women had not yet achieved any extraordinary compositions but maintained that this was the result of their relatively recent emancipation, so there had not been enough time for their development as composers. She ended by predicting great future accomplishments for women in this area.

The 1890–91 season was a very busy one. Bloomfield-Zeisler played Chopin's Concerto no. 2 in F minor at the Worcester Festival, receiving marvelous reviews. She was soloist with the Boston Symphony in a Saint-Saëns concerto in Baltimore and played the Rubinstein G minor Concerto in Washington, D.C. In January and February she appeared with the New York Philharmonic Society, and she repeated the Chopin concerto with the Boston Symphony in New Haven and with Theodore Thomas at the Music Hall Concerts in Chicago. Generally acknowledged to be "among the first pianists in the country,"[43] she was chosen in July to be one of the three examiners in piano for the American College of Musicians, a newly formed organization intending to give accreditation to music teachers; she was the only woman examiner they employed that year.

The following year she appeared several times with Thomas's orchestra, playing the Chopin Concerto no. 2 and giving the U.S. premiere of Saint-Saëns's Concerto no. 4. (A couple of years later, at the height of the Dreyfus Affair, she played the same concerto in Paris, at a time when Saint-Saëns had just refused to preside over the recently organized Musicians Union there, and consequently the performance was roundly booed.[44]) In 1892–93 she made an extended western tour with Thomas and his orchestra, and she helped, along with voice teacher Sara Hershey Eddy, organize the women's music section of the World's Columbian Exposition in Chicago in 1893, at which she herself performed the Schumann Concerto in A minor and appeared in Beethoven's Triple Concerto with Max Bendix, violin, and Bruno Steindl, cello.

That fall she again went to Europe, but following a concert in Vienna early in 1894 she collapsed from nervous strain and canceled all her appearances for a time. The tour proved successful nevertheless, and the following season she undertook another, sailing for Europe in October 1894 and performing in Germany, Austria, Hungary, France, Italy, and England. In 1895–96, however, she remained in America. One reviewer said whereas Paderewski confined himself to playing only three or four concertos per season, Bloomfield-Zeisler would play not only the Rubinstein D minor, Saint-Saëns D minor, and Chopin F minor concertos, for which she was already famous, but the Schumann A minor and Beethoven E-flat concertos as well.[45] By the end of the season, July 1896, she had made some fifty appearances, twelve of them with orchestra, and had made plans to tour the Pacific coast the following season, where she would give some thirty recitals in two months.

This schedule, although busy, does not seem especially arduous compared with those of Urso, Powell, and Carreño. But Bloomfield-Zeisler also was raising three sons and expressed pride in the fact that she was neither giving up her art nor neglecting her home. Conflicts undoubtedly arose from time to time, even given her relative wealth and an era of faithful servants, and her life could not always have been easy. Nevertheless, she continued to perform. On March 24, 1900, she celebrated the twenty-fifth anniversary of her debut at the Central Music Hall in Chicago. Around this time she began regularly spending summers in Europe, in some years either going early in late spring or staying late through fall in order to take part in the concert season there. She appeared with the major European orchestras—the Berlin Philharmonic, the London Symphony, and the Lamoureux Orchestra of Paris, among others—and gave solo recitals. In 1903 it was announced that she would head the piano department of the Bush Temple of Music in Chicago, which presumably would keep her closer to home and make her a colleague of Rivé-King's.

In February 1905 the *Etude* cover story, by William Armstrong, was entitled "Mrs. Bloomfield-Zeisler on Study and Repertory." Some of her comments in this interview are illuminating. Mozart, she said, was very difficult to play well; every flaw shows, and one cannot be sentimental, implying that bravura can cover up flaws with some other composers' works. Bloomfield-Zeisler loved to play Grieg, especially his *Ballade,* and Tchaikovsky. She tried to include some contemporary pieces in all her recitals—works by Schütt, Poldini, Moszkowski, Godard, Chabrier—but she neglected to mention any woman composer, not Amy Beach or even Cécile Chaminade, some of whose piano works were, for a time, in the standard repertory. Clearly her approach had much in common with Carreño's, who was most famous for her performance of the Grieg concerto and who also promoted contemporary composers, most notably MacDowell but also others. Bloomfield-Zeisler's repertory was huge. She once gave eight recitals in the space of eighteen days in which no work was ever repeated.[46]

As for teaching, Bloomfield-Zeisler said she could not really describe her method in general, since she preferred to take up one problem at a time. In a number of short articles published in the 1880s, she was more explicit on subjects such as expression in piano playing (she maintained that not only touch but the different kinds of tone produced, and shading, or phrasing, affect expression), the use of the pedal, and other particulars. More insight comes from an article published some years later by Theodora Troendle,[47] who had been her pupil and then her assistant in Chicago from 1913 to 1920. Bloomfield-Zeisler, she said, was famous for her bell-like *pianissimo,* was extremely good at using the pedal to vary tone color, and insisted on memorizing everything, at least in part because she was very nearsighted. Among her dicta to pupils, the most important were: (1) avoid fast, unfirm, or uneven practicing; (2) do not overlook the usefulness of the metronome, but differentiate between faulty time and faulty rhythm; (3) haste makes waste, so practice slowly and carefully; (4) pedaling and phrasing differentiate the gifted amateur from the true artist; (5) when learning a piece, concentrate on one phrase at a time; (6) consider carefully all criticism and advice, and make sure it really does apply to you before using it constructively; (7) success comes from charm, and true charm is the product of sincerity and simplicity; (8) quality is more important than quantity. Like Leschetizky, she emphasized a loose wrist and fingers made strong through training, especially with the exercises of Czerny, who had been Leschetizky's teacher.

In 1908 Bloomfield-Zeisler said that a foreign debut still was necessary for an American artist in order to win acceptance at home.[48] As for the state of music in America, she believed that Chicago, New York, and Boston all had better music than Vienna, and what was more, performers were paid approximately five times as much in the United States as they received in Europe. On the other hand, the pace of the American tour was much faster. "In one week," she said, "one appears in five [U.S.] cities as widely apart as Novgorod, Berlin, Vienna, and Paris."[49]

In 1910 Bloomfield-Zeisler was a veteran of thirty-five years on the concert stage, yet her ability was still undiminished. "Her style of playing," said one critic, "is vigorous, clear, and yet capable of great tenderness."[50] She was still undertaking large tours, too. In 1912 her six-month European tour took her to Dresden, Vienna, Munich, Hamburg, London, and Paris and included both orchestral concerts and recitals. This, however, was the last of her major tours abroad.

For the next fifteen years Bloomfield-Zeisler devoted herself principally to teaching in Chicago. On February 25, 1925, she gave a farewell concert in celebration of the fiftieth anniversary of her debut. Two and a half years later, after a period of ill health, she died at home of a heart attack.

Two other nineteenth-century women pianists, Amy Fay and Adele Aus der Ohe, must be included here, one because she was also an influential teacher and writer, and the other because, although a German, she made many American tours and for a time settled in the United States.

Amy Fay was born in 1844 in Mississippi.[51] Her mother, Charlotte Emily Fay, was a fine pianist, and Amy began to play by ear and compose from the age of four. When she reached age five her mother began to give her formal lessons, which continued for a time. But when Amy Fay was twelve, her mother died. Meanwhile, her older sister Melusina had married the son of a Harvard professor and Amy later went to live with her in Massachusetts. There she began to study Bach with John Knowles Paine and to attend classes at the New England Conservatory. She also studied in New York. At the age of twenty-five she went to Europe, where she studied for a year with Taussig in Berlin, for three years with Kullak, and for a summer with Liszt at Weimar. Liszt reputedly considered her one of his most promising pupils.

In 1875 she returned to the United States after a total absence of six years and made her debut with the Mendelssohn Glee Club in New York. She then returned to Massachusetts, where she performed with the Theodore Thomas orchestra at Sanders Theatre in Cambridge, and at the Worcester Festival of 1878, where she became the first performer to play an entire concerto, rather than just one or two movements. John Sullivan Dwight called her style brilliant and hard but not poetic.[52]

Late in 1878 Fay moved to Chicago, where she divided her time about equally between performing and teaching. She devised a kind of lecture-recital called "Piano Conversations," in which she first discussed pieces and then played them. In 1890 her younger sister Rose became Theodore Thomas's second wife. In that year Amy Fay moved to New York, where she remained active giving lecture-recitals, teaching, and working in music clubs, including a dozen terms as president of the Women's Philharmonic Society of New York, founded by her sister Melusina in 1899. She died in 1928.

The principal reason for Fay's importance is not her ability as a performer, lecturer, or even as a teacher, but a book she wrote about her studies in Europe. Entitled *Music Study in Germany* and originally published in 1880, it consists of her very vivid impressions and sharp observations of an American music student's life abroad. Since European study was still considered a *sine qua non* for American musicians, the book had a much wider audience than might be expected. It went into about twenty printings, as well as being translated into French and German. In 1891, a decade after the book's original publication, a writer on music books was still saying, "Perhaps no book on musical topics is more widely read than Amy Fay's 'Music Study in Germany.'"[53]

Germany was, for most of the nineteenth century, considered by Americans to be the wellspring of good music. The finest musicians, orchestras, conductors, and teachers, it was widely believed, were either German or German-trained. The personnel of American orchestras was largely German. Practically all American musicians of note went to Germany to study, and, as Bloomfield-Zeisler pointed out, a foreign debut was considered indispensable. Amy Fay thoroughly enjoyed and profited from her six years in Germany, and she said that girls were freely admitted to the study of piano there. In the end, however, she advised no American to go to Europe to study music, since the United States now had William Mason, William H. Sherwood, Julia Rivé-King, and many other fine teachers.

One piano student Fay had heard in Germany was Adele Aus der Ohe, about ten years old at the time and a pupil of Kullak's son. Fay reported that she heard the child play a Beethoven concerto perfectly and was astounded at the ability of one so young.[54]

Adele Aus der Ohe was born in Hanover in 1864, the daughter of a university professor.[55] By the time Fay heard her, she had been studying with Kullak in Berlin for three years. At age twelve she became a pupil of Liszt's and studied with him for seven more years. Not surprisingly, she became especially noted for her interpretations of Liszt's works.

In 1886 she made her American debut in Liszt's Piano Concerto no. 1 in New York, and she undertook extended American tours for each of the next seventeen years. She was especially in demand as a soloist with the Boston Symphony, with which she performed fifty-one times between 1887 and 1906. She also frequently appeared with the Brooklyn Philharmonic, New York

Philharmonic, and Chicago orchestras, and she played at the Worcester Festival in 1887, 1889, and 1898. Her repertory was exceedingly large—she played concertos by Chopin, Liszt, Tchaikovsky, Schumann, Beethoven, Rubinstein —and by 1889 she had the reputation of earning more than any other pianist in the United States. Said one correspondent, "She deserves to."[56]

Not everyone admired Aus der Ohe's style. James Huneker said she had a strong touch and reliable technique but was deficient in musical disposition and "has a large following among those who prefer physical power to poetry."[57] But another writer said of her rendition of Beethoven's "Emperor" Concerto, "We knew her great technique, her brilliancy, her dash and magnetism, but to see her abnegate all self-assertion, and carefully and conscientiously reproduce the composer's thought without any effort at effect, was a welcome surprise. She is a great artist."[58]

Aus der Ohe also gave recitals and played chamber music; she appeared a number of times with the leading string quartet of the time, the Kneisel Quartet, in Schumann's Piano Quintet, op. 47. In May 1891 she took part in the festival to dedicate Carnegie Hall in New York, performing the Tchaikovsky Concerto in B-flat minor under the composer's baton. She repeated this work, again with Tchaikovsky himself conducting, with the Boston Festival Orchestra in Philadelphia and Baltimore. In 1897 she filled in for the pianist Moritz Rosenthal, who was ill, in a company tour for which he had been engaged, and she performed the identical works that he had planned to play. In the same year, her own Suite in E major for piano was performed at the nineteenth annual MTNA convention, and she played it again in a New York recital the following year.

In 1904 it was announced that Aus der Ohe was moving to the United States permanently, although she continued to perform in Europe as well. In 1909 she was given the title Royal Prussian Court Pianist, the first woman so honored by Emperor Wilhelm II. Soon afterward a crippling illness forced her to retire. She returned to Germany, and in the runaway inflation following World War I her savings became completely worthless. The war's end saw her living impoverished in Berlin, and eventually *Etude* published an appeal for contributions to a relief fund for her.[59] On this she managed to subsist until her death in 1937.

Another American woman pianist who appeared regularly from about 1900 to 1925 was Augusta Cottlow, born in 1878 in Shelbyville, Illinois. She studied with Carl Wolfsohn in Chicago and made her debut there in 1888 or 1889, followed by a New York appearance in 1891. She then went to Berlin to study with Ferruccio Busoni and made a number of European tours. Her next appearance in the United States was in 1900 at the Worcester Festival, where she played Tchaikovsky's B-flat minor Concerto. She returned there in 1908, playing MacDowell's Concerto in D minor. She seems to have toured and played without interruption until about 1910, and then returned to Europe, where in 1912 she married Edgar E. Gerst of Berlin. She returned to the United States in 1917 and gave regular recitals in New York until the early 1920s. In 1925 the *Musician* published her memoirs, *My Years with Busoni.* She died in 1954.

By 1900 women pianists were not a novelty, in Europe or in America. However, while they constituted by far the majority in music schools and conservatories and vastly outnumbered men as teachers, relatively few women pianists became influential, either through performance or through teaching. Even disregarding nationality, names such as Artur Schnabel, Walter Gieseking, Rudolf Serkin, Artur Rubinstein, Vladimir Horowitz, and Mieczyslaw Horszowski, and, in more recent times, Van Cliburn, Glenn Gould, Claudio Arrau, Emil Gilels, Alfred Brendel, Mischa Dichter, Eugene Istomin, Gary Graffman, Garrick Ohlsson, John Browning, Eugene List, Peter Serkin, Daniel Barenboim, and Vladimir Ashkenazy are much more numerous and readily recognizable than the handful of women pianists known internationally during the same era: Olga Samaroff, Guiomar Novaes, Myra Hess, Lili Kraus, Gina Bachauer, Alicia de Larroccha, Rosalyn Tureck. And of this last group, only Samaroff and Tureck are Americans.

Olga Samaroff was born in 1882 in San Antonio, Texas, and was named Lucie Jane Olga Agnes Hickenlooper.[60] Her first piano teacher was her grandmother, Lucie Palmer Loening Grunewald, for whom she was named, but she later decided to take a more euphonious and exotic name—Samaroff was the name of another branch of her family. European study was still considered essential, so she went first to the Paris Conservatory, where in 1894 she became the first American girl to win a scholarship for piano classes, and then to Berlin, where she studied with Ernst Jedliczka. She also studied at the Peabody Conservatory in Baltimore with Ernest Hutcheson and composition with Otis Boise. While still in her teens she married a Russian, Boris Loutzky, and retired from performing, but the marriage was annulled after three years.

Returning from Europe, she wanted to make her debut as a concert pianist, and in September 1904 she asked Henry Wolfsohn, the leading New York manager at the time, to handle it for her. Wolfsohn refused because she had no European notices to her credit, and she could not afford to return to Europe to acquire them. Her family, not wealthy to begin with, had lost all its property in the terrible Galveston flood of 1900 and had moved to St. Louis. Wolfsohn suggested that she take a gamble, hire an orchestra, and perform at Carnegie Hall. For this occasion she changed her name to Olga Samaroff and, risking the sum total of her family's funds, hired Walter Damrosch and the New York Symphony Orchestra for January 18, 1905. She played two concertos, Schumann's in A minor and Liszt's in E-flat, as well as a number of solo pieces by Chopin. The gamble paid off, and thereafter she played in numerous private musicales and eventually with other orchestras in the United States. Later that year she went to London to give her first solo recital, and in the same year Charles A. Ellis of Boston, manager of the Boston Symphony Orchestra and a select group of individual artists, became her manager.

Samaroff was delighted with Ellis, for he got her the highest fees any woman pianist had ever earned, $500 to $600 per concert. Women were generally paid less than men, and, Samaroff later wryly said, they were therefore considered a good bargain by organizers of subscription concert series and private musicales. During this period, a Metropolitan Opera star might earn $3000 a performance, but no woman pianist ever earned more than $600. In 1908 Teresa Carreño was engaged for a series of concerts at $400 per performance, which she considered munificent.[61] What was more, as Bloomfield-Zeisler had said, American fees were higher than European ones. Samaroff said she believed this discrimination in pay had been changed by Myra Hess after World War I, and she hoped her information was accurate.

Samaroff remained with Ellis until 1911, when she married Leopold Stokowski, then conducting the Cincinnati Orchestra, and gave up her concert career. "Just like a woman," Ellis reportedly said. The following year Stokowski became conductor of the Philadelphia Orchestra, and by 1914 Samaroff decided to resume her own career. In 1917 she played the Saint-Saëns Concerto in G minor at the Worcester Festival, accompanied by her husband. Several accounts of this occasion note that she was now fully recovered from some unspecified serious illness, perhaps a nervous breakdown. Among her projects was commemorating the 150th anniversary of Beethoven's birth by learning all thirty-two of his piano sonatas. She began performing them in 1920, each recital preceded by a lecture from Stokowski, and thus became the first American pianist to perform all thirty-two in concert.

During this period, she began to write about music, and several of her articles appeared in *Etude* and other journals. These and a number of books she wrote in the 1930s and 1940s give evidence that Samaroff was a serious musician. In an article entitled "Self-expression at the Keyboard," for example, she stressed that understanding the music is quite as essential as feeling, and that true artists avoid sentimentality and exaggeration.[62] She made a large number of recordings for the Victor Talking Machine Company, and the royalties from these enabled her to buy a house at Seal Harbor, Maine, where she spent summers and later invited her favorite pupils.

Although their marriage was troubled for some years, Samaroff bore a daughter in London in 1921. Stokowski was in Philadelphia at the time. In 1923 they were divorced, but they remained on friendly terms. She left Philadelphia for New York, where she spent the winters in rented apartments and summers in Maine. For about two years she was successful in giving recitals, but in 1925 she fell, tearing ligaments in her arm and shoulder. She had to cancel all her engagements, and this proved to be the end of her concert career. Meanwhile, however, she had signed a contract to teach piano at the newly formed Juilliard Graduate School of Music, where her colleagues included her former teacher, Ernest Hutcheson, as well as Josef and Rosina Lhévinne and other notable masters.

Shortly after her accident, Samaroff was offered the job of music critic for the *New York Evening Post,* to replace Ernest Newman. She held the post for two seasons, but resigned when the paper refused her request to expand the department.

Upon leaving the *Post,* Samaroff decided not to resume performing. She loved teaching and wanted to help young musicians, as well as continue with her writing. In 1928 she helped found the Schubert Memorial, a foundation to help give young musicians opportunities for performance with a major orchestra. It established an annual contest whose winner had the privilege of performing a solo work with the Philadelphia Orchestra at a regular subscription concert. In 1935, once Samaroff was no longer associated with the program, the winner was one of her most gifted pupils at Juilliard, Rosalyn Tureck, who that year made her debut with the Philadelphia Orchestra.

In addition to teaching at Juilliard, Samaroff began in 1929 to commute regularly to Philadelphia and teach an advanced piano class at the Philadelphia Conservatory of Music. One of her pupils there was Eugene List, who at thirteen was granted a fellowship to the school and under her tutelage became a successful concert artist.

In the 1930s Samaroff began to lecture extensively on music appreciation and published a number of books on the subject, the most important of which was *The Layman's Music Book,* published in 1935 and enlarged and revised in 1947 as *The Listener's Music Book.* In 1936 the U.S. State Department sent her as the official American delegate to the first International Congress of Musical Education in Prague, Czechoslovakia. Two years later she was the only woman among twenty-one delegates to Belgium to serve on the international jury of the Concours Eugène Ysaÿe. She also received an honorary degree of doctor of music from the University of Pennsylvania. She died in 1948.

Her own success notwithstanding, Samaroff had no illusions about the difficulties faced by women in a highly competitive field. One way to overcome the difficulties, to gain an edge on the competition, was to specialize. A brilliant Polish pianist, Wanda Landowska (c. 1880–1959), did just that. Partly through expeditious timing and partly through her enormous talent and hard work, Landowska virtually singlehandedly revived the baroque harpsichord and its music. She was not the first to think of rebuilding and reviving this instrument, but she became the first great twentieth-century performer on it, and she gave impetus to its rebirth. She taught many others how to play the harpsichord, and she inspired outstanding contemporary composers—de Falla, Stravinsky, Poulenc, and others—to write for it, both orchestral music and solo works. Long before she died, Landowska's name had become practically synonymous with the harpsichord, and it has remained so to this day.

Samaroff's pupil Rosalyn Tureck also chose to specialize, not in an instrument but in a composer. In October 1977 she celebrated the fortieth anniversary of her first playing the complete forty-eight preludes and fugues of J. S. Bach's *Well-Tempered Clavier* and his *Goldberg Variations* in New York. That first performance, when she was only twenty-two, took place in a series of six concerts in New York's Town Hall. The anniversary concert began with a single long concert at Carnegie Hall, at which Tureck played the *Goldberg Variations* first on the harpsichord, as the composer had intended, and then on the piano, "with a touch and technique she has devoted her musical life to perfecting."[63] This concert was followed by five more at which she played the forty-eight preludes and fugues. Indeed, Tureck had at various times played Bach on harpsichord, piano, clavichord, organ, and even on an electronic keyboard instrument known as the Moog Synthesizer. She performed Bach all over the world and became as much identified with this composer as Landowska had been with the harpsichord.

Tureck was born in Chicago in 1914. She began to play the piano at age four and started lessons at eight, making her debut with two solo recitals a year later. She studied first with Sophia Brilliant-Liven, who had been a pupil of Anton Rubinstein, and then with Jan Chiapusso, a great student of Bach who first aroused her interest in the baroque composer. He encouraged an intellectual approach to Bach, and Tureck began to study the harpsichord, clavichord, and organ in order to gain a better understanding of baroque performance practice. At fifteen she was giving all-Bach recitals in Chicago, and the following year she went to New York to study at Juilliard, where she became a pupil of Olga Samaroff's.

In those days the music of Bach was far from being either well known or popular with audiences. In fact, in a newspaper interview in 1977 Tureck said, "I can remember . . . having people ask me, 'Who is Goldberg?'" She went on to say that the study, teaching, and even the performance of Bach had improved enormously in the last thirty years.[64] Much of that was a result of Tureck's own work, for, in addition to playing Bach's music, she conducted research, recorded, lectured, and wrote about Bach. Her writings include a three-volume work, *An Introduction to the Performance of Bach,* which contains fourteen pieces of music and essays on ornamentation, phrasing, touch, and other questions of performance style.

When Tureck began her career, Bach's keyboard music was considered excellent for use as finger exercises but very stuffy and dry. Moreover, many—including Landowska—felt that Bach's music should not be performed on the piano, which did not even exist during his time, but on the harpsichord, clavichord, or organ. Tureck, on the other hand, believed that it is the conception of the music rather than the instrument it is played on that gives a performance of Bach's works authenticity. At the age of not quite seventeen, in what she later described as a kind of mystical revelation, she realized that she would have to develop an entirely new and different piano technique in order to play Bach's music properly on the piano. And she spent the next forty years developing such a technique.

At first she had great difficulty convincing others that Bach was indeed worth playing. In fact, she said in 1977 that early in her career she did not believe she would be understood until she was seventy. One early experience reinforcing this pessimism was the Naumburg Competition of 1934, in which she advanced to the finals and presented an all-Bach program as her final recital. She lost. One judge did not approve of her ornamentation in the *Goldberg Variations,* ornamentation itself being out of fashion then, but principally the jury refused her the much coveted Naumburg Prize because they believed nobody could or should make a career of Bach. Three years later, however, a year after her graduation from Juilliard, Tureck's Bach series won her the first Town Hall Award for the most distinguished performance of the season, and the award was presented to her by the president of Town Hall, Walter W. Naumburg.

At the same time she was giving all-Bach programs, Tureck was also giving more conventional piano recitals, playing Chopin, Debussy, and Scriabin. She played the Brahms B-flat Concerto with the Philadelphia Orchestra and Beethoven's "Emperor" Concerto with the New York Philharmonic, pieces that were still considered by many to be "men's work." The double bind of the woman musician still persisted in the 1930s. Tureck wore shapeless black dresses so as not to distract the audience by her appearance. Feminine sentiment was allegedly admired, but the greatest compliment was to tell a woman that she played like a man. On the other hand, masculine women were also suspect. On the whole, it was simply preferable to *be* a man. Tureck did not let this attitude stop her. A favorite piece of hers was Brahms's *Variations on a Theme by Handel,* which was supposed to be too difficult for any woman pianist except perhaps Clara Schumann. But Tureck played it with great success.

Tureck also was interested in the music of her own time. Several composers wrote works for her, and she introduced compositions by William Schuman, Aaron Copland, and other contemporary composers to both American and European audiences. In 1952 she founded Composers of Today, an organization intended to bring contemporary composers together with performers, and to promote the performance of new works. Before its dissolution after 1955, the group introduced works by Messiaen, Krenek, and Hovhaness to New York audiences, and presented the first concert of taped electronic music in the United States.

In 1953 Tureck made her London debut, and soon afterward established residence there. She also tried her hand at conducting. In 1958 she conducted the New York Philharmonic, leading the orchestra in two Bach concertos from the keyboard. The next year she formed her own chamber ensemble in London, the Tureck Bach Players, and in 1966 she founded the International Bach

Society, dedicated to promoting research on and performance of Bach's works and, most particularly, to closing the gap between musicologist and performer. For a long time, Tureck believed, the tradition of how to play Bach's music was lost. By studying the sources and putting into practice what is learned, this great tradition could be revived.

In 1974 Tureck was appointed to a fellowship at St. Hilda's College, Oxford University, an honor hardly ever bestowed on a woman and especially not an American one, and subsequently she was made an honorary life fellow. But in 1977 she decided to move back to the United States and to continue her multifaceted career of performance, writing, and study. Thanks to her, by that time no one thought it strange that an artist should devote herself so overwhelmingly to J. S. Bach. In subsequent years Tureck founded the Tureck Bach Institute, which in the 1984–1985 season presented six concerts in honor of the composer's tricentennial; it concluded on March 31, 1985, Bach's birthday, with a performance of the *Goldberg Variations*. And in 1998, at age eighty-four, she was persuaded to make her sixth recording of this monumental work, a recording of which *Boston Globe* reviewer Richard Dyer said, "Her mind-hand coordination seems unimpaired and her understanding of the music continues to develop and deepen. . . . One listens in awe to the variety of dynamics and articulation she achieves; the amazing 'orchestration' of the voices, each of which has its own color; the spring of her rhythm; the suppleness and expressivity of her ornaments."[65]

At least two notable pianists began in the 1970s to specialize in performing music by women composers. Neither played such music exclusively, but both embarked on a degree of affirmative action in this respect. Joanne Polk, based in New York, had studied with Byron Janis, Martin Canin, Samuel Sanders, and Nina Svertlanova. She studied at Juilliard and the Manhattan School of Music, where she later became director of chamber music and ensembles. In 1998 she embarked on a series of recordings of the complete piano music of Amy Beach. Prior to this project, Polk recorded the lieder, or art songs, of Clara Schumann and chamber music by Judith Lang Zaimont. Virginia Eskin, born in New York in 1940 and based in Boston, studied under Gina Bachauer in London, and performed as a soloist with many orchestras in the United States, Europe, and Israel, as well as collaborating with several notable string quartets. But when she began to record music, she concentrated on neglected American composers such as Arthur Foote and George Chadwick, and particularly on women, among them Rebecca Clarke, Marion Bauer, Ruth Crawford, and Amy Beach. She frequently performed Clara Schumann's and Amy Beach's piano concertos, along with concertos by Rachmaninoff and other well-known men composers. She also has made a number of recordings of ragtime music. In 1994 she was awarded an honorary doctorate by Keene State College in recognition of her contribution to women's music. In the late 1980s she joined the adjunct faculty of Northeastern University, where she teaches undergraduate courses, and in 1998 she also took over as host of one of National Public Radio's longest-running classical music programs, *A Note to You.*

Still another kind of specialization for pianists takes the form of team-work—that is, pairing off with another pianist and tackling the two-piano and four-hands (on one piano) literature. Many outstanding pianists have per-formed as duopianists once in a while, as Bloomfield-Zeisler did with her teacher, Annette Essipoff, in London in 1888. There have been husband-wife duopianists—Robert and Gaby Casadesus of France, Ethel Bartlett and Rae Robertson of England, and briefly Teresa Carreño and her third husband, Eugène d'Albert—father-son duopianists—Rudolf and Peter Serkin of the United States—and many unfamilial pairs—Carreño and Wilhelm Backhaus, for one.

The hazards of two-piano performance are considerable. Touring pianists frequently complain about the instruments they must use, and usually for good reason. To find two pianos of acceptable, let alone excellent, quality is under-standably even rarer. Moreover, ideally they are grand pianos placed so that the two performers can see one another. As with other chamber music, a certain amount of eye contact is necessary simply for the performers to stay together. Upright pianos, apart from their other drawbacks, make this awkward.

Another problem is tuning. Violinists can adjust the tension of their strings on the spot; with a piano this takes far more time and skill. The com-poser Mary Howe, who for many years gave two-piano concerts and recitals with Anne Hull, wrote very amusingly about one concert in a small southern city where the pianos provided not only were uprights but one of them was tuned at least a quarter tone higher than the other. Such incidents are funny in retrospect but harrowing at performance time.

Difficulties notwithstanding, a number of duopianists have been long-lived and successful. Among them were two sisters, Rose (1870–1957) and Ottilie Sutro (1872–?) of Baltimore. Their father, Otto Sutro, was a patron of the arts and a founder of the Baltimore Oratorio Society. They both began piano lessons with their mother, and in 1889 they were sent to Berlin, where they studied with Karl Barth. They made their debut in London in 1894 and were highly acclaimed; the same year they returned to the United States and made their first American appearance in Brooklyn, New York, which marked the beginning of an extensive American tour. They then returned to Europe and were invited to play for Queen Victoria. A number of composers wrote works for them—they premiered Max Bruch's Concerto for two pianos, com-posed for them, with the Philadelphia Orchestra in 1916. In 1924 in Paris they premiered Amy Beach's *Suite for Two Pianos,* op. 104, which was dedi-cated to them. In 1930, by now well into middle age, the Sutro sisters were still performing. In that year they undertook a series of concerts in Washington, D.C., devoted to the work of American composers.

Two other sister duopianists are Katia and Marielle Labèque. Born in southwestern France, they are gaining recognition internationally. The sisters' first lessons were with their Italian mother, a well-known teacher. Later they attended the Paris Conservatory and both won first prizes. Their repertory ranges from Bach and Mozart to Stravinsky, Gershwin, Bernstein, and avant-garde contemporary composers. Audiences and reviewers alike have been delighted with their fine musicianship and, when the music allows it, their fiery, dramatic performances.

A discussion of great women pianists would be incomplete without mentioning a few of those who made a brilliant beginning but for one reason or another never fulfilled their early promise. This unfortunate outcome applies, of course, to child prodigies in every area, and quite regardless of sex. Hazel Harrison (1883–1969) was born in LaPorte, Indiana, and learned to play the piano at an early age.[66] Despite her modest circumstances and limited opportunities—hers was one of few African-American families in the community—she managed to go to Germany and in 1904 appeared with the Berlin Philharmonic, playing the Chopin E minor and Grieg A minor piano concertos. Billed as Hazelda Harrison, she garnered excellent reviews. Upon returning to the United States, she appeared in a number of recitals during the next few years, and in 1911 returned to Germany and studied with Busoni. At the outbreak of World War I she returned to America, teaching and giving recitals. No American orchestra engaged her as a soloist, presumably because of her race. From 1931 to 1934 she headed the piano department at Tuskegee Institute in Alabama, and from 1934 to 1959 she taught at Howard University, both highly respected African-American institutions. Unable to get appropriate management, she acted as her own concert manager and periodically took leave from teaching to perform. During a three-year leave from Howard, she performed about 100 concerts throughout the United States. Later, dissatisfied with retirement, she taught at Alabama State College for another five years (1959–64) and continued to teach privately almost until her death at age eighty-six.

Another pianist child prodigy, but one who never reached her full potential, was Hephzibah Menuhin, born in San Francisco in 1920. After only eighteen months of formal study, she debuted as a pianist at the age of eight, playing the Bach "Italian" Concerto, a Beethoven sonata, and Chopin's *Fantasy Impromptu*.[67] She did not appear in public again for six years, and then only as the accompanist of her gifted brother, violinist Yehudi Menuhin, in sonata recitals. Her mother did not believe she should have a separate career. In 1936 Marutha Menuhin was quoted as saying that Hephzibah yearned for her own career but "I tell her the only immortality to which a woman should aspire is that of a home and children," and in 1938 she wrote in an article in a women's magazine, "We have always praised Hephzibah far more for a well-balanced, well-executed dinner cooked by her than for any concert she has ever played with her brother."[68] In 1938 Hephzibah married an Australian and gave up playing for many years. She was later divorced and resumed public appearances, most often with her brother.

In January 1978 Yehudi Menuhin gave a recital in New York that marked the fiftieth anniversary of his New York debut; with him was Hephzibah, whom the *New York Times* referred to as "his perennial accompanist." In his autobiography, published the previous year, Menuhin wrote of his sister, "She could have been a leading virtuoso touring three hundred days a year. She chose otherwise." But then, though he goes on to say she has found fulfillment in her life, her second husband and his social work, and her own music, he maintains that she prefers chamber music to "the lonely glory of solo playing," and "She needs an object of inspiration, preferably her brother, in addition to the music; as in another sphere she needs to know she is fulfilling her husband's intentions."[69]

Ruth Slenczynski, born in 1925 in California of Polish parentage, began studying at the age of three under her father's extremely harsh tutelage, and made her debut in Oakland, California, at the age of four. A fantastically intelligent and talented child, she became, as she later recounts in her moving autobiography,[70] a virtual slave to her father, who forced her, from the age of three, to practice nine hours a day, slapped her face for every wrong note she played, and exploited her as a performer, financially and in just about every other way. At fourteen, she rebelled and gave up the piano entirely for a time. She married early, and her husband, George Born, pressed her, although more gently, to resume her career. She eventually became a successful teacher and writer of technical books about the piano, but she never entirely shook off the traumas of her childhood and, as a performer at least, never reached the heights that she had so nearly scaled earlier.

Finally, there was Philippa Schuyler, born in 1931 in Harlem in New York City of a black father and white mother. She made her debut at the age of four, playing her own compositions before the National Piano Teachers Guild. Among her many teachers was pianist and conductor Antonia Brico. At age ten she had finished eighth grade and was giving solo recitals all over the United States, and at age eleven she composed *Manhattan Nocturne* for a full symphony orchestra. At age fifteen she played her composition *Rumpelstiltskin* and the Saint-Saëns G minor Concerto with the New York Philharmonic. She traveled widely, became a news correspondent in addition to pursuing her career in music, and was tragically killed in Vietnam at the age of thirty-five.[71]

In the late 1970s several promising women pianists were on the American concert scene, but none had yet won worldwide recognition. Ruth Laredo made her New York Philharmonic debut in 1974 at the age of thirty-seven, eight years after her first New York solo recital. Thereafter she appeared as soloist with most principal American symphony orchestras as well as leading chamber orchestras. Born in Detroit in 1937, she studied with Rudolf Serkin and became, during her marriage to violinist Jaime Laredo, chiefly an accompanist for her husband. When the couple parted, she resumed her solo career. In the mid-1970s she became known for her recordings of the complete Scriabin sonatas and of Ravel's works, and she began recording the complete piano works of Rachmaninoff, a five-year undertaking that won numerous awards. She also became a commentator on piano literature on National Public Radio and a regular columnist for *Piano Today*.

In 1977 Ursula Oppens was one of four young artists to win the Avery Fisher Career Grant, entitling her to appearances with the New York Philharmonic and six other orchestras and a $1000 cash prize. Oppens studied piano with her mother, Edith Oppens, as well as with Leonard Shure and Guido Agosti. She also studied at Juilliard with Felix Galimir and Rosina Lhévinne. She made her New York debut in 1969. A specialist in contemporary music— she helped found and performed with the new music group Speculum Musicae in 1971—she premiered works by Rzewski, Lutoslawski, Harbison, Nancarrow, Picker, Wuorinen, and Wolff, among others. She also performed with numerous chamber groups and in recital, as well as with major orchestras in the United States and Europe. In 1994 she was appointed professor of music at Northwestern University.

Martha Argerich was born in Argentina in 1941 and performed widely in the United States. Winner of important piano competitions at only sixteen, she won acclaim for her interpretations of nineteenth- and twentieth-century virtuoso piano works. She has worked with numerous important conductors and particularly closely with Charles Dutoit—she was his first soloist at the beginning of their careers. After her appearance in New York with Dutoit and the Montreal Symphony, a *New York Times* reviewer wrote of her performance of a Liszt concerto:

> From a purely technical point of view, much of what Ms. Argerich did was stunning, not least because she is able to make it look so easy. Of particular note was the unusual combination of delicacy and insistent power that she brought to rapid passages. Elsewhere the sheer grandeur of her sound had an electrifying effect on the orchestra.[72]

Among the younger pianists on the rise in American music at the end of the twentieth century is Anne-Marie McDermott,[73] who made her Carnegie Hall debut at age twelve, playing the Mendelssohn Concerto in G minor. She studied at the Manhattan School of Music and went on to win a number of important prizes, among them the Avery Fisher Career Grant. In 1995 she was named an artist member of the prestigious Chamber Music Society of Lincoln Center. Two years later she made her debut with the New York Philharmonic in a Mozart concerto. In the late 1990s she became increasingly involved with chamber music, including the ensemble Opus One with Ida Kavafian, violin, Steven Tenenbaum, violin, and Peter Wiley, cello.

Another pianist active in chamber music is Lois Shapiro.[74] Born in 1950 in Newburgh, New York, she studied at Oberlin, at Fontainebleau with Nadia Boulanger, at the Peabody Institute with Leon Fleisher, at Yale, and at the New England Conservatory. She has performed both as a soloist and a chamber musician throughout the United States, Europe, and Latin America. Her repertory ranges from eighteenth-century music on period instruments—she is an accomplished fortepianist—to contemporary works. She premiered a number of new works, including several written expressly for her. In 1999 Richard Dyer of the *Boston Globe* wrote of her:

> She is a wonderful artist and a dangerous person to work with . . . what makes her dangerous is her imagination and insight. . . . Shapiro has the great gift of making everything she does sound inevitable even when it is surprising.

In 1995 Shapiro formed the piano trio Triple Helix with Bayla Keyes, violin, and Rhonda Rider, cello. They became artists-in-residence at Skidmore and Wellesley colleges. At this writing Shapiro is on the faculties of Wellesley College, Brandeis University, and the Longy School of Music.

4

THE FIRST
"LADY COMPOSERS"

*T*HE FIRST AMERICAN school of musical composition developed from the singing masters and their need for teaching tools. As discussed in Chapter 1, these Yankee "tunesmiths" of the eighteenth and early nineteenth centuries began fashioning music for their pupils and eventually published hundreds of songs. Except for a few isolated individuals, another group of American composers with common bonds did not arise until the third quarter of the nineteenth century.[1] Its center, too, was New England, where between approximately 1850 and 1875 more than a dozen significant composers were born. This group is frequently called the New England school, or sometimes the second New England school, the first being that of the Yankee singing masters, but it might just as well be called the school of Paine and Chadwick, its most influential exponents. From their respective posts at Harvard University and the New England Conservatory of Music, these two men exerted a powerful sway over their pupils and the entire American musical world of their time.

John Knowles Paine (1839–1906) was Harvard's first professor of music, occupant of the first such university chair in the United States, and he ran the department of music from 1875 until his death. He also was the first American composer to write in the larger musical forms—he wrote a Mass, oratorios, and symphonies. His pupils included Arthur William Foote (1853–1937), who composed chamber music and organ and choral works; Frederick Shepherd Converse (1871–1940), who composed symphonies, operas, oratorios, and more; Daniel Gregory Mason (1873–1953), the grandson of music educator Lowell Mason; and John Alden Carpenter (1876–1951), who composed songs and orchestral works.

George Whitefield Chadwick (1854–1931), who had studied in Germany, taught at the New England Conservatory for a half-century; he was its director from 1897 to 1931. He composed operettas, symphonies, and other orchestral works, choral works, and songs. His pupils included Horatio William Parker (1863–1919), who composed two operas and many choral works, the best of which is *Hora Novissima,* and taught at Yale for twenty-five years; Edward Burlingame Hill (1872–1960), who later taught at Harvard; and Margaret Lang and Mabel Wheeler Daniels, whose accomplishments are discussed later in this chapter. Chadwick also shared with Paine in educating Converse and Mason. And at Yale, Horatio William Parker's most famous pupil was Charles Ives (1874–1954), long unrecognized but by the late 1990s considered the most innovative and talented of the entire group.

Also active in Boston during this period was Alsatian-born Charles Martin Loeffler (1861–1935). He played first violin with the Boston Symphony for several decades and became one of the first American impressionist composers.

The first outstanding American woman composer emerged at this same time: Amy Marcy Cheney Beach, or, as she signed all her works, Mrs. H. H. A. Beach. She was neither the first nor the only American woman to write music, but she was the first to hold her own among highly educated and, for their time, sophisticated musicians like Chadwick and Parker. Indeed, her success led one writer to conclude with great enthusiasm that the prejudice militating against women composers in Europe was absent in the United States.[2] Unfortunately this conclusion was far from valid.

Women composers, even more than performers, faced considerable odds. Part of the reason is that composition is a very difficult field, for women and men alike. From playing an instrument to writing music is just a short step, and countless musicians have taken it. But to compose in a concentrated way poses the same requirements as the serious pursuit of painting, poetry, or any other art: a certain amount of schooling and enough money to support one's efforts. The survival of a piece of music, however, requires even more. Works must be written down in order to be performed by others, and they must be accessible—that is, they must be published. Their availability must be made known through further performance and other means of advertising. Often, a work's survival depends on its being recorded, so that it can be heard not just by the relatively small audience of concert-goers but in homes via CDs or tapes and broadcasts. All this involves convincing a number of persons—performers, publishers, record companies—that a composition is good enough to warrant their investment of time and money.

Clearly these requirements pose problems for any would-be composer, regardless of sex, and undoubtedly the challenge of fulfilling them has suppressed hundreds of thousands of musical works. But for women who wished to compose, this challenge was compounded by lack of education and lack of financial support, not to mention lack of positive encouragement. There have been no great women composers, said critic Ernest Newman as late as 1910, because they have no opportunity, no patronage, no support for the long period of technical study that is necessary. Economic necessity leads them either to marriage or to gainful employment; neither is conducive to composition. Moreover, when they do manage to compose, they cannot get their works published or performed. Some have gotten around this difficulty by publishing under masculine, or at least ambiguous, pseudonyms, and some by financing their own performances, as Carlotta Ferrari paid for the production of her opera, *Ugo,* in Milan in 1857. But how many can afford that?[3]

Despite these handicaps, women have been composing music since the time of Sappho, who lived in the seventh century BC and none of whose compositions has survived. The handful of women living before 1800 whose works did survive, though only in small part, tended to belong to one of three social groups: the convent, the nobility or near nobility, or a family of professional musicians, usually supported by a wealthy patron.[4] Only women in these circumstances were sufficiently supported to pursue composition. The convent provided not only education but performance opportunities, usually in the form of a choir. Thus some songs by an anonymous tenth-century Benedictine nun from near Gandersheim, Germany, and some plainsong and a morality play by the twelfth-century Hildegard of Bingen have survived. Hildegard even has seen a considerable revival of interest during the late twentieth century. Wealthy and politically powerful women similarly were able to acquire an education and, often, to hire musicians to perform their works. In the Renaissance a number of Italian noblewomen composed music—Maddalena Casulana, Vittoria Alioti, Isabella Leonarda, and others—as did such better known women as Anne Boleyn, Mary Queen of Scots, Elizabeth I of England, and, later, Marie Antoinette of France, Catherine the Great of Russia, and Princess Anna Amalia of Prussia, sister of Frederick the Great.

Daughters in families of professional musicians often were taught music along with sons. Such was the case for Francesca Caccini (1588–c. 1640), daughter of composer-singer Giulio Caccini. She wrote operas, opera-ballets, and many songs, both sacred and secular, and was director of music at the Medici court in Florence. Another musician's daughter was Elisabeth-Claude Jacquet de La Guerre (c. 1664–1727), a famous harpsichordist who wrote an opera entitled *Uphale et Procris,* performed in Paris in 1694, as well as keyboard works, cantatas, trio sonatas, a Te Deum performed in 1721, and sacred and secular vocal music. She was a protégé of France's music-loving Louis XIV.

Of course, being a member of a musical family does not guarantee either talent or success. Indeed, it carries the risk of being overshadowed by a more talented or more favored relative. This happened in the eighteenth century to Mozart's sister Nannerl, who allegedly was as gifted as her brother, and several generations later to Mendelssohn's sister Fanny, who went so far as to publish some of her compositions under her brother's name.

Even when circumstances permitted a woman to compose, she still lacked social support—sometimes she even faced active opposition. Such antagonism ranged from not being taken seriously or being treated condescendingly—one writer said women especially excel in writing children's music, work that required "perfect sympathy with child-life"[5]—to bald denials that a woman even can have musical talent—"A woman seldom writes good music, never great music."6

Those who deny women's capabilities often point out that there has been no female Bach or Beethoven. Why this should be so has been a subject for speculation by leading American music journalists since the 1880s. The views presented range from wholly unsympathetic (women just do not have the talent, perseverance, concentration, or dedication) to ludicrous (women cannot compose because they cannot sing bass7) to very sympathetic (women have not been given the same chance as men, at least not until very recently).8 Even Fannie Bloomfield-Zeisler, who presumably realized she was the equal of practically any male pianist of her day, said that in the creative arts, specifically composition, women are not the equal of men but they should nevertheless cultivate the very best they can muster. If they work hard, develop the greatest possible competence, and aim at clearness of thought and symmetry of form, they might perhaps become as great as men within the limits of their own sphere. "May it then be said," Bloomfield-Zeisler concluded, "She came, was heard, and conquered."9

If, by some lucky fluke, a woman should produce a respectable composition, it was argued that she could do so only at the expense of her womanhood. For example, one writer pointed out that even if matrimony and lack of strength and endurance did not deter a woman composer, she still needed a considerable amount of "fight" to make her way. Even many men found themselves temperamentally ill-equipped for such battle, and if a woman should be suited for it, it would diminish her "womanly qualities." What then would become of her power of writing "womanly music"?10 Like the violinists and pianists who were suspect, or even condemned, for playing "just like a man" or condescendingly praised for their "feminine playing," the woman composer found herself damned if she did and damned if she didn't. Composing was inherently a masculine province. If women succeeded at it, they were betraying their femininity, except insofar as they expressed feminine delicacy and other approved virtues in a sentimental love song or graceful piano piece for the salon. Indeed, one present-day musicologist suggests that this is the very reason the popular nineteenth-century parlor song became a feminine genre: if they were not actually written by women, since men wrote them, too, they were at least written to be sung by women and for female audiences.11 Even when a writer proudly pointed to the many works produced by women composers, only their songs were usually selected, despite the many other forms in which they wrote.12

These attitudes prevailed in Europe13 and America alike, and if there were few women composers in nineteenth-century Europe, there were fewer still in America. In the United States, after all, the tradition of native composition still lay in the hands of the singing masters, none of whom was a singing mistress. Nevertheless, by 1800 some works by women, principally songs, had been published in the United States, and possibly more are hidden behind masculine pseudonyms.[14] Oscar Sonneck's compendium of music published in America in 1800 or earlier[15] cites four women composers by name and one anonymous "lady of Boston." The most prolific of them was Mary Ann Pownall (1751–1796), the English actress-singer who had come to America in 1792 and collaborated on at least two books of music with James Hewitt, father of organist Sophia Hewitt, as well as writing numerous songs of her own. Another was Harriet Abrams (1758–1822), who wrote "Crazy Jane" and other popular songs.

Women also are represented, still sparsely but in growing numbers, in the music published between 1800 and the 1860s.[16] Two hymns by a Miss M. T. Durham appeared in 1835 in the hymn collection *The Southern Harmony,* a notable exception to the more usual parlor songs and dances. Another important work of this period is German-born Adele Hohnstock's "Polka," consisting of an introduction, theme, and three variations requiring considerable technique from the pianist. Simplified versions of this work for dancing, called "Hohnstock Polka," continued to be published for many years. In 1844 Marion Dix Sullivan composed "The Blue Juniata," the first commercial hit by a woman; Mark Twain reported hearing it at a minstrel show. Jane Sloman, the young English pianist born in 1824 who settled in America, published songs and solo piano pieces into the 1850s. She also published *The Melodist,* a collection of "gems from celebrated composers" that was dedicated to her father and went into several editions.[17] Augusta Browne (1821–1882), who in the late 1840s played the organ at Dr. Cox's church in Brooklyn, New York, apparently gave some organ recitals as well. She wrote keyboard music, anthems, and songs, among them "Grand Vesper Chorus," of 1842, for four-part chorus. Two of her songs, "The Music We Love Most" and "The Mexican Volunteer's Quickstep," were among the new publications received by the *Musical Gazette* of Boston in 1847.[18]

In 1838 there appeared at least two instrumental works by women, *Victoria Waltz* with variations, for piano, by Mrs. Nixon of Cincinnati (published by Dubois and Bacon, New York), and *New Brighton Quadrilles,* also for piano, by Mrs. George Dearborn (published by J. F. Nunns, Philadelphia).[19] "Are We Almost There," a sentimental ballad by Florence Vane, was published in Boston in 1845, and undoubtedly many other songs of this kind appeared elsewhere. Somewhat later came the ballads, sacred songs, and piano pieces of Faustina Hasse Hodges (1822–1895). Daughter of organist Edward Hodges (1796–1867), she was an organist herself. She published songs and keyboard music from the 1850s until her death, and one of her songs, "The Rose Bush" (1859), supposedly sold 100,000 copies.[20] Susan McFarland (1836–1918), who published under her married name, Mrs. E. A. Parkhurst, was well known in the 1860s, especially for her temperance ballad and chorus, "Father's a Drunkard and Mother Is Dead."

Relatively little is known about these women other than their names and an occasional date of publication. Even the music itself is difficult to find, and indeed much of it may not be worth rediscovery. As for the larger forms of composition—symphonies, concertos, oratorios—women are conspicuous by their absence. Of course, not many such works were produced by American men composers between 1800 and 1850. One of the very few was a grand opera, *Leonora* by William Henry Fry (1813–1864)—the first ever composed by an American—produced in Philadelphia in 1845. For the most part, the American concert scene was dominated by the European repertory, and only an occasional short work by an American, usually a song or piano solo, would be performed in a program of otherwise entirely European compositions. Not until John Knowles Paine returned from three years of study in Berlin (1858–61) and wrote his first large choral composition could America claim a native composer of larger works.

Most of the composers of the New England school founded by Paine went to Europe for several years' study, usually to Germany. There were two important exceptions. Arthur Foote was trained entirely in the United States under Paine and Benjamin J. Lang, although he did travel in Europe. And Amy Marcy Cheney Beach, the first American woman to write a Mass and a symphony, did not even visit Europe until 1910, and by then she had been composing for a quarter of a century.

Amy Marcy Cheney was born on September 5, 1867, in Henniker, New Hampshire, the only child of paper manufacturer Charles Abbott Cheney and Clara Imogene Marcy Cheney.[21] She showed musical inclinations very early, already singing many songs accurately at the age of two and composing her first pieces at four. In 1871 the family moved to Chelsea, near (now in) Boston, and soon afterward Amy's mother, who was an excellent pianist and singer, began to teach her piano. She attended a private school and in 1875, at seven, she appeared as pianist at a church musicale, playing a Chopin waltz and, as an encore, "Mama's Waltz," which she had written at four or five.[22] In that year the family moved to Boston, where Amy resided for the next thirty-five years.

From 1876 to 1882 she studied piano with the highly regarded Leipzig-trained teacher Ernst Perabo, and from 1881 to 1882 she studied harmony with organist Junius W. Hill. On October 24, 1883, she made her professional debut at the Boston Music Hall, playing the Moscheles G minor Concerto with an orchestra conducted by Adolph Neuerdorff and, as a solo, Chopin's Rondo in E-flat. She played in several recitals the following year and received good reviews for her rendition of works by Bach, Beethoven, and Chopin. In March 1885 she played the Chopin F minor Concerto with the Boston Symphony, the first of more than a dozen appearances with that orchestra over the years, and a few weeks later she appeared with the Theodore Thomas Orchestra at the Music Hall, playing the Mendelssohn Concerto in D minor. That marked the virtual end of her professional concert career for the next quarter of a century, for in December 1885, a few months after turning eighteen, she married Dr. Henry Harris Aubrey Beach, a prominent Boston surgeon. A widower in his forties, actually a few months older than Amy's father, Beach was a distinguished amateur musician, and he encouraged his young wife to concentrate on composition. Except for occasional appearances, usually to play her own works in charity benefits, she did just that.

Amy Beach's formal training as a composer was minimal. When her mother asked Wilhelm Gericke, conductor of the Boston Symphony, to recommend a composition teacher, he advised that she teach herself by studying the great musical masters. Beach therefore proceeded to train herself, and in the process she translated into English the treatises of Berlioz and Gevaert on instrumentation and orchestration. At first she confined her own attempts to the smaller forms. In December 1886 the *Musical Herald* announced the publication of "Ariette," a setting of a Shelley poem that the reviewer said was "dainty yet sufficiently passionate," and "the guitar effect is well sustained throughout." A year later, perhaps influenced by her translations from the French, she produced the song "Jeune Fille et Jeune Fleur," which a reviewer pettishly said should be sent to a French critic, and weren't there any English poets Mrs. Beach could "employ her excellent muse upon?"[23] In 1888 she played her own cadenza, which was published later that year, in performance of Beethoven's Piano Concerto no. 3 with the Boston Symphony. Of the published version, her first publication of instrumental music, the reviewer said it was interesting but too long for its purpose; in sum, it was a fine piece of bravura work and an excellent study piece, but as a cadenza it violated good taste.[24]

But she continued to make progress. Of her new duet, "Sea Song," a vocal canon, Louis Elson, a well-known critic of the era, said it betrayed considerable skill in polyphonic work.[25] Moreover, despite her youth and sex she was already recognized by Boston's musical establishment; at the commencement exercises of the New England Conservatory in 1891 Amy Beach, then twenty-three, served on the piano awards committee, along with Arthur Foote and Edward MacDowell. And in December of that year, commenting on her anthem, "Praise the Lord All Ye Nations," Elson said, "Boston at last possesses a female composer of merit able to cope with the large as well as the small forms of musical creation."[26]

This judgment was premature, but only by a couple of months. In February 1892 Beach's first large work, Mass in E-flat, op. 5, for full chorus, soloists, orchestra, and organ, was presented by the Handel and Haydn Society under conductor Carl Zerrahn. Later that year her scene and aria "Eilende Wolken," for contralto and orchestra, from Schiller's *Maria Stuart,* was performed by Mrs. Carl (C. Katie) Alves and the New York Symphony Society under Walter Damrosch, the first work by a woman composer at these concerts.

The Mass in E-flat was, on the whole, a success. Most critics liked it, though a few quibbled about portions of it, and the audience gave the composer a standing ovation. This enthusiastic reception notwithstanding, the Mass in E-flat, which had taken the composer three years to complete, was strictly a *succès d'estime.* It was not performed again until years after Beach's death and then only rarely. Nevertheless, it proclaimed Beach's ability to produce a score for large forces, and it no doubt helped her obtain the commission to write a work for the dedication of the Woman's Building of the World's Columbian Exposition to be held in Chicago the following year. In only six weeks Beach produced *Festival Jubilate,* op. 17, which was performed May 1, 1893, by a mixed chorus of 300, soloists, and an orchestra conducted by Theodore Thomas.

Though much was made of women musicians at the women's division of the exposition, Beach's was the only large-scale work for chorus and orchestra by an American woman that was played during the following four months of festivities, and even then the performance was confined to the Woman's Building. W. Waugh Lauder, special exposition correspondent for the *Musical Courier,* said of the work, "It was thoroughly scholastic . . . the success of the afternoon. It made a deep and satisfying impression, and gave an official seal to woman's capability in music."[27] The *Musical Herald* called the work exceedingly well written, pleasing, and musicianly.[28] And Rupert Hughes later said, "The work is as big as its name. It may be too sustainedly loud, and the infrequent and short passages of *piano* are rather breathing spells than contrasting awe, but frequently this work shows a very magnificence of power and exaltation. And the ending is simply superb."[29] Another of Beach's works played at the exposition was her *Romance,* op. 23, for violin and piano. It was dedicated to Maud Powell, who played it along with the composer, and was so well received it had to be played a second time.[30]

The 1890s were an exceptionally prolific period for Beach. By 1896 she had produced more than sixty shorter works for piano, violin, or voice, and several cantatas. Outstanding among the shorter works and singled out for special praise by critics were *Four Sketches,* op. 15, for piano ("In Autumn," "Phantoms," "Dreaming," "Fireflies"), and the song "Ecstasy," op. 19, which became one of the most popular of her many songs.

Beach's next major work was her *Gaelic Symphony,* op. 32, the premiere of which was an important event. It took place on October 30, 1896, with Emil Paur conducting the Boston Symphony Orchestra. Scored for full orchestra, it was the first symphony ever produced by an American woman, and the first such work ever performed by an American orchestra.[31] Beach's symphony, in four movements, is in the traditional mold. The first movement, Allegro con fuoco, is in sonata form, and it introduces the themes resembling Gaelic folk tunes for which the work is named. The second movement opens with a lilting siciliano, has a brisk scherzo midsection, and returns to the siciliano at the end. The third movement, Lento con molto espressione, again has a melody of Celtic character, followed by second and third themes that undergo elaborate development. The final movement, fast and brilliant, is again in sonata form.

The *Gaelic Symphony*, which is rather long, is very much a work of its time, both in its incorporation of folk motifs, a popular late-nineteenth-century device, and in its overall harmonic vocabulary, directly traceable to Wagner and Brahms. One present-day writer believes all Beach's instrumental works are derivative, though probably not consciously so, and that those of her early period all echo Wagner and Brahms, whereas later she reflected elements of the styles of Debussy, Reger, and MacDowell.[32] Certain stylistic traits of Beach's own also are present in the symphony, particularly the flowing melodies—characteristic of all her work, vocal and instrumental—and the persistent use of chromaticism, the use of all tones, not just those of the particular given key, especially at points of climax. The symphony also shows, to some extent, Beach's perennial tendency toward overelaboration, but it further demonstrates a technical mastery that is truly surprising for a largely self-taught composer.

Unlike the Mass in E-flat, the *Gaelic Symphony* was performed numerous times during the next twenty years or so, not only in Boston but in New York, Brooklyn, Philadelphia, Pittsburgh, Chicago, Detroit, Buffalo, Minneapolis, San Francisco, and many smaller cities. Nevertheless, some critics continued to insist that Beach was at her best in smaller works, especially the songs and chamber pieces that she continued to turn out.[33] Among these was the Sonata in A minor, op. 34, for violin and piano, first performed by Franz Kneisel and the composer in 1897 in Boston. Elson regarded this work, along with the *Gaelic Symphony*, as the most important music produced by an American woman.[34]

Not everyone admired Beach's music, to be sure. Further, some of the criticism, both favorable and unfavorable, invoked the double standard by which the music of women composers was so often judged; that is, it was either "too feminine" or "too masculine."[35] For example, *Etude* said Beach's Violin Sonata was excellent, feminine in sentiment but worked out in a broad, masterful spirit worthy of a man.[36] A month earlier it had praised the *Gaelic Symphony* on more neutral grounds, for having more "music imagination" than her earlier works and for exhibiting both originality and profundity of thought. Herbert Hall did not like the Violin Sonata at all; he believed Beach should concentrate on simplicity and "not draw her ideas out to an infinitive point."[37] Nevertheless, the sonata won favor with performers such as pianist Teresa Carreño, who played it with Carl Halir in Berlin.

In March 1898 Beach appeared in a program of her own works as a benefit for the Elizabeth Peabody House in Boston. She and violinist Olive Mead played several of her works for violin and piano, among them *Romance*, op. 23. The program also included the song "Forget-me-not," to words by Beach's husband, as well as settings of poems by Burns, Shakespeare, Heine, Goethe, and Hugo. It must have been just about this time that Beach was working on her op. 44, three settings of poems by Robert Browning that include two of her most famous songs, "The Year's at the Spring" and "Ah, Love But a Day!" The first, relatively simple, sounds much like a Schubert lied, and the second, more chromatic, like a Brahms song. Both these songs, which were frequently performed for many years, show several basic traits of all Beach's vocal music: they lie well for the voice, with comfortable intervals and tessitura, and the setting of the words is skillfully handled. They are, of course, very sentimental, and, although once praised for their sincerity and depth of feeling[38] they seem somewhat silly today. Yet they are melodic, well crafted, and eminently singable, which is undoubtedly why so many recitalists chose them for so long.

In April 1900 Beach herself appeared with the Boston Symphony in the premiere of her last big orchestral work, the Piano Concerto in C-sharp minor, op. 45. During the remaining forty-four years of her life—she was only thirty-two in April 1900—Beach continued to write songs, choral works (including one large cantata), chamber music, and piano pieces, but she never again wrote a purely orchestral piece.

She dedicated the Piano Concerto to Teresa Carreño. A long work in four movements, it has a brilliant and difficult piano part. The first movement, Allegro moderato, takes up fully one-half the length of the concerto. In modified sonata form, it presents the main theme first lyrically by the orchestra, then passionately by the solo piano. The coda of this movement includes a richly worked cadenza. The second movement, the brisk Scherzo, is a *perpetuum mobile* (perpetual motion) for the piano, with the orchestra playing two countermelodies against the piano's constantly shifting rhythms. The third movement, Largo, is a lament built on two brief ideas, one stern, the other lyrical. It proceeds without interruption into the final movement, Allegro con scioltezza (fast and fluent), a vivacious rondo in 6/8 time, with a quasi-bolero rhythm marking the second theme. This is the most interesting of all the movements, both rhythmically and melodically. The central section is a slow part in which, in indistinct rhythms, the piano plays a free-flowing fantasy of the main thematic material marked by drifting fragments of melody and flashbacks to earlier themes. With mounting excitement in a stretto (ever narrower, ever faster) coda, the concerto concludes with extremely rapid octave passages by the piano.[39]

Like the *Gaelic Symphony,* the concerto was a resounding success, and it was played with major orchestras in the United States (Chicago, Pittsburgh, St. Louis, Los Angeles) and, some years later, in Europe (Berlin, Leipzig, Hamburg, with the composer as soloist). It was last performed with Beach as soloist by the Boston Symphony under Karl Muck in 1917. It was then reintroduced nearly sixty years later, in 1976, by Mary Louise Boehm with the American Symphony under Morton Gould. Although it has been criticized as oversentimental, a quality many find especially prevalent in Beach's writing for the piano,[40] it shows a mature mastery of form and undeniable lyrical talent. The composer's skill and imagination are evident throughout.

Until the end of World War I all of Beach's big works except the Mass—the *Gaelic Symphony,* Violin Sonata, and Piano Concerto—were performed quite frequently, both in America and Europe. The Violin Sonata was performed in Paris by Ysaÿe and Pugno in 1900 and in London by Sigmund Beel and Henry Bird in 1904. The *Gaelic Symphony* was performed in 1915 by the Philadelphia Orchestra under Leopold Stokowski, by New York's Manhattan Symphony under Henry Hadley in 1931, and by the Woman's Symphony Orchestra of Boston under Alexander Thiede in 1940; the Los Angeles Symphony performed the first movement alone in 1972. The Piano Concerto, introduced in Germany by Carreño, was often played by major orchestras there, especially during Beach's stay abroad.

An interview published in *Etude* in 1904 gives a vivid picture of the composer. Amy Beach was then in her mid-thirties, childless, and by virtue of her own talent and her husband's position, very much a lady of quality. Said William Armstrong:

> She is a woman of charmingly simple manners. . . . She is of medium height. Her eyes are of a grayish blue, large and smiling. Her complexion is fresh and brilliant. Her blonde hair, primly parted, is brushed back smoothly from her face. The manner of her wearing it, and the quaint style of her dress, rather that of the early seventies [1870s] than of today, make her appear older than she in reality is.[41]

The interview, which took place at Beach's Boston home on Commonwealth Avenue, continues, "She composes when she feels the inclination moves her to it." When not writing, she studied the piano, and she was, said Armstrong, very interested in housekeeping. She spoke about the classics of the piano literature, of the at that time neglected works she loved, among them the Schubert impromptus and sonatas, the lesser Chopin mazurkas, Mendelssohn's *Songs Without Words,* some Liszt works no longer played. Her favorites, however, were Bach, Beethoven, and Brahms.

Those who knew her recall Amy Beach as a woman of considerable personal charm. Called Aunt Amy by the younger generation, she was unfailingly courteous to all and especially kind to young students, though she herself never taught. Amy Beach Clubs were formed in many towns, often initiated by a local piano teacher who admired Beach, and enthusiastically joined by many others. Though her husband encouraged her to compose, one cannot help but wonder if he did not restrict the expression of her undeniable talent. His very position in upper-class Boston society—intellectual and artistic, but also somewhat stuffy—probably imposed rather rigid standards of respectability and gentility. Moreover, the Beaches seldom traveled, and so had little exposure to other worlds.

Amy Beach surely realized this, for after her husband's death in 1910 and her mother's in 1911—Clara Cheney lived with the Beaches for the last decade of her life—she undertook her first journey to Europe, and she remained there for nearly four years. Though her stay there did not greatly influence her style of composition, she did resume more frequent public performances, appearing with German orchestras in her Piano Concerto and with chamber groups in her Violin Sonata and her Piano Quintet in F-sharp minor, op. 67, written in 1908. This last piece, too, has been criticized for oversentimentality, but a later critic singled out the slow movement for its "scrumptiously Straussian melody," although he considered the rest rather dull, and another characterized the music as rich and dark, with soaring lines and inventive chord progressions.[42]

Beach returned to America in 1914. She had adopted a more modern style of dress and coiffure, and she resumed playing in public here. She began with a program of her own works in New York's Aeolian (later Town) Hall, which included the Violin Sonata, Piano Quintet with the Olive Mead Quartet, and the long Prelude and Fugue, for piano. For the next couple of years she traveled across the country for performances of her works, appearing in Milwaukee, Chicago, St. Louis, Toronto, Baltimore, Boston, Philadelphia, and San Francisco. Also during this period her *Panama Hymn* was accepted by the Panama Pacific Exposition as its official anthem.

In 1915 Beach gave an interview to the *Los Angeles Examiner* in which she cited "ten commandments" for young composers:

1. Perfect the technique of composition, beginning with the simplest rudiments.
2. Begin with small things, ideas that can be expressed in small forms.
3. Develop all the possibilities of a small form.
4. Learn to employ as much variety in form as possible. Avoid becoming stereotyped in expressing melodic, harmonic, or rhythmic ideas.
5. Analyze the old masters, especially their examples in the same form (as, for a fugue, Bach's *Well-Tempered Clavier*).
6. Study the string quartets of Haydn, Mozart, and the early Beethoven; analyze and learn them by heart.
7. Listen to good string quartets at their rehearsals and concerts; take along a score and follow it.
8. Hear good choral music.
9. Learn the masterworks of the symphony as played by fine orchestras; be thorough in studying symphonic works.

10. Remember that technique is only a means to an end. You first must have something to say: "If you feel deeply and know to express what you feel, you make others feel."[43]

Deep-feeling and emotional as Beach herself was, she believed in a firm technical foundation for expressing her sentiments.

Though Beach told John Tasker Howard that she divided herself about equally between composing and performing, her public appearances from 1920 on became much rarer. In 1915 Beach had given up her Boston house and after a good deal of touring and a long stay in California and more than a decade in Hillsborough, New Hampshire, she eventually made New York her base, at least in winter. One of the last big pieces she composed was *The Canticle of the Sun,* op. 123, performed at the Worcester Festival in 1931 and numerous times thereafter in various New York churches, including St. Bartholomew's, which she attended. In Worcester she told Raymond Morin, "One thing I have learned from my audiences is that young women artists and composers shouldn't be afraid to pitch right in and try. If they think they have something to say, let them say it. But let them be sure to build a technique with which to say it. The technique mustn't be visible, but it must be there."[44]

Concerning the status of women composers, in 1915 she said that she herself had never felt limited as a woman and had encountered no prejudice; she believed the opportunities for men and women were equal.[45] Certainly she had no trouble in getting her works published—in 1940 only two of her 150 opus numbers were still unpublished: a one-act opera, *Cabildo,* op. 149, and String Quartet, op. 89, in one movement, which finally was published in 1993. One of her last works, Piano Trio, op. 150, was published in 1939.[46] By then quite a few of her works were out of print, but, considering the half-century of her activity as a composer, that is not too surprising.

On the other hand, Beach could not have overlooked the fact that she was almost invariably singled out as the leading *woman* composer, not as the leading American, or New England, or even Boston composer. In July 1924 she became president of the newly founded Society of American Women Composers.[47] The following year she was represented at a Women Composers Festival held in Washington, D.C., sponsored by the National League of American Pen-Women, and she continued to be more or less active in the women composers' group for the next decade. At the very least, through her membership in the group she acknowledged her kinship with other women composers. The very fact that they joined together and regularly arranged for performances of their works indicates a perceived need for more performance opportunities.

Always a devout Episcopalian, in the 1920s and 1930s Beach wrote a considerable amount of church music. In addition to the early Mass in E-flat, she had by 1910 written several anthems, including Service in A, op. 63, and the three-movement motet *Help Us, Oh God,* op. 50, for a cappella chorus. The motet's last movement is one of the few fugues she wrote, and a fine one at that. She wrote a number of other anthems and motets, a Te Deum in F, a Communion service, and, in addition to *Canticle of the Sun,* the cantata *Christ in the Universe,* op. 133, for soloists, chorus, and orchestra or organ. The very last composition she produced, "Though I Take the Wings of Morning," op. 152, was also sacred, on a text paraphrasing Psalm 139. One writer thinks this is the single best work she ever produced, showing "a lack of chromaticism, a simplicity of style, plus a reticence in the piano part [that] allow the musical ideas to show through."[48]

Beach also produced secular choral works and, of course, more songs, much in the vein of the earlier ones but none as successful as the Browning songs or "Ecstasy." Indeed, it has been said that her style—sentimental but technically sound, somewhat complicated by the overuse of chromaticism but lush in musical imagination—changed little between op. 1 and op. 152.[49] The only exceptions, Tuthill suggests, are the Variations, op. 80, for flute and string quartet, published in 1916, and the String Quartet, op. 89, in one movement. The former, consisting of a theme and six variations, not only displays her technical command of harmony and counterpoint, but her genuine understanding of the balance of parts in chamber music, where each instrument is equally important. She had trouble conveying this idea when one of the instruments was the piano. In the quartet, Beach for the first time departed from traditional tonality, introducing what for her was an unusual amount of dissonance. And though Beach may have clung to essentially the same style, she continued to try her hand at new forms. Her first attempt at opera, *Cabildo,* was written in 1932, at the age of sixty-five.

Beach spent her winters in New York in a women's residential hotel (her alleged love for housekeeping must have died with her husband), but in summer she returned to New England. There she went to her summer home on Cape Cod in Centerville, which had been paid for with royalties from "Ecstasy" alone, or to the MacDowell Colony in Peterborough, New Hampshire, or to a room she kept in Henniker, New Hampshire, to spend time with relatives and friends. She retained her legal and voting address there throughout her life. "Life in the woods is my greatest joy," she told John Tasker Howard, "with my friends and all that they have meant to me."[50] She was a close friend of Marian MacDowell's, to whom she dedicated her *Three Piano Pieces,* op. 128. It was at the MacDowell Colony that Beach befriended many young musicians and fellow women composers, among them Mabel Daniels and Mary Howe, and there she composed the Piano Trio, op. 150, in the summer of 1938.

On May 8, 1940, Beach was honored at a dinner in New York's Town Hall Club, attended by some 200 musicians, composers, and friends. Marian MacDowell, the composer Douglas Moore, and pianist Olga Samaroff were among those who paid tribute to her. In her speech on that occasion, Samaroff

said that although women were handicapped in music, Amy Beach had not fal-
tered in courage and had set an example to her personally, as well as to many
other women. Both *Romance* and the Piano Trio were played that day.[51] Four
and a half years later Beach died, on December 27, 1944, at the age of seventy-
seven. Her music was no longer in vogue, and that, together with her persistent old-fashioned use of her husband's name and her uncanny physical resem-
blance to a benignly smiling Queen Victoria, made her a figure of fun to some.
Yet, considering that she was largely self-taught and entirely American-trained,
her achievements were quite remarkable for her generation, and some of her
music can hold its own in any age.

Though Beach's *Gaelic Symphony* was the first symphony written by an
American woman, it was not the first orchestral work by a woman performed
by the Boston Symphony. That honor belonged to Margaret Lang, whose
Dramatic Overture, op. 12, was performed under Artur Nikisch on April 7,
1893. At that time the composer was twenty-five years old. Later that year her
overture *Witchis* was performed in Chicago by Theodore Thomas and his
orchestra.

Margaret Ruthven Lang was, like Amy Beach, born in 1867, and her
orchestral works were received with great enthusiasm in the 1890s. But there
the similarity between the two women ends. Lang was the daughter of a highly
successful and prominent Boston musician. She studied, both in Boston and
abroad, with the most eminent teachers of the time. Her works run to fifty-
seven opus numbers but, except for three overtures and a few other orchestral
works, her output was confined to songs and choral music, and her last published work appeared in 1916, when she was not yet fifty. For the remainder of
her long life—she lived to the age of 104—she apparently never composed
again.

Unlike Amy Beach, Lang was no child prodigy. Her mother was a talented amateur singer and her father an eminent conductor, organist, and
teacher. Benjamin J. Lang, born in 1837 in Salem, Massachusetts, served as organist for the Handel and Haydn Society of Boston from 1859 to 1896, and
as its conductor from 1896 to 1898. He was instrumental in building up two
other musical organizations, the Apollo Club, a male chorus formed in 1871,
which he directed until 1901, and the Cecilia Society, a mixed chorus formed
in 1877, which he led until 1907. The latter is credited with giving more first
American performances of great works, including Bach's B minor Mass, than
any other Boston group. A church organist, Lang also produced a number of
compositions—songs, duets, and an oratorio, *David*—but he allowed none
of them to be published, "rightly judging them to have no lasting merit," according to one writer.[52] He died in 1909, leaving an estate of $600,000. One
must conclude that he had a shrewd head for business, music being an impe-
cunious profession even then. And money, of course, made it possible for his
daughter Margaret, who never married, to become a composer.

One of three children, Margaret Lang first studied under one of her father's pupils, and then studied piano with her father and violin with Louis Schmidt of Boston. At twelve she wrote her first piece, one movement of a piano quintet. In 1886 she went to Munich and studied violin with Drechsler and Ludwig Abel, as well as composition with Victor Gluth. When she returned to Boston in 1887 she continued her musical education, studying orchestration with George Chadwick and composition with Edward MacDowell. Finding it difficult to work at home without interruption, she rented a room in the neighborhood to use as a studio. Allegedly it contained a shelf full of "rejected manuscripts," pieces with which Lang was not satisfied. During this period she also went to see individual members of the Boston Symphony to discuss the capabilities of their respective instruments, so that she might write better for them.[53]

Her father's position in Boston's musical world provided Lang with an entrée. A number of her works were performed by the Cecilia Society and the Apollo Club. The *Musical Herald* of March 1889 reports "a very pretty quartette by a young Boston composer, Miss M. R. Lang," at a recent Cecilia Society concert, and the *Musical Record* of June 1889 notes that a recent Apollo Club concert included her "Maiden and the Butterfly," a song Rupert Hughes later described as being "as fragile and rich as a butterfly's wing."[54]

The following year the Apollo Club performed one of Lang's best works, *The Jumblies,* a series of settings of limericks by Edward Lear for baritone solo, men's chorus, and two-piano accompaniment. The *Musical Herald* critic said of the work, "It is impossible to deny Miss Lang's facility in composition or the grace with which she states her ideas, and while she has constructed a rather formidable work upon Lear's innocent text, she has shown an original bent in her harmonies, and a sympathetic study of the voices."[55] A number of these settings are musical pastiches—takeoffs on forms such as the development section of a late romantic symphony, a barcarolle, a waltz—executed with great delicacy and wit. *The Jumblies* was repeated at a Mendelssohn Glee Club concert in New York on February 10, 1891, and was most favorably received. A portion of the work was revived at a special Handel and Haydn Society concert in October 1975, in arrangements for mixed chorus, solo voice and piano, women's voices, and more.

In February 1893 the Cecilia Society, in two concerts at the Boston Music Hall, included the song "Love Plumes His Wings," which Francis H. Jenks of the *Musical Herald* described as "very delicate and bright." A few weeks later, on April 8, the Boston Symphony performed the *Dramatic Overture,* of which the same critic wrote, "Miss Lang's work is an ingeniously devised and constructed composition with evidences of thought at every turn."[56]

The Bureau of Music of the 1893 World's Columbian Exposition of Chicago had asked for new American works, and twenty-one American composers had responded, but only four instrumental compositions were chosen for public performance. One of them was Lang's overture *Witchis,* op. 10, which was performed in August under Theodore Thomas and later was repeated by Bendix. In the next few years she wrote another overture, *Totila,* op. 23, and three arias for solo voice and orchestra—*Sappho's Prayer to Aphrodite,* for contralto, performed in New York, 1896; *Armida,* for soprano, performed by the Boston Symphony on January 13, 1896; and *Phoebus' Denunciation of the Furies at His Delphian Shrine,* for baritone and orchestra.

The only other performance of a large work of Lang's appears to have been that of the Choral Music Society of Boston on January 10, 1917, performing *The Heavenly Noel,* for mezzo-soprano solo, women's chorus, organ, piano, harp, and string quartet. Philip Hale said of this work, "The music, published last year, is not too deliberately quaint, nor is it affectedly modern. It reflects the spirit of the text."[57] And the *Boston Transcript* review said, "The least pretentious proved the most distinctive and meritorious." It called the setting "freshly imagined, dexterously conducted, and abundant in unobtrusively ingenious and prettily fanciful play with the timbres of the women's voices and the heightening strings."

As it happens, neither reviewer mentioned Lang's outstanding characteristic, her highly individual treatment of harmonies and her exploration of dissonance. Unlike Beach, however, who was accused, often justly, of overcomplicating her works with unnecessary key changes and chromaticism, Lang's harmonies have, as Rupert Hughes put it, "the appearance of spontaneous ease, and the elaborateness never obtrudes itself upon the coherence of the work." Moreover, he adds, her songs "are singable to a degree unusual in scholarly compositions."[58]

After producing more than 100 songs, Lang simply stopped composing. She lived out her life on Brimmer Street, in Boston's Back Bay, regularly attending the concerts of her beloved Boston Symphony. On her 100th birthday the Boston Symphony, under conductor Erich Leinsdorf, honored her by playing "Old Hundredth" and a Bach cantata. She died on May 30, 1972, six months before her 105th birthday.

A contemporary of Lang's who also studied piano with Benjamin J. Lang and composition with George Chadwick was Helen Hood, born in 1863 in Chelsea, Massachusetts.[59] She, too, went abroad to study for a time, with Moszkowski and Scharwenka in Berlin, and returned to spend the rest of her life in Boston. And she, too, was represented at the 1893 World's Columbian Exposition in Chicago. Although Hood wrote two suites for violin, piano pieces, a piano trio, a string quartet, and a Te Deum, she was noted principally for her songs. Unlike Lang's songs, which were closer in approach to the German lied, Hood's were principally "parlor songs," graceful, melodious, sentimental ballads, popular in their time but of passing interest. She died in 1949.

Still another pupil of Chadwick's was Mabel Wheeler Daniels, who brought with her to Germany a letter of introduction to composition professor Victor Gluth from Margaret Lang. Born on November 27, 1879, in Swampscott, Massachusetts, Mabel Daniels came from a musical family.[60] One grandfather, William Daniels, was an organist and a member of the Handel and Haydn Society from 1844 to 1886; the other grandfather was a choir director. Both her parents sang with the Handel and Haydn Society, and her father, George F. Daniels, served as the society's president from 1899 to 1908.

Daniels began piano lessons at an early age and wrote her first piece, *Fairy Charm Waltz,* at ten. She had a good soprano voice, and at Radcliffe College she joined the glee club and soon was given leading roles in the operettas it presented. She became the glee club's director, and wrote two operettas for it in 1900, *A Copper Complication* and *The Court of Hearts.* After graduating magna cum laude in 1900, she studied composition with George Chadwick, who became a close friend, and then, in 1903, she went to Germany to work with Ludwig Thuille. She was the first woman to be admitted to the score-reading class at the Royal Conservatory in Munich. Apparently five years earlier women had not even been allowed to study counterpoint at the conservatory. In 1903 they could, but few chose to. Also, the faculty included two women professors and thirty-eight men.

After two winters in Germany, where the conservatory awarded her a medal, Daniels returned to the United States and joined the mixed chorus of the Cecilia Society in order to learn more about orchestration and scores, since she herself played no orchestral instrument. During this time she also wrote a book about her experiences in Germany, *An American Girl in Munich (Impressions of a Music Student),* which was published in 1905. Less influential than Amy Fay's book of 1880, *Music Study in Germany,* it nevertheless presents an interesting picture of the life of American students abroad.

In 1908 the Boston Pops under Gustav Strube performed Daniels's first work for full orchestra, *In the Greenwood.* In 1911 she won two prizes from the National Federation of Music Clubs, one for the song "Villa of Dreams" and the other for two three-part songs for women's voices with violin and piano accompaniment. She also wrote *The Desolate City,* a cantata for baritone solo, chorus, and orchestra, which Marian MacDowell asked her to conduct at a MacDowell Colony summer festival in 1913. MacDowell was so impressed that she invited Daniels to return the following summer as a colonist, or resident artist, and Daniels, accepting the invitation and returning many times thereafter, wrote many of her later works during her stays there. Daniels also became a corporate member of the Edward MacDowell Association. The prelude *Deep Forest,* one of her most frequently performed works, was inspired by one of her summers in the New Hampshire woods. Originally written for chamber orchestra, it was first performed by the Barrère Little Symphony; later it was revised for full orchestra and in this form was performed by Serge Koussevitsky, John Barbirolli, Hans Kindler, and other important conductors. Daniels herself conducted it with the Chicago Symphony on August 1,

1915, in a program of American compositions at the Pan-Pacific International Exposition in San Francisco.

Meanwhile Daniels was active in other areas as well. From 1911 to 1913 she directed the Radcliffe Glee Club and served as music director for the Bradford Academy, and from 1913 to 1918 she was director of music at Simmons College. She later became a member of the advisory committee on music for the Boston public schools, served as a trustee of Radcliffe College, and was an active member of the Society of American Women Composers. She was a good friend of many women composers, especially Amy Beach, Margaret Lang, and Helen Hopekirk (Hopekirk rode along in her carriage during a suffragist demonstration in Boston in 1915).

In 1929 Daniels wrote *Exultate Deo,* op. 33, for mixed chorus and orchestra, for the celebration of Radcliffe's fiftieth anniversary. It was later performed by the Boston Symphony and Cecilia Society under Koussevitsky, and became one of Daniels's best known choral works. The cantata consists of four sections: the first and last ring out in praise of God, assisted by trumpet fanfares; the second describes the instruments that shall join together in praise; and the third is a short prayer of trust in God.

Though she produced a number of other works, the next important one—and some believe the most important of all her compositions—was *The Song of Jael,* op. 37, which had its premiere at the Worcester Festival of 1940. A cantata for soprano solo, mixed chorus, and orchestra, it was based on the poem "Sisera" by Daniels's close friend, Edwin Arlington Robinson, and was the first of her works to use modern idioms. The story concerns a Jewish woman, Jael, who killed the tyrant Sisera while he slept and became a heroine to her people. The music consists of three sections, essentially two hymns of triumph separated by a shorter Andante pastorale. The *Boston Post* critic said its outstanding feature was the striking and highly original handling of the choral sections, but there were also many effective parts in the orchestral score, and the soprano solo, performed at Worcester by Rose Bampton, was dramatic and impressive.

In her later works Daniels continued to use modern idioms, although with some caution. Among these are her 1940 *Pastoral Ode,* op. 40, for flute and strings, given its premiere by members of the Boston Symphony; her 1943 *Three Observations for Three Woodwinds,* a short, charming, satirical piece that the composer said was not intended to be taken too seriously; her 1947 *Digressions for String Orchestra,* op. 41, no. 2; and her 1948 *Two Pieces for Violin and Piano.* Her last completed composition, finished in 1961, was *Piper, Play On!,* op. 49, a choral work based on an ancient Greek text. Daniels's previous big choral work had been written for the seventy-fifth anniversary of Radcliffe, *A Psalm of Praise,* op. 46, for mixed chorus, three trumpets, percussion, and strings. It was first performed by the Harvard Glee Club and Radcliffe Choral Society under G. Wallace Woodworth in 1954, with the piano playing the string parts. Two years later it was performed by the Boston Symphony, making Daniels the first woman ever to have had three different works performed by that orchestra: *Exultate Deo*, 1932; *Deep Forest*, 1937; and *A Psalm of Praise*, 1954.

Though Daniels was active in groups of women composers, she had some mixed feelings about this issue. Concerning the premiere of *The Song of Jael* at Worcester in 1940, she later recalled with amusement that she was called to the stage to take bows with conductor Albert Stoessel and then encountered a man at intermission who said, "That Jael piece was tremendous, and what a climax with the brass and drums and cymbal all going like mad while the chorus sings 'Jael has killed Sisera!' But tell me, what was that woman doing who came on to the stage when they applauded?"

Yet Daniels herself believed that women musicians and composers are handicapped in at least two ways. First, they have more exacting time-consuming obligations than men do, by which she meant not social functions but the ordinary routines of life, domestic and other. Second, she believed that most women do not have the physical strength to compose an extended list of symphonies, operas, string quartets, and other kinds of concerted music. The sheer burden of writing down, day after day, notes, dynamics, accents, and phrasing for all the different parts of an orchestral work is extremely hard work. For this reason, she said, women have usually stuck to the smaller forms. Four requisites, she maintained, are indispensable to any woman composer, over and above talent: a strong constitution, perseverance, ingenuity, and above all, courage.[61]

Awarded honorary degrees in music from Tufts and Boston universities, Wheaton College, and the New England Conservatory of Music, Mabel Daniels was highly respected throughout her long life. She was kind and generous to many young musicians and students, offered several composition prizes anonymously, set up a loan fund for music majors at Radcliffe, and established a scholarship at the New England Conservatory of Music, where she also served as a trustee. She died on March 10, 1971.

The last important "lady composer" of New England, Helen Hopekirk, was a Scot by birth. Like Amy Beach, she began her career as a pianist, and it was in that capacity that she first came to Boston. She eventually settled there permanently, devoting herself to composition and teaching.

Helen Hopekirk was born near Edinburgh in 1856 and studied with G. Lichtenstein and A. C. Mackenzie.[62] She spent two years at the Leipzig Conservatory and later studied piano with Leschetizky in Vienna. She made her debut in Leipzig in 1878 and her English debut at the Crystal Palace in London the following year. In 1882 she married a Scottish music critic and landscape painter, William A. Wilson, and in 1883 she made her first American tour, playing with the Boston Symphony on December 8, 1883, and giving a New York recital a couple weeks later. She continued to study and perform in

Europe during the 1880s, visited the United States again during the 1890–91 season, and moved to Boston permanently in 1897. From 1892 on she had been living in Paris, concentrating primarily on composition. Her Sonata in E minor, for violin and piano, was first played in Boston at a concert of the Kneisel Quartet in March 1891. The *Musical Herald* critic liked the piece, calling it "a little classic in point of dignity of form." The themes were good; the repetition of the first movement's subjects was somewhat excessive but showed a sure musical touch. The slow movement was "really imaginative." And the Finale was "vivacious," though its ideas were slight.63

In 1897, after her husband was severely injured in a traffic accident and could no longer work, she accepted George Chadwick's offer of a job teaching piano at the New England Conservatory. The Wilsons remained in the United States for the rest of their lives, except for one year spent in Edinburgh (1919–20), and both became American citizens. Hopekirk, who retained her maiden name for professional use, taught at the conservatory for four years, and in 1901 resigned, thereafter teaching only privately at her home.

Hopekirk's first major composition was her *Concertstück* for piano and orchestra, composed in Paris in 1894 and first played in Edinburgh by the Scottish Orchestra under Georg Henschel in November of that year. The American premiere took place seven years later, on April 15, 1904, with the Boston Symphony and the composer as soloist. The form of this work is that of a piano concerto in one movement, molded on classic lines in the opening section but then becoming more free. Although the program notes describe the unifying effect of a theme presented in the prelude that appears and reappears throughout, the *Boston Transcript* critic said the piece was rich in ideas but lacking in unity, though many of the themes were charming. Besides the Violin Sonata, several other of her compositions had been heard in America. In June 1899 her song "Under the Still White Stars," with violin accompaniment, won a prize in the *Musical Record* contest in the category of concert songs. Then in 1900 the Boston Symphony performed her Piano Concerto in D major, which was never published.

For the next couple of decades Hopekirk continued to appear once or twice a year in recitals of chamber music or of her own works. In 1904, in an interview with Edith Lynwood Winn published in the August issue of *Etude,* she said her ancestors were Celts and she had become interested in Gaelic song. The following year she published *Seventy Scottish Songs,* which went into a number of editions and was considered very successful. Her next major published work was *Iona Melodies* of 1910, four short piano works that show the influence of both Edward MacDowell and Scottish folk song. In an interview published in the *Musician* in 1912, Hopekirk said that she spent each morning composing and practicing and each afternoon teaching. Also, part of each year she spent in Europe, where she devoted her time entirely to composition. In 1919 she and her husband went to spend an entire year in Scotland, and at the time of their departure her friends presented her with a silver bowl; among the donors' names engraved on that bowl was M. R. Lang, so presumably Margaret Lang and Helen Hopekirk were good friends.

In 1925 Hopekirk became musical adviser for the Dana Hall Music School at Wellesley. The following year her husband died, but she continued to be active, giving recitals regularly and composing. She made her last public appearance in a recital of her own compositions before the Pianoforte Teachers Society of Boston in April 1939, a month before her eighty-third birthday. She died in November 1945 at the age of eighty-nine. She appears not to have composed any large-scale works after the early concertos, but she produced another violin sonata, more than 100 songs, and many piano pieces.

Hopekirk's attitude toward other women musicians was also somewhat ambivalent. Like so many others, she wanted to be judged not as a woman composer or a woman pianist but as an individual making a contribution. Yet in 1901 she wrote a curious letter to *Etude* concerning piano teachers. She believed that the ability to teach was found equally in men and in women, she said, but she opposed "the thoughtless plunging into teaching, by women, that is so prevalent." She went on:

> In this country there is a perfect mania to become a teacher of some sort or other among people who, in Europe, would not feel themselves demeaned by doing housework well. Many girls would be much better employed and more comfortable keeping houses orderly and nicely— say for other women who through their work lack the time for personal supervision—than in giving cheap, bad piano-lessons and swelling the ranks of the victimizers of our much-abused piano.[64]

At the same time, Hopekirk was an ardent suffragist and had great respect for the compositions of Mabel Daniels.

One more pianist-composer of European birth had enough impact in New England to be mentioned with this group of women. She was Adele Lewing, born in 1866 in Hanover, Germany, where her maternal grandfather, A. C. Prell, was a cellist in the court orchestra.[65] She began her musical studies early and made her debut as a pianist at the age of twelve. She studied in Leipzig under Reinecke, graduated with high honors from the conservatory there, and then went to America, where she first taught and gave concerts in Chicago but later moved to Boston. On May 10, 1892, she gave a concert devoted entirely to her own compositions at the Meionaon in Boston, performing some twenty-five songs and piano works. In 1893 she played another program of her own piano compositions at the Woman's Congress of the World's Columbian Exposition in Chicago, and a number of her songs were sung there as well. Soon afterward she went to Vienna to study piano with Leschetizky and composition with Robert Fuchs, and she remained there for three years.

In October 1896 Lewing returned to New York and announced that she would teach the Leschetizky method and accept concert engagements. Her first concerts, in Carnegie Hall and Steinway Hall in December 1896, were well received. The following July her composition *Meditation* was played at the nineteenth annual convention of the Music Teachers National Association. In 1899 she married Dr. Benjamin W. Stiefel of New York, and the following year her song "Fair Rohtraut" won the *Musical Record's* first prize for a concert song. She continued to be active, teaching and composing, until her death in 1943, at the age of eighty-two.

Clara Kathleen Barnett Rogers was another European-born woman influential in Boston's musical world during the latter part of the nineteenth century.[66] As Clara Doria she had made a name for herself as an opera singer. Born in England in 1844, the daughter of composer John Barnett, she graduated from the Leipzig Conservatory and also studied at Berlin and Milan. During her student years she composed a string quartet but was excluded from the composition class because of her sex. She came to the United States in 1871 on tour with the Parepa-Rosa opera company and several years later settled in Boston. In 1878 she married Henry Munroe Rogers, a Boston lawyer, and retired from professional performance, although she continued to participate in private musicales and amateur musical clubs and in 1902 joined the voice faculty of the New England Conservatory. In 1883 she helped form a Bach Club in order to study cantatas, and she was active in the Manuscript Club, founded in 1888, whose chief aim was to perform the works of young, unknown composers. At one of its early meetings she performed the piano part of her own Violin Sonata in D minor, together with Charles Loeffler; the same meeting also featured a group of songs by Margaret Lang and a suite by Arthur Foote.

Rogers's other compositions include the aforementioned string quartet, a cello sonata, some piano pieces, and a large number of art songs. Of her *Six Songs* for soprano or tenor, published in 1882, the *Musical Herald,* after a detailed description of each song, said, "The set as a whole is one of the most poetic and genuinely beautiful that we have seen for a long time."[67] This was high praise indeed, for during this period dozens of newly published songs were listed in every issue. Rogers composed a second set of songs, also titled *Six Songs,* which was reviewed in the *Musical Herald* in April 1884, and two months later her Scherzo in A major for piano received a highly favorable review. Much later she deplored the fact that women students of her time had no opportunity to learn orchestration or composition, for if she had learned the technique of writing for instruments she would have attempted orchestral composition.[68]

Critic William Upton also admired Rogers's songs, which he said had great spontaneity and showed consummate skill in interpreting various moods. Artistically, he felt the best of her songs were the last—especially her 1900 "Sudden Light," op. 33, no. 1, and her 1903 "Overhead the Treetops Meet," op. 36, which he described as "choice songs of rare flavor, showing a high grade of musicianship."[69] After Rogers joined the voice faculty of the New England Conservatory, she published a number of books on singing, among them *My Voice and I* (1910), *English Diction in Song and Speech* (1912), and *The Voice in Speech* (1915). She also wrote two autobiographical books, *Memories of a Musical Career* (1919) and *Clara Kathleen Rogers, The Story of Two Lives: Home, Friends, and Travel* (1932). She died in 1931.

Though Boston was an outstanding American musical center during the last quarter of the nineteenth century, it certainly was not the only home for women composers during this period. At least three women of the same era, all of them known principally for their vocal compositions, pursued active careers elsewhere. The oldest of them was Mary Elizabeth Turner Salter (1856–1938), born in Peoria, Illinois.[70] She studied for a time at the New England Conservatory and with Hermine Rudersdorff near Boston and briefly held the job of soprano soloist in Boston's St. Paul's Church. She followed Rudersdorff to New York, and in 1881 she married the organist and music teacher Sumner Salter, subsequently moving with him to Syracuse, Buffalo, Atlanta, New York City, and finally Williamstown, Massachusetts, where he became director of music at Williams College. This marriage produced five children, and when domestic duties began to interfere with her concert career as a singer, Mary Salter began to compose. She had had only a few formal piano lessons as a child and no formal training in theory or composition, but she ended up writing more than 200 songs, as well as a number of anthems and other choral works, of which about 100 were published. Among her best-known works were *The Cry of Rachel, The Pine Tree,* and *A Christmas Song.*

The other two women were midwesterners. Carrie Jacobs Bond (1861–1946) became famous for her popular songs, two of which are still sung, "I Love You Truly" and "A Perfect Day." The former was her first published song; the latter sold some seven million copies in sheet music and five million records. Born and educated in the small town of Janesville, Wisconsin, Bond began to compose at the age of thirty-two to support herself and her young son after her husband's death. She promoted her songs by singing them at parties, dinners, and other entertainments, for which she was paid $10 per appearance; when publishers rejected her material, she started her own printing business. In the end she had written about 175 songs. They were in effect a blend of the parlor song and art song, and although originally intended for recitalists, they became part of the popular culture. She also published her autobiography, *The Roads of Melody,* in 1927. Bond's contemporary, Jessie L. Gaynor (1863–1921) of St. Louis, Missouri, became famous mostly for her children's songs, although she also wrote numerous piano pieces, piano-teaching material, and vocal quartets. She studied piano with Louis Maas and theory with A. J. Goodrich and Frederic Grant Gleason, and she taught in Chicago, St. Louis, and St. Joseph, Missouri.

Of a later generation but also remembered principally for their vocal compositions, though each published many other kinds of music as well, are Harriet Ware, Mana-Zucca, and Lily Strickland. Harriet Ware (1877–1962) was born in Wisconsin and studied in New York, Paris, and Berlin. Her *Women's Triumphal March* was made the national song of the Federation of Women's Clubs in 1927, and her symphonic poem, *The Artisan,* was performed by the New York Symphony Orchestra in 1929. She also wrote cantatas, a choral cycle, many songs, and an opera, *Undine.*

Mana-Zucca (c. 1887–1981), born Augusta Zuckerman in New York City, was a piano prodigy who made her debut with the New York Symphony at age eight. She studied in the United States and Europe and gave a program of her own compositions in New York in 1917. She wrote a piano concerto, which she performed with the Los Angeles and National Symphony orchestras, a violin concerto, a piano trio, and many short piano pieces and songs. Allegedly she published more than 1000 compositions. Her most famous song is "I Love Life," to words by her husband, Irwin M. Cassel.

Lily Strickland (1887–1958) was born in South Carolina, studied music in New York, and published many songs, choral works, and piano pieces. Her piano compositions tended to have descriptive titles, such as *Cherokee Indian Dances, Moroccan Mosaics,* and *East Indian Nautches.* One of her best known works was the song "Lindy Lou," which became a standard encore in song recitals.

In another area of nineteenth-century American composition—church music—surprisingly few women's names are known. Although the organist and choir director in most American Protestant churches is a woman and many of these women have composed music, little of it is published or circulates beyond their own churches. Thus, though the *Musical Herald* of November 1881 says that contrary to popular thought there have been many fine women hymnists, almost six decades later, in 1939, Clement Harris said that of 150 women composers listed in music dictionaries and biographical works, only about one-sixth showed any predilection for sacred music.[71] Likewise, Ellinwood's 1953 biographies of American church musicians comprise ninety-eight men and three women, two of whom were Roman Catholic nuns.[72] Eva Munson Smith, herself a composer, made a collection of hymns by women that was published in 1885.[73] Representing more than 820 authors, it contains about 2500 hymns with *texts* written by women. The preface states that only at the last minute was it decided to include music in the book, and consequently fifty-two women composers of hymns are represented as well; Smith adds that given more time she surely would have found a great many more hymn tunes by women. Since then the situation has changed only very slowly. Of the 720 hymns in the 1982 hymnal of the Episcopal Church, for example, only nine were composed by women, three of them by Jane Manton Marshall. The 1993 Episcopal hymn supplement, *Lift Every Voice and Sing II,* billed as an African-American hymnal for its many spiritual settings, includes among 281 hymns twenty-five composed by women, two of those by African-American composer Doris Akers.

Although the sheer number of women composers increased vastly after the mid-1880s,[74] public performance of their works did not, neither by symphony orchestras nor by groups presumably sympathetic to women, such as the Music Teachers National Association (MTNA). At the tenth annual MTNA meeting, held in Boston in 1886, a program of all-American works included compositions by Parker, Chadwick, Paine, Rohde, Maas, Buck, Foote —not one by a woman. Nor were there women performers, except for a few singers and the women's chorus. "It is an oversight that speaks volumes and puts out of sight the much vaunted American estimation of feminine talent," protested Amelia Lewis.[75]

The representation of women at the World's Columbian Exposition of 1893, with its separate Woman's Building and special programs of women's music, was, generally speaking, a case of separate but less than equal. In May, the opening month of the exposition, the big Music Hall hosted thirty-seven musical programs by visiting orchestras, quartets, and choruses, including no works by women; the Woman's Building held two programs. At the concert that opened the Woman's Building, there was no orchestra, just an organ, for compositions written and performed by women.[76] In two special concerts of American music presented at the Music Hall on May 23 and 24, no woman composer was represented. The only work by a woman played at the Music Hall was Lang's *Witchis* overture. Yet there was no lack of women composers. In 1896 the Manuscript Society of New York, founded in 1889 to give its members a chance to hear their own works played, had 1000 members, and practically every one of its concerts included works by women. The society's members included Beach, Lang, Rogers, Hood, and others.[77]

Neither the New York Philharmonic nor the Boston Symphony had performed a single work by a woman until the latter played Lang's *Dramatic Overture* in 1893. Between then and the start of World War I, works by only three women, Beach, Lang, and Hopekirk, were played by the Boston Symphony, as compared to works by 249 men. The records for New York and Boston did not improve markedly after 1914. Boston performed Beach's piano concerto once more in 1917; three works by Daniels, once each; Leginska's *Two Short Pieces for Orchestra* in 1924; and three works by the Frenchwoman Germaine Tailleferre in 1925, 1926, and 1927. New York did Mana-Zucca's *Fugato-Humoresque on "Dixie"* in the 1916–17 season, Marion Bauer's *Sun Splendor* in the 1947–48 season, and Julia Perry's *Study for Orchestra* in 1965.[78]

In 1975 *Musical America* asked five of the major U.S. orchestras what works by women they had performed in the past decade. Cleveland had done none; Detroit had done Warren's *Crystal Lake* in 1974; New York had done the same Warren work in 1974 and two works by Ruth Crawford Seeger in

1971 and 1974; San Francisco had performed *Sun* by Tonia Scherchen in 1973; and Los Angeles had done the Warren work in 1965. The Los Angeles orchestra also, in 1972 at the University of California, performed a special program devoted to women composers, with works by Beach, Warren, Seeger, Gladys Nordenstrom, and two non-American women.[79]

Only after 1975 did women begin to be represented more, although still with the fanfare accompanying a novelty. In November 1975 the New York Philharmonic did a program of music composed entirely by women and led by a woman conductor, Sarah Caldwell. Ironically, it was a benefit for the orchestra's pension fund that, considering the number of men versus women players, chiefly helped men. Even as late as 1978, the performance of a work by Barbara Kolb on the regular subscription series of the Boston Symphony prompted a special interview in the *Boston Globe,* radio talks, and other publicity that rarely accompanies the first performance or the local premiere of a piece of contemporary music. In the 1997–98 season, the Seattle Symphony, New York Philharmonic, San Francisco Symphony and Pittsburgh Symphony were the only major orchestras among fifteen surveyed that performed works by women composers.[80] In the 1999–2000 season the Boston Symphony included works by exactly two women composers, Thea Musgrave and Russia's Sofia Gubaidulina. Far from being the conquerors that Fannie Bloomfield-Zeisler predicted, women composers were just beginning to be heard.

5

APARTHEID—THE
ALL-WOMEN'S ORCHESTRAS

THE STEP from "lady violinists" to "ladies' orchestras" would seem but a short one, but in reality it was a giant stride, and one toward a dead end. That women instrumentalists should have been excluded from conventional orchestras—which might just as well have been called "gentlemen's orchestras"—is hardly surprising. Despite the increase in women instrumental players, particularly violinists, in the second half of the nineteenth century, despite the growth of music schools and conservatories, despite a spate of articles saying, "Why shouldn't women play instruments?" women were not encouraged to play professionally, either as soloists or in ensembles.

A major reason for their exclusion was economic. Any post given to a woman meant one less opening for a man. And the very fact that women had been allowed to play instruments other than keyboard instruments for only a short time led to the conclusion that few competent women players were available, especially for the woodwind, brass, and percussion sections.

In any event, women were largely excluded. The *Boston Herald* of December 12, 1878, for example, reported a real novelty: a new orchestra in Louisville was going to admit women, and a number of violinists, violists, and cellists were about to join, along with a woman cornetist. But the Harvard Symphony Orchestra, said the *Herald* reporter, "an old conservative society," would not admit women players. The Chicago Symphony during its first season (1892–93) had one woman harpist, Mrs. Lawrence A. Winch, and one man harpist; the following season it employed Mrs. C. Wunderle as harpist, probably the wife of C. Wunderle who played both cymbals and viola.[1] The Philadelphia Orchestra, in contrast, did not employ a woman harpist or any other woman instrumentalist on a regular basis until the 1930–31 season. (See Chapter 10 and the Appendix for late-twentieth-century practices in orchestral hiring.)

The harp was sanctioned for women, and women string players were growing in numbers. But orchestras also include brass and woodwinds. Could women play those as well? Contrary to Victorian belief, women had been playing wind instruments for centuries. The flute was played by women in numerous ancient cultures; Sumerian, Egyptian, Greek, and Roman iconography shows women playing flutes. Early Christianity began to forbid such active music-making by women, although this proscription did not apply to prostitutes or the lower classes.[2] Peasant women of all cultures had always made and played pipes and flutes.[3] During the Renaissance, respectable women again were permitted to play instruments—flutes, along with lutes, viols, virginals—but this applied largely to courtly ladies. A few of these women formed little orchestras of their own. Tarquinia Molza was a composer who organized and conducted her own women's orchestra at the Italian court of Ferrara.[4] Eighteenth-century Venice had all-female orchestras made up of musically trained orphans that were named for their sponsoring charitable institution, such as the Mendicanti, heard in 1774 by Charles Burney, the English music historian.[5]

These groups were largely, if not entirely, made up of string and keyboard players. As late as 1880 Maria Bianchini of Venice, a concert flutist, was still a great novelty. Critic Eduard Hanslick pointed out, though, that she had predecessors in Madame Rousseau in 1827 and Lorenzine Meyer from about 1830 to 1840. Hanslick praised Bianchini's performance, saying that "she avoids the ugly contortions of the lips and short-breathed blowing which may so easily jeopardize the aesthetic effect of flute-playing. Managed as it was on the occasion in question, the flute is decidedly not an unfeminine instrument."[6] In response, an American reader wrote to the *Musical Record* that America had a comparable lady flutist: Emilie Schiller, a flute teacher in Chicago and "a virtuoso much admired."[7] Nine years later the same journal reported, "New York has a lady flautist, of whom great things are expected,"[8] and in 1900 it announced that a Danish flutist, Julie Peterson, was coming to settle in the United States. Peterson's name had appeared earlier in an ad placed by flute manufacturer John C. Haynes and Company, in which she was described as "a world-renowned concert flute virtuoso and teacher."[9]

If flutists and other woodwind players were rare, one would think women brass players would be scarcer still. Yet as early as 1873 Nellie Daniels, cornet soloist, joined Spaulding's Concert Company,[10] and a few months later a Ladies Cornet Band, led by Georgie Dean Spaulding with her gold cornet, played in Vermont.[11] In 1875 it was announced that Anna Berger, cornetist, would take lessons from Matthew Arbuckle,[12] and in 1879 another ladies' cornet band was organized in Tipton, Indiana.[13] In the early 1880s at least one woman cornetist, Fannie Rice of Lowell, Massachusetts, advertised her services for concerts or entertainments.[14] A child prodigy, Ida Clark of Chicago, aged thirteen, appeared in 1885,[15] and in the same year Eva Hewitt reportedly "played so beautifully that she has astonished Levy and received an engagement for New Orleans, where she will be a novelty next season."[16]

By 1889 Anna Berger had profited enough from Arbuckle and her other teachers to go on tour, and she was well received at Covent Garden and London's Promenade concerts.[17] The following year the *Musical Herald* reported:

"Madame Anna Teresa Berger, an American (wife of the manager Leigh Lynch) has electrified English audiences at Covent Garden by her cornet playing. She played fifty nights in succession and has accepted offers from France, Germany, and Russia."[18]

Even more unusual was the achievement of saxophone virtuoso Elise Hall, who was always listed in programs as Mrs. R(ichard) J. Hall, for her instrument was uncommon for men players as well. A pupil of Georges Longy's, principal oboist of the Boston Symphony and founder of the Longy School of Music in Cambridge, she became manager of the second Orchestral Club of Boston, founded in 1899, which Longy conducted. Critic Philip Hale praised her playing at an Orchestral Club concert, commending her technical mastery, musical intelligence, and beautiful tone.[19] She was the first amateur ever to appear with the Boston Symphony Orchestra, playing the long solo in Bizet's *L'Arlésienne Suite* no. 1 in the subscription concerts on December 24 and 25, 1909, "because no [other] competent saxophonist" could be found.[20] A number of composers—among them Vincent d'Indy, Charles Loeffler, and Georges Longy himself—wrote compositions especially for Hall. She had received most of her musical education at the Paris Conservatory, renowned for its school of wind playing, and in 1909 she reportedly was taking up another instrument as well, the new double-bass clarinet.

There were others too, for by the late nineteenth century women's brass bands had become more common. Indeed, a letter to the *Musical Record* in 1882 claims a considerable history for this phenomenon. The writer, J. Heneage Carter of Louisville, maintains that he managed the first female brass band in the United States:

> Twenty years ago [in 1862] I had a number of young girls—from ten to fourteen years of age—who were engaged to give a military drill in the performances of my company. My orchestral leader suggested that I should try and form these girls into a brass band. I almost scouted the idea, but, shortly after, a man desired me to engage him as a cornet player. I did so, and asked him to co-operate with my leader to see what they could do with the girls in brass band playing. The result was that my "young female brass band" was soon formed, and the people of the cities of New England, and other sections, abundantly testified to the popularity of my troupe. Had I not taken the celebrated Berger Family into my service, and had them taught to play brass music, the public would probably never have heard Miss Anna Teresa Berger (Mrs. Leigh Lynch) playing cornet solos. . . . My company was known as the Carter Zouave Troupe.[21]

In 1888 the 120-woman Ladies Band of Audubon, Iowa, performed at the annual meeting of the Northwestern Band Association,[22] and by 1895 the *Musical Record,* announcing the formation of another new women's band in

Michigan, commented that this "hobby" seemed to prevail to a considerable extent in the West. By then Boston had had its own Ladies' Military Band for some years. Organized in 1890, it consisted of thirty "young ladies" who toured the United States and Ontario in the 1898–99 season, directed by Mr. D. W. Howard, and played at the Pan-American Exposition in September 1901.[23] Also, an ad in the *Musical Review* of October 1899 touts the Ladies' Talma Band, an eighteen-woman wind ensemble, as the chief attraction at Norumbega Park, a Boston resort.

Beginning in the late 1870s, a special variety of women's orchestra became popular. It was modeled after the Vienna Ladies Orchestra, which had first come to America on tour in 1871 and aroused considerable interest. One reviewer said:

> One of the musical sensations of next season will be the female orchestra, consisting entirely of female performers, which Mr. Rullmann has brought over from Vienna, and who will make their appearance at Steinway Hall in September. Judging from their photographs, they must be quite pretty.[24]

The Vienna group was organized in 1867 by Josephine Weimlich, who at first formed a string quartet that expanded. By 1871 it had about twenty players: four first violins, three second violins, one viola, two cellos, one double bass, one flute, one piccolo, one harp, one parlor organ, and three drums. The ensemble performed mostly light music—waltzes, portions of operettas by Strauss, von Suppé, and other popular composers of the time, and an occasional movement from a symphony. The *Metronome* critic did not like the group at all, terming them "another foreign fraud" because they lacked horns, trumpets, trombones, clarinets, oboes, and bassoons, and therefore were not really an orchestra.[25]

Originally, the Vienna Ladies Orchestra came to the United States as concert artists, but by 1873 they were roaming about the land as "lager-beer musicians," playing in restaurants and beer gardens. Moreover, common report had it that the women were very poorly paid, earning no more than $15 or $20 per week even though they played every night until after midnight.[26]

Their detractors notwithstanding, the Vienna Ladies Orchestra soon had numerous American imitators which became closely associated with German-American entertainment. In New York they played in the German music halls of lower Manhattan, such as the Bowery Garten, Atlantic Garten, and Volksgarten. In fact, they were often known by the German term for ladies' orchestra, *Damen Orchester.* Their appeal, like that of the brass bands, was based entirely on their oddity; the curiosity value of women playing cornets and double basses was such that audiences would come for that alone.[27] Moreover, if any instrument was lacking and no woman player could be found, they used one or more men instrumentalists dressed in women's clothes to preserve at least the illusion of an all-female ensemble. The most famous of these groups was the Ladies Elite Orchestra, which performed at the Atlantic Garten for more than thirty-five years. Its repertory varied during this long period, but for the most part it played popular songs as well as selections from opera—both grand and light—between vaudeville acts.[28]

New York had the largest number of these ensembles, but they existed elsewhere as well. Ohio had at least two, one at Schumann's Garden and the other at Meyer's Music Hall,[29] while Boston had Kampa's Ladies Orchestra, made up of six sisters,[30] and John Braham's Female Theater Orchestra, based at the Oakland Garden. Of the last group a reviewer wrote:

> Lady artists, a lady chorus, a lady ballet, an orchestra composed of ladies, lady ushers, lady doorkeepers, and lady ticket-sellers held possession of Oakland Garden, Boston, during the presentation of "An Adamless Eden." Who shall say that "Woman's rights" are not progressing?[31]

The first to deny the truth of this, in all likelihood, would have been the very performers in question, who could enter the entertainment world only through the back door. After all, blacks formed their own minstrel troupes and, as late as the 1940s, their own baseball league because that was the only way they could appear in public. Women likewise formed their own orchestras, and exploited their novelty value, in order to play their instruments and be paid for it, however little. Said one member of the Ladies Elite Orchestra, "If I had the chance to substitute for a man I should do so in a minute, and should look for more and better opportunities to follow."[32] Nor did Jackie Robinson turn down a contract with the Brooklyn Dodgers when it finally came along.

In the case of orchestral musicians, economic discrimination was supported by prejudices and stereotypes. If women were considered on the same level as men, they would presumably compete with men for the same jobs. But if they could not play the same instruments at all, or not as well, or if they could not play the same kind of music, their threat was automatically diminished. Thus initially women were told they were not strong enough to play large, heavy instruments—tubas and double basses, for example—or not skilled enough for some of the others, such as oboes and clarinets and drums. The prejudice about tubas and basses has survived to the start of the twenty-first century. If women proved that they could indeed play these instruments, they were told they were not talented or dedicated enough to play serious music and had to confine themselves to the lighter repertory.

The rapid growth of American music schools and conservatories in the late nineteenth century aggravated the problem. What would become of all the women musicians they were turning out in growing numbers? They could not all become teachers, for that market would soon be glutted, and further, on the assumption that teachers would train still more musicians, the problem would be compounded for future generations.

The solution was segregation. Women could, on the one hand, form professional all-women's ensembles, which would survive, despite their alleged inferior quality, because of their novelty appeal and because they were willing to play any music, anywhere, any time, that would appeal to a paying audience. Or they could, on the other hand, remain dedicated amateurs, performing serious music if they wished, since they were not paid for playing anyway.

As a result, the late nineteenth century saw the formation of two kinds of women's orchestra. The one was professional, in that performers were paid, and played mostly popular but some serious music, often in conjunction with other kinds of popular entertainment, principally vaudeville. The other was amateur, that is, unpaid, even though its members might be highly trained and of professional caliber. Boston and New York each had several ensembles of both kinds, and some that fell between the two categories. The Ladies (Amateur) Orchestra of New York gave charity concerts in 1888 and 1889.[33] The first Orchestral Club of Boston, formed in 1885, included both men and women, though the latter were in practice confined to the violin section. It included some pupils of Julius Eichberg's, among them Lillian Chandler, Jennie Ladd, Georgia Pray (who was a cellist but played violin here), Edith Christie, Lettie Launder, and Fannie Grebe.[34] In contrast, the Beacon Orchestral Club of Boston, conducted by violinist Marietta B. Sherman, consisted wholly of women playing ten violins, two violas, one cello, one trombone, one flute, two cornets, one clarinet, and one piano.[35]

Boston also had two semiprofessional ensembles. The twenty-five-piece Englesbian (Lady) Orchestra, under conductor J. E. Dandlin, performed at the Brookline Town Hall on January 24, 1888, featuring as soloists cellist Georgia Pray, cornetist Lizzie Howe, and several men; the program announced that the group was available for concerts and other "occasions," suggesting that fees might be involved.[36] During the same year, Marion Osgood's Lady Orchestra reportedly enjoyed a successful season; all the "young ladies" in this group were said to have considerable concert experience.[37] Again, it is not clear if this ensemble was paid or not. Definitely unpaid, however, were the Ladies Philharmonic Orchestra of Boston, formed about 1892 under Arthur W. Thayer, and the Women's String Orchestra of New York, formed in 1896 under Carl V. Lachmund. The latter consisted of twenty-eight string players, among them violinist Jeanne Franko.[38] Both these groups were devoted to serious music exclusively, and each survived for about ten years. A typical program was that presented by the Boston women on January 23, 1900: Mendelssohn's Italian Symphony, Tchaikovsky's *Nutcracker Suite* in its Boston premiere, and Schubert's "Unfinished" Symphony.[39]

Of the professional ensembles, by far the most prominent and longest lived was the Fadette Women's Orchestra of Boston, founded in 1888 by violinist Caroline B. Nichols.[40] Named for Fanchon Fadette, the heroine of George Sand's novel *La Petite Fadette,* who brought joy to her townspeople, this ensemble survived until 1920 and in all yielded more than $500,000 to more than 600 performers. It presented more than 6000 concerts in the United States and Canada, playing symphonies, all the classical overtures, selections from seventy-five grand operas, and numerous salon pieces and popular songs.

The Fadettes' founder and conductor, Caroline Nichols, was yet another pupil of Julius Eichberg's. Born in 1864 in Dedham, Massachusetts, the daughter of a choir director, she also studied violin with Leopold Lichtenberg and Charles Loeffler, and theory with Percy Goetschius and J. B. Claus. Her motive in founding the Fadettes was quite straightforward: to provide employment for herself and other women musicians. She began, on October 1, 1888, with a group of six players, which by 1890 had grown to fifteen. Supported by Nichols's brother-in-law, George H. Chickering, president of the Chickering Piano Company, the Fadettes gave a few recitals in Chickering Hall. Esteemed musician Benjamin J. Lang was among those who praised their performance. The group soon grew to twenty: four first violins, two second violins, one viola, one cello, two double basses, one flute doubling on piccolo, one clarinet, two cornets, two French horns—allegedly the only two women horn players in the entire United States[41]—one trombone, two percussionists on tympani and drums, and one harp.

In 1895 the group was incorporated in Massachusetts and given a charter with exclusive rights to its name. Three years later it toured the East, the West, and the South, ending with a six-week junket through Canada. Then, in the summer of 1902, Keith engaged the Fadettes for a two-week tryout in his Boston theater and promptly invited them to remain for the rest of that season, displacing an ensemble of Boston Symphony players—all men, of course—who were understandably disgruntled at losing their summer jobs, especially since the Fadettes included a few of their own former pupils. That fall they also joined the first of their fifteen tours on the Keith winter circuit. They performed in so-called "first-class," meaning respectable, vaudeville theaters all over North America, interspersing musical performances with comic routines and skits. In one such skit, the orchestra members would pretend to quarrel and leave the stage one by one, forcing the conductor, Nichols, to take up first one instrument and then another in order to keep the music going. One of the group's innovations was that they would play pieces by popular request; indeed, their official program booklet eventually listed a repertory of 600 pieces from which the audience could make requests.

For a time the Fadettes also accompanied silent films at Roxy's Theatre in New York, but the musicians' union put a stop to this undertaking. Eventually Nichols retired to Boston, where for a time she trained new orchestra members. In the end, it was said, she had trained more young women for professional, wage-earning, self-supporting orchestral jobs than any other individual. She died in 1939, at the age of seventy-five. In June 1952 nine survivors of the original Fadettes assembled in Boston to celebrate the fiftieth anniversary of their first season with Keith.[42] The total they looked back on was staggering: 2025 concerts in parks and summer resorts, 3050 concerts in vaudeville theaters, 364 in Boston alone.

The Fadettes were unique, and not just for their long life. They were the only professional women's orchestra of their time that directly and successfully competed with men's ensembles. Not only did they oust established Boston Symphony players from their summer jobs, but Caroline Nichols often found herself on the same podium as John Philip Sousa, Walter Damrosch, and Victor Herbert—all highly respected conductors. The Fadettes may have begun with purely novelty status, but they eventually transcended it.

In 1903 discrimination against women orchestral players officially ended when the Musicians Union, in order to join the American Federation of Labor, was forced to admit women for the first time (see Chapter 10 for more about the union's role). Although thirty-one women, and 4469 men, were enrolled in New York at that time,[43] in the following decades only a few women harpists found their way into major orchestras, and the women's orchestra movement was no means obsolete. As late as 1936 *Women in Music,* edited by conductor Frederique Petrides, claimed that there were 522 women playing in eight women's orchestras—and this did not include jazz orchestras or chamber ensembles with fewer than fifteen players. The two largest women's orchestras then were the Women's Symphony of Long Beach (California), with 105 players, and the Woman's Symphony of Chicago, with 100; the Los Angeles Women's Symphony had only seventy members but was the oldest still in existence, then in its forty-fifth season.[44]

The women's orchestra movement was far from being an exclusively eastern phenomenon.[45] Early in the 1890s San Francisco had a Saturday Morning Orchestra of twenty-six players, all women, playing nine violins, three violas, four cellos, two double basses, one flute, three cornets, one trombone, one harp, one snare drum, and one tympani. Its first conductor was a Professor Rosenwald, but in October 1895 he was replaced by Alfred Roncovieri. The Los Angeles Women's Symphony was founded in 1893, under conductor Harley Hamilton. It began with twenty-five players, and expanded to seventy by 1936. In its early decades it was principally an amateur group, although it always had a few professional musicians in its ranks. It regularly gave anywhere from three to eight concerts per year, playing at first the lighter repertory but in time attempting symphonies and other classical works. It gradually acquired professional status and lasted until the 1960s. The Cleveland Ladies Orchestra, on the other hand, which gave daily concerts during the summer of 1900 at Atlantic City's Royal Palace Hotel, was a professional group that stuck to the popular repertory. The Women's Orchestra of Minneapolis, founded in 1910, consisted of twenty-nine players, twenty-two of them women. Most likely its two bassists, two cornetists, two cellists, and one euphonium player were men, but this is a matter of conjecture.

The Women's Orchestral Club of New York, organized in 1914 under Theodore Spiering, was all female. An amateur group, it was founded in order to give women ensemble practice, and it survived for at least three seasons. Oddly enough, for nearly twenty years, there already had been a New York organization that should have provided such opportunities. This was the quasi-professional Women's Philharmonic Society of New York, which was founded in 1899 by Melusina Fay Peirce, sister of pianist Amy Fay. By 1910 it had more than 200 members, including both performers and teachers. Though all its members were professional musicians—they included Amy Fay, violinist Jeanne Franko, and singer and voice teacher Eugenie Pappenheim, among others—the society seems to have functioned as a nonprofit philanthropic organization, its object both to provide performance opportunities and to give scholarships to students in piano, violin, voice, and composition. It supported both an all-women's orchestra and a chorus, and it presented four large concerts each season, usually in Carnegie Hall, as well as monthly musicales. Presumably the performers were not paid, though admission may have been charged to pay for the hall rental and other expenses. The Women's Philharmonic Society of New York was still alive as late as 1916, when it gave an orchestral concert. However, as the *Etude* reviewer of that occasion points out, while the all-women's orchestra included one double bass and several flutes, clarinets, and cornets, there were no "heavy" brass, no trombone or tuba, a piano being substituted to play these parts.[46]

In the 1920s a few orchestras finally began to hire women other than harpists. In 1925 *Etude* announced that five women—four violinists and a cellist—had been engaged by the San Francisco Symphony, the first time a first-rank orchestra had made such a move, and commended conductor Alfred Hertz "for his courage."[47] Many women harpists were already being employed, and both the Cleveland and Minneapolis orchestras had a few women violinists; moreover, in smaller city orchestras many players were women.[48]

Obviously these new opportunities represented just a drop in the bucket, for women's orchestras continued to be founded all over the country. The year 1925 saw the formation of the Long Beach (California) Women's Symphony under conductor Eva Anderson. It had 102 players and gave more than 100 concerts in its first decade. The Women's Symphony of Philadelphia was founded in the same year by trumpeter Mabel Swint Ewer. Conducted by J. W. F. Leman, its seventy members performed the standard orchestral repertory into the late 1930s. Also in 1925 the American Women's Symphony Orchestra of New York was organized and conducted by the Dutch composer Elizabeth Kuyper, who had led similar ensembles in Europe. The Chicago Woman's Symphony Orchestra survived from 1925 through the end of World

War II. Its 100 players were at first conducted by Elena Moneak, then by Ebba Sundstrom from 1928 to 1937, and thereafter by various men conductors.

In most instances women's orchestras were begun by a local instrumentalist or conductor who wanted to create performance opportunities for herself and other local women. But at least two such ensembles were founded by women conductors who had led all-male orchestras and who decided to start women's orchestras in cities that appeared to have sufficient numbers of unemployed women instrumentalists. These two were the Boston Woman's Symphony Orchestra, established by Ethel Leginska, and the Woman's Symphony of New York, founded by Antonia Brico. Both ensembles lasted for a number of years, then admitted a few men players, renamed the group for its conductor—Leginska's Symphony Orchestra and Brico Symphony Orchestra—and soon afterward disbanded.

If playing in an orchestra was a male province, conducting was far more so. What more outspoken role of leadership could there be than leading an orchestra? "A conductor," said one woman of her profession, "controls the orchestra in order to embody the expression of the composer and to project the music itself."[49] Traditionally such control, especially over an all-male orchestra, requires a forcefulness that was encouraged only in men. Even in the late nineteenth century women conductors were extremely rare. By the turn of the century only two American women had become well-known conductors, Caroline Nichols of the Fadettes and Emma Steiner, who conducted principally light opera. Hermine Rudersdorff, a German soprano who settled in America in the 1870s and became a famous voice teacher, conducted the Handel and Haydn Society of Boston in the quartets of Mendelssohn's *Elijah* in 1872. She did it so well that "it was said that she could have conducted singers, orchestra, and all if given the chance."[50] She was not. Selma Borg, a Scandinavian, conducted one performance at Boston's Music Hall in June 1879.[51] Though both Rudersdorff and Borg were Europeans, the situation for women was no different in Europe. Amy Fay, writing about her stay in Germany from 1869 to 1875, reported:

> Did you read my letter to N.S., in which I told her about Alicia Hund, who composed and conducted a symphony? That is quite a step for women in the musical line. . . . All the men were highly disgusted because she was allowed to conduct the orchestra herself. I didn't think myself that it was a very *becoming* position, though I had no prejudice against it. Somehow, a woman doesn't look well with a baton in her hand directing a body of men.[52]

In addition to superb musicianship, a successful conductor usually must have a vivid personality that can command both the orchestra and the attention of the audience. The latter quality was possessed in abundance by Ethel

Leginska, one of the most colorful women musicians of her time. Born in 1886 in Hull, England, and originally named Ethel Liggins, she, like many performers, changed her name to sound more exotic.[53] She began her musical career as a pianist, studying first in England and then at Hoch's Conservatory in Frankfurt. At fourteen she allegedly ran away to Vienna to study with Leschetizky, where she remained for three years and was among the few students he consented to teach gratis. She made her orchestral debut at age sixteen in London, under conductor Henry Wood. For a time she pursued a successful career as a concert pianist in Europe, and in 1912 she came to the United States, making her New York debut that fall. She appeared in New York every subsequent season through 1919, receiving very favorable reviews; critic Richard Aldrich said she showed great delicacy of interpretation, was marvelous in Beethoven's "Waldstein" Sonata, and played Bach, Mozart, and Schubert very well. She also was known for her all-Chopin recitals.

In 1907 Leginska had married Roy Emerson Whithorne, an American composer from Cleveland who served as her manager for a time, and in 1915 the newspapers were full of their sensational divorce suit, complete with a custody fight over their six-year-old son. Leginska claimed that Whithorne had deserted her and insisted she could earn enough to support the child. (She later lost custody of her son to her ex-husband's parents.) She gave numerous interviews to newspapers during this period, explaining that the only way a woman could succeed as a concert pianist was to stand on her own feet and emulate a man in her dress and hairstyle. Contending that the conventional bare-shouldered evening dress of women artists was a terrible handicap in concert halls that were often unheated, she devised her own costume of a black silk skirt and black velvet jacket over a white brocade vest and silk shirt with a mannish collar and cuffs. She also affected a hairstyle resembling that worn by Paderewski and Liszt. She showed a definite knack for promotion, and not only in her unconventional dress, which aroused both interest and much publicity. When she caught her finger in a door in 1916, she promptly sent an X-ray of the bruised finger to *Musical America,* which published it. She also omitted intermission breaks from a long, difficult program at Carnegie Hall in 1916, a feat that made headlines.

In 1919, after seven seasons of constant touring throughout the United States, Leginska announced that she would retire from performing for a season and devote herself entirely to composition and teaching. At that time one journal described her as "the Paderewski of women pianists."[54] She had spent the summer of 1918 studying composition with Ernest Bloch, and during the next few years she produced a considerable number of compositions, including such orchestral works as the symphonic poem *Beyond the Fields We Know* (1921), *Two Short Poems* (1922), and the four-movement suite *Quatre Sujets Babares* (1923). Her *Four Poems* for string quartet was premiered by the London String Quartet at London's Aeolian Hall on June 14, 1921, and her *Six*

Nursery Rhymes for soprano and small orchestra (1923) was given three performances by the Boston Philharmonic in 1926. She also produced numerous songs and piano works.

In 1924 Leginska embarked on yet another career: conducting. In October she conducted the Paris Conservatory Orchestra, and in November she allegedly led the London Symphony, Berlin Philharmonic, and Munich Konzertverein orchestras. In newspaper interviews and publicity releases in the United States, Leginska claimed to have been the first woman to conduct the previously mentioned ensembles, but she may have embroidered her feats somewhat; Antonia Brico also said she was the first woman to conduct the Berlin Philharmonic, in 1930, and her claim is better documented. In any event, Leginska was back in the United States early in 1925, and in January proceeded to conduct the New York Symphony Orchestra at Carnegie Hall in Beethoven's Symphony no. 7, in the first appearance of a woman on the Carnegie Hall podium. In April she led the People's Symphony of Boston, and in August the Los Angeles Symphony.

The following year Leginska founded a new 100-member Boston Philharmonic Orchestra—all men except for the harpist and pianist—which was intended to make good music available to the masses by charging very little for tickets—twenty-five cents admission, fifty cents and up for seats. She led this ensemble in its first concert on October 24, 1926, in overtures by Weber and Wagner, Beethoven's Symphony no. 5, the premiere of Peterka's *Triumph of Life,* and Liszt's *Hungarian Fantasy,* for which Leginska performed the piano solo as well. This concert received excellent reviews in all the Boston papers, the *Herald, Globe, Transcript,* and *Christian Science Monitor.* But the ensemble survived just one season. Nevertheless, in March 1927, Leginska offered to conduct and train, without a fee, the Boston Women's Symphony Orchestra, which made an introductory appearance on March 23 and gave its first real concert December 12, to mixed reviews. This ensemble was made up of about sixty-five performers, all women, and frequently played works by women composers. The third concert, on April 14, 1928, featured Radie Britain's *Symphonic Intermezzo* and an arrangement by Mabel Wood Hill of Bach's Prelude and Fugue for strings, as well as Leginska's own *Fantasy* for piano and orchestra, which, according to the *Boston Herald,* was "not old-fashioned," for it had "fascinating discords, and modern rhythms."

In its second season, Leginska took the Boston Women's Symphony on tour for six weeks to Chicago, St. Louis, Milwaukee, Buffalo, Cleveland, and Washington, D.C., presenting fifty-two programs in thirty-eight cities. For its February concert it played the Boston premiere of Leginska's *Triptych* for eleven solo instruments. By 1930, according to the printed program, the Boston Women's Symphony had, in its three years, played more than 200 symphonic concerts in twenty-one states. For its program of January 29, 1930, a few men appeared with the orchestra, and its name was now Leginska's

Women's Symphony Orchestra. Leginska later explained that when Boston women could not be found for certain parts, she could not afford to import women players from other cities and simply had to substitute local men instrumentalists. But this turned out to be the ensemble's last concert.

Leginska did not give up, however. In 1932 she started another women's orchestra, this time called the National Women's Symphony and based in New York City. It gave its first concert in Carnegie Hall on March 12, 1932, playing Schubert's Symphony in B-flat, Glinka's Overture to *Russlan and Ludmilla,* and the Mozart Piano Concerto in A major, with Leginska conducting from the piano. The group was well received but appears to have disbanded soon afterward.

Between 1930 and 1932 Leginska also found time to compose her first opera, *The Rose and the Ring,* based on a satire by Thackeray. It was not performed until 1957, in Los Angeles. She had done some opera conducting as well, presenting *Carmen* in English at Boston's Jordan Hall in May 1929. She then wrote another opera, *Gale,* and herself conducted the premiere, with the Chicago Civic Opera Company and John Charles Thomas in the title role, on November 23, 1935. She continued to make guest-conducting appearances, but by 1939 she had moved to Los Angeles, and there she devoted herself almost entirely to teaching piano. In the 1940s she established a series of public piano recitals devoted to the works of individual composers, and in the 1950s she was still presenting her pupils in musicales, often including some of her own piano pieces and songs. A woman of considerable talent and energy, she remained active until she died at the age of eighty-three, in 1970.

Less flamboyant than Ethel Leginska but just as determined to pursue a conducting career was Antonia Brico, who was born in Holland on June 26, 1902 and was brought up in California.[55] In 1923 she graduated from the University of California at Berkeley, where she assisted Paul Steindorff in directing the chorus and in his work at the San Francisco Opera. She then studied piano for two years with Sigismund Stojowski in New York and went on to Berlin, where she studied privately with Karl Muck and at the State Academy of Music. She spent from 1925 to 1930 at the academy's master school of conducting, becoming its first American graduate. She made her debut with the Berlin Philharmonic on February 14, 1930, conducting a Dvořák symphony, a Handel concerto grosso, and the Schumann Piano Concerto in A minor, with Valesca Burgstaller as soloist. There followed four years of conducting appearances in Germany, Poland, and other European countries, although she took time to come to America in 1930 for appearances with the Los Angeles Symphony at the Hollywood Bowl and the San Francisco Symphony.

In 1933 Brico returned to the United States, making her New York debut at the Metropolitan Opera House with the Musicians Symphony Orchestra. She conducted a second concert there but then was denied a third appearance because the baritone John Charles Thomas refused to work under a woman conductor. Ironically, he changed his mind the very next year and worked with Leginska in Chicago. Sporadic conducting assignments followed—one with the Detroit Symphony in 1934; others in Buffalo, New York, and California; two with the National Symphony in Washington, D.C., in the summer of 1935; and the New York Civic Opera at Brighton Beach in 1936. But with far too little opportunity to exercise her métier, Brico decided to form her own orchestra, the New York Women's Symphony, to prove finally that women could be competent musicians. The ensemble, consisting of eighty-six players, made its first appearance at Carnegie Hall on February 18, 1935, performing Schumann's Symphony no. 1, Handel's Concerto Grosso in D minor, and Tchaikovsky's Overture to *Romeo and Juliet*. Pianist Olga Samaroff addressed the audience during the intermission. The concert received excellent reviews, and two more concerts followed that spring. In 1935–36 the New York Women's Symphony undertook a full season at Carnegie Hall. In 1937 Brico publicly challenged the pianist José Iturbi, who in a speech had said that women were incapable of greatness in either music or sports, to bring a group of men musicians to compete against a group of women before a panel of blindfolded judges. "I am sure that at least half of the players selected would be women," she said, "and after this proof has been given and more women trained for orchestral work, we shall have mixed orchestras of men and women."[56] Iturbi hastily backed down, saying he had been misquoted.

In 1938, believing she had proved her point that women could play as well as men and that she should now hire simply the best available players, she admitted ten men to the orchestra and renamed it the Brico Symphony. Despite enthusiastic reviews of its concerts, the ensemble did not survive much longer. Brico continued to make guest appearances, and she was the first woman to conduct the New York Philharmonic at Lewisohn Stadium in the summer of 1938. That same summer she was awarded an honorary doctor of music degree from Mills College, taught a master class in conducting at Golden Gate College in San Francisco, and conducted a series of municipal concerts in San Francisco and Oakland. In 1939 she led the Federal Orchestra concerts at the New York World's Fair, and she subsequently conducted a number of concerts by choral groups in the metropolitan area.

In 1942 Brico moved to Denver, Colorado, where she devoted herself largely to teaching piano and conducted whenever she could. Soon after World War II ended, she went to Europe for a five-month tour, conducting and appearing as a pianist in Stockholm, Vienna, Amsterdam, London, Prague, and Zagreb. The highlight of this trip was conducting the Helsinki Symphony in 1946 in an all-Sibelius program at the express invitation of the Finnish composer, with whom she had become good friends.

Quite unlike Ethel Leginska, Antonia Brico believed a conductor should not present his or her own interpretation of a composition but should serve the composer's intention and purpose. "The music I am conducting at the moment is my favorite," she once said, "I try hard to put everything into it."[57] Self-assured but unassuming, she wore, when conducting, a simple black dress with a white collar and cuffs, designed to blend with the orchestra and background rather than stand out in any way.

For the next three decades Brico had to content herself with conducting various amateur orchestras in Denver, performing only a half-dozen times a year; the rest of her time she spent teaching and lecturing. In 1973 the folk singer Judy Collins, a former piano pupil of Brico's, together with director Jill Godmilow made a documentary film about her old teacher. Called *Antonia: A Portrait of the Woman,* it presented a poignant picture of a talented woman musician who had no instrument to play, which is how Brico herself described her lack of an orchestra. The film aroused new interest in its subject, leading to Brico's debut as a recording artist and engagements with a number of symphony orchestras. Although delighted with her revived conducting career, Brico did not abandon her old pupils. She continued to teach piano and conducting, coach opera, and lead her old ensemble, the Denver Businessmen's Orchestra, which had renamed itself the Brico Symphony in her honor.

Brico was not reticent about describing the difficulties she had encountered. Despite the support of artists such as conductor Bruno Walter, composer Jean Sibelius, and pianist Artur Rubinstein, orchestra boards would not engage her, managers would not accept her, artists refused to work with her—solely because she was a woman. Manager Arthur Judson, the most powerful man in American music—he managed most leading conductors as well as both the New York Philharmonic and Philadelphia orchestras—would not engage Brico as a Philharmonic guest conductor because, he maintained, the orchestra's women subscribers would not like to see a woman on the podium. Minnie Guggenheimer, who managed the Lewisohn Stadium concerts, was outraged at the idea of a woman conducting and allowed Brico to appear only because 4000 persons had signed a petition for it. Long unrecognized, Brico in her seventies began to build a new career, determined to make the best of the years ahead, as she had of the leaner years in the past. She died in 1989.

Besides Leginska's and Brico's ensembles, several other women's orchestras were founded in the 1930s: those of Youngstown, Ohio, in 1930, under Margaret Walter; Hollywood, California, in 1932, under Anna Priscilla Risher; Portland, Oregon, in 1934, under D'Zama Murielle; Pittsburgh, in 1935, under Carl Simonis; Little Symphony of Cleveland, in 1935, under Ruth Sandra Rothstein; Commonwealth Symphony of Boston, in 1936, under Solomon Branslavsky, the only WPA-funded orchestra consisting entirely of women;[58] Women's Chamber Orchestra of New York, in 1937, under Jeanette Scheerer; and the Baltimore Women's String Symphony Orchestra, in 1937, under Stephen Deak.[59]

The longest-lived of these ensembles by far was the Cleveland Women's Orchestra, founded in 1935 by violinist Hyman Schandler of the Cleveland

Orchestra in order to give talented violin students an opportunity to play. At the inaugural concert that November, pianist Rosalyn Tureck was soloist in Beethoven's "Emperor" Concerto. Schandler conducted the orchestra for fifty-six years, until his death at age ninety-two. He was replaced by Robert Cronquist in 1990. At this writing the orchestra was completing its sixty-fourth season. Although many of its approximately seventy members are professional musicians and music teachers, for the most part the women members are volunteers. Only the conductor, concertmaster, and occasionally some key players are paid. Sometimes, but rarely, a male player is recruited for a concert, only when no woman is available for it. Soloists often, but not always, are women. The orchestra presents two to three concerts per year and three to four outreach programs in retirement homes, hospitals, schools, and so on.[60]

Another leading women's ensemble of this era was the Orchestrette Classique of New York, founded in 1933 by Frederique Joanne Petrides (1903–1983).[61] Later renamed Orchestrette of New York, the group survived until 1943. A Belgian-born violinist and an outspoken feminist where women musicians were concerned, Petrides also published the monthly newsletter *Women in Music* from 1935 to 1940, and used its pages to publicize the achievements of women musicians, past and present. The Orchestrette was a 30-woman chamber group that was ahead of its time in several respects. For one thing, it performed baroque music with the forces for which it had originally been composed—that is, a chamber orchestra, rather than the 100-piece symphony orchestra then used for such compositions. Virgil Thomson, reviewing one of the Orchestrette's programs, said, "To hear the music of the great eighteenth century masters . . . in such appropriate acoustical frame is to begin to know something of what that music really sounded like in the ears of its makers and of its contemporary listeners."[62] The Orchestrette also performed a considerable amount of contemporary music, often giving first performances of new works. And finally, it often performed works by women composers. Its pianist for some years was the composer Julia Smith. The group performed many of her works, and she dedicated her *Hellenic Suite* to Petrides. After the Orchestrette ended, Petrides continued to conduct, founding the Hudson Valley Symphony Orchestra in the 1940s, an orchestra made up of men players from the New York Philharmonic in the 1950s, a Festival Symphony in the 1960s, and an ensemble of players from the American Symphony Orchestra in the 1970s.

The 1930s enjoyed the success of another women's ensemble, the Women's Symphony Orchestra of Boston, founded in 1939 by conductor Alexander Thiede. It lasted until 1944, when it was merged with the Civic Symphony Orchestra of Boston.[63] Consisting of sixty-five players, it was set up as a kind of subscription cooperative; to join, one had to subscribe to four concerts for $4. Any leftover proceeds from subscriptions would be distributed among the active members at the end of the season. Men could subscribe but could not become active members. At least one composition by a woman would be performed at each program, and indeed the orchestra did perform Daniels's *Deep Forest* on January 16, 1940, Beach's *Gaelic Symphony* on March 12, 1940, and other works by women. In its third season it sponsored a composition contest won by Radie Britain with her symphonic poem, *Light,* performed on May 25, 1941.

The Boston Women's Symphony was, by and large, a community orchestra, differing from other such ensembles mainly in that it admitted only women players. Its performers included shopgirls, housewives, secretaries, music teachers, and music students, as well as some professional musicians. Seven of its members had played with the Fadettes thirty years earlier, and practically all had been members of Leginska's Symphony. The tuba player, Thelma Goodwin, had played that instrument since the age of nine; she learned from her father, also a tuba player. She was also a church organist and had eight children. The third trombone was a sixteen-year-old high school student. The first trombone, Belle Mann, was a former Fadette and had for a time conducted her own ensemble. The Boston Women's Symphony annually gave four concerts at Jordan Hall and one summer concert at the MacDowell Colony in New Hampshire. Its only male member was the conductor, Alexander Thiede, who was quoted as saying that a women's orchestra needs a male conductor because women accept criticism better from a man. In the end, although its programs were regarded as interesting and the reviews were favorable if not overwhelmingly enthusiastic, the group merged with the Boston Civic Symphony; the women's group had often performed the compositions of the Civic Symphony's conductor, Joseph Wagner.

During World War II, the women's orchestra movement came to an end. Although a few of the orchestras survived the war years, principally as amateur organizations, few new ones were founded after 1945.[64] Civic and community orchestras increasingly allowed women to join,[65] and the orchestras of smaller cities began to admit more women as well. In the major orchestras, however, women remained a very small minority. In 1978 Kay Gardner founded the Boston-based New England Women's Symphony, which was intended primarily to provide a podium for women conductors and to perform compositions by women. It gave three concerts in its first season but was forced to disband for lack of funds during the next year.

In the last decades of the century, the situation for women in larger orchestras gradually improved from about 1980 on. Nevertheless, a handful of new women's ensembles were founded. One was the Columbus (Ohio) Women's Orchestra, an offshoot of Women in Music—Columbus, a member of the National Federation of Music Clubs that had existed since 1882. In 1977 the club president, Isabel Chandler, founded a women's symphony orchestra, which gave its first concert in April, 1978. The ensemble has continued to give four concerts per year; only the conductor is paid. In 1998 Emelyne M. Bingham was appointed music director.[64]

A somewhat different ensemble was the Women Composers Orchestra of Baltimore. Founded in 1985 by musicologist Selma Epstein and conductor Deborah Freedman as the Maryland Women's Symphony, it changed its name in 1989 and survived until 1996. The ensemble was conducted by women but included both male and female professional instrumentalists selected by blind audition. All performers were paid, but owing to financial constraints performances often were limited to chamber music. The ensemble was devoted entirely to performing the works of women composers whose birth dates span the years from the twelfth to the twentieth centuries, and it performed a number of world premieres, numerous American premieres, and many Maryland premieres. When financial support waned, it finally disbanded.[65]

The only wholly professional women's orchestra formed since 1980 is the Women's Philharmonic, based in San Francisco. Formerly called the Bay Area Women's Philharmonic, it gave its first concert in 1981 and as of this writing has thirty-nine tenured players. It hires more players as needed, depending on each concert program—the May 1999 program involved sixty-five players—and all players are paid. The orchestra is dedicated to the advancement of women composers, conductors, and performers, and in the first sixteen seasons it commissioned thirty-six new works by women while programming music from more than 150 composers. In that period it won thirteen ASCAP (American Society of Composers, Authors and Publishers) awards for programming. The conductor for the first five seasons was Elizabeth Seja Min, who founded the orchestra with Miriam Abrams and Nan Washburn. Washburn stayed with the orchestra for many years and then turned to conducting. In 1999 she was named conductor of the Plymouth (Michigan) Symphony and the West Hollywood Orchestra. Min was replaced by JoAnn Falletta, who in turn was replaced by Taiwan-born Apo Hsu.[66] Critical response to the orchestra has been laudatory, with such comments as "a virtuoso orchestra . . . expert in every style" (*Washington Post*), "a significant force in American symphonic music" (*Los Angeles Times*), "bringing in a breath of fresh air, performing both new music and newly discovered music" (*Morning Edition,* National Public Radio).

This chapter would not be complete without at least mentioning the many all-woman bands formed in the 1930s and 1940s by jazz and pop musicians who were not welcomed in all-male ensembles.[67] Actually, their history goes back to the 1880s, when a number of African-American women who played brass and reed instruments formed their own ensembles. The Colored Female Brass Band, led by cornetist Viola Allen, performed in and around Michigan. There were all-women minstrel ensembles such as Madame Rentz's Female Minstrels. The Lafayette Ladies Orchestra in New York City, taken over by trombonist and pianist Marie Lucas in 1915—she replaced her father—was not only an all-women's ensemble but trained others, both men and women, to play drums and trumpets in theater orchestras.

Often these players were male jazz musicians' wives or relatives. Thus Fletcher Henderson's wife, Leora Mieux, played trombone and formed her first all-woman band in 1927. On the other hand, both Lester Young's sister Irma, who played saxophone and ukulele, and Jack Teagarden's sister Norma, who functioned as both pianist and bandleader, worked in otherwise all-male bands. Lil Hardin Armstrong, for a time married to Louis Armstrong, formed an all-women's swing band in 1932; it lasted until 1936, when she switched to an otherwise all-male band. In the 1930s and 1940s numerous all-woman groups formed, both black and white and sometimes mixed, largely because of the difficulty of gaining access to all-male jazz bands. The women's ensembles emphasized a sexy, glamorous image, especially for the singers and leaders, and like the classical women's ensembles they probably contributed to the double standard. However, two outstanding groups, both all black, helped women improve their position: the Melodears, formed in 1934 and led by singer Ina Ray Hutton (the stage name for Odessa Cowan, 1916–1984), and the International Sweethearts of Rhythm, formed in 1937 and disbanded late in the 1940s. Both were widely accepted as first-rate jazz ensembles. The Sweethearts eventually included Latino, white, and Asian women as well. In 1978, at the second Women's Jazz Festival in Kansas City, twelve of the original Sweethearts of Rhythm were honored. There was also Phil Spitalny's All-Girl Orchestra, with his wife Evelyn on violin. This all-white group played light dance music and semiclassical selections more than jazz and lasted from 1934 to 1955.

During World War II all-woman big bands entertained U.S. troops overseas. Generally they were segregated by race, black groups performing for black soldiers and white groups—such as Al D'Artega's All-Girl Band, Joy Cayler's band, and Ada Leonard's All-American Girls—for white regiments. The mostly black International Sweethearts of Rhythm were an exception in that they also performed for white soldiers.[68] The bands were wildly welcomed, but not entirely for their playing. Their glamorous image and reminders of home stirred the men overseas. "We could have spit on the floor and they would have applauded," remarked trumpeter Jane Sager in 1995.

By the late 1940s the big band era was just about over, and men musicians returning from World War II largely ousted women who had taken their place. Owing to changes in taste and economics, the large bands all disbanded. A few women succeeded in forming successful all-female small groups, and some leaders of the 1930s and 1940s led more commercial bands, some of them all-male. Recording opportunities for women also dropped. As a result, some women went to Europe, especially to Paris.

A few women pursued a dual career in jazz and classical music. June Rotenberg started playing bass at age thirteen, her first teacher a bass player in the Philadelphia Orchestra. After graduating from high school, she went to New York in the early 1940s, auditioned for a scholarship with the National

Orchestral Association from the New York Philharmonic, and played jazz at night in order to make a living. She eventually worked with jazz pianist and composer Mary Lou Williams. Six months of the year she played with the St. Louis Symphony, and in 1950 she began playing both solos and chamber music at Pablo Casals festivals. Natalie Clair, another jazz bass player, joined the Cleveland Orchestra. Laura Bohle (later Sias) played bass with Al D'Artega's All-Girl Band during World War II and returned home to a scholarship at the Eastman School of Music and a chair in the Rochester Philharmonic. In addition she conducted a series of all-women's swing bands and combos in the Rochester, New York, area.[69]

Still another bass player, Lucille Dixon, had more difficulties. As she put it, "I thought I had two strikes against me—being a woman and being black. Then I realized I had *three* strikes: I was playing a man's instrument." In the early 1940s she got work in the all-male Earl Hines band. She left in 1945, founded her own Lucille Dixon Orchestra, but did not enjoy traveling. She finally got a job at the Savannah Club and stayed until 1954, when she went to Panama with her new husband and joined the National Symphony of Panama. In 1956 she returned to the United States, and in 1960 began to play with classical ensembles, specifically the Ridgefield Symphony, Boston Women's Symphony, and Scranton Symphony. In 1965 she became manager of the Symphony of the New World, an orchestra she formed for young musicians. When it disbanded in 1974, she returned to working dinner theater and playing in community orchestras. Though technically retired by 1993, she continued to sit in with bands in Puerto Rico, where she spent part of each year.[70]

In the decades after World War II a few women formed important ensembles, notably jazz pianist-composers Carla Bley and Toshiko Akiyoshi, who are further described in Chapter 7. But in general the picture in jazz was similar to that in classical music. Trumpeter Jane Sager once said, "There's only one way to play music and that's with authority—it doesn't mean man or woman." Not everyone believed that. Certainly not Billy Tipton, a gifted saxophonist and pianist, who died from a bleeding ulcer in 1989 at age seventy-four. He never visited a doctor, no matter how ill he was, and a funeral director finally explained his odd behavior to one of his three adopted sons: Tipton was a woman. He began his masquerade during the big band era of the 1930s, in order to get work. Kitty Oakes, the woman he claimed as his wife for nineteen years, said he gave up everything for his music, and no one ever suspected the ruse. He never gave his social security number to a booking agent and never went swimming with his sons.[71] Gender continues to play a role in both jazz and classical orchestras. In the late 1980s and early 1990s a number of new all-women's jazz ensembles were formed. Among the best of them were Maiden Voyage, Straight Ahead, and DIVA. DIVA, a big band with fifteen players, including the leader, drummer Sherrie Maricle, performed its first concert in 1993. It concentrated on contemporary jazz arranged by band members and by renowned musicians specifically for the individual personalities of the band members, some of whom had formerly played with other important big bands.

Some women, however, never want to play in all-women's groups or all-woman jazz festivals for fear of being ghettoized. For them "apartheid" is as undesirable as it was for blacks in South Africa.[72]

6

AMERICAN COMPOSERS
IN EUROPEAN IDIOMS

FROM THE VERY START the music of Europe dominated the concert halls of America. Serious native American music remained little more than a curiosity until the emergence of the New England school of composers in the latter half of the nineteenth century. Even then, most of these composers had received their training in Europe, and when they had not, the best of what they produced was most often an amalgam of the musical language that dominated late nineteenth-century Europe, the late romanticism of Brahms and Wagner, Tchaikovsky and Dvořák.

There were, of course, a few important exceptions. Charles Ives (1874–1954), far ahead of his time, used American idioms—hymn tunes, popular songs, and marches—along with both conventional devices and innovations such as conflicting rhythms and keys, dissonant harmonies, optional parts, and the like. Charles Tomlinson Griffes (1884–1920) combined elements of Oriental music, unusual harmonies, and some impressionistic devices. Alsatian-born Charles Martin Loeffler (1861–1935), a resident of Boston for much of his life, wrote music that reflected his European—especially his French—training, with definite leanings toward modality, chromaticism, and new tone colors, all features of impressionism.

Although Germany had been the wellspring of romanticism, which was the dominant nineteenth-century style, the search for new modes of musical expression began principally in France, and the first composer to succeed in this endeavor was Claude Debussy (1862–1918). The style he developed is generally called impressionism, a term Debussy himself rejected but that nevertheless has validity. Borrowed from the visual arts, impressionism describes music that evokes mood and atmosphere through the use of pure tone color—the individual characteristic sounds of the different instruments—rather than traditional melody or harmony. Impressionistic music therefore produces an effect of vagueness of form, even when the harmonies themselves follow a very strict formal pattern. Probably the most important contribution of impressionism was its use of new harmonies and scales, which greatly expanded the tonal possibilities available to composers.

The musical form that became the principal vehicle of impressionism was the symphonic poem or tone poem, an orchestral work in a single, fairly long movement, which, however, unlike the earlier tone poems of the nineteenth-century romanticists, did not necessarily follow a specific program. Sometimes the impressionist tone poem was a description of some natural phenomenon, usually named in the title, such as Debussy's *Prélude à l'après-midi d'un faune* and *La Mer,* or Respighi's *Pines of Rome.* Some impressionist works were more programmatic, and often they employed exotic devices, that is, elements from non-European music, such as Persian or Balinese; among these is Griffes's *Pleasure Dome of Kubla Khan.* Still others evoke a specific national tradition, such as Debussy's *Images* (which includes "Ibéria") and Ravel's *Rapsodie espagnole.*

By the early 1900s Debussy's influence was strongly felt. His *La Mer* of 1905 was followed in 1907 by Ravel's *Rapsodie espagnole,* and the English composer Frederick Delius, who lived in Paris from the late 1880s on, was producing orchestral works in a similar vein at about the same time. The Spanish composer Manuel de Falla lived in Paris from 1907 to 1914 and was personally acquainted with Debussy, whose influence is apparent in his *Noches en los jardines de Espana* of 1916, though later de Falla turned away from impressionism.

With these and other composers, French impressionism had direct influence and was most apparent in works published from about 1905 to 1925. By the mid-1920s other influences had become important in the European mainstream, notably the neoclassicism of Prokofiev and Stravinsky, and the serial techniques of Schoenberg and others. The legacy of impressionism, while not exactly lost, had been, as it were, internalized, to be drawn on as needed for writing music that was essentially in quite another vein.

Yet just about the time that most European composers had turned to other styles, two American women composed impressionist music. Both Marion Bauer and Mary Howe had been in Europe in the early 1900s and had undoubtedly been exposed to at least some impressionist music. Bauer studied in France in 1906 and 1907, was in Berlin from 1911 to 1912, and again was in France from 1923 to 1926. Howe studied piano briefly in Dresden and was making almost annual journeys abroad between about 1901 and 1912. Neither woman composed any large-scale works until after 1925, but when they did, the impressionist influences from their formative years were unmistakably present.

Mary Carlisle Howe was born on April 4, 1882, in Richmond, Virginia, and grew up in Washington, D.C.[1] Her father, Calderon Carlisle, was an international lawyer. Her mother, Kate Thomas, had studied voice. Educated privately, Mary became a fine pianist, and by the age of eighteen she was accompanying at private recitals. In her wealthy and socially prominent milieu, public performance was still frowned on, but playing at private social gatherings was quite acceptable.

Just after Christmas in 1900 Mary went to Baltimore's Peabody Conservatory for an audition with Ernest Hutcheson, playing Schumann and Debussy. She was accepted as a student and commuted regularly from Washington to study piano with Hutcheson and later with Harold Randolph. In 1901 her father died, and Mary began to go abroad frequently with her mother. In the spring of 1904 she spent four months in Dresden, studying piano with Richard Burmeister. She continued to play in private recitals, abroad and at home, even tackling the difficult Schumann A minor Concerto, with a second piano playing the orchestral part. During the Taft and Roosevelt administrations, she was often a guest at the White House, and she played chamber music at Washington's Friday Morning Music Club.

In 1912 Mary married her brother Mandeville's law partner, Walter Bruce Howe, and devoted the next few years to starting a family; her son Bruce was born in 1912, another son, Calderon, in 1916, and a daughter, Mary (called Molly), in 1918. At the Peabody Conservatory she had become acquainted with another pianist, Anne Hull, and in 1912 the two women gave the first of a long series of two-piano performances. At first they performed chiefly before music clubs, in private homes, and at the Peabody, from which Hull had graduated. From 1920 on they played with a number of symphony orchestras, on tour with the Russian Symphony under Modest Altschuler, with the Baltimore Symphony, Cleveland Orchestra, and others.

About 1920 Howe began to devote herself more and more to composing. She had returned to the Peabody to study composition formally with Gustav Strube. On March 3, 1920, at a "Manuscript Evening" held there, Colin McPhee performed Howe's *Three Preludes* for piano. The following year her *Berceuse* for piano was played, and in 1922 she graduated, passing the first formal examination she had ever taken. In 1923 Howe appeared with the National String Quartet to play her Andante and Scherzo for piano quintet. During this period, her two-piano performances with Hull continued as well; in 1924 they made their New York debut in a two-piano recital at Aeolian (later Town) Hall, performing a Bach chorale transcribed by Hull, three Spanish dances transcribed by Howe, and works for two pianos by Mozart, Schumann, Glière, and others. The reviews were universally enthusiastic.

In the early 1920s Howe had become acquainted with pianist and composer Amy Beach, and in 1925 the two women gave the Washington premiere of Beach's *Suite for Two Pianos* in a benefit concert for the MacDowell Colony. Howe visited the Colony the following summer, and from about 1927 on, sponsored by Beach and another composer friend, Ethel Glenn Hier, she was a fellow there nearly every summer for the next twenty years. Though she usually stayed only for a few weeks, not wanting to leave her family for longer periods, she felt her time there was extremely productive.

Howe also attended the Festival of Chamber Music established by music patron and composer Elizabeth Sprague Coolidge in Pittsfield, Massachusetts, where she heard for the first time works by Schoenberg and Hindemith. There she encountered her friend Carl Engel, chief of the Music Division of the

Library of Congress. Howe helped organize the first Coolidge Festival in Washington, held in 1924 at the Freer Gallery, and the Chamber Music Society that eventually became the Friends of Music of the Library of Congress. Engel also helped arrange performances of Howe's works.

In 1925 Howe attended the premiere of her *Chain Gang Song* for chorus and orchestra at the Worcester Festival. This represented her first public success as a composer. In retrospect, she said,

> The first time I heard a piece of my own orchestral writing played, I got a real kick out of it. I finally began to rate respectably as pianist and composer. . . . This was the public rehearsal at Worcester, 1925, of my *Chain Gang Song* for chorus and orchestra, with about 275 voices and the New York Symphony [under Albert Stoessel], and there it was out of my hands and about to come to life.[2]

Chain Gang Song is based on three tunes sung by a road gang of prisoners in the western North Carolina mountains. Howe said,

> It means to me, rounding a bend on horseback on a hot Southern afternoon and coming on a gang of twenty or so black convicts in striped clothes, guarded by a lean ornery looking white man with a shot gun. Iron ball and chain on many feet, and they sang while they drilled the hole for the dynamite charge. One man held and aimed the iron drill, and two more slugged at it with heavy shoulder weight iron hammers, rhythmically, so the three could know inevitably when the hammer blows would fall.[3]

Chain Gang Song was hailed as a strong, effective work. One critic said, "a powerful piece of writing with no trace of femininity and astonishing skill in the handling of her resources."[4]

In 1926 conductor Georges Barrère asked Howe to orchestrate two of her shorter works—*Stars,* originally for piano, and Scherzo for piano quintet—and in March 1927 he conducted his Little Symphony in New York in both pieces and *Chain Gang Song.* Barrère became one of Howe's staunchest champions; in 1930 he performed her new work, *Sand,* which he repeated the following year on a program that also included the first performance of Mabel Daniels's *Deep Forest.*

A short but difficult work, *Sand* is essentially a tone poem in miniature. Howe intended for it to convey the consistency, the grains, bulk, and grittiness, and the potential scattering quality of sand itself. The intriguing staccato effects she used in this piece led Leopold Stokowski to say it had given him an entirely new view of what could be done with staccato. Stokowski conducted *Sand* with the Philadelphia Orchestra in 1934. Though Howe herself said that her "back foot is in the garden gate of the Romantics, but I feel no hesitation in thumbing the passing modern idiom for a hitch-hike to where I want to go,"[5] she used dissonances sparingly. But *Sand* is very much an impressionist work, exploiting, as it does, the characteristic sounds of the instruments to evoke a desired atmosphere. *Stars* is also impressionistic, and the two orchestrated works are frequently performed together. In *Stars* the composer wished to convey the gradually overwhelming effect of a starry night, opening with a sonorous ensemble of strings and expanding to use the full orchestra.

About 1930 Hans Kindler, principal cellist with the Philadelphia Orchestra, asked Howe to help raise $40,000 for a new Washington, D.C., orchestra. An energetic, strong-minded woman with connections in both wealthy and musical circles, Mary Howe helped him raise the required sum. In 1931 the National Symphony Orchestra was born. For the next eighteen years Howe, together with her husband and Kindler, worked hard to support the orchestra. In addition to its Washington concerts, it undertook regular symphonic series in other cities and became known for its imaginative programs, combining music from all periods and presenting many new works. Eventually Kindler had a falling out with members of the orchestra's board and resigned in 1948, but Howe remained on good terms with his successor, Howard Mitchell, and continued to work for the orchestra.

Kindler had performed some of Howe's works in recitals, her *Ballade fantasque* for cello and piano, and *Canción romanesco* for string quartet.[6] Under him the National Symphony regularly performed her tone poems and her *Castellana* for two pianos and orchestra, a brilliant, showy piece. Built on four folk tunes she had learned from her father's Spanish cousins, this work became one of Howe's most popular and was often performed by her and Anne Hull.

The two-piano recitals also continued through the 1930s, though by then Hull had moved to New York and was pursuing a busy teaching career. Hull became, in effect, the New York custodian of Howe's compositions and did a great deal to promote their performance, in New York and elsewhere. Together Hull and Howe often performed *Castellana*, Howe's transcriptions of several Bach arias, and her *Three Spanish Folk Tunes* ("Habanera de Cinna," "Petenera," and "Spanish Folk Dance"); of these works, her *Sheep May Safely Graze*, the transcription of Bach's aria, has become a standard work in the two-piano literature.

Howe's views on women composers were unequivocal:

Women composers should be played more than they are. I don't think conductors have a prejudice against women composers now. But no one puts women writers or women painters in a class any more, and they still do so with women composers. I know I considered it a handicap to be a woman when I started composing. I'm not a feminist. But I think I would have gotten along faster if I'd been a man.[7]

Despite Howe's wealth, social position, and connections in the musical world, she was discriminated against. In fact, the conductor William Strickland, who knew her well, believed that both her position and her sex militated against her: The former marked her as a dilettante, and the latter prevented her from being taken seriously.

Howe had early become a member of the Society of American Women Composers, founded around 1924, and her music was regularly performed at its concerts. She also befriended and retained contact with many other women musicians and composers. She gave one of the first performances of her Violin Sonata with violinist Leonora Jackson McKim. Pianist Olga Samaroff played Howe's *Nocturne* on her tour in 1924 and remained a friend for many years, as did Amy Beach and Ethel Glenn Hier. Conductor Antonia Brico performed *Sand* with the National Symphony at a summer concert in 1940 and another of Howe's symphonic poems, *What Price Glory,* the following summer. Howe also kept up her connection with the Friday Morning Music Club well into the 1940s.

Shortly before the United States entered World War II, Howe completed her last two orchestral works, *Paean* and *Potomac.* The former, a symphonic poem, is thought by some to be her best orchestral score; the latter, a suite consisting of a prelude and three movements, was given its premiere by Albert Stoessel with the New York Symphony at Chautauqua in 1942. Busy with Red Cross work and other volunteer activities during the war, Howe still continued to compose. In 1943 she wrote *Prophecy, 1792,* a setting of part of William Blake's "Song of Liberty," for the Army Music School Choir, which performed it at the National Gallery that September.

Throughout the 1930s, in addition to orchestral works, Howe had continued to write chamber works, choral music, and many solo songs. In April 1939 a recital devoted entirely to Howe's songs was held at Washington's Phillips Memorial Gallery. It included settings of poems by Rainer Maria Rilke, Elinor Wylie, and others, and prompted warm praise from critics:

> Mrs. Howe has a remarkable talent in lyric style. . . . She does not bend the text to the melodic line, or use any of the strategems of emotional appeal, save in one or two instances of obvious strophe form imposed by the nature of the poem. Her music grows out of the text and exists with it in artistic symbiosis.[8]

Seven volumes of her songs were published in 1959. Among the best are the settings of Elinor Wylie's poems, especially "When I Died in Berners Street," which has been called "a perfect union of text and music" and "one of the finest American songs produced to date."[9] It is every bit as good as the songs of Debussy, with which it has inevitably been compared.

Howe herself disclaimed allegiance to any school. "If I want to use dissonance," she said, "I use dissonance. If I want to express feeling, I express feeling. I write what I want to write." She admired many contemporary American composers, especially Aaron Copland, Gian Carlo Menotti, Paul Creston, and Louise Talma; she had heard some of Talma's works played at the Library of Congress and called her "a very talented young woman."[10] She also was a great admirer of Nadia Boulanger, with whom she had studied in 1933, during a year spent in France.

Howe continued to be active throughout the 1950s. In 1952 the National Symphony under Howard Mitchell gave an all-Howe program featuring *Stars, Sand, Dirge, Paean, Castellana,* and a number of the songs. The following year there was an all-Howe concert in New York at Town Hall, with soprano Katherine Hansel and the Howard University Choir performing *Prophecy, 1792; Cavaliers; Williamsburg Sunday;* and numerous songs. Again the reviews were universally favorable. Frances Perkins of the *New York Herald Tribune* said the songs showed "notable ability for presenting the texts and musical projection of the expressive atmosphere of the poems was constantly persuasive," while the choral writing was "lucid and skilfully wrought." The *New York Times* critic agreed: "Mary Howe's musical idiom is a refreshing one. The musical structure has clarity and design throughout."

In 1954 Walter Howe died, and by then their children were settled in careers of their own. The following year Mary Howe went to Vienna, where William Strickland led the Vienna Symphony in a performance of *Stars, Sand,* and *Rock;* the last was another short tone poem, here given its premiere. The Vienna orchestra, Strickland recalled more than twenty years later, was notoriously hard on foreigners and could scarcely be expected to open its arms to a foreign woman composer. But Howe won them over readily, and, in fact, it was at the request of the orchestra's principal wind players that she composed *Suite for Wind Quintet. Stars, Sand,* and *Rock* were again performed together by the National Symphony in Washington, D.C., in February 1956 and won the composer a standing ovation by the Constitution Hall audience.

On Mary Howe's eightieth birthday she was given a party attended by some 200 guests at the Mayflower Hotel in Washington, D.C. Among the music performed was *Interlude Between Two Pieces* for flute and piano, a two-piano version of *Stars,* the Violin Sonata in D, choral works, and many songs. Among the last tributes Howe received was an honorary doctor of music degree from George Washington University. She died in 1964.

The other woman who absorbed French impressionism at an early age and used its idioms in her own compositions years later was Marion Bauer, who is remembered as much as a champion of contemporary music and a teacher as a composer. Marion Eugénie Bauer was born on August 15, 1882, in Walla Walla, Washington, the youngest of seven children.[11] Her parents were of French lineage, her mother a gifted linguist and her father an amateur musician. Her first music lessons were with her oldest sister, Emilie Frances, a pianist and later a music critic.[12] Marion was educated in the West, and after graduation from high school she went to New York to live with Emilie Frances, by then established as a critic there.

Bauer's first studies in New York were with Henry Holden Huss; later she also worked with Eugene Heffley and Walter Henry Rothwell. In 1906 she went to France, where she studied piano with Raoul Pugno, the famous violinist. Through him she met Nadia Boulanger, who began to teach her harmony. In exchange Bauer gave both her and Pugno's young daughter lessons in English, thus helping to finance her year of music studies. She later said that she must have been the first American pupil of Boulanger, who was to teach a whole generation of American composers.

In 1907 Bauer returned to the United States and spent the next four years in New York, teaching piano and theory and continuing her own studies. During this time, her first published song, "Light," was introduced by the famous contralto Ernestine Schumann-Heink. In 1910 Bauer again went to Europe, this time to Berlin, and studied counterpoint and form for a year with Paul Ertel. She was still composing songs that clearly showed the influence of French impressionism, and in 1912, when she returned to America, she obtained a seven-year contract with the music publisher Arthur P. Schmidt.

Bauer continued to write songs, but she gradually expanded into piano works and then chamber music. One composition from this period is a tone poem for violin and piano, *Up the Ocklawaha,* which she wrote in 1913 for her friend, violinist Maud Powell, and describes Powell's trip up this Florida river. She also wrote *Fair Daffodils* (1913), a trio for women's voices; *The Lay of the Four Winds* (1915) for men's voices; and *Allegretto giocoso* (1920) for eleven instruments, her most ambitious instrumental work so far.

In 1923 Bauer returned to Europe for a third time, this time to France, where she studied fugue with André Gédalge, the teacher of many celebrated composers, including Ravel, Milhaud, and Honegger. She remained in France until January 1926. But then her sister fell ill, and Bauer returned to her bedside and remained with her until her death later that year. She then lived with her sister Flora, an arrangement that continued until Flora's death in the early 1950s.[13]

Very early in her career Bauer had begun to write for music journals in both Europe and America. In 1926 she replaced her sister Emilie as New York correspondent of the *Musical Leader,* an important Chicago journal, for which she reviewed an immense number of concerts and recitals; she held this post until her death. She also began what was to be an important collaboration with Ethel Peyser on popular books of music history, the first of which, *How Music Grew,* was published in 1925. Their *Music Through the Ages* appeared in 1932, and *How Opera Grew* in 1956. In addition, Bauer alone wrote *Twentieth-Century Music* (1933) and *Musical Questions and Quizzes* (1941), as well as contributing articles and chapters to Oscar Thompson's *International Cyclo-pedia of Music* and *Musicians and Great Modern Composers* and writing for many music journals.

Bauer's own compositions were not radically innovative, but they were skillfully wrought. Of her *Four Songs,* op. 16 (1924), William Upton said, "In easy command of modern technique, in rich pictorial quality, in vivid play of the imagination and sustained dramatic interest, these songs may worthily take their place beside Griffes' own."[14] Like Griffes and other impressionist composers, Bauer often used "exotic"—that is, non-Western—elements in her music, which in her case ranged from American Indian to African material. In this vein are her *Indian Pipes* (1927) for orchestra and *Lament on African Themes* (1928) for chamber orchestra. During the same period she also wrote Violin Sonata, op. 18, published 1928, String Quartet, op. 20, first performed in 1928, and *Four Piano Pieces,* op. 21, premiered in 1930.[15]

In 1926 Bauer joined the faculty of New York University, the first woman in its music department, where she taught music history and composition for the next quarter of a century. Later she also taught at the Juilliard School, and she taught summer sessions at several well-known institutions, including Mills College, Carnegie Institute of Technology, and the Cincinnati Conservatory of Music. She was not in the forefront of the avant-garde in her own compositions, although her later works became increasingly dissonant and she wrote some serial piano pieces in the 1940s and 1950s, but she was extremely sympathetic to those who were. In 1932 she initiated a series of lecture-recitals with pianist Harrison Potter to explain modern music to the general public. Four years earlier she had begun a twenty-year stint as annual lecturer at the Contemporary Trends Series of the Chautauqua Institute in New York State. She was the only woman on the executive board of the American Composers Alliance, founded by Aaron Copland in 1937,[16] and she served on the boards of the League of Composers, beginning in 1926, and the Society for the Publication of American Music, all organizations working to foster the cause of contemporary American music. Bauer tirelessly defended this cause in many quarters. Typical is her article "Why Not Teach Music of Today?" in the November 1951 issue of the *Associated Music Teachers' League Bulletin,* in which she said, "It's a vicious circle! Publishers don't publish modern teaching pieces because teachers don't buy them. Teachers don't teach modern music because publishers don't publish it." And everyone, Bauer continued, was partly to blame. Teachers did not want to take the trouble to find and buy and test new music; parents complained about unusual-sounding pieces; composers did not bother to write good teaching pieces. "Dissonant sounds do not disturb the young pianist," said Bauer, "if there is a rhythmical interest or a melody that may be easily followed, or an entertaining subject or a pattern that is easy to get hold of." But children must have the chance to get used to new styles of music, or they never will be accepted. "Do not forget that . . . all music was modern once."

Bauer herself did continue to write teaching pieces, as well as more choral, chamber, and orchestral music. Her Viola Sonata, op. 22 (1935), was often performed. Her *Symphonic Suite for Strings* was given its premiere at Chautauqua in 1941; *American Youth Concerto* for piano and orchestra was written for and performed at New York's High School of Music and Art in 1943; *China,* a setting of a poem by Boris Todrin for mixed chorus and orchestra, was performed at the Worcester Festival in 1945; and the tone poem *Sun Splendor,* originally for piano and later orchestrated, was performed by the New York Philharmonic under Leopold Stokowski in 1947. Other works include Concertino for oboe, clarinet, and string quartet (1939–43) and Symphony no. 1 (1950).

In 1951 the Phi Beta National Fraternity of Music and Speech sponsored an all-Bauer program at New York's Town Hall, which included the first performance of her new Trio Sonata no. 2, op. 47, for flute, cello, and piano, commissioned and played by the Sagul Trio (Edith Sagul, Marilyn Beabout, and Mary Stretch). The program also premiered her *Moods for Dance Interpretation,* op. 46 (1950), for dancer and piano. Of this program Olin Downes of the *New York Times* reported, "The music is prevailingly contrapuntal and dissonance is not absent. Yet the fundamental concept is melodic, the thinking clear and logical, the sentiment sincere and direct."[17]

Four years later Marion Bauer died, a few days before her sixty-eighth birthday. At her funeral the musicologist Gustave Reese, a longtime friend and colleague at New York University, said that in the 1920s Marion Bauer had been very much a modernist and the outstanding woman among American composers. What he omitted to say and perhaps did not realize was that she frequently was the only woman among a group of men. As early as 1921, when she was a founder of the American Music Guild, formed for the purpose of hearing and criticizing each other's works, she was also its only woman member. The 1947 performance of her *Sun Splendor* was the only composition by a woman performed by the New York Philharmonic in a quarter of a century. She was the only woman who was consistently quoted in settings such as the Yaddo Festival of Contemporary Music held in the early 1940s.

There were a number of reasons why she was accepted when other women, some of them just as competent, were not. For one thing she, like many of the young American men composers of the 1920s—and unlike many prominent women composers, including Beach and Daniels—had studied in France during the early 1920s, and from that time France replaced Germany as *the* music center. Second, her position as a working music critic gave her considerable influence; she was in a position to help or put down new works, so inevitably her favor was courted. And finally, her intelligent approach to new music and her ability to explain it lucidly in lectures and in her book, *Twentieth-Century Music,* earned her universal respect.

As for her own views about women, she said, "My early aspiration was not to listen to the sly remarks of intolerant men regarding women composers

. . . that if given a reasonable chance for development, an individual talent, regardless of sex, can progress and grow."[18] Generous in helping students and younger composers, Bauer numbered many women musicians among her friends. Some of her own compositions are dedicated to Maud Powell, Amy Beach, and Ruth Crawford, among others. The last was to become one of the most innovative of all American composers.

Ruth Crawford was a close friend of Bauer's from their first meeting at the MacDowell Colony in 1929. Like Charles Ives, she was one of the great originals in American music, and Bauer was among the first to give her public recognition. A good many of Crawford's works give, at least on first hearing, the sense of diffuseness and vagueness that often is associated with the impressionist music of Debussy and others. Nothing could be further from the truth. In all but her earliest works, the music of Ruth Crawford, who continued to use her maiden name professionally after marriage, is very tightly organized with respect to just about every element—pitches, intervals, rhythms, meters, dynamics, instrumentation, text. Though she was exposed to late romantic and impressionist music, the twelve-tone music of the Viennese school of Schoenberg and Hauer, and the expressionism of Alban Berg, she assimilated elements from all these and formed her own highly individual style. Moreover, some techniques she developed anticipated by twenty or thirty years the experiments of post-World War II composers in Europe and America.

The daughter and granddaughter of Methodist ministers, Ruth Porter Crawford was born on July 3, 1901, in East Liverpool, Ohio, the younger of two children.[19] Her father held many pulpits during Ruth's early childhood, and the family moved frequently, from Ohio to Missouri to Indiana, and finally, in 1911, to Jacksonville, Florida. About that time her father became ill, and three years later, when Ruth was fourteen, he died. After this her mother rented out rooms to help support Ruth and her brother, Carl.

Crawford's first music studies were with her mother, but at age six she went to a professional piano teacher. She continued to study music through high school, but she was also very interested in writing, especially poetry. After graduating from high school she began to earn her own living, teaching piano at the School of Musical Art and music at a settlement kindergarten in Jacksonville. In 1920, having saved just enough money to support a year's study, she went to Chicago and enrolled in the American Conservatory there. After that first year, she supported herself by ushering coats in theaters on the Loop, and, in 1922, having earned the American Conservatory's teacher's certificate, she began teaching piano and theory. At first she taught privately and then, from 1924 on, at the American Conservatory and from 1926 also at Elmhurst College. In 1923 her mother joined her in Chicago, and they lived together until Mrs. Crawford's death in 1928.

Crawford's first courses at the American Conservatory were in piano and harmony, but later she took up counterpoint, composition, and orchestration, earning a bachelor's degree in 1924 and a master's with highest honors in 1929. A number of musicians Crawford met during these years had a profound influence on her music and her life. Her first teacher of harmony and counterpoint at the conservatory, violinist Adolf Weidig, was one of the first to encourage her to concentrate on composing. Djane Lavoie-Herz, with whom Crawford studied piano for four years, regularly held musical evenings in her Chicago studio where Crawford met the composers Henry Cowell, Edgard Varèse, and Carlos Chávez; art critic Alfred Frankenstein; Adolf Weiss, a Chicago Symphony bassoonist who had studied with Arnold Schoenberg and was enthralled with the Viennese composer's twelve-tone system; and Dane Rudhyar, a French-born composer with mystical leanings who introduced her to the music of Scriabin. It was here, also, that Crawford first heard the music of Igor Stravinsky, Paul Hindemith, Darius Milhaud, and Ralph Vaughan Williams. Frankenstein in turn introduced her to the poet Carl Sandburg, whose children she taught piano for a time. She contributed some of the piano accompaniments for Sandburg's collection of folk songs, *The American Songbag,* and this association awakened what was to be a lifelong interest in folk music. Probably the most important of her new friends was Henry Cowell. It was Cowell who first helped Crawford publish her compositions; it was he who persuaded her to leave Chicago for New York in 1929; and it was he who introduced her to Charles Seeger.

By 1929 Crawford was considered one of the most promising young musicians in Chicago, and in fact she had already produced nearly half of her total compositional output. In the end, she wrote but thirty-two compositions in all, and even that figure is reached only by counting each song and prelude as a separate work. Among the earliest of her works to survive[20] are *Five Preludes* for piano (1924–25), Violin Sonata (1926), and *Suite for Small Orchestra* (1926), written while she was studying under Weidig. The preludes, never published and first performed at Town Hall in New York by Gitta Gradova, are still late romantic in style, though at least one scholar, Mary Matilda Gaume, saw in them some characteristics of Crawford's later style: a twisting and quite chromatic melody; no key signatures, though the music is not yet atonal for it still has a tonal center, or key, and the harmonies and chord progressions are based on the traditional triads of tonal music; and repeated patterns and sequences in which the repetition often is not quite exact but involves slight changes. These pieces, like most of Crawford's compositions, are short; Prelude no. 1 is only twelve measures long, and the longest, Prelude no. 2, consists of forty-six measures.

The *Suite for Small Orchestra,* scored for flute, clarinet, bassoon, violins, cellos, and piano, consists of two movements, the first somber and slow, the second lively and jaunty.[21] In the first movement, static ostinato patterns in groups of six, five, four, three, and two notes are set against sustained pedal tones in the cello and piano parts. The pedal tones consist chiefly of tone clusters, adjacent notes that might be played by simply putting one's forearm down on the keyboard, for example. The second movement, in contrast, trips along almost mechanically, relieved by a flowing melody full of triplets. This work, too, was never published; it received what was presumably its premiere performance only in 1969 at West Texas University and was recorded in 1975.

There followed another set of piano pieces, *Nine Preludes* (1927–28), first performed in 1928 at one of the Copland-Sessions concerts devoted to new music in New York. These compositions are more impressionist and rhapsodic in character and include the only two works Crawford ever dedicated to anyone: no. 6, to Djane Lavoie-Herz, and no. 9, to pianist Richard Buhlig, who played it in San Francisco in 1928, as well as in New York.

Crawford's next instrumental work was *Suite no. 1 for Five Wind Instruments and Piano,* written in 1927 and revised in 1929. Neither version was ever published. It was followed in 1929 by *Suite no. 2 for Four Strings and Piano,* in three movements. Crawford spent the summer of 1929 at the Mac-Dowell Colony, where she became close friends with Marion Bauer and produced her first vocal works, *Five Songs,* settings of poems by Carl Sandburg. All five are for medium or low voice, suitable for either a man or a woman singer, and use panchromatic harmony—that is, the simultaneous sounding of chromatic notes—and tone clusters. That fall she moved to New York, and soon afterward Henry Cowell persuaded Charles Seeger, his own former teacher, to take Crawford as a pupil. At first Seeger did not take kindly to the idea; he had a low opinion of women composers and some very radical ideas about composition. But Cowell convinced him that Crawford was no run-of-the-mill student, and Seeger finally agreed to take her on.

Cowell later described Seeger as "the greatest musical explorer in intellectual fields which America has produced, the greatest experimental musicologist. . . . [He] suggested more fruitful pathways for musical composition than any other."[22] Seeger was fifteen years older than Ruth Crawford. A graduate of Harvard, he had taught at the University of California from 1912 to 1919, a time when Debussy's impressionism was considered the most modern kind of music. There he developed the idea of dissonant counterpoint, a technique in which the discordant, tension-filled intervals of dissonance are the desired norm, the agreeable, restful intervals of consonance are undesirable, and the texture of the music is not primarily chords but a fabric of separate melodic lines. Such a texture, he believed, would make the musical structure more apparent to listeners, since separate lines are easier to discern than the individual notes in a chord.

In Ruth Crawford Charles Seeger found a kindred spirit. They both were fascinated with Schoenberg's twelve-tone system, where a row of twelve tones, used in a fixed order, becomes the organizing principle of a composition. This row or series—hence the term "serial music"—is used over and over throughout a work. No pitch may be repeated before all the others have sounded, but the series may be varied in accordance with certain rules; for example, notes may be moved up or down an octave, or a fifth, or the entire series may be inverted, or appear backward, or both backward and inverted. Much as they liked this system, however, Crawford and Seeger agreed that it was too rigid and that the music produced was too diffuse. The tonal organization should be more obvious to listeners.

Crawford's next compositions, produced during the winter of 1929–30, were essentially exercises in dissonant counterpoint assigned by her new teacher. In effect, the purpose was to take a single melodic line and keep it dissonant for as long as possible, using only major and minor seconds, sevenths, and ninths and augmented fourths, and avoiding all the consonant intervals, thirds, perfect fourths and fifths, sixths, and octaves. Crawford's first of these exercises, *Piano Study in Mixed Accents* (1930), consists entirely of octave passages, the same in the right- and left-hand parts, with no chords. The melodic line moves from the low end of the keyboard to the high end and down again, and there are three optional dynamic patterns: loud throughout; soft to loud to soft; or loud to soft to loud. *Four Diaphonic Suites* (1930) are similar exercises, this time in dissonant two-part polyphony.

In 1930 Ruth Crawford won a Guggenheim Fellowship in composition for a year abroad, the first woman ever selected. That fall she sailed for Europe, and she spent most of her year there composing. For several months she stayed in Berlin, where she wrote *Chant,* a group of three choral pieces, two of which were not premiered until sixty years later. In Berlin she also wrote part of her String Quartet, the song "In Tall Grass," and some unspecified shorter pieces. She went for what she called "too short a time" to Vienna, where she had long talks with Alban Berg, whose opera *Wozzeck* had impressed her profoundly, with the twelve-tone composer J. M. Hauer, and with Egon Wellesz. She met Bela Bartók in Budapest, and in Munich she heard a choral work by Werner Egk. She then spent a number of months in Paris, where she met Maurice Ravel and finished her String Quartet.

Because she did not produce a major symphonic work the Guggenheim Fellowship was not renewed, an irony since during the year abroad she produced her most remarkable composition to date, the String Quartet. It also became her best-known work. She herself recognized its value: "I am sure that the work I did during this time was by far the best I had done—a fact which I attribute not so much to Europe itself (though the experience abroad was invaluable to me in a general sort of way) as to the financial freedom to work and to the natural course of my growth."[23] The String Quartet was first performed by the New World String Quartet at the New School in New York on November 13, 1933, and was published in 1941. The third movement, Andante, was recorded a few weeks later and records were sent to critics, which made it quite well known. The third movement can be performed alone by a string orchestra—a part for double bass was added for this purpose—so it has been heard not only as chamber music but also as orchestral music. In the 1970s, when so many of her compositions still were available only in manuscript from the Library of Congress, it was performances of the String Quartet and the Andante that sparked new interest in Crawford's work.

The String Quartet is a remarkable piece. The first movement, Rubato assai, has fourteen changes of tempo in seventy-eight measures, and twelve different time signatures. The texture is contrapuntal, with each instrument having its own dissonant line. In contrast to the generally subdued dynamics of most of her earlier works, Crawford here made more use of sudden, intense dynamic changes and high dynamic levels. The basic tonal material is again short motifs, not themes or melodies, and the composer notes: "The melodic line, as indicated by 'solo' in each part, must be heard continuing throughout the movement."[24] In the second movement, Leggiero, there is more rhythmic drive, and the four instruments play follow-the-leader through five basic motifs, stated first by one and then the other. In the third movement, Andante, all four parts change pitch slowly and together, but they are differentiated from one another by their dynamic patterns, which are so staggered that each instrument alternately emerges and then sinks back into the total mass of sound, going from very soft to very loud and then back again. The fourth movement, Allegro possibile, "as fast as possible," consists of two contrapuntal lines, one played by the first violin and the other by the three remaining instruments in unison and octave doublings. The first violin starts with a single-note unit, which is increased, one note at a time, to a twenty-one-note unit. At the same time, it begins very loud and becomes softer and softer. Halfway through the movement, the entire process is repeated in reverse and transposed up one step, so groups of fewer and fewer notes are played louder and louder. In the meantime the other three instruments play the same design in reverse, beginning with a twenty-note unit, decreasing to one note, and reversing the process at midpoint.[25]

In 1931 Crawford returned to America, and in October 1932 she married Charles Seeger. She continued to compose, producing the third of the *Three Songs of Carl Sandburg,* orchestral parts for all three of them, and *Two Ricercari,* two songs to political texts, "Sacco, Vanzetti" and "Chinaman, Laundryman." Written in 1932, the *Ricercari* are settings of poems by H. T. Tsiang that were published in 1928 in the *Daily Worker,* the leading American Communist newspaper. Their choice reflected Crawford's concern with social and economic conditions, an interest shared by her husband and many other intellectual liberals of this period. Sacco and Vanzetti were two Italian-Americans executed for the murder of a guard during a robbery, even though many believed they were innocent of the crime and had been accused chiefly because of their radical political beliefs. "Chinaman, Laundryman" concerns the miserable conditions of the exploited immigrant in his laundry sweatshop. For "Sacco, Vanzetti" Crawford noted on the manuscript, "It is essential that the audience understand the words. If the effort to secure the pitches as written should interfere with the clear rendition of the words, these pitches should be regarded as general rather than as specific indications." Some of the pitches are actually indefinite, marked only by an arrow pointing up or down to indicate that a pitch should be higher or lower than the preceding pitch. This technique, called *Sprechstimme,* meaning "speaking voice," was used early in the 1900s by Schoenberg and others.

Crawford's *Three Songs* (1930–32) use some of these same devices but are still more complex. They are scored for alto voice, oboe, percussion, and piano, a group the composer called "concertanti," plus an orchestra, called "ostinati." All are settings of poems by Sandburg and were published in 1933 along with dates of composition: "Rat Riddles," March 1930; "In Tall Grass," January 1931, written in Europe; and "Prayers of Steel," November 1932. This group was the first of Crawford's output to receive more than a local hearing. It was one of two compositions, along with Aaron Copland's *Piano Variations,* selected to represent the United States at the Festival of the International Society for Contemporary Music, held in Amsterdam in 1933. Crawford was the first American woman so honored.

With these songs Crawford's original work came to a halt. Both she and Seeger had become attracted to left-wing political causes and proletarian music. Moreover, in 1933 Michael, their first child, was born. He was followed by Margaret (1935), Barbara (1937), and Penelope (1943). In addition, Seeger's three children from his first marriage lived with them. Seeger had no regular job and they were living a hand-to-mouth existence, but in 1935 he was offered a full-time job at a federal relief agency in Washington, D.C., and the family moved from New York. Occupied with raising her family, Crawford discovered a new musical world in folk music, and she began to arrange folk tunes as piano pieces for students. At this time John and Alan Lomax were collecting and recording folk songs in rural areas, and in 1937 they asked Crawford to transcribe their recordings. During the next fifteen years Crawford transcribed some 1000 songs from field recordings in the nearby Archive of American Folk Song in the Library of Congress, and the income from this work helped support the family. For many of the songs she also wrote piano arrangements and accompaniments, some of which were published in the Lomax collections *Our Singing Country* and *Folksong: USA.* Others appeared in some of Crawford's own books for children, *American Folk Songs for Children, Animal Folk Songs for Children,* and *American Folk Songs for Christmas.* During this period, Crawford also taught music, not only to her own children—one stepson, Pete Seeger, and two of her own children, Michael and Peggy, became professional folk singers—but at a number of local schools. She had a marvelous faculty for conveying her own delight in the spontaneous vitality of folk song to others, especially the young. She also taught piano privately, to as many as twenty or thirty students a week.

Although she tried to begin work on a second string quartet, the demands on her time did not allow it. Crawford produced only one original composition during these years: *Rissolty, Rossolty* (1939), a work for small orchestra commissioned by the CBS American School of the Air and performed over the radio on January 23, 1940. It is based on three folk tunes woven into a complicated pattern without, however, obscuring their dance-like quality and rustic flavor.

In 1952 Crawford returned to composition. In that year she wrote *Suite for Wind Quintet* and submitted it to a competition sponsored by the District of Columbia chapter of the National Association for American Composers and Conductors. It won first prize and was performed on December 2, 1952, by the National Woodwind Quintet in Washington. In three movements, the quintet combines elements of Crawford's earlier style—dissonance, contrapuntal texture, chromatic motifs instead of a melody, ostinati—and elements of her earlier compositions with later influences, especially her interest in folk music, evident in the quintet's strong rhythmic pulse.

This was Crawford's last complete work. In 1953 she became ill with what turned out to be a rapidly advancing cancer. On November 18, 1953, she was to appear at a children's folk festival in Washington, D.C., but had to cancel at the last minute; Michael and Peggy took her place. On that same day she died. For some years thereafter Crawford was remembered principally for her work in folk music. Her obituary in *Musical America* was typical: "folk singer, composer, leading collector of children's folk music."[26] But gradually her music began to be recognized for the milestone it was, and it surfaced in more and more concerts of "contemporary" music. *Piano Study with Mixed Accents* and the Andante for string orchestra found their way into New York Philharmonic concerts in 1974 and 1971, respectively; her *Suite for Piano and Woodwind Quintet* (1927–29) was played by members of the Boston Symphony at Tanglewood in 1976; and *Three Songs by Carl Sandburg* turned up again in New York in 1977. Gradually the musical world began to realize that Crawford had been among the best and most original of all American composers of the first half of the twentieth century. Yet when Charles Seeger died in 1979 at age ninety-two, the *New York Times* obituary mentioned his musical children but not Ruth Crawford.

One of the most important influences on American composers of this period was a French teacher of composition, Nadia Boulanger (1887–1979).[27] Of the women discussed in this book, the following studied with or were advised by her: composers Marion Bauer, Mary Howe, Louise Talma, Elinor Remick Warren, Margaret Bonds, Julia Perry, Evelyn LaRue Pittman, Peggy Glanville-Hicks, Thea Musgrave, and Joyce Mekeel, and conductors Lorna Cooke de Varon, Frances Steiner, and Catherine Comet.

Trained at the Paris Conservatory, where Gabriel Fauré was among her teachers, Boulanger began to teach privately in 1904 when she was only seventeen and five years later joined the Conservatory faculty. In 1913 her best-loved pupil, her younger sister Lili, became the first woman to win the Grand Prix de Rome for her cantata *Faust et Hélène,* and Boulanger decided to devote herself entirely to teaching and give up composition, for which she believed she had little talent compared to her sister's. Her sister died of tuberculosis five years later, and after Lili's death Nadia's pupils became, in effect, her family.

In 1920 Boulanger became a professor at the École Normale de Musique, teaching harmony, counterpoint, accompaniment, the history of music, and, after Paul Dukas died in 1935, composition. She remained there until 1939. But her principal influence over American composers was exerted at a summer school of music founded in 1921 at Fontainebleau near Paris, the American Conservatory, whose director she became in 1949. Three young Americans—Aaron Copland, Melville Smith, and Virgil Thomson—more or less independently found their way to her, and they were followed before long by Elliott Carter, Theodore Charles, Herbert Elwell, Roy Harris, Douglas Moore, Walter Piston, and Roger Sessions.[27] As Copland later said, "No one to my knowledge had ever before thought of studying composition with a woman. . . . Everyone knows that the world has never produced a first-rate woman composer; so it follows that no woman could possibly hope to teach composition."[28] Copland wrote his Symphony for organ and orchestra for Boulanger, and she was soloist in its premiere in New York with the Boston Symphony Orchestra under Walter Damrosch on January 11, 1925.

Highly knowledgeable about many kinds of music, both ancient and modern, Boulanger had a gift for teaching the techniques essential to composition —harmony, counterpoint, ear training—and, whatever her own prejudices, for allowing her pupils to develop their own individual styles. Looking back a half-century, Virgil Thomson said she "put me at ease in front of music paper. She taught me that writing music was a normal thing to do, like writing a letter. You simply put down what you mean. Her gift as a teacher was to force you to mean what you had said."[29]

Boulanger herself was by temperament, if not by training, a neoclassicist, and her favorite contemporary composer for many years was Igor Stravinsky. The detachment, the clarity, the strict forms of baroque and classical music, combined with the tonal and harmonic freedom to which the impressionists first pointed the way, had enormous appeal for her. Or, as one writer put it:

> Historically Nadia Boulanger came at a very opportune moment. French music had reacted against Romanticism, and was therefore placed in a very advantageous position to welcome the new developments of the twentieth century . . . In her own mind she always sought after a distillation of expression that was more in sympathy with classicism than romanticism. She was on the side of those who looked outwards, rather than in.[30]

For Boulanger the touchstone of great music was that it satisfy the mental faculties but also touch the heart. For her, Stravinsky's music, at least until 1950 or so, met those requirements. For intellectual understanding she turned to old music, and in the mid-1930s she became one of the first to teach by performing and analyzing the music, especially the choral masterpieces, of Bach and Monteverdi, Schütz and Carissimi, Palestrina, Taverner, Tallis, and Binchois. A keyboard artist of concert caliber, she continued to perform throughout the 1930s and also took up a new career, conducting. She said it was the need of students studying Bach by singing his cantatas that had turned her to conducting. In 1936 and 1937 she conducted the Royal Philharmonic Orchestra of London in Gabriel Fauré's Requiem; she was their first woman conductor. She also was the first woman to conduct the Boston Symphony, the Philadelphia Orchestra, and the New York Philharmonic, and she came to Washington, D.C., in 1938 to conduct the premiere of Stravinsky's *Dumbarton Oaks Concerto.*

Though pupils flocked to Boulanger from all over the world, she never attained the stature in France that she had elsewhere. Her closest ties were with America, which in the 1920s and 1930s she believed was about to embark on a golden age of music such as Russia had seen in the 1850s. She spent World War II in America, living mostly in the Boston area but giving concerts and recitals in many places. She returned to Paris after the war and continued to teach well into her nineties. Virgil Thomson called her "a one-man graduate school for musical Americans," one so powerful that "legend credits every United States town with two things—a five-and-dime and a Boulanger pupil."[31]

One of Boulanger's star pupils at the American Conservatory, and the only American she ever permitted to teach there, was Louise Talma, whose compositions embody much of Boulanger's teaching. Talma became the first woman to receive a Guggenheim Fellowship in composition twice, in 1946 and 1947; the first woman to be awarded the Sibelius Medal for composition, in 1963; and the first woman composer to be elected to the National Institute of Arts and Letters, in 1974. She also became the outstanding American woman neoclassical composer, at least for the first four decades of her career.

Louise Juliette Talma was born of American parents on October 31, 1906, in Arcachon, France.[32] Her father, a pianist, died not long after her birth. Her mother, Alma Cecile Garrigue, was an opera singer but gave up her own career to direct her daughter's musical education, teaching her solfège and piano. For her formal education she brought the child to New York, where she attended high school and then studied at the Institute of Musical Art (later the Juilliard School) with theoreticians George Wedge and Percy Goetschius and the composer Howard Brockway. Money was scarce, but Talma was able to go to Europe in 1926 and spend the summer at the American Conservatory at Fontainebleau. She returned there every summer for the next fourteen years. Originally intending to become a pianist, Talma was convinced by Nadia Boulanger that she could be an outstanding composer. Winters she taught at the Manhattan School of Music and then at Hunter College, where she began teaching in 1928 and celebrated her fiftieth anniversary in 1978—after reaching mandatory retirement age she simply stayed on without pay.

Talma's earliest compositions were songs and piano pieces. In 1929–30 she wrote *Three Madrigals* and *La Belle Dame sans merçi,* commissioned by Gerald Reynolds for the Women's University Glee Club. About this time, however, her mother became paralyzed, and Talma had to concern herself with earning enough to support them both. To keep her job at Hunter, she needed to obtain a degree, which at first had not been required; so Talma, who had attended night school for years, completed her degree requirements and by 1933 received a bachelor of music degree from New York University and a master of music degree from Columbia University. Even so she was not made a full professor at Hunter until 1952.

Consequently, the 1930s were a less productive period, although Talma did produce a number of songs, the song cycle *Five Sonnets from the Portuguese,* and *In Principio Erat Verbum* for chorus and organ. In 1943 her mother died and Talma felt freer to return to creative work, but for a time, at least, she found herself blocked. That summer she went to the MacDowell Colony and completed her Piano Sonata no. 1, which she performed in New York for the League of Composers on January 21, 1945. The following year she completed *Terre de France,* a song cycle for soprano and piano that sets five poems by French poets paying homage to France. These songs are still tonal and even reminiscent of impressionism. They were sung over radio station WBAF in New York, with the composer at the piano, in January 1946, and again in September at the Yaddo Festival.

In 1944 Talma wrote her first big orchestral work, *Toccata for Orchestra,* which was premiered by the Baltimore Symphony under Reginald Stewart on December 20, 1945. Olin Downes said, "It reminds me more of one of the baroque eighteenth century toccatas in the variety and style presented."[33] *Toccata for Orchestra,* which won the Juilliard Publication Award in 1946, opens with a brilliant trumpet fanfare, continued by the strings and woodwinds. The theme is then stated by violins and violas; it is cast in one of the dominating rhythms of the work, a Latin figure in 4/4 time with two dotted quarter notes plus one quarter note. It is followed by a very soft but rhythmically spirited section, and then a presto section with legato triplets. About halfway through the twelve-minute work a new theme is presented, first by the oboe, then by strings and brass. The texture here is more chordal and denser, and the rhythm less syncopated. This section is followed by a return to the brilliant mood of the beginning, with its syncopated rhythm, but slower and less frantic, until the majestic end.

An excellent pianist and organist, Talma became a fellow of the American Guild of Organists, having decided to study organ in order to play Bach's organ works as they were intended to be played. She continued to write keyboard compositions as well as songs and chamber music. These were, after all, the principal kinds of composition produced during the baroque period, whose forms—toccata, fugue, canon, cantata—attracted the twentieth-century neo-classicists. Her *Alleluia in the Form of a Toccata* (1944), written about the same time as *Toccata for Orchestra,* features jazz rhythms and a percussive style reminiscent of Stravinsky's music. A second piano sonata, which was begun about the same time but not completed until 1955, still shows the dry, spare style and transparent texture of much of her work but incorporates some serial elements.

In the 1950s Talma became interested in twelve-tone music, a development that her longtime teacher, Nadia Boulanger, regarded as "a musical heresy."[34] Boulanger believed that carried to its logical conclusion serialism, particularly that of the postwar composers such as Anton Webern, would dehumanize music. Talma nevertheless found their work interesting. Arthur Berger, also a former Boulanger pupil, thought it was Irving Fine's espousal of the twelve-tone idiom in his String Quartet of 1952 that prompted Talma to adopt it, but rather than adopting the style completely she absorbed the technique of row-writing into her customary manner.[35] This second period of her output has been called "serial neotonal."

Talma's *Six Etudes* for piano (1953–54), each quite short, employ a tone row for demonstrating a variety of pianistic techniques. "Allegro—for contrasts," no. 1, sets brilliant virtuoso passages against quiet, simple ones; "Prestissimo—for staccato," no. 2, has an interesting syncopated rhythm; "Allegro—for sostenuto pedal," no. 3, uses fast passages above a sustained pedal; "Allegro—for wide skips," no. 4, uses huge horizontal skips up and down the length, of the keyboard; "Allegro grazioso—for crossed hands," no. 5, is a quiet, flowing piece; and "Molto adagio—for increase of notes per beat," no. 6, begins with one note per beat, then two per beat, and so on, progressing to chords per beat, and then slows back to one note per beat. Nearly a quarter of a century later, in 1978, Talma wrote a similiar work, *Textures,* in which each of five interconnected sections concentrates on a different pianistic texture.

In 1955 Talma was awarded a Senior Fulbright Research Grant and went to Rome for ten months to work on what became one of her most discussed works, *The Alcestiad,* an opera with a libretto by Thornton Wilder. She later recalled that it was a chance hearing of a piano work of hers that prompted Wilder to propose they do an opera together. "You can imagine how I felt," she said, "Since so many composers had been trying to get him to collaborate on an opera."[36] The three-act opera took somewhat longer to complete than her stay in Rome and received its premiere in German translation on March 1, 1962, at Frankfurt-am-Main, Germany. It received eight performances and was the first work by an American woman to be produced by a major European opera house. Despite the warm reception, it was not performed again, and to Talma's particular regret, it was never done in the original English.

In 1959 the Koussevitsky Music Foundation awarded Talma a commission to write a chamber work, and the result was *All the Days of My Life,* a cantata for tenor, clarinet, cello, piano, and percussion, completed in 1965. Both this and a number of Talma's subsequent important works—*The Tolling Bell* for baritone and orchestra (1969), *Summer Sounds* for clarinet and string quartet (1973), and *Voices of Peace* for chorus and strings (1973)—are twelve-tone in construction. *The Tolling Bell* is a triptych dedicated to the MacDowell Colony, where Talma frequently worked in the summer from 1943 on, though she did return to Fontainebleau during the summers of 1949, 1951, and 1961. Like some of her other vocal works, it is based on texts from several authors, in this case the soliloquy Shakespeare gives to Hamlet, the "Ah, Faustus" speech from Marlowe's *Doctor Faustus,* and a sonnet by John Donne. The work falls into three sections, the first and third meditative and the middle one more dramatic. Its framework is a twelve-tone row (G-D-E-B-Bb-Db-Eb-C-Gb-F-Ab-A), but it is used in a fairly free manner. At the same time, the texture is characteristically spare and transparent. There is little doubling of parts, that is, each instrument plays its own line. At least one writer, the composer Elaine Barkin, finds in it a number of techniques typical of American neoclassicism, especially in the style of Arthur Berger.[37]

Summer Sounds is also loosely serial. Its four movements are named "Dawn," "Morning," "Noon," and "Night," a departure from the neoclassic idea that only vocal music should have specific extramusical associations. This work reminds one listener of Janáček in its use of animal and bird sounds as material, especially in the clarinet-dominated "Noon,"[38] whereas for another critic it recalls the "night music" of Mahler and Bartók.[39]

Though honors and prizes were not slow in coming to Talma, performances were infrequent. When she was elected to the National Institute of Arts and Letters in 1974, she was given a citation that states in part: "Many of her admirers, who had grown accustomed to seeing or hearing her referred to as one of our foremost women composers, have noticed with pleasure in recent years that she is being referred to more and more often without any qualification at all as one of our foremost composers." How much of that was due to a growing appreciation of her work and how much to society's changing views of women is anyone's guess. Though Talma herself, like so many others, rejected being identified as a "woman composer," she clearly benefited from the wave of concerts of "women's music" of the late 1970s. Her String Quartet, for example, was given its first performance in twenty-three years when the Aviva Players, a group devoted to promoting women performers and composers, included it in a program in New York.[40] One reviewer said the piece showed its age but was eminently respectable in craftsmanship, and as a major effort by a well-known musician and teacher it should have been performed a couple of decades earlier, when it might have sounded fresher and more adventurous.[41] Neoclassicism may have been out of fashion just then, but that does not negate the value of a well-crafted, expressive composition.

In the final decades of her life Talma abandoned serialism entirely for what has been called a neotonal style. In this music certain pitches serve as the tone centers of a composition by being asserted and reasserted throughout. During these years she wrote fewer works for solo piano but numerous chamber pieces, such as *Ambient Air* (1983) for flute, violin, cello, and piano, and *Seven Episodes* (1987) for flute, violin, and piano; numerous vocal pieces, such as *Thirteen Ways of Looking at a Blackbird* and *The Lengthening Shadows* (1993); and numerous sacred choral pieces. She died in 1996.

The twelve-tone school exerted a more direct influence on Dika Newlin than on Talma. Newlin studied with Arnold Schoenberg for three years, from 1938 to 1941, and for about twenty-five years all her compositions were constructed on a twelve-tone row.

Dika Newlin was born in 1923 in Portland, Oregon, but grew up in East Lansing, Michigan, where her father, a professor of English, taught at Michigan State College.[42] Her parents were not musicians, but her grandmother, Eva Hummer Hull, was a piano teacher, organist, and pianist, and her uncle, Alexander Hull, a composer. Dika began piano lessons at the age of six with Arthur Farwell, who encouraged her early interest in composing. At the age of eight she wrote *Cradle Song* that was performed by the Cincinnati Symphony in 1935, and later also by other orchestras, including the Los Angeles Philharmonic and the NBC Symphony. Academically precocious as well, she was a sophomore at Michigan State at the age of thirteen. By then she had heard of Arnold Schoenberg, who had fled Nazi Germany for America, and in her junior year she enrolled for study at the University of California at Los Angeles, where he was teaching. In the summer of 1939 she returned to complete her bachelor's degree at Michigan State and then went back to Los Angeles for two more years and a master's degree. By that time she was a dedicated Schoenberg disciple.

In 1941 Newlin went to Columbia University, which in 1945 granted her its first doctor of philosophy degree in musicology. Her dissertation on Bruckner, Mahler, and Schoenberg was published in 1947 and became a standard reference work on these composers; a revised edition appeared in 1978. While in New York she also studied composition with Roger Sessions and piano with Artur Schnabel. After receiving her doctorate, she taught for six years, at Western Maryland College and then at Syracuse University. She still kept in touch with Schoenberg and returned to California to work with him during the summers of 1949 and 1950. About this time she decided to write his biography and applied for a Fulbright grant to do research on his early years in Vienna. Schoenberg himself was never to know that her application was approved, for he died in the summer of 1951.

Newlin spent 1951–52 in Europe, mostly in Austria doing research, but also performing in Vienna and Paris, lecturing on American music in several Austrian cities, and making some recordings with violist Michael Mann. She also performed the piano part of her Piano Trio, op. 2, in Salzburg at the 1952 Festival of the International Society for Contemporary Music. Although Newlin has been called "an American composer who speaks Viennese,"[43] this was her only prolonged stay in Austria.

Upon returning to America in 1952, she became head of the newly formed department of music at Drew University in New Jersey, a post she held until 1965. She then taught at North Texas State University for eight years, returning east in 1973 to direct the electronic music laboratory at Montclair State College in New Jersey. In 1976 she resigned and devoted herself fully to writing and composition for the next two years. In 1978 she accepted an invitation to develop a new doctoral program in music at Virginia Commonwealth University in Richmond.

An excellent pianist, Newlin wrote many of her most important works for that instrument, beginning with her 1947 *Sinfonia,* for piano, which is not a twelve-tone work but uses many unusual tone colors. Her 1948 Piano Trio is fully twelve-tone, based on the row G-F-A-B-G♯-D-C♯-F♯-E-C-B♭-E♭. She wrote it at least partly because none of the major twelve-tone composers— Schoenberg, Berg, or Webern—had written a piano trio. It follows a structure favored by Schoenberg, which Newlin called the "portmanteau" form, that is, with all movements built into one. An introduction is followed by a first movement with three principal ideas: Moderato grazioso, a slow, graceful waltz; Poco piú lento, a more passionately lyrical theme; and Con brio alla marcia, a lively martial theme. The second movement, a scherzo, has two trios, in which the ideas of the first movement are transformed and developed further, ending with a very slow section. The final movement combines the fast and slow themes and continues to rework this material, ending with a chord that contains all twelve tones of the row.

From the same year as the Piano Trio dates Newlin's best-known orchestral work, *Chamber Symphony* for twelve solo instruments, which was dedicated to Schoenberg. It was first performed in 1949 in Darmstadt, Germany, and did not get its American premiere until 1960. Her other important keyboard works are *Variations on a Theme from "The Magic Flute"* (1956) for piano, two variations on the March of the Priests from Act 2 that portray the dark–light contrast so important in Mozart's opera; *Sonata da Chiesa* for organ (1956), a chorale prelude on "O Mensch bewein deine Sünde gross," flanked by a praeambulum in French overture rhythm and a fugue; and *Fantasy on a Row* (1957), which musicologist Konrad Wolff regards as most typical of her piano style in that "traditional elements of music are completely fused with the present-day melodic and harmonic language." Wolff continues, "To me, this is the most Schoenbergian quality of Dika Newlin's work, setting her apart from almost all other American twelve-tone composers."[44] In this piece the first six tones of the tone row quote the opening viola recitative of Mahler's Symphony no. 10, identical with respect to both pitch and rhythm, whereas the remaining six tones emphasize the dissonant interval of the fourth plus the octave. The Postlude, which is to be played very slowly and without expressive dynamics, is based on the chorale "Ach Gott, vom Himmel sieh darein" used by Bach in his cantata BWV 2.

About 1970 Newlin became attracted to some of the newer developments in music and began to use both taped and computer-generated sounds in her own compositions. Her first important work of this kind was *Big Swamp* (1972), which includes both taped computer-generated sounds and live performance on man-made bird and animal calls. Her *Atone* (1977), for "diverse voices and instruments," uses aleatory elements, that is, some choices are left up to the performers. Newlin's advice to young composers is, among other things, "Be aware of and enter into contemporary forms of expression, such as multimedia, musical theater, group-improvised composition, electronic music, environmental music. Be aware that today *everything* one learns and does can be part of a musical composition."[45] In the late 1970s she herself was working on group-improvised composition and verbal scores, as well as continuing her work in musicology; an analysis of Schoenberg's music, an anthology of writings about film music, and a study of Schnabel's teachings were among her current projects. Her book, *Schoenberg Remembered: Diaries and Recollections, 1938–1976,* was published in 1980. In the 1990s Newlin turned to both composing and performing rock and other kinds of popular music, and also film music.

Not all the European idioms that persisted into the twentieth century were new. Many composers, in both Europe and America, clung to nineteenth-century romanticism, writing highly expressive, often emotional, largely tonal music. Among these "neoromanticists" are such Americans as Howard Hanson, Samuel Barber, Gian Carlo Menotti, and a very successful woman composer, Elinor Remick Warren, best known for her orchestral and choral works.

Warren was born on February 23, 1900, in Los Angeles, California, which remained her lifelong home. [46] At the age of five she was picking out pieces on the piano, and her mother, an excellent amateur musician, wrote some of them down. Soon after her fifth birthday she began piano lessons with Kathryn Cocke, who remained her teacher throughout childhood. From her she also learned harmony, general musicianship, and good working habits; she later said that her debt to her old teacher was enormous, and many years later, when she went to study with Nadia Boulanger, Boulanger was amazed to hear about Warren's excellent early training.

Warren's first songs were published when she was still a sophomore in high school. She graduated, studied for a year at Mills College, and then went to New York "with a sheaf of songs" that were immediately accepted for publication. She also continued her piano studies. Her accompaniment teacher, Frank La Forge, introduced her to many singers, some of whom performed her songs. Later she toured with some of these same singers as accompanist and solo pianist. Among them were Lucrezia Bori, Florence Easton, Lawrence Tibbett, and Richard Crooks, all of the Metropolitan Opera, as well as Rose Bampton, Nelson Eddy, Kirsten Flagstad, Dorothy Kirsten, and Eileen Farrell. Warren also played numerous concerts and recitals of her own, and was soloist with several symphony orchestras. One of her first large works, *The Harp Weaver,* for women's chorus and orchestra, was performed in New York in 1936 by the New York Women's Symphony under Antonia Brico.

In 1936 Warren married Z. Wayne Griffin, a Los Angeles businessman who warmly encouraged her in her career. She continued to perform after marriage, even after two sons and a daughter had been born, but her interest in composition, always considerable, began to supersede her interest in the piano; she later said, "I had continued composing right up until I went to the hospital, with all three children." She gradually gave up touring and began to write for instruments, at first orchestrating some of her many songs, and then branching out into compositions for orchestra alone and for orchestra with chorus. Though she had earlier studied both the larger forms and orchestration, she spent a number of years continuing these studies on her own. Finally, in 1959, she decided to go to Paris to study with Nadia Boulanger, spending an intensive three months there in daily lessons. Warren later said that Boulanger had enlarged her scope considerably, especially in the matter of orchestration, which led her to revise some of her earlier works.

Soon after Warren's return from France, the well-known Chicago baritone and music patron Louis Sudler commissioned a cantata, which became *Abram in Egypt.* Set for baritone solo, chorus, and orchestra, with a text based on Genesis and the recently discovered Dead Sea Scrolls, it received its first complete performance at the Los Angeles International Music Festival on June 7, 1961, along with works by Igor Stravinsky, Walter Piston, and Roy Harris. An earlier orchestral work of Warren's is *Suite for Orchestra,* first performed in 1955 by the Los Angeles Philharmonic. Both works are neoromantic in style. The suite was inspired by the vast mountain panorama seen from the composer's ranch, high in the Sierra Nevada: "Although my Suite has no story or program behind it, the overtones of this pageantry of the sky and the long shadows of the towering mountains are doubtless in the fabric of the work."[47] *The Crystal Lake,* a shorter work from 1958 similarly inspired by the High Sierras landscape, was performed by the New York Philharmonic in 1974 as one of a half-dozen works by women played between 1965 and 1975; the Detroit Symphony also performed it in 1974.[48]

A Requiem Mass was commissioned by Roger Wagner for his chorale and was first performed by that group in Los Angeles in 1966. Set for mixed chorus, mezzo-soprano and baritone solos, and orchestra, with a text partly in Latin and partly in English, it was warmly received: "Choral writing is superbly idiomatic, solos beautifully integrated, the orchestration equally effective and colorful," said Martin Bernheimer of the *Los Angeles Times. Symphony in One Movement* was commissioned by Stanford University and received its premiere performance there in 1971. *Singing Earth,* for high voice and orchestra, a setting of a Carl Sandburg poem, was revised in 1977–78. Also in 1977 came the first performance of another setting of a Sandburg poem, *Good Morning, America!* for narrator, chorus, and orchestra, by the Honolulu Symphony with Efrem Zimbalist Jr. as narrator. It had been commissioned by Occidental College.

Warren won many honors. She was awarded an honorary doctor of music degree by Occidental College and received first prizes in numerous biennial contests of the National League of American Pen Women from 1964 on. In all, more than 200 of her works were published, for chorus and orchestra, orchestra, voice, piano, and chamber ensemble. At the age of eighty-seven she accompanied Marie Gibson in a new recording of twenty-six of her art songs. Warren died in 1991.

Flutist Katherine Hoover is another American who composed in traditional European forms—quartet, quintet, trio, divertimento, tone poem, sinfonia, concerto—but treated the music in novel ways. Born in 1937 and educated at the Eastman School of Music, she majored in theory and flute.[49] "I was writing little bits and pieces and taking composition," she later said, "but nobody looked at my work. As the only female taking theory and composition classes, I wasn't worth the trouble."[50] Her tone poem *Eleni: A Greek Tragedy* (1987) incorporates folk melodies with contemporary harmonies. Her *Quintet da Pacem* (1989) for piano and strings is lyrical, and her Clarinet Concerto (1987), written for jazz clarinetist Eddie Daniels, exploits the instrument's virtuoso qualities. Long on the faculty of the Manhattan School of Music, Hoover also became active as a conductor. The commissioning, rehearsing, and premiere of her *Dances and Variations* (1996) at the Kennedy Center became the subject of a prize-winning documentary film entitled *New Music.* Concerning women composers, Hoover said, "Critics have written that it's absolutely true . . . there are no masterpieces by women. That was said to be the case in the visual arts also, but this myth was exploded when they started bringing back pictures from the past."[51]

Impressionism, neoclassicism, serialism, and neoromanticism, the principal European styles of composition of the first half of the twentieth century, engaged American women composers just as they did men. However, a return to tonality and lyricism did not always signify a return to older styles, as evidenced in the music of Ellen Taaffe Zwilich and Jennifer Higdon. At the same time, some composers continued to use or reflect intrinsically American idioms—folk music of the South and West, including slave songs, spirituals, square dance music, jazz, and even the music of Broadway.

7

GRASS ROOTS—COMPOSERS
IN AMERICAN IDIOMS

M USICAL NATIONALISM, conventionally associated with the second half of the nineteenth century, has in truth emerged in many periods. Musical composition, like any other art, represents the sum of the creator's experience. With some artists the absorption of national or folk elements is more profound than other influences, and their work inevitably reflects these elements, either by design or unconsciously.

In music such elements surface in many ways—in melodies, in rhythms, in characteristic harmonies. Composers may literally quote all or part of folk songs, or they may invent tunes that closely resemble the spirit and idioms of folk songs. The overall composition, moreover, need not be in any particular style. Since nationalism was most prominent in nineteenth-century Europe, it has come to be associated with the dominant musical style of that time, romanticism, but this need not be so. Both Charles Ives and Aaron Copland incorporated American folk idioms in many of their works, which otherwise show many stylistic differences.

Folk music, both song and dance, is an oral tradition passed on by imitation from generation to generation. In order to make formal use of folk music, it must be generally known and available. In Europe the political nationalist movement spurred the collection, writing down, and arrangement of folk music, and in America much the same process took place. One of the earliest publications of music by an American woman was, as it happened, just such a compendium, in this case a collection of camp-meeting hymns made by Peggy Dow, wife of a Methodist preacher, Lorenzo Dow. It was published in Philadelphia in 1816.[1] In this province, today generally called "ethnomusicology," many American women were active, collecting and preserving camp-meeting hymns and spirituals, slave songs and Creole ballads, songs of the Appalachians and the Southwest, and American Indian music. The very first collection of slave songs published in book form, *Slave Songs of the United States* (1867), was the work of two men and one woman, William Allen, Charles Ware, and Lucy McKim Garrison. A pianist, Garrison (1842–1877) wrote down the slave songs she had heard in the South and published two of them in *Dwight's Journal of Music* in 1862, "Roll, Jordan, Roll" and "Poor Rosy."[2]

Without recording equipment, transcribing folk music was a very tricky business. Folk songs often, if not generally, differ from one performance to the next; indeed, in some cases such performance practice is a basic feature of the music. Even in 1862 Garrison was aware of this problem:

> It is difficult to express the entire character of these negro ballads by mere musical notes and signs. The odd turns made in the throat, and the curious rhythmic effect produced by single voices chiming in at different irregular intervals, seem almost as impossible to place on the score as the singing of birds or the tones of an Aeolian Harp.[3]

Inevitably the ethnomusicologist's own musical background—at that time usually conventional European music—influenced his or her transcriptions.

Despite these difficulties, some outstanding work was done by three women who studied American Indian music.[4] Alice Cunningham Fletcher (1838–1923) did the first important work, beginning about 1882. A fellow at Harvard University's Peabody Museum of American Archaeology and Ethnology, she wrote a treatise on the songs of the Omaha Indians and articles on the music of the Sioux and Pawnee Indians; her book, *Indian Story and Song from North America* (1900), was one of the earliest authoritative works on this subject.

The second woman, Natalie Curtis Burlin (1875–1921), who had studied piano and theory in Germany and France, worked among the Indians of the Southwest, particularly the Hopi and Zuni, beginning about 1900. She published her findings in 1907 in *The Indian's Book,* which contained more than 200 songs of eighteen tribes. Later she also collected and recorded songs of blacks in the South for the Hampton Institute, published in four volumes in 1918–19.

Finally, Frances Densmore (1867–1957), who had studied piano with Leopold Godowsky and counterpoint with John Knowles Paine, became interested in Indian music at the 1893 World's Columbian Exposition in Chicago, where Alice Fletcher gave a talk on the subject.[5] From 1907 on Densmore worked for the Bureau of American Ethnology of the Smithsonian Institution. She investigated the music of many tribes, recording and transcribing songs, and is said to have made the most comprehensive survey and objective analysis of their music.

Many other women also contributed to recording American musical traditions. Josephine McGill, Ethel Park Richardson, Dorothy Scarborough, and Susannah Westmore recorded and notated the songs of southern Appalachia. Emily Hollowell, Nina Monroe, Maude Cuney Hare, and Mildred Hill recorded and transcribed black slave songs, spirituals, and Creole ballads.

Allena Luce and Elizabeth Waldo collected the songs of the Southwest.[6] Camille Nickerson was particularly interested in the Creole folksongs of her native Louisiana. A professor at Howard University from 1926 to 1962, she collected these songs, arranged them for the concert platform, and published many of them. From the 1930s to 1950s she toured periodically in the United States and France as the Louisiana Lady, singing Creole songs and wearing Creole dress. Harriet Gibbs Marshall established the Center for Negro Music, which was to be a repository for both folk music and published works of black composers.[7]

All these women were *transcribing* the music of an oral tradition. They were not using elements of that tradition in their own compositions, as Ruth Crawford did in *Rissolty, Rossolty* or Mary Howe in *Chain Gang Song.* The remainder of this chapter concerns women composers who did just that.

A characteristically American musical idiom is that of the rural West and Southwest, the songs of cowboys and the dances of hoedowns, the tradition of ranch life and rodeos, which often includes Spanish-American elements as well. Unique to the United States, this idiom is clearly evident in much of the music of two natives of Texas, Julia Smith and Radie Britain.

Julia Frances Smith was born on January 25, 1911, in Denton, Texas, one of seven children.[8] She was educated at North Texas State University and the Juilliard School in New York, where she studied piano, composition with Rubin Goldmark and Frederick Jacobi, and orchestration with Bernard Wagenaar, graduating in 1939. She also attended New York University, where Marion Bauer was among her teachers, and where she earned her master's and doctorate. Although Goldmark, her composition teacher, had also taught Aaron Copland, Smith herself never heard Copland's music until after Goldmark's death. In 1933 she attended the New York premiere of Copland's ballet, *Billy the Kid,* and was much taken with its use of American materials. She wrote her doctoral dissertation on Copland; in book form, it became one of the standard reference works on him.

Smith was a fine pianist, and she became pianist for the Orchestrette Classique, an all-women's ensemble whose conductor, Frederique Petrides, introduced her to her future husband. Smith married Oscar A. Vielehr, an engineer and inventor, in 1938. He proved to be a great help to her, copying her music at times and always encouraging her in both performance and composition.[9] Smith continued to perform, both with orchestras and in recital, for the next thirty years or so. In 1957, believing that Copland's works for piano were still neglected, she gave an all-Copland piano recital in New York's Town Hall, and during the next ten years she performed these works in colleges and universities all over the United States.

Smith's first important composition, *American Dance Suite* for orchestra, based on four American folk tunes, was premiered by the Orchestrette Classique at Aeolian (later Town) Hall, New York, on February 10, 1936. It was later revised and was reworked into a version for two pianos. The following year the Orchestrette performed the premiere of Smith's *Episodic Suite,* originally written in 1935 for piano but revised in 1936–37 for orchestra. Tuneful and discreetly dissonant, it shows touches of the humor that is characteristic in the best of Smith's compositions; in 1940 Smith herself conducted it with the Dallas Symphony Orchestra.[10] In 1941 the Orchestrette gave still another premiere, this time of *Hellenic Suite,* dedicated to Petrides. Based on Greek folk melodies, this three-movement suite has not been performed as much as her works based on American materials.

During this same period, Smith composed the first of her six operas, the two-act *Cynthia Parker.* Based on the life of a woman in early Texas history, it was produced in 1939 in Denton, Texas, with Metropolitan Opera soprano Leonora Corona in the title role. Another work of distinctly American heritage is *Liza Jane,* written in 1939–40 when CBS commissioned her to produce a short orchestral work based on American folk themes; it has been widely performed in both the United States and Europe.

From 1940 to 1942 Smith taught theory and counterpoint at Juilliard, and from 1944 to 1946 she taught at New Britain (Connecticut) State Teachers College. During this period, she also founded the department of music education at Hartt College of Music, in Hartford, Connecticut, where she taught from 1941 to 1946. Always interested in music education, Smith wrote many teaching pieces, a string method with Cecile Vashaw, and a number of works for band, including *Remember the Alamo!* (1964).

Smith's other important orchestral compositions include *Folkways Symphony* (1947–48), based on folk and cowboy songs, and Concerto for piano and orchestra (1938–39, revised 1970–71). The revised version was first given a complete performance by the Dallas Civic Symphony in 1976. The work's three movements and its themes reflect both folk and jazz idioms. The first movement, in sonata form, consists of an extended introduction, a first theme marked Alla marcia vivace (a lively march), and a second, more lyrical theme. The second movement, in three-part song form, begins with a sustained horn solo. The final movement, in free rondo-sonata form, brings the work to a playful, joyous conclusion.[11]

Smith wrote for smaller forces as well. Among them are her only twelve-tone piece, *Characteristic Suite* (1949) for piano, of which Virgil Thomson wrote, "Her music is jolly, and even in twelve-tone syntax, easy to take";[12] the piano trio *Cornwall* (1955); and the sprightly String Quartet (1962–64) with syncopated, dance-like rhythms, especially in the brilliant last movement, which call to mind the hoedowns and other celebrations of rural America. Notable among Smith's operas are *The Gooseherd and the Goblin* (1945–46), a one-act commissioned by and performed more than thirty times by the Hartt College of Music Opera Workshop; *The Shepherdess and the Chimneysweep,* a one-act Christmas opera performed many times since its premiere in 1968;

and *Daisy,* a two-act opera about the life of Juliette Gordon Low, founder of the Girl Scouts of America, which received its premiere in 1973 in Miami, Florida, and was given nineteen special bicentennial performances in 1976, as well as more performances in succeeding years.

In the late 1960s Smith, long active in a number of composers' organizations, compiled a *Directory of American Women Composers* for the National Federation of Music Clubs, which published it in 1970. It was the first book of its kind. "I really had to stop my own work entirely to do this," she later said, "but I felt that it was important that someone do it—at least make a start toward recognition of the really fine work (in some cases) of our women composers."[13] In November 1976 Smith helped organize an international program sponsored by the National Federation of Music Clubs and devoted to works by women, held at Columbia University; her Piano Concerto was among the compositions performed. Active to the end, in 1989 she was preparing for a trip to Fort Worth, Texas, for a performance of her one-act opera *Cockcrow* (1953) when she died.

The other composer whose music shows her Texas roots is Radie Britain. She was born on March 17, 1903, on a ranch near Amarillo, Texas.[14] She began her music studies at the age of seven at Clarendon College, in Texas, and graduated with high honors. She then went to the American Conservatory in Chicago, where she studied piano with Heniot Levy and organ with Von Dusen, receiving her bachelor of music degree in 1920. She returned to Texas to teach at Clarendon for about four years, and then went to Europe, where she studied composition with Albert Noelte in Germany for two years and made her debut as a composer in Munich, with four songs. She also spent one summer in Paris, where she studied organ with Marcel Dupré. After returning to America, she taught for some ten years at the Chicago Conservatory of Music. During these years, she married and had one daughter, Lerae, but the marriage did not last. In 1939 she moved to California and taught piano and composition in Hollywood for about ten years. Also in 1939, she married Edgard Simone, a sculptor who died in the 1950s. In 1959 she married Ted Morton, prominent in aviation; her *Cosmic Mist Symphony* of 1962 is dedicated to him.

Unlike many composers who confine themselves chiefly to small forms at the outset, Radie Britain early produced a number of works for full orchestra. Her first big success was her *Heroic Poem* for orchestra, in commemoration of Lindbergh's first transatlantic flight. It won both an International Hollywood Bowl Prize in 1930 and in 1945 the first Juilliard Publication Award ever given to a woman composer. Even earlier, in 1928, Britain's *Symphonic Intermezzo* had been performed by the Chicago Woman's Symphony under Ethel Leginska. Other early orchestral works include two composed at the MacDowell Colony in 1935—*Light,* dedicated to Thomas Edison, which won a first prize from the Boston Women's Symphony and was performed by the Chicago Woman's Symphony, and *Southern Symphony,* a larger work in four movements. Her string quartet from the same year, *Prison Lament,* was performed at the White House in 1936 at the special request of First Lady Eleanor Roosevelt.

More than fifty of Britain's works received international or national awards, and she herself was awarded the honorary degree of doctor of music from the Musical Arts Conservatory of Amarillo. Though she also wrote many chamber works, ballets, operas, pieces for piano, two pianos, organ, harp, violin, choral works, and songs, it is for her orchestral compositions that Britain became best known. Many of her works celebrate her native Texas, the cattle country, and the southwestern desert, as can be seen from descriptive titles such as *Ontonagon Sketches* (1939), *Drouth* (1939), *Red Clay* (1946), the piano trio *Cactus Rhapsody* (1953), and *Cowboy Rhapsody* (1956). Some of the Spanish influence important in the Southwest emerges in works such as *Rhumbando* (1975) for wind ensemble. Her large-scale orchestral work, *Cosmic Mist Symphony,* won the first national award of the National League of American Pen Women in 1964 and was performed by the Houston Symphony Orchestra under A. Clyde Roller. Her *Pyramids of Giza* (1973) for orchestra was first performed in New York in 1976. Another late work, *Musical Portrait of Thomas Jefferson,* for string quartet, was premiered in Sacramento in 1978 and received a standing ovation. In the same year her *Fantasie* for oboe and piano won an award from the Texas Composers Guild. Her other late works include *Ode to NASA* (1981) for brass quintet and *Anwar Sadat (In Memory)* (1982). Britain died in 1994, and her music is collected at the University of Southern California School of Music in Los Angeles.

A composer whose works sometimes show Native American influences is Ruth Lomon. Born in Canada in 1930, she moved to the United States about 1951. A pianist and teacher as well as composer, Lomon began going to Los Alamos, New Mexico, in the late 1960s, and became increasingly interested in the Southwest and its native traditions. The first of her pieces to reflect this was *Dust Devils* (1977) for harp, inspired by the tumbleweed. There followed *Celebrations* (1978), for two harps, and *Five Ceremonial Masks* (1980) for solo piano, both reflecting her reaction to Navajo ceremonies. *Imprints* (1987), a concerto for piano and four percussion instruments, was influenced by the Peyote ceremony, and her second string quartet, *The Butterfly Effect* (1989), quotes outright Geronimo's personal song. Later works include Requiem, a setting of the Mass that incorporates poems on the death of her sister, and an oratorio in commemoration of the Holocaust, in progress at the time of this writing.

Another rich American musical tradition is that of the South, particularly, although not exclusively, that of southern blacks. Slave songs, spirituals, gospel hymns, and minstrelsy not only gave rise to the popular genres of blues, jazz, and modern soul and gospel music, but were absorbed by and reflected in a large body of music produced by serious composers. According to Frederick Douglass, on many plantations slaves were expected to sing as well as to work;

for teamsters and field-workers it was a means of letting the overseer know where they were and that they were moving along with their work. These work songs, often plaintive even though wild or rapturous in character, shared certain fundamental musical traits: a steady, usually 4/4 beat; considerable syncopation; four-bar phrases; simple basic harmonies; a great deal of riffing repetition; and free improvisation by the singers.[15]

Most attractive to early collectors of southern folk music was black religious music, today lumped together under the catchall term "spirituals."[16] The most common structure for spirituals was a call-and-response form, in which solo verses, sung by a leader, alternated with the refrain, sung by a group. The leader began the words of each verse, often improvising, and the others struck in with the refrain or occasionally joined the soloist when the words were familiar. A genuine spiritual was an unceasing variation around a theme; it changed with each performance as the leader's words were elaborated on by the chorus at different points in time, singly and together. There was no singing in parts as with conventional hymns or chorales; rather, the harmony was often jagged and dissonant, with the various parts breaking in anywhere. Chants and hums also were used to reinforce the verse at various points.[17]

Another feature of the southern folk tradition was the minstrel show. Originally an entertainment put on by slaves for their owners, in time it was imitated by white songwriters and entertainers who regarded the black as a figure of fun. By the 1820s white men were blacking their faces with burnt cork and mimicking black songs and dances and telling jokes based on slave life. The first organized full-length minstrel show was produced in 1843 in New York by Daniel Decatur Emmett and his troupe of Virginia Minstrels, which soon had many imitators. To obtain material, white minstrels visited plantations, listened to the songs of blacks working in the fields, on steamboats and docks, and in tobacco factories. Combining this kind of music with the sentimental parlor ballads in vogue at this time produced a new musical form, the minstrel song, whose greatest exponent was Stephen Foster (1826–1864).[18] His "Old Black Joe," "Swanee River," "Camptown Races," "My Old Kentucky Home," "Old Folks at Home," and other songs became immensely popular among blacks as well as whites and, in time, joined the roster of genuine American folk songs.

After the Civil War, genuine black minstrel companies were organized. These troupes existed side by side with white companies, remaining a very popular form of American entertainment until 1910 or so. Minstrel shows included several kinds of song: sentimental ballads, spirituals and other religious songs, operatic airs, and comic songs.

Minstrelsy was one of two major vehicles carrying southern music to the North and West. The other was the touring choral group, whose first and most famous representative was the Fisk Jubilee Singers. Soon after the Civil War ended, black schools began to be founded in the South. One of the first was

Fisk University in Nashville, Tennessee, opened in 1866. To help raise funds for Fisk's building program, in 1871 the school sent a small group of excellent singers on tour. After a shaky beginning, they scored their first big success in Boston in 1872 at a huge World Peace Jubilee, which inspired their name. Thereafter they toured all over the United States and even in Europe, raising, in only seven years, the unheard-of total of $150,000.[19]

Other schools followed Fisk's lead, sending out groups to sing spirituals and plantation songs. The spirituals they performed were adaptations rather than the genuine article. In their formally organized concerts, much of the improvisatory nature of the true spiritual was abandoned. Nevertheless, the melodies and something of the original performance style were retained. In time more and more spirituals became widely familiar, disseminated through both performance and publication. As they were written down, the different possibilities for arrangement became apparent. Both choral and solo arrangements were written, and later even purely instrumental arrangements were made of what had originally been vocal music.

At the same time, more and more blacks, taking advantage of new educational opportunities, took up the formal study of music, which in the late nineteenth century meant principally the study of European music. In the work of these composers, trained in the traditional European forms of composition—art song and symphony, march and overture—the native idioms appeared in new guise.

Among serious composers, the first outstanding black woman was Florence Smith Price. Her work reflects her training, which was dominated by white American men steeped in European musical traditions, but it also reflects her southern roots. Price was born on April 9, 1888, in Little Rock, Arkansas, where her father was a dentist.[20] Her early musical training was given her by her mother, a soprano and pianist. For a time she attended elementary school in Chicago but she returned to high school in Little Rock, graduating at fourteen. She then went to the New England Conservatory in Boston, where she majored in piano and organ, and received her artist's diploma in organ. She also studied composition and counterpoint with George Chadwick and Frederick Converse, and as a student wrote a string trio and a symphony.

At nineteen she returned to Arkansas and took on her first teaching job in a school that included both elementary and high school grades; later she took over the music department at Shorter College in North Little Rock. In 1912 she married Thomas J. Price, a lawyer. They had three children: two daughters, Florence and Edith, and a son named Thomas, who died quite young and in whose memory she wrote the song, "To My Little Son."

While raising her family, Price became a highly respected music teacher in Little Rock, giving private lessons in violin, piano, and organ. But in 1927, with racial tension high following a lynching, the family decided to move to Chicago, where Price continued to teach, compose, and perform whenever possible. She became a close friend of Estella C. Bonds, with whom she lived during a brief period of hard times, and she gave Estella's daughter Margaret, who is discussed later in this chapter, lessons in piano and composition. Price herself also went back to school, studying composition with Carl Busch, Wesley La Violette, and Arthur Olaf Anderson; at various times she was enrolled at the Chicago Musical College, Chicago Teachers College, Chicago University, and American Conservatory of Music, studying not only music but also languages and the liberal arts.

In 1932 Price won two Wanamaker Foundation awards, one of $500 for her Symphony in E minor and another of $250 for her Piano Sonata; the remainder of the $1000 stipend was won by Margaret Bonds for a song. The winning symphony was performed on June 15, 1933, by the Chicago Symphony Orchestra under Frederick Stock, at the Century of Progress Exposition. Other of her orchestral works were performed by the WPA Symphony Orchestra of Detroit and the Chicago Woman's Symphony—Bonds performed the solo part of Price's Concerto in F minor with the Chicago group in 1934.[21] Price's Piano Quintet was played at the University of Illinois and by the Forum String Quartet of Chicago.

Price was prolific. She wrote art songs, spiritual arrangements, works for piano and organ, four symphonies, three piano concertos, and a violin concerto. She made considerable use of characteristic black rhythms and melodies in her works, especially in the Symphony in E minor, *Concert Overture on Negro Spirituals, Three Little Negro Dances,* and *Negro Folksongs in Counterpoint* for string quartet. This last was originally for string orchestra, commissioned by conductor John Barbirolli.

Humble in demeanor and deeply religious, Price often used the music of the black church and made a number of arrangements of spirituals. Her *Two Traditional Spirituals,* "I Am Bound for the Kingdom" and "I'm Workin' on My Buildin'," published in 1949, were dedicated to the black contralto Marian Anderson, who frequently performed them. The most famous of Price's arrangements was "My Soul's Been Anchored in de Lord," published in 1937 in an arrangement for voice and piano; she later made another arrangement for voice and orchestra, and both were recorded. Price's arrangements are, on the whole, simple chordal settings that allow the melody to dominate. In "My Soul's Been Anchored," however, she created a striking rhythmic setting, with both the accompaniment and the vocal part syncopated but in contrasting rhythms. Her *Three Little Negro Dances,* highly syncopated settings of "Hoe Cake," "Rabbit Foot," and "Ticklin' Toes," was originally a piano work that later was arranged for band and frequently was performed by the U.S. Marine Band. Price died in Chicago on June 3, 1953.

The second black woman composer of note was Price's one-time pupil, Margaret Bonds, who made a conscious effort both to develop black idioms in larger musical forms and to promote the music of black Americans. Margaret

Bonds was born in Chicago on March 3, 1913, and began her musical studies with her mother, Estella C. Bonds.[22] A church organist and highly accomplished musician, Estella Bonds was an important figure in black artistic circles, and young Margaret met such leading artists as the sculptor Richmond Barthe, the poets Langston Hughes and Countee Cullen, the soprano Abbie Mitchell, and the popular composer Will Marion Cook. She became especially close friends with Hughes, many of whose poems she later set to music. Abbie Mitchell introduced her to the works of the black composer Harry T. Burleigh, who not only used black idioms but quoted spirituals in his own compositions.

In high school Bonds studied composition with Florence Price and with another black composer, William Dawson. She also worked closely with a number of singers, earning money as an accompanist in supper clubs and shows. Among her jobs was accompanying the dancer Muriel Abbott in the Empire Room at Chicago's Palmer House. She also copied parts for black composers. She later recalled,

> Our collective security stretched out a hand to visiting artists, and when composers like Will Marion Cook had an opportunity to present a Negro choir on NBC, I was sent to extract all of his choral parts, which, incidentally, he changed daily. Even now, when I write something for a choir and it's jazzy and bluesy and spiritual and Tchaikowsky all rolled up into one, I laugh to myself, "That is Will Marion Cook."[23]

Also while she was still in high school, Bonds joined the National Association of Negro Musicians, helped establish its junior division, and through it worked hard to promote black music and black musicians.

Despite the difficulties posed by the Great Depression, Bonds went to Northwestern University, one of a small minority of black students there, and by the age of twenty-one she had earned both her bachelor's and master's degrees. She then opened a school for ballet, art, and music, but in those hard times it did not thrive. In 1939 Bonds left Chicago for New York City. For a time she worked as a music editor, and she published several popular songs, among them "Peach Tree Street," "Georgia," and "Spring Will Be So Sad." In 1940 she married Lawrence Richardson, a probation officer in the New York court system. They had one child, Djane, named for pianist Djane Herz, with whom Bonds studied at the Juilliard School. She also studied composition, both at Juilliard and privately, with Roy Harris, Robert Starer, and Emerson Harper.

While in New York Bonds met Nadia Boulanger and hoped to study composition with her, but the French teacher turned her down flat. Boulanger admired the composition Bonds showed her—it was *The Negro Speaks of Rivers* —but told her she should go on as she was and not study with anyone. No doubt Boulanger realized that Bonds had grasped European compositional techniques but her style combined these with black improvisation in such a way that her own natural direction might easily have been stifled by further study of European idioms.[24]

From the 1940s to the 1960s Bonds continued to compose, perform, and teach. She formed the Margaret Bonds Chamber Society to present black musicians in works by black composers, and she herself continued to appear on the concert stage, both as a piano recitalist and as soloist with the Chicago Symphony, Chicago Woman's Symphony, New York Symphony, and other orchestras. She served as music director and pianist for numerous theatrical productions. She also taught at the American Theater Wing and at various times was music director of the Stage for Youth, East Side Settlement House, and White Barn Theater.[25] Herself a resident of New York's Harlem, she was minister of music at a local church and helped establish a Cultural Community Center there.

Bonds's own compositions show the influence of the blues and jazz she heard so much during her youth in Chicago, and they often include either spiritual melodies or original melodies in spiritual style. Understandably, they also are very pianistic, and often quite difficult technically; Bonds herself was an excellent pianist. She gradually won increasing recognition, first the Wanamaker Award for a song in 1932, then a Roy Harris Fellowship, and in the 1960s several awards from ASCAP. She was particularly proud of the Northwestern University Alumni Medal awarded her in 1967; at the time she had attended Northwestern, black students, few in number though they were, still were barred from many university facilities.

In 1967 Bonds moved to Los Angeles, where she devoted the remaining years of her life to teaching music to inner-city children. In 1972 the Los Angeles Symphony under Zubin Mehta performed the premiere of her Credo for chorus and orchestra. She died a few months later.

Bonds wrote art songs, choral works, orchestral works, piano pieces, and popular songs—more than 200 works in all. Among the best is the song *The Negro Speaks of Rivers,* a setting of Langston Hughes's first published poem, with jazzy augmented chords. In 1967 Bonds wrote,

> Thirty years ago a teacher of mine objected to the music. It was "too far out," then, not only because it had a Negro spiritual flavor, but because in the last part of the song, when the poet speaks of America, it becomes very "jazzy." My teacher said that maybe it would be all right if I took out those "jazzy augmented chords." I changed not a note, because God had "gotten at me" for several hours during the song's creation, and I believed that I had recorded what He wanted me to record.[26]

Unfortunately, Marian Anderson, to whom Bonds showed the song, also did not like it; she never performed it, although she later sang a more somber setting by Howard Swanson.

Also notable is Bonds's *The Ballad of the Brown King,* originally for voice and piano and later enlarged for chorus, soloists, and orchestra. Another setting of a Hughes poem, it tells of the three kings who attended Jesus's birth and particularly of Balthazar, who is portrayed as a black or "brown" man. Performed by the Westminster Choir in New York in December 1960, the work is in nine movements and blends a variety of traditions: spirituals, jazz, calypso rhythms, and some blues and folk styles, as well as the traditional European choral tradition, here seen in the quasi-recitative sections.

Three Dream Portraits, published in 1959, also settings of Hughes's poems, is a series of mood paintings imbued with jazz style. "Minstrel Man" has repeated bass patterns in the accompaniment that are reminiscent of ragtime, and there is frequent use of the lowered seventh chord found in spirituals, blues, and jazz. "To a Brown Girl Dead," a setting of a poem by Countee Cullen, is in the style of a funeral dirge, and "I Got a Home in That Rock," a spiritual arranged for solo voice and piano or orchestra, has an accompaniment in jazz-blues style. Other of Bonds's spiritual arrangements are "Dry Bones," "Lord, I Just Can't Keep from Crying," "I'll Reach to Heaven," "Sit Down, Servant," "This Little Light of Mine," and "Ezekiel Saw the Wheel." In addition, Bonds wrote several scores for stage works, notably *Shakespeare in Harlem,* two ballets, a symphony entitled *Peter and the Bells, Spiritual Suite* for piano, and Mass in D minor.

Like Margaret Bonds and Florence Price, Julia Perry arranged some spirituals, and like them she wrote a considerable amount of vocal music, but in her work black idioms are incorporated far more subtly, and they rarely predominate. Indeed, as a former student of both Nadia Boulanger and the Italian avant-garde composer Luigi Dallapiccola, Perry, one might argue, would be more appropriately discussed with other composers in European idioms. But like Bonds and Price, Perry was born black, and the black experience in America during the first half of the twentieth century nearly always involved, from the musical standpoint, considerable exposure to gospel, jazz, blues, and other American idioms. Thus, even though Perry was trained along conventional—and not so conventional—European lines, her vocal settings and her use of rhythm reflect her American experience.

Julia Amanda Perry was born on March 25, 1924, in Lexington, Kentucky, but her family soon moved to Akron, Ohio.[27] Her physician father was also a pianist. Her two older sisters studied violin, and her mother saw to it that the children practiced. Julia, who from the first wanted to be a composer, graduated from Akron High School and in 1943 went to the Westminster Choir College in Princeton, New Jersey, where she studied piano, violin, voice, conducting, and composition. During the summer of 1946 while still a student, she went to Birmingham, Alabama, where she trained a young choir and taught it one of her own compositions. Perry received her master's degree from Westminster in 1948, having written a secular cantata, *Chicago,* for her mas-

ter's thesis. She then moved to New York City and continued her studies at
Juilliard. During this period, her cantata *Ruth* was performed at the Riverside
Church in April 1950, and several of her compositions were published. She
also worked for a time as assistant coach at the Columbia Opera Workshop,
which in 1954 performed her first opera, the one-act *The Cask of Amontillado,*
based on a short story by Edgar Allan Poe.

In 1951 Perry worked with the Italian composer Luigi Dallapiccola at the
Berkshire Music Center in Tanglewood, and as a result she applied for a Guggenheim Fellowship to study further with him in Italy. In 1952 she went to
Europe, where she also studied with Nadia Boulanger, and in that year she
received the Boulanger Grand Prix for her Viola Sonata. Perry was awarded a
second Guggenheim Fellowship in 1954 and returned to Italy to study with
Dallapiccola again. In the summers of 1956 and 1957 she studied conducting
at the Accademia Chigiana of Siena, and in 1957 she organized and conducted
a series of concerts in Europe under the sponsorship of the U.S. Information
Service.

In 1959, after a total of five and one-half years in Europe, Perry returned
to America and devoted herself largely to composition and some teaching. In
1967 she taught at Tallahassee's Florida Agricultural and Mechanical College, and in 1969 she was visiting lecturer at Atlanta College. In 1971 Perry
suffered a paralytic stroke and was subsequently hospitalized for a number of
years. By the late 1970s, she had recovered enough to leave the hospital and
taught herself to write with her left hand so as to resume composing. She died
in 1979.

Perry's early works in particular incorporate black musical idioms. "Free
at Last," published in 1951, and "I'm a Poor L'il Orphan" are arrangements of
spirituals. In *Song of Our Savior,* for a cappella chorus, written for the Hampton Institute Choir, she used the Dorian mode (instead of the diatonic scale)
and a hummed ostinato, as well as the call-and-response structure in one section. But it was not long before Perry began to combine traditions more freely.
One of her most striking works is the Stabat Mater, composed in 1951 and
dedicated to her mother. Set for contralto solo and string orchestra, it makes
free use of dissonance but is still tonal. It uses modern devices such as quartal
harmony, which is based on fourths instead of the traditional thirds and fifths,
an occasional whole-tone scale, and cluster chords, which are made of adjacent
notes. The overall work is very dramatic, almost operatic in character.

From her early concentration on vocal music, Perry turned increasingly,
from the 1950s on, to instrumental compositions. By 1971 she had produced
twelve symphonies, beginning with Symphony no. 1, for violas and string
basses, which she revised in 1962, and continuing with symphonies for full
orchestra, string orchestra, concert band, marching band, and orchestra with
chorus. Significantly, the first major work she produced after her illness was
another symphony, no. 5, in 1976.

Perry's *Short Piece for Orchestra,* also revised in 1962, was performed by the New York Philharmonic in 1965. From its rather wild, loud, brassy opening it moves to Andante lento featuring the woodwinds and strings in long, lyrical passages. It then accelerates to return to the first tempo, with the horns announcing a return to the tumult of the opening, punctuated by percussion. This work has a great deal of rhythmic interest, with considerable use of syncopation. More experimental in nature is *Homunculus C.F.,* for ten percussionists, composed during the summer of 1960. Scored for timpani, various cymbals, snare drum, bass drum, wood blocks, xylophone, vibraphone, celesta, piano, and harp, the work is based on the chord of the fifteenth, the "C.F." of the title, that is, a succession of superimposed thirds with an E root, beginning on E above middle C: E-G#-B-D#-F#-A#-C#-E#. It is not in any major or minor key, and the composer herself termed the work "pantonal," using any and all available tones. The name "Homunculus" refers to the test-tube creature brought to life by Wagner, Faust's young apprentice, alluding to the experimental nature of the piece. The work falls into four sections, the first purely rhythmic, using only unpitched percussion instruments; the second principally melodic, using timpani, harp, and two cymbals; the third harmonic; and the fourth combining harmony, melody, and rhythm.

Perry's other instrumental works include her 1959 Requiem for orchestra, also called *Homage to Vivaldi,* based on themes by the baroque composer; a number of shorter orchestral works; chamber music; a violin concerto; twelve symphonies; and two piano concertos. She also produced a number of vocal works: a three-act opera, *The Symplegades,* concerning the seventeenth-century Salem witchcraft panic, which took more than ten years to write; an opera-ballet to her own libretto based on Oscar Wilde's fable, *The Selfish Giant; Five Quixotic Songs* (1976) for bass-baritone solo, two clarinets, viola, baritone horn, and piano; and *Bicentennial Reflections* (1977) for tenor solo and six instruments.

A number of other black women composers must be mentioned. Evelyn LaRue Pittman, born in Oklahoma in 1910, pursued an active career in teaching, choral conducting, and composition.[28] Much of her original work was prompted by the need for new teaching materials for her pupils and music for choral groups under her direction. The Evelyn Pittman Choir performed for twelve years during the 1930s and 1940s. Educated at Spelman College, in Atlanta, the University of Oklahoma, the Juilliard School, and with Nadia Boulanger, Pittman wrote *Rich Heritage,* a collection of songs and stories concerning eminent blacks, first published in 1944 and updated in 1968; *Cousin Esther,* a folk opera performed in Paris in 1957; *Freedom's Child,* an opera about Martin Luther King Jr. first presented in Atlanta in 1972 by her own Woodlands High School students from Hartsdale, New York; and many arrangements of spirituals and choral works that show the influence of black church music in particular.

Lena Johnson McLin similarly wrote much music for her pupils and for choirs she directed.[29] Born in Atlanta in 1929, she was later a resident of Chicago, where she did graduate work in theory, counterpoint, and electronic music. Her compositions, which include cantatas, Masses, spiritual arrangements, anthems, operas, songs, piano works, orchestral works, and electronic music, incorporate not only the older black idioms of spirituals and work songs but the twentieth-century idioms of blues and gospel, jazz and rock. Notable among her works are *The Torch Has Been Passed,* for a cappella chorus, based on a text by President John F. Kennedy concerning the achievement of world peace; *If They Ask Why You Can,* a gospel song dedicated to her brother, the Reverend B. J. Johnson III; *Let the People Sing the Praises of the Lord,* an anthem for chorus, piano or organ, and trumpet, notable for its driving rhythms, syncopation, and quartal, often dissonant, harmonies; and *Free at Last,* a cantata about Martin Luther King Jr., which includes five spirituals but treats them largely in the style of freely invented gospel song.

Undine Smith Moore became known mostly for her choral compositions and arrangements of spirituals.[30] Born in 1904, she graduated from Fisk University and studied at the Juilliard, Eastman, and Manhattan schools of music. She later taught at Virginia State College from 1927 to 1972 and helped found Virginia State's Black Music Center. She herself said her rhythms, choice of scale structures, use of call and response, and general use of contrapuntal devices are among the characteristics making her music uniquely black. These devices extended to both her choral and her instrumental compositions. In an interview with James A. Standifer in 1980 she said, "I hope that everything that I have written reflects my blackness. I cannot say, but I hope so."[31] Her favorite composition was *Scenes from the Life of a Martyr (to the Memory of Martin Luther King, Jr.),* written in 1982, which was nominated for a Pulitzer Prize. She died in 1989.

Zenobia Powell Perry, born in 1914 in Oklahoma, graduated from Tuskegee Institute in 1938. Tuskegee did not have a music department at the time, but Perry was alto section leader and accompanist for the choir under William Dawson, whom she considered an important mentor. She later studied at the University of Northern Colorado and University of Wyoming. At Wyoming and later at Aspen she studied with Darius Milhaud, an important influence on her music. Perry taught at Central State University in Ohio from 1955 to 1982, and has written a Mass, an opera, band and orchestral works, chamber works, and piano pieces.[32]

Betty Jackson King, born in 1928 in Chicago, began her musical studies with her mother, Gertrude Jackson Taylor, founder of the Imperial Opera Company, which fostered the vocal development of young singers.[33] Her father was a pastor of the Community Church of Woodlawn, so she heard hymns and spirituals from an early age. She received bachelor's and master's degrees from Chicago Musical College of Roosevelt University and taught at a number of schools befores settling in Wildwood, New Jersey, where she taught and directed the high school choir until she retired in 1989. Her output is mostly vocal music: two operas, a cantata, a Requiem, many choral works, art songs, and arrangements of spirituals. She also composed organ and piano works and some chamber music. Elected president of the National Association of Negro Musicians in 1979, King emphasized the importance of preserving African-American spirituals and urged black composers to use African-American folk themes in their art music. She died in 1994.

Younger African-American women composers include opera singer Dorothy Rudd Moore, born in 1940, who helped found the Society of Black Composers in 1968, and whose compositions include the opera *Frederick Douglass* and *Modes* (1985), a three-movement string quartet. Her music is mainly contrapuntal.

Of course, not only black composers have made use of southern idioms or become known for their arrangements of old hymns and spirituals. One of the most renowned and successful American choral arrangers is Alice Parker, whose arrangements of folk songs, carols, and spirituals were for many years performed and recorded by the Robert Shaw Chorale. Also a composer in her own right, Parker wrote principally choral music, both sacred and secular, as well as several operas.

Alice Parker was born on December 16, 1925, in Boston, Massachusetts, and studied piano, organ, clarinet, and violin.[34] She graduated from Smith College in 1947, having majored in organ and composition, and went on to New York to the Juilliard School, where she worked with Julius Herford, Vincent Persichetti, and, most important, Robert Shaw. After getting her master's degree in choral conducting in 1949, she went to work for Shaw, whose highly successful choral group had begun touring and so brought an end to his teaching. From 1949 to 1968 Parker was employed as arranger for the Robert Shaw Chorale, producing hundreds of arrangements of folk songs, hymns, and carols, many of which have become standard works in the choral repertory. She also assisted Shaw in planning programs, writing program notes and record jacket notes, conducting section rehearsals, and doing many of the musical chores involved in conducting a famous choral ensemble. At the same time, she taught music at several private schools, but from about 1965 on she devoted herself increasingly to her own composition. In 1954 Alice Parker married Thomas F. Pyle, a baritone soloist and choral singer, and later a contractor for choral singers; they had five children. Parker accompanied her husband in recitals and often composed music for him. He died in 1976.

Though she also wrote keyboard works and instrumental chamber music, it is for her vocal music and her more than 400 published arrangements of folk songs, hymns, and carols that Parker became best known. Inevitably it reflects her longtime association with American idioms. For example, *Commentaries*, a 1978 cantata for women's voices and full orchestra, sets five poems by the nineteenth-century New England poet Emily Dickinson as a kind of contra-puntal commentary on arrangements of sacred and secular songs of the same period, principally from the South. The music quotes an old hymn tune with a text from a hymn collection published in Virginia in 1835, an Appalachian love ballad with old English roots, a black spiritual, a Quaker hymn, and a mountain hymn. In 1971 Parker had completed her first opera, *The Martyrs' Mirror,* a church opera first performed that October in Pennsylvania and given more than thirty performances in the next three years. Scored for solo-ists, two choirs, and small instrumental ensemble, it tells the story of four sixteenth-century Swiss Anabaptists who were executed for their religious beliefs. The choral score is based partly on old Mennonite hymn tunes—the Mennonites were a sect descended from the Anabaptists—combined with an instrumental accompaniment in more contemporary style. Parker's next opera, written in 1974–75, is *The Family Reunion,* a one-act opera set in rural America in the 1850s; it quotes folk songs, marches, dances, and hymns of that period, among them "Home, Sweet Home," "Where Have You Been, Billy Boy," and "Work for the Night Is Coming." *Singers Glen,* an opera in a prologue and two acts, was written in 1978 and first performed in Pennsyl-vania that same year. It concerns the life of Joseph Fuchs (1778–1862) of Singers Glen, Virginia, a Mennonite who published, between 1832 and 1862, ten editions of a hymn-tune collection called *Genuine Church Music.* The twenty-fifth edition of Fuchs's collection, entitled *Harmonia Sacra,* was pub-lished in 1993. Parker's opera quotes a number of hymns from the collec-tion, and one scene is devoted to the meeting of a singing school, classes set up in the mid-1700s to improve the music skills and hence the singing of congregations.

Parker's other works include *Martin Luther King: A Sermon from the Mountain* (1969), a cantata based on texts from the black leader's writings and his favorite biblical texts and spirituals; *The Time of Ingathering* (1970), for alto solo, chorus, and organ; *Melodious Accord* (1974), a cantata for chorus, harp, and brass quartet; *Songs for Eve* (1975), for vocal quartet and string quar-tet, a setting of twenty-eight short poems by Archibald MacLeish; *There and Back Again* (1976), for chorus and woodwind quartet; and a number of works for chorus and orchestra, notably *Gaudete. Six Latin Christmas Hymns* (1973) and *The True Use of Music* (1976). *Journeys. Pilgrims and Strangers* (1976), also for chorus and orchestra, concerns the different heritages of America's early settlers, with texts from early hymns and spirituals. Her later pieces include *That Sturdy Vine: Mennonite Singing* (1991) and *Singing in the Dark* (1995), for men's voices and orchestra, which was commissioned by Chanti-cleer. Other choral works include *Sacred Madrigals* (1989), *A Canonic Mass* (1993), *And Sing Eternally* (1996), setting traditional hymns, and *Sing Now of Peace* (1999), setting texts from the Bible, Shakespeare, and American Indian verses for chorus, vibraphone, and percussion.

In 1985 some of the singers and choral directors inspired by her teaching persuaded Parker to start Melodious Accord, a sixteen-voice professional chorus that presents an annual concert series in New York and has made numerous recordings of her work. It also presented symposia, encouraged new composers, offered postdoctoral seminars, and published a newsletter. In addition to composing, Parker continued to travel widely, conducting workshops, concerts, and "sings" in which the participants learn to make music. In June 1999 in the Melodious Accord newsletter, Parker wrote: "The basis of my teaching, then and now, is the conviction that melody—song—is what brings us to music in the first place." The statement of purpose of Melodious Accord is

> that melody is an unparalleled means of communication for human beings; that when we use our ears and voices we enrich our lives through creating communities of sound; and that singing together brings immediate benefits–physical, mental and spiritual—to those who join in this most participatory of all the arts.[35]

Two generations earlier, composer-conductor Gena Branscombe was similarly attracted to vocal music, choral conducting, and the use of American historical subjects in her compositions.[36] Born on November 4, 1881, in Picton, Ontario, Branscombe lived and worked in the United States, except for brief intervals abroad, from 1896 until her death in 1977; she became a U.S. citizen in 1910. Two of her most important compositions reflect her dual Canadian-American background, one celebrating the Pilgrims of the *Mayflower* and the other the early settlers of Quebec.

Branscombe began improvising on the piano from about the age of four or five, and was accompanying an older brother in public by the age of six. At fifteen she entered Chicago Musical College, where she studied piano with Florenz Ziegfeld and composition with Felix Borowski. She received her bachelor's degree in 1900, having continued piano studies with Arthur Friedheim, Hans von Schiller, and Rudolph Ganz. In 1903 she joined the college's piano faculty and began studying songwriting with Alexander von Fielitz. Four years later she moved to the state of Washington, where she headed the piano department of Whitman College for the next two years. She then went to Europe, studying composition for a year with Engelbert Humperdinck in Berlin and piano again with Ganz, who by then had returned to Germany. Branscombe returned to America and on October 5, 1910, she was married to John Ferguson Tenney of New York. They had four daughters.

Branscombe's first important composition was *Festival Prelude* for orchestra, which was performed at the MacDowell Colony Festival in 1914, and later in New York and at the San Francisco Exposition. Five years later she composed the text and music of her next large work, *Pilgrims of Destiny,* for soloists, chorus, and orchestra, which, however, was not performed in its entirety for another decade. Branscombe herself was not of Pilgrim stock, but her maternal ancestors had come to New York, then called Nieuw Amsterdam, in 1638 and settled near Fishkill, New York, until their land was confiscated during the Revolutionary War and they moved to Canada. *Pilgrims of Destiny* celebrates the courage and vision of the young English Pilgrims who sailed on the *Mayflower*, and fittingly, it received its first complete performance in 1929 at Plymouth, Massachusetts, by the New England North Shore Festival Chorus, augmented by local choruses, and the Boston Festival Orchestra under Arthur B. Keene. Branscombe's other large historic work, *Quebec*, a symphonic suite for tenor solo and orchestra, was taken from an opera she never finished, *The Bells of Circumstance*. The suite concerns the French who settled in the icy wilderness of Quebec in the early sixteenth century and was first performed by the Chicago Woman's Symphony, with the composer conducting. It was later performed elsewhere and broadcast both in America and Canada.

By 1921 Branscombe had become interested in conducting, and for the next ten years she studied intermittently with Frank Damrosch at the Institute of Musical Art (later the Juilliard School); Albert Stoessel and John Warren Erb at New York University; Chalmers Clifton of the American Orchestral Society; and Walter Rothwell. Her earliest compositions were songs, but she had written a number of choral works as well, both for mixed chorus and for women's voices, and in 1934 she founded her own women's chorus, the Branscombe Choral, which she led for the next twenty years. From 1923 on she also conducted the MacDowell Club Chorus (later Chorale) of Mountain Lakes, New Jersey, and she frequently appeared as guest conductor in performances of her own choral compositions in the United States, Canada, and England. In the 1940s she conducted the Contemporary Club Chorale of Newark, New Jersey, the New Jersey State Chorus, and the first organized American Women's Voluntary Services chorus, which sang in uniform throughout World War II.

One of the high points of Branscombe's conducting career came in 1941, when she was chosen by the General Federation of Women's Clubs to conduct a national chorus of 1000 voices for its golden jubilee in celebration of women's achievements. Held in Atlantic City, New Jersey, its final concert featured works by women composers, selected by Branscombe herself.

Branscombe's own favorite among her choral works was *Coventry's Choir*, a setting of a poem by Violet Alvarez about the bombing of the great English cathedral during World War II. Scored for soprano solo, four-part women's chorus, and orchestra, it received its first complete performance by the Branscombe Choral in Town Hall, New York, on May 2, 1944. Other important choral compositions were *Youth of the World*, a cycle for women's voices and orchestra, written in the early 1930s and often performed over the years in England, Holland, and Canada, as well as many American cities, and *A Joyful Litany* as late at 1967.

Branscombe was active in the National Federation of Music Clubs for many years, serving it in a variety of capacities. She was president of the Society of American Women Composers from 1929 to 1931 and maintained lifelong friendships with many of its members, especially Harriet Ware, Amy Beach, Mary Howe, and Mabel Daniels. Also, she was active in the General Federation of Women's Clubs and served as chairman of American Music and Folksong; in this capacity she made up numerous programs of works by women composers and American composers for use by clubs affiliated with the General Federation.

In 1973, by then in her nineties, Branscombe was asked by the organist Frederick Swann to compose an Introit, Prayer Response, and Amen for a special service at the Riverside Church, New York. This was her last commission. She died on July 26, 1977, at the age of ninety-five, and the Introit, Procession, and some of her other works were performed at her funeral.

Always a vigorous supporter of women musicians, Branscombe once said, "Having a home, a husband, and children to love and serve brings enrichment of life to a woman, but being a part of the world's work in humbly serving and loving the illumined force which is music brings fulfillment."[37] Later, in 1962, she wrote,

> Had there been time, space, money, I could have done hundreds of programs devoted entirely to the works, large and small, of women composers. I have found women, in groups and individually, generous, chivalrous, efficient, and intelligent—a joy to work with. . . . It's a good life, being a woman composer, worth all the hard work that goes into it.[38]

A special U.S. Information Services article on Branscombe's life and work to be used abroad on radio, television, and in printed media said, "She has done perhaps more than anyone else to revitalize and expand the repertory for the nation's many women's choral groups."[39]

Although this book is largely concerned with "serious" music, it would be remiss to omit the role of women in other important genres of indigenous American music—blues, ragtime, and jazz. Many of the performers and composers in these genres were classically trained, but some others who were not also made enormous contributions. At the same time that Amy Beach and Margaret Lang were writing symphonic music, some women were writing a totally different kind of music, keyboard ragtime. Although the best known of the turn-of-the-century ragtime composers were men, the majority of pianists at that time were women, mostly middle- and upper-class white women, and a few of them wrote piano rags that were every bit as successful as Scott Joplin's smash hit, *Maple Rag*.[40] It is impossible to chronicle all these many women, but one may mention a few outstanding ones. May Frances Aufderheide (1890–1972), from an upper-middle-class Indiana family, studied piano with her aunt, May Kolmer (1877–1956), who had played with the Indianapolis Symphony. Aufderheide's first published composition was *Dusty Rag* (1908), and eighteen more piano rags followed in the next decade. She appears to have given up music soon after her marriage. Another rag composer was Julia Lee Niebergall (1886–1968), from a musical family in Indiana. Her *Red Rambler Rag* (1912) was extremely popular. The most successful woman's rag composition of all was *Pickles and Peppers* (1906) by Adaline Shepherd (1883–1950). She, too, gave up music after her marriage.

Whereas ragtime attracted white women composers and pianists, from the 1920s on the women jazz singers and pianists who also composed were mostly African-American.[41] Among the earliest were singer-composers Gertrude "Ma" Rainey (1886–1939), the so-called mother of the blues, and Alberta Hunter (1895–1984). Ma Rainey apparently never learned to read music but composed at least two dozen of the blues songs she performed. Hunter's "Down Hearted Blues" was recorded by singer Bessie Smith in the 1920s and eventually sold an estimated million copies, for which Hunter was still collecting royalties up to her death. In 1954 she abruptly abandoned music and worked as a nurse for more than twenty years, but she was coaxed out of retirement in 1977. Bessie Smith (1895–1937) herself did not compose but was considered the first truly great singer in the African-American tradition; her art bridged the transition from blues to jazz. Her singing, one writer said, bridged elements of spirituals and gospel, the rural blues of Ma Rainey, and the music of the tent show and black vaudeville.[42] Her contemporary, Ethel Waters (1896–1997), also started as a blues singer and like Smith ended making a contribution to jazz. Of the outstanding jazz singers who followed, Billie Holiday (1915–1959) was a masterful improviser, which cost her jobs in her early years. She, too, composed a number of songs that became classics, the most famous of which is "God Bless the Child," with lyrics by Arthur Herzog. Others were "Don't Explain," "Fine and Mellow," "Billie's Blues," and "Preacher's Boy," this last cowritten with Jeanne Burns.

Pianist and bandleader Lil Hardin Armstrong (1902–1971) started at age six on the organ, and had two-and-a-half years of music education at Fisk University. Married for a time to trumpeter Louis Armstrong, whose name she adopted and kept after they separated, she composed approximately fifty pieces between 1925 and 1927. Among the most popular were "Struttin' with Some Barbecue" and "Brown Gal." She helped bandleaders such as "King" Oliver and her husband to write down arrangements, which at that time were mostly played from memory. In the late 1920s and early 1930s she obtained a teacher's diploma in music from the Chicago College of Music and a postgraduate degree from the New York College of Music. Later she also led an all-woman swing band as well as an all-male band. By her own estimate she composed some 150 pieces of music during her lifetime.[43] A contemporary of hers was Lovie Austin (1887–1972), who was not only leader and pianist in a famous theater pit band but wrote all its orchestrations. Her compositions included "Graveyard Blues," written for Bessie Smith.

Perhaps the most notable pianist-composer was Mary Lou Williams (1910–1981). Born Mary Elfrieda Scruggs (1910–1981), she was playing the piano by the age of four and soon entertained at parties, silent movies, and brothels. Had she been white, wrote biographer Linda Dahl, she quite conceivably would have become a classical concert pianist. But she was black, poor, and in need of immediate employment.[44] By the late 1920s, now married to baritone sax player John Williams, she moved to Kansas City and played with various jazz bands throughout the 1930s. Although she had never studied theory, she asked others about chords and voicing registers, and soon was supplying numerous arrangements to swing bands. In the end she produced some 350 works in all. Boogie-woogie piano was the rage, with tunes such as her "Little Joe from Chicago." In the 1930s she wrote such popular tunes as "Froggy Bottom," "Cloudy," and "Roll 'Em," a hit for Benny Goodman. Her first extended composition was *Zodiac Suite* (1945), twelve tone poems on astrological themes, conceived as mood portraits of individual musicians. Considered one of the earliest modern jazz symphonic works, it premiered on her own New York radio show and the following year was performed in part by the New York Philharmonic at Carnegie Hall, with the composer at the keyboard. In 1957 she converted to Roman Catholicism and began to compose music with spiritual and religious themes. Her *Music for Peace Mass,* also called *Mary Lou's Mass* (1969), for jazz combo and solo vocalists, was commissioned by the Vatican and choreographed by Alvin Ailey. It was praised as "an encyclopedia of black music." Until her death she continued to perform, often in all the styles of jazz developed throughout her lifetime. As artist-in-residence at Duke University from 1977 to 1980, she included a historic jazz demonstration in her performances.[45] She left her entire estate to the Mary Lou Williams Foundation to enable gifted youngsters aged six to twelve to study one-on-one with professional jazz musicians. As for her views on women in jazz, she said, "You've got to play, that's all. They don't think of you as a woman if you can really play. . . . If they have talent, the men will be glad to help them along."[46]

Still other African-American women are important in the history of jazz. Trinidad-born Hazel Scott (1920–1981) trained at Juilliard, played a variety of instruments, worked with Lil Hardin Armstrong's all-woman orchestra, and by age eighteen was fronting a band and writing most of her own arrangements and some original pieces. She was known for "swinging the classics." British-born Marian McPartland (b. 1918) was groomed for a concert career at London's Guild Hall School of Music but was far more interested in jazz. In 1945 she married Dixieland trumpeter Jimmy McPartland and moved to the United States. Notable for her taste and keen sense of harmony, she soon set out with her own trio. In the 1960s she began writing songs that were recorded by such artists as Tony Bennett, Sarah Vaughan, and Peggy Lee. She also gave concerts and played in piano bars. Beginning in 1979 she hosted a popular radio program, *Piano Jazz*, on National Public Radio. Originally in a two-piano format, it included such guests as Mary Lou Williams and Hazel Scott. Later she also invited classical pianists, among them Ruth Laredo, and non-pianists like Dizzy Gillespie. In spring of 1999, with McPartland in her eighties, the show was celebrating its twentieth anniversary; it had won numerous awards. McPartland also received honorary doctorates from a number of colleges. One reason for her long-lived success was her joy in playing both old and new styles of jazz: "I love to go back and play older things but, as I've heard new music, I've wanted to be doing that, too."[47]

Outstanding among the women jazz composers of the next generation were two pianists, Toshiko Akiyoshi and Carla Bley.[48] Akiyoshi, born in 1929 in Manchuria, was raised in Japan. By the early 1950s she was playing piano in coffeehouses and on Japanese television. In 1956 she came to the United States to study at Berklee College of Music in Boston and that year she made her debut at the Newport Jazz Festival. In 1963 she debuted as composer-conductor at New York's Town Hall, and two years later she married saxophonist-flutist Lew Tabackin and formed a quartet with him. Soon after, they formed a jazz orchestra, which did spectacularly well both in Japan and the United States. Akiyoshi's music is complex, representing a cultural blend of Japanese music and American jazz. She also includes Japanese instruments and folk-song elements in many works. Her *Kogun* is dedicated to a Japanese soldier who hid in the Philippines for thirty years following the end of World War II; *Tales of a Courtesan* is about the falsely romanticized Western image of courtesans.

Carla Bley, composer, keyboard and saxophone player, and band leader, was born in 1938 in California. She began playing the piano early, mostly church hymns and classical music. She came upon the New York jazz scene in the late 1950s and began composing for various players at the urging of her first husband, Paul Bley. In 1964 she founded the Jazz Composers Guild and soon afterward her own record label. Her reputation was made by *Escalator over the Hill*, an opera covering six record sides and taking five years to produce (1967–72). Telling the story of a wandering rock band, it borrows from musical sources around the world, including jazz. By the late 1970s she had formed her own ten-piece orchestra that played only her music, which crossed lines between jazz, rock, and "new music." Her compositions draw on a wide variety of musical idioms: Spanish civil war songs, marching band music, Indian ragas, the Beatles, and Kurt Weill, among others. In the 1990s she worked with her second husband, bassist Steve Swallow, in duos and in larger groups, and wrote on commission for orchestras.

Unlike Bley and Akiyoshi, Melba Liston was born poor and black, in 1926 in Kansas City.[49] At age six or seven she got her first trombone, an instrument her mother could ill afford, and at ten she entered a musical program run by Alma Hightower, who made passing on black culture her life's work. At sixteen she turned professional and played for a pit band that called on her for arrangements and new compositions. From the late 1940s on she was playing with Count Basie and then Dizzy Gillespie, whose band included John Coltrane and Jimmy Heath. She became known not only for her playing but for her compositions and fine arrangements. She also led her own band until she became ill and subsequently returned to California. In the 1960s she worked with pianist Randy Weston, and her collaborations with him produced harmonically complex music, thick with dissonances. She then spent a decade teaching in Jamaica. After she returned to the United States, a stroke left her partly paralyzed, but she continued to arrange music with Weston. Their collaboration endured into the 1990s, producing dramatic pieces. In May 1993 she was inducted into the Pioneers Hall of Fame at the International Women's Brass Conference. Liston was one of the few successful women who admitted that in jazz, as in classical music, there was considerable prejudice against women instrumentalists and that it was difficult to win acceptance, let alone rise to the top of their profession. Although opportunities widened in the 1980s and 1990s, most established male jazz leaders still do not call women for gigs; even men who accept invitations in women's groups still rarely think about paying the women back by calling them for work. Liston died in 1999, six days after Harvard University sponsored a major tribute to her.

An important contemporary of Liston's was another African-American woman, trumpeter Clora Bryant, a brilliant jazz musician. Bryant began her career studying trumpet at Prairie View University in Texas. She went on to play with some legendary jazz figures—Dizzy Gillespie, Quincy Jones, Ray Charles, Duke Ellington, Louis Armstrong, and Count Basie. In 1993 she won the Distinguished Achievement Award for her contributions to African-American music from the University of Massachusetts. She also received three National Endowment for the Arts grants. At this writing she gives frequent master classes in jazz history and is writing her autobiography.

The second half of the twentieth century also saw some international "fusion," that is, combining musical idioms from different countries. Among women composers exemplifying the style are Cuban-born Tania León, Chinese-born Chen Yi, and Macao-born Lam Bun-Ching. All three women moved to and studied in the United States, and their music blends elements of their original heritage with prevailing American idioms.

León, born in Havana in 1943, was steeped in Cuba's popular music but studied classical music at the Carlos Alfredo Peyrellade Conservatory.[50] In 1967 she emigrated to the United States and worked for a dozen years for the Dance Theater of Harlem, as accompanist, music director, conductor, and composer. She also attended New York University, where her studies ranged from jazz to Elliott Carter. In 1979 she returned to Cuba and rediscovered her Afro-Cuban musical heritage, which was to influence her compositions of the 1980s and 1990s. Indeed, her tastes and fluency in many genres reflect not only Latin influences, but Asian and African-American idioms, jazz and popular music, opera, dance, and other theater music. Often she combined these elements with contemporary techniques. Among her works are the 1986 *A La Par* (Going Together), a three-movement work for piano and percussion with highly complex polyrhythms, representing her first attempt at Afro-Cuban-modernist fusion. Her *Indigena* (1991), for a chamber ensemble, evokes the Carnival season and its music; in fact, one portion directly quotes a Carnival melody. She also wrote an opera, *The Scourge of Hyacinths* (1994). A multifaceted musician, she has worked as conductor, pianist, music director, and composer. Moreover, she stridently resists categorization. She does not want to be identified as a woman, a black, Hispanic or Latino, but just as a musician, or composer, or conductor. In 1985 she joined the faculty of Brooklyn College Conservatory of Music in composition and conducting, and from 1993 to 1995 she served as a new music adviser to the New York Philharmonic Orchestra. At the time of this writing she is serving as Latin American adviser to the American Composers Orchestra and is a cofounder of the annual *Sonidos de las Americas* (Sounds of the Americas) festival. Other compositions of the 1990s include *Crossings* (1992), for brass ensemble, commissioned for President Bill Clinton's inauguration; *Drummin'* (1997), an interactive multimedia work involving dance and video as well as orchestra; *Singin' Sepia* (1996) for soprano, clarinet, violin, and piano, a song cycle setting poems by Rita Dove; and *Sol de Doce* (The Sun at Twelve), for twelve solo voices, written in 1997.

Chen Yi, born in China in 1953, began her musical studies as a violinist and came into contact with the traditional music of her country during the Cultural Revolution when she was forced to relocate to the countryside for two years.[51] At age seventeen she was released to serve as concertmaster and composer for the Beijing Opera Troupe. After Chinese schools were restored she continued her violin studies and began a systematic study of Chinese traditional music. In 1986 she came to the United States for further study at Columbia University, studying with Chou Wen-chung and Mario Davidovsky. She then served for three years as composer-in-residence with the Women's Philharmonic and subsequently joined the composition faculty of Peabody Conservatory. In 1998 she was appointed to the faculty of Kansas City Conservatory. In her compositions, comprising both intimate and large-scale works for both Western and Chinese instruments, Chen Yi distills the essential character and spirit of both Chinese and Western art music. Her Piano Concerto (1992) and Symphony no. 2 combine the Western orchestral medium with traditional Eastern pentatonic scales. *Shuo* (1994), for string orchestra, includes a Chinese folk melody treated contrapuntally. *Song in Winter* (1993) is a trio for harpsichord, di (a kind of flute), and zheng (a zither).

Chinese Myths Cantata (1996) incorporates traditional Chinese string instruments—erhu, pipa, yangqin, guzheng—into the traditional Western orchestral sound. "In the *Cantata*," wrote composer Elaine Barkin, "the synthesis of East and West is smoothly achieved."[52] In 1999 Chen Yi won the first $25,000 Eddie Medora King Award for musical composition at the University of Texas, Austin, for her skillful drawing together of music of the East and West.

Lam Bun-Ching, born in 1954 in Macao to Chinese parents, graduated in music from the Chinese University of Hong Kong and won a doctorate from the University of California, San Diego, where she studied composition with Robert Erickson, Bernard Rands, and Pauline Oliveros.[53] She won numerous awards, including the prestigious Prix de Rome. Her origin is evident in *Saudades de Macau* (1990), a reflection on her memory of her birthplace. In her later works particularly she leans on Chinese traditions but blends them with the post-modern techniques she acquired in California. They include a shadow-puppet opera, *The Creation of God* (1993), *Circle* (1992) for orchestra, and *Walking Walking, Keep Walking* (1991), a setting of Han dynasty poems for tenor and Chinese instruments.

As the world becomes smaller through improved communications, music, like other fields, is likely to become globalized; more and more multicultural compositions will become part of the musical landscape.

8

OPERA COMPOSERS
AND CONDUCTORS

*V*OCAL MUSIC has long been more hospitable to women musicians than instrumental music has been. Women singers were accepted long before women instrumentalists. Although in the earliest operas the female roles were sung by countertenors and castrati, by the early eighteenth century women were allowed onstage, and within another 100 years the prima donna was placed on a pedestal and made a public idol.

The same was true of vocal composition. Women songwriters were winning acceptance by 1800 or so, and in fact the nineteenth-century sentimental ballad—the parlor song—was intended to appeal chiefly to women and was often composed by a woman. The next logical step was a more ambitious vocal composition, with music for choruses, for several soloists, or both—oratorio or opera.

Among the first American women to compose an opera was Constance Faunt Le Roy, a granddaughter of Scottish industrialist and reformer Robert Owen. She was born in Indianapolis in 1836 and spent part of her childhood in New Harmony, the utopian colony in Indiana established by her grandfather. Her mother was a fine pianist and harpist, and her father an amateur composer. In 1852 she was sent to Germany to study harp and piano; she remained there for five years and during this period developed an interest in composition. After returning to New Harmony, she married the Reverend James Runcie in 1861 and proceeded to write a great many songs, both words and music. She also wrote one romantic opera, *The Prince of Asturias,* which allegedly was considered for production by "a prominent eastern manager" but presumably was never performed, or if it was, only locally.[1]

Considerably more prolific and more successful was an American singer who wrote more than 100 songs and, during the last twenty years of her life, took up the cause of opera in English, composing nine operas herself. Eleanor Warner Everest Freer was born on May 14, 1864, in Philadelphia.[2] Her parents were Cornelius Everest, a prominent teacher of music theory and a church organist, and Ellen Amelia Clark Everest, a singer. Her early musical training

192

came from her parents, who, at the suggestion of the renowned soprano Christine Nilsson, sent her to Paris in 1883 to study at the music school of Mathilde Marchesi. She remained there for three years, her fellow students including Nellie Melba, Emma Eames, and Emma Calvé, all of whom became world-famous opera singers. In 1886 she returned to Philadelphia and began teaching voice, the first pupil whom Marchesi officially sanctioned to teach her famous method. By 1889 she also was commuting to New York twice a week to teach the Marchesi method at the National Conservatory of Music. In 1891 she married Archibald Freer of Chicago, and the following year the young couple went to Leipzig, where he studied medicine and she continued her music studies and bore their only child, Eleanor.

In 1899 Freer and her family returned to Chicago, where she became active in music clubs and began to study composition with Bernard Ziehn. By 1902 she had begun to compose, which occupied her fully—except during World War I, when she devoted herself to volunteer war work—until her death in 1942. At first Freer wrote many art songs, mostly settings of English poems since she believed the repertory already included settings of the best French, German, and Italian poems but that English had been sadly neglected. The most ambitious of these was her cycle of all forty-four of Elizabeth Barrett Browning's *Sonnets from the Portuguese,* but she also set poems by Robert Browning, Coleridge, Donne, Crashaw, Herrick, Longfellow, Lowell, Milton, Shelley, Shakespeare, and Tennyson.

Shortly after World War I Freer wrote her first opera, the one-act *Legend of the Piper,* about the Pied Piper of Hamelin, completed in 1921 and first performed in 1924 in South Bend, Indiana. It was performed in Chicago in 1925 by the American Theater for Musical Productions and again in Nebraska in 1926 on a double bill with her next opera, *Massimiliano, or the Court Jester,* also in one act. In her first opera, Freer used graceful melodies, easy rhythms, and relatively uncomplicated orchestration to present an old folk legend. In *Massimiliano,* the romantic tale of a court jester in love with a noblewoman, she used more modern harmonies but nevertheless produced very singable melodies. Four more one-act operas followed: *The Chilkoot Maiden,* based on an Alaskan legend and first presented in Skagway, Alaska, in 1927; *A Christmas Tale,* adapted from a French play; *A Legend of Spain,* based on a fifteenth-century Spanish story and performed in 1931; and *The Masque of Pandora,* written in 1927 and first performed in 1930, an adaptation of a poem by Longfellow. Her remaining operas are *Preciosa* (1928), *Joan of Arc* (1929), *Frithiof* (1929), *Little Women* (1934), and *The Brownings Go to Italy* (1936). She died in 1942.

Another woman who studied voice with Marchesi in Paris and composition with Ziehn in Chicago was Jane Van Etten, born in St. Paul, Minnesota.[3] She also studied voice in London, where she made her debut in the opera *Faust* in 1895, and later toured in both England and the United States. In 1901 she

married Alfred Burritt Andrews and retired from public performance, settling
in Evanston, Illinois. She then began to study with both Ziehn and Alexander
von Fielitz and soon published some songs. Her one-act opera *Guido Ferranti,*
performed in Chicago on December 29, 1914, by the Aborn Brothers' Century Opera Company, was, according to opera chronicler Edward Ellsworth
Hipsher, the first opera by an American woman presented by a well-known
company. He may have meant the first "serious opera," for composer Emma
Steiner's *Fleurette* and other light operas preceded it by some years. Van Etten's
libretto was based on a play by Oscar Wilde, *The Duchess of Padua,* and the
music was in the style of late nineteenth-century Italian opera, as represented
by Puccini and Mascagni. Though *Guido Ferranti* won critical acclaim, it
appears not to have been performed again.

A contemporary of Freer's and a native of Philadelphia was Celeste de
Longpré Massey Hecksher, who became very prominent in that city's musical
affairs.[4] Born in 1860, she began to compose about 1890, served for a long
period as president of the Philadelphia Opera Society, and wrote two operas,
The Flight of Time and *The Rose of Destiny.* The latter was performed at the
Metropolitan Opera House of Philadelphia on May 2, 1918. She also wrote an
orchestral suite, *Dance of the Pyrenees,* which was performed by the New York
Symphony, Philadelphia Orchestra, and Chicago Symphony, as well as songs
and piano works. She died in 1928.

In the early 1900s California was the home of at least three women composers of opera. Elsie Maxwell, of San Francisco, wrote songs, instrumental
music, a comic opera, and at least one grand opera, in English. In 1909 she also
was working as a music critic,[5] and in 1916 her suffragette operetta, *Melinda
and Her Sisters,* with a libretto by Mrs. O. H. P. Belmont, was presented in
New York at the Waldorf Astoria Hotel with a cast headed by Marie Dressler.[6]

Abbie Gerrish Jones, born in 1863 in Vallejo and raised in Sacramento,
began her music studies with voice lessons but soon turned to theory and composition.[7] She first published some compositions at the age of eighteen. She
wrote works for solo piano, piano and violin, and more than 100 songs, and at
least six operas—*Priscilla, Abon Hasson, The Aztec Princess, The Milk-Maids
Fair, The Andalusians,* and *Two Roses.* In 1906 her Prelude for piano won a
prize offered by the pianist Josef Hofmann. Like Maxwell she was for some
years a music critic, writing for the San Francisco paper *Pacific Town Talk* and
the *Pacific Coast Musical Review.* She also was the West Coast correspondent
for the *Musical Courier.* Her music drama, *The Snow Queen,* was performed in
Cleveland and New York as well as California. She later moved to Seattle,
where she died in 1929.

The third woman, Mary Carr Moore, was born in 1873 in Memphis,
Tennessee.[8] In 1881 she and her family moved to California, where she studied both voice and theory. Her first opera was *The Oracle,* for which she wrote
the libretto and sang the leading role in a San Francisco production in 1890.

Her four-act grand opera *Narcissa, or The Cost of Empire,* composed from 1909 to 1911, premiered in Seattle in 1912, with Moore conducting. It also was given a one-week run in San Francisco in 1925, where Moore staged and conducted the performance with an eighty-piece orchestra. With a libretto by her mother, Sarah Pratt Carr, *Narcissa* tells the story of Narcissa Whitman and her husband, Marcus Whitman, missionaries who were massacred in the Oregon Territory in 1847. Moore's opera *Los Rubios,* commissioned for the celebration of the 150th anniversary of the founding of Los Angeles, received its premiere on September 8, 1931. The following year came the premiere of her two-act *Davide Rizzio,* to an Italian libretto by Emanuel M. Browne about Mary, Queen of Scots. Moore also wrote the opera *Legende Provençale* (1928–35), which was never performed. She also produced numerous choral works, many songs, and instrumental pieces. Her suite, *Four Love Songs,* for voice, strings, and piano, won an award in 1932 from the National League of American Pen-Women. She continued to compose into the late 1940s and died in California in 1957.

None of the American women opera composers named thus far in this chapter ever had an opera performed in an internationally known opera house, in either Europe or America. Yet the precedent had been set, at least in Europe. The French composer Marie Félicie Clémence de Reiset, Vicomtesse de Grandval (1830–1907), who had studied composition with Flotow and Saint-Saëns, had no fewer than five operas produced in Paris between 1859 and 1869, first *Le Sou de Lise* and last *Piccolino,* and another, *Mazeppa,* in Bordeaux in 1892.[9] Of course her rank and wealth may or may not have influenced these performances. Perhaps she financed them herself. This was not the case, though, with Ethel Smyth, whose first opera, *Fantasio,* to a libretto in German by the composer Henry Brewster, was produced in 1898 in Weimar, Germany.[10] Born in England in 1858, Smyth studied at the Leipzig Conservatory and in Berlin. She presented several orchestral works in London in 1890. Her first major success was the performance of her Mass in D in London in 1893. From then on she devoted herself principally to composing operas, both serious and comic, and some songs. A militant leader in the women's suffrage movement, she also composed its theme song, "The March of the Women." She was honored in 1923 by being made a dame of the British Empire.

An Englishwoman who worked chiefly in Europe, Smyth would have no place in this book except for the fact that her opera *Der Wald* (The Forest), to a German libretto by her and Brewster, was the first and at the time of this writing still the *only* opera composed by a woman to be presented at the Metropolitan Opera. It was performed there twice during the 1902–3 season because Maurice Grau, then manager of the company, believed it had considerable novelty appeal. He, however, died suddenly before the first American performance. It also was performed once in Boston. Of Smyth's four more operas, her next opera, *The Wreckers,* proved to be her single most successful work; it had librettos in French, German, and English, but to the best of my knowledge, it has not been performed in America. Henry Wood, Sir Thomas Beecham, Bruno Walter, and Arthur Nikisch were among the conductors of her works. She died in 1944.

Although the Metropolitan Opera did not perform another work by a woman, on November 17, 1925, its house was the site of a special program to honor a woman on her golden anniversary as a composer and conductor of operas. Ironically none of her works was ever produced there, nor did she ever conduct there. The woman so honored was Emma R. Steiner. The program included the overture to her opera *Fleurette* (1877), and scenes from her three-act light opera *The Burra Pundit* (1907) and the two-act comic opera *The Man from Paris* (1900). The program ended with her orchestral song, "The Flag—Forever May It Wave" (1918), dedicated to her grandfather, Colonel Stephen Steiner, who led the American victory at North Point, near Fort McHenry, during the War of 1812, and incorporating some melodies from that period.

Steiner was born in 1852 in Baltimore, Maryland.[11] Her father was Colonel Frederick B. Steiner, and her mother was a fine pianist. She was writing simple tunes by the age of seven and produced a piano duet at age nine, but her parents did not encourage her musical ambitions. About a year later a number of Baltimoreans interested in music advised her father to send her to Paris to study, but nothing came of the suggestion. Nevertheless, she was determined to continue and by age eleven had begun working on a grand opera, *Aminaide,* for which she completed one and one-half acts. One scene of this opera was produced at Baltimore's Peabody Conservatory, whose director at the time, the Danish composer Asger Hamerick, liked it very much. Steiner herself did not study at the Peabody, however. Unfortunately the score of *Aminaide* was lost along with many of her other belongings in a New York City warehouse fire in 1902.

It is not known exactly when or how Steiner managed to break away from her family and pursue a career in music. One account has it that she sang in the chorus of several touring companies and was finally asked by manager Edward E. Rice to rehearse his opera company's orchestra. Another says that she began to compose waltzes and other popular music in order to earn money and so attracted the attention of opera managers, who then asked her to assist them. However it happened, by the time she was twenty-one Steiner had left Baltimore for Chicago, where one of her earliest jobs, perhaps her first, was as assistant music director to Rice in the Rice and Collier "Iolanthe" Company.

The Gilbert and Sullivan comic operas were immensely popular in America in the 1880s and 1890s, and managers formed touring companies that took each new opera from town to town. For example, the *Musical Record* of January 3, 1880, announced under the headline "A Lady Conductor" that Miss Fannie Arnold was to bring out Sullivan's *Sorcerer* in Brownville, Nebraska, conducting it herself. Arnold explained, "Tho' we are miles and miles from Boston, America's musical centre, yet in our small way we have considerable music here." Steiner conducted for a number of companies that presented these and other light operas. She worked three seasons with George Baker's company, unspecified periods with Grau and Fitzgerald and the Julius Howe Company, and finally one season in New York with Heinrich Conried, who the following year, 1903, became the manager of the Metropolitan Opera. Conried allegedly told Steiner that he would gladly have appointed her conductor at the Met if only he had dared.

By 1902 Steiner was relatively well known. Her opera *Fleurette* had been produced in San Francisco in 1889 and in New York in 1891. A reviewer said that its music was far superior to that usually heard on the comic opera stage, calling the Act I finale brilliant and effective, worthy of composers of much greater fame, clearly indicating that Steiner could undertake serious opera if she wished. As a conductor, Steiner was "easy, self-contained, and careful," and the production was a success despite an unsympathetic orchestra and inferior company. Moreover, said the reviewer, the libretto, by Edgar Smith, was just plain terrible; "more Steiner is wanted, and less Smith."[12]

In 1894 Steiner conducted the eighty-man Anton Seidl Orchestra, one of the best of its time, in New York City in a program of her own works. In 1896 *Freund's* reported that she was seriously ill with pneumonia,[13] potentially fatal in that pre-antibiotic era, but she recovered and in 1897 announced that she would soon start a series of instrumental and vocal concerts with forty members of the New York Metropolitan Orchestra, leading them in works by Wagner, Flotow, Liszt, and Meyerbeer.[14] By then she herself had written at least two other operas, *Day Dreams,* based on Tennyson's *Sleeping Beauty,* and *Brigands.*

Shortly after the turn of the century Steiner again became ill, and then was troubled with failing eyesight. The doctors ordered complete rest, which she must have interpreted to mean a radical change. She went to Nome, Alaska —in those days one of the last frontier outposts—and carrying provisions and tools on her back became the first white woman to go to the tin fields 100 miles northwest of Nome. She later was credited with discovering important tin deposits there. She spent ten years in Alaska, prospecting, mining, and traveling. After her return to New York she often gave lectures, illustrated by slides, on Alaska's natural resources.

In 1921 Emma Steiner presented *Harmony and Discord,* a program of her own works, at New York's Museum of Natural History. It included songs, arias, an oboe solo, and the vocal quartet from *The Man from Paris,* and received quite favorable reviews. During her career, she produced seven operas, a number of musical dramas, ballets, and many songs and dances. The score for a dance for piano and orchestra, *Gavotte Menzeli,* published in 1914, designates this work as opus no. 400. Toward the end of her life she founded the

Home for Aged and Infirm Musicians, for which she and her friend Margaret I. MacDonald donated property at Bay Shore, Long Island. This home also received the proceeds of her 1925 "golden jubilee" concert at the Metropolitan Opera House. By then Steiner had conducted more than 6000 performances of more than fifty different operas and operettas. According to the *New York Times,* work and worry over the new musicians' home brought on a nervous collapse, followed by heart trouble, which eventually caused her death on February 27, 1929.

It was another fifty years before a woman appeared on the podium of the Metropolitan Opera. On January 13, 1976, Sarah Caldwell became the first woman to conduct there. She was engaged for eleven performances of Verdi's *La Traviata* that season, and the first performance, in which her good friend, soprano Beverly Sills, sang the title role, was an artistic triumph. Said one of New York's most respected critics, who also happened to be an expert on Verdi:

> Until "La Traviata," the Met season lacked first-rate conductors. Miss Caldwell's arrival there—it was her debut in the house—brought a triumph for her and confirmation of her great power to animate a score and reveal its composer's intentions. By the stopwatch, and by tradition, many of her tempi must probably be counted fast—as fast, even, as the metronome markings in Verdi's score! But there was no sense of hustle— only Verdian vitality, tension, vigor, dramatic impetus. The singers were not straitjacketed. When a phrase needed to expand, or a syllable to be dwelt on, or an attack to be delayed for an instant, Miss Caldwell was there. She also showed an uncommon command of dramatically striking timbres and of instrumental balances in support of, not in competition with, the individual voices.[15]

This certainly is high praise for a woman whose first strength long had been acknowledged to be her sense of theater and skillful staging, and whose emergence as a conductor came relatively late and, she once said herself, almost by accident.

Sarah Caldwell began her musical studies on the violin, and at one point in her life she nearly accepted an offer to join the violin section of the Minneapolis Symphony.[16] But her dual interest in the theater and music won out, and she turned the offer down. Caldwell was born in 1928 in Maryville, Missouri. She grew up in Fayetteville, Arkansas, where her mother moved when her second husband, Henry Alexander, became a professor of political science at the University of Arkansas. Her mother, educated at Northwestern University and the Juilliard School, taught piano during Sarah's childhood. Sarah herself took up the violin and was giving recitals by the age of ten. At fourteen she graduated from high school and then studied for a time at Hendrix College and the University of Arkansas. In her late teens she went to Boston to attend the New England Conservatory, and it was there that she first became interested in opera.

In the early 1940s Caldwell staged Ralph Vaughan Williams's *Riders to the Sea* at Tanglewood, and shortly afterward conductor Serge Koussevitsky named her to the faculty of the Opera Workshop at Tanglewood, which was headed by Boris Goldovsky. Goldovsky, a Moscow-born pianist and conductor who had been in America since about 1930, later recalled that he first met Caldwell about 1942 and she became his personal assistant soon afterward, working with him for about a decade at Tanglewood, Worcester, Boston, and the New England Conservatory. In 1946 Goldovsky founded the New England Opera Theater of Boston. He hoped to make it into a permanent Boston company and a vehicle for carrying out his concept of opera. Unlike many music directors, Goldovsky regarded theater to be as important as music, and he believed that in opera the two are intricately entwined. Although he and Caldwell eventually came to a parting of the ways, she always acknowledged that he had been a great teacher, with many ideas far ahead of his time.

In the mid-1950s the old Boston Opera House was torn down and Goldovsky abandoned his Boston ambitions and turned to a touring company, the Goldovsky Grand Opera Theater. By then Caldwell, who in 1952 joined Boston University's opera department, had begun to plan for her own Boston company, and in 1957, with only $5000, she founded the Opera Group (later Company) of Boston. It gave its first production the following year, and in subsequent seasons, though it presented only about four productions per season for a total of twelve to sixteen performances, it became known as one of the most innovative companies in the United States. Working as producer, stage director, sometime conductor, and—in a sense most important of all—fund-raiser, Caldwell presented the Boston public with many "firsts"— the first American productions of Schoenberg's *Moses und Aron* (1966) and Rossini's *Semiramide;* the first American stage appearance of the great Australian soprano, Joan Sutherland; the first *Boris Godunov* in Mussorgsky's own orchestration (1966); the first five-act *Don Carlos* in Verdi's original French edition (1972); and in 1972 the first complete version of Berlioz's *Les Troyens* ever staged in the United States (the Metropolitan Opera followed suit two years later).

By 1978 the company was operating on a $1.5 million budget, and Caldwell was trying to raise funds for building a proper opera house, having for years performed in college gyms, converted movie theaters, convention halls, and dirt-floored arenas. The next decade, however, brought insurmountable financial problems, some relating to the opera house and others to the 1988 festival Making Music Together, conceived by Caldwell to bring together Americans and artists from the former Soviet Union. She was forced to stop working in Boston in 1990, but she continued her efforts to remedy the problems of the opera house. She also traveled frequently to Russia, where she became principal guest conductor of the Ural Philharmonic. In 1998 she staged the premiere of a two-act chamber opera, *The Black Swan,* by composer Thomas Whitman and librettist Nathalie Anderson, at Swarthmore College, marking her first return to opera. The following year she accepted an appointment as distinguished professor and chair of the opera department at the University of Arkansas, but still hoped to revive her Boston company as well.

According to *Boston Globe* critic Richard Dyer, who closely followed Caldwell's career over the years, her eloquent advocacy of opera as an important and exciting art took three principal forms: her musical preparation and conducting, her stage direction, and her skill as an impresario, that is, in choosing repertory and convincing patrons to underwrite her choices. Caldwell was initially an indifferent conductor with little of the conventional technique of wielding a baton. She sometimes forgot an upbeat or downbeat, or could not reestablish order when the orchestra fell apart, or herself became so absorbed in the action onstage that she forgot to conduct at all. But she managed to pull through and continued to attract fine musicians because of her sheer enthusiasm, her attention to tone and the shape of a melodic line, and her feeling for the pace of an opera.[17] In time her technique improved, so much so that from about 1975 on she was invited to conduct symphony orchestras all over the United States and Europe, as well as operas in New York and elsewhere.

As a stage director, Caldwell was considered by many to have no equal. At her best, her ideas enhanced the meaning of the music and drama in a striking visual way; for example, in *Moses und Aron* she placed the two main characters back to back on a slowly revolving circular platform, illustrating in one bold stroke the underlying meaning—that they represent two complementary aspects of a single personality.

Though Caldwell was asked to conduct the New York Philharmonic in a special concert celebrating women composers in 1975, and much was made, a few months later, of her being the first woman to conduct the Metropolitan Opera, she herself denied having difficulties because of her sex. This is particularly interesting in that reviews of her performances—especially in earlier days—often referred to her physical appearance in terms not only unflattering but of a kind rarely if ever used for a man on the podium. Fortunately she chose to ignore them, and perhaps other slights as well, for her talent in creating exciting opera performances was undeniable. Eve Queler, who in 1967 founded her own orchestra to present operas in concert form, also said she never felt discriminated against as a woman, but in the same interview she stated, "I know that some orchestra managers, when approached to engage me, turned me down because 'we already have hired our woman guest conductor for the season.'"[18]

Eve Rabin Queler was born in 1936 in New York and began piano lessons at the age of five.[19] Her first ambition was to be a concert pianist, and to this end she practiced constantly, gave recitals, and entered competitions. After a year off following graduation from the High School of Music and Art, where she played French horn in the orchestra, she enrolled at both City College of New York and the Mannes School of Music. At the former she met Stanley Queler, whom she married while he was still attending law school. Unable to afford further music study for the time being, she gave up the idea of a concert career and decided to become an accompanist, taking on various assignments as pianist and organist.

In 1957 their first child, Andrew, was born, and six months later Queler was engaged as rehearsal accompanist and coach at the New York City Opera. It was a bad year for her. She had thirteen operas to learn, a baby to care for, and little experience. She was not rehired the following year, and at this point Queler decided to return to Mannes and study conducting with Carl Bamberger. A second child was born, a daughter, but Queler continued her studies, with Joseph Rosenstock of the Metropolitan Opera and Igor Markevitch of the Monte Carlo Orchestra.

In 1967, in part to test her conducting ability, in part to provide instrumental students with a chance to learn opera repertory, which was largely overlooked at conservatories, Queler established the Opera Orchestra of New York. At first it only rehearsed; then it performed an opera in concert form in a junior high school auditorium. As the orchestra developed, it moved to more prestigious halls, and in 1972 it made its debut in Carnegie Hall, where it continued to appear. By then, its student musicians had grown into or been replaced by professional instrumentalists, and its singers, instead of young beginners, were opera stars from the Metropolitan and other companies. In addition, instead of performing the standard repertory, Queler had begun to present rarely performed operas—Donizetti's *Parisina d'Este,* Meyerbeer's *L'Africaine,* Zandonai's *Francesca da Rimini,* Verdi's *Lombardi,* Massenet's *Le Cid.*

Oddly enough, Queler did not list herself as a conductor on her resumé until the fall of 1970, when she was appointed associate conductor of the Fort Wayne (Indiana) Orchestra. For one season she moved to Indiana, returning to New York only when she had a week or more off. But at the end of the year, rather than moving her family to the Midwest, she decided to give up the job. From that time on, she was offered more and more guest-conducting assignments, in Europe and in the United States, for both staged productions of operas and, increasingly, wholly symphonic concerts. In 1975 she conducted the San Antonio Symphony, which she regarded as a breakthrough for a woman, and in the summer of 1976 the Philadelphia Orchestra at Saratoga. There followed appearances with the Hartford Symphony, New Jersey Symphony, Colorado Springs Symphony, and Cleveland Orchestra. Also, in 1978 she appeared for the first time in the pit of the New York City Opera, marking her first opportunity to conduct a fully staged production in New York. The work was Mozart's *The Marriage of Figaro,* and despite the handicap of performing with no orchestral rehearsal, the performance was a success.[20]

Conducting is a demanding job. For her Opera Orchestra, Queler found she had to go through approximately fifty neglected scores for every opera she finally chose to perform. Moreover, when she began conducting purely instrumental works, she had to learn, or relearn, the symphonic literature to know it sufficiently well. She always conducted from memory.[21] "Conducting," she once said, "involves endless studying of scores. In a sense I'm lucky because I can do a lot of studying in my head and that means I can work on an opera almost any time. I can hear any part of a score at will—if I can't hear a piece at will, I know I'm not familiar enough with the music and have to go back and study the score."[22] In the late 1990s Queler was still conducting neglected operas. Of her performance of Halévy's *La Juive,* a *New York Times* reviewer wrote: "Ms. Queler conducted the orchestra and excellent Dallas Symphony Chorus in a surely paced and spacious performance of this over-three-hour score. . . . Once again she has rendered opera a service by championing an overlooked work. Her legacy will be large."[23]

In 1966, just before Queler founded the Opera Orchestra of New York, another woman, Judith Somogi, was hired as assistant conductor with the New York City Opera, but it was some years before she conducted a performance herself. When Somogi was first hired, her job had no title. She began as a coach, that is, a pianist who helps singers prepare their roles. She went on to conduct backstage ensembles, help prepare the chorus, play piano accompaniments during rehearsals, and occasionally help out in the orchestra, playing the celesta or another instrument. Then, on March 17, 1974, she led Gilbert and Sullivan's *The Mikado,* the first time a woman had conducted the company.

Judith Somogi was born in 1943 in Brooklyn, New York, and grew up in Lynbrook, Long Island.[24] She first studied violin and then piano, but did not decide to become a professional musician until her last year in high school. She went to the Juilliard School, where she majored in piano and received both bachelor's and master's degrees. She put in a seven-year stint as organist and choir director of a local church, where she hired soloists and guest organists, conducted oratorios, and acquired considerable conducting experience. She also spent one summer at the Oberlin Music Theater, where she conducted *The Mikado* and *La Traviata.* She was hired as one of Leopold Stokowski's three assistants at the American Symphony Orchestra, which she conducted in nearly three dozen children's concerts. She also spent a summer studying chamber music at Tanglewood, she played for ballet and voice classes, and she served as music director of the American Savoyards, an off-Broadway Gilbert and Sullivan troupe. After she was hired by the New York City Opera, she spent three summers as assistant to conductor Thomas Schippers at the Festival of the Two Worlds in Spoleto, Italy. Then Christopher Keene, whom she had come to know at Spoleto, engaged Somogi to conduct Menotti's *Amahl and the Night Visitors* and *Help! Help! The Globolinks* at the ANTA Theater on

Broadway during the Christmas season of 1971, marking her New York conducting debut.

Though her New York City Opera debut in *The Mikado* was warmly praised, Somogi really came into her own later the same season when she conducted the company in Verdi's *Traviata*. In this performance, wrote *New York Times* critic Donal Henahan, she "met the challenge of the Verdi opera with the utmost aplomb and professionalism . . . and demonstrated not only intimacy with the score and technical security, but also the ability to control the pace and flow of the performance, which some conductors never learn to do with any consistency."

In May 1975 Somogi became the first woman to conduct a Naumburg concert, a long-standing series of free summer concerts, in New York's Central Park. Engagements followed with the Tulsa Philharmonic, Syracuse, Duluth, Oklahoma City, and Milwaukee Symphony orchestras, and with the Tulsa and San Diego operas. In 1977 Somogi was appointed music director of the Utica (New York) Symphony. In spring of that year she had made her conducting debut with the New York Philharmonic in a Promenades concert, of which Henahan wrote, it "left no doubts about her basic musicianship and competence as a baton wielder."[25] Somogi also continued to work with the New York City Opera, conducting a number of productions, and she conducted the live television broadcast of Douglas Moore's *The Ballad of Baby Doe* in 1976.

When asked about her views about women conductors, Somogi once half-jokingly suggested that opera was an ideal vehicle because the conductor was virtually hidden in the orchestra pit. By the winter of 1975–76, however, she said, "When I take my bow at a New York City Opera performance, and the audience realizes that a woman is conducting, there's a kind of 'Yeah, team' response from men and women alike. Of course, part of that reaction is because the idea of a woman conducting is still so new to most people. What we need now is a whole *army* of women pursuing conducting careers."[26] And in 1977 she said she believed there was no prejudice against women in the major orchestras and opera houses or the top echelons of management, though there still might be some among smaller organizations.[27] In fact, the opposite was true. The major orchestras were the last to engage women, and the smaller ones generally have the largest proportion of women players (these statistics are discussed further in Chapter 11).

Somogi capped off her career with a move to Germany to become principal conductor of the Frankfurt Opera, serving there from 1982 to 1988, and making only occasional guest appearances in the United States. She died of cancer in 1988, at the age of forty-seven.

Somogi's call for an "army of women conductors" was not shared by Alberta Masiello (1915–1991),[28] a widely respected opera coach and assistant conductor at the Metropolitan Opera. Born in Italy in 1915 and trained as a pianist at the Milan Conservatory, Masiello originally intended to be a concert pianist. She came to the United States in 1939 and studied further at the Juilliard School. She had a brief career as a mezzo-soprano, singing in night clubs and at the fledgling New York City Opera during the 1940s, but she soon devoted herself to vocal coaching, working privately in New York. In 1954 she took her first job as assistant conductor with the Chicago Lyric Opera, where she remained for three seasons before joining the Met as a rehearsal pianist in 1959. She also coached a number of famous singers, including the great soprano Maria Callas.

Though Masiello's name had been suggested to the Metropolitan Opera management before, allegedly there was not even a women's restroom in the part of the house where coaching and rehearsals took place. But in 1959 this obstacle was somehow overcome, and Masiello was hired. She rose from rehearsal pianist to assistant conductor, coaching all the principal artists and playing all the rehearsals for the operas she prepared, chiefly the Italian repertory, but she never conducted a performance at the Met. At one time the New York City Opera invited Masiello to conduct as well as coach, and the Metropolitan Opera appears to have extended a similar invitation, but Masiello would not consider it. In 1976 she told an interviewer:

> I am too old for pioneering in this respect—much too old. I think the time is coming when some lady will come through and be a great conductor. But my principle has always been that a great opera conductor really has to start from the bottom, to go backstage and try to understand all the ingredients that go into the soup. . . . You see, I have been a pianist, a singer, a coach. I have also conducted—not very much. But I should go to the podium of the Metropolitan and conduct? No. That would be against my principles.[29]

Another highly respected conductor is Jane Glover, a native of Britain who became well known in Europe through the 1980s, especially for conducting baroque music. She made her American debut at the Glimmerglass Opera Festival in 1994 with a Monteverdi opera and returned during the following three summers. She also conducted Glimmerglass productions at the Brooklyn Academy of Music in 1996 and the New York City Opera in 1997. Also known for choral conducting, she made several notable appearances with choruses in the United States, including Boston's Handel and Haydn Society.

Although both the Metropolitan and New York City opera companies— as well as some smaller organizations—had begun to lift their bars against women conductors, they remained remarkably slow to perform an opera by a woman composer. But in 1963 the Ford Foundation awarded a commission to Peggy Glanville-Hicks to compose a new opera for the San Francisco Opera, and in 1977 the New York City Opera presented the American premiere of

Thea Musgrave's *The Voice of Ariadne,* with the composer conducting. As it happens, neither woman was American by birth, but both lived in America for extended periods and their work had considerable impact in the United States.

Peggy Glanville-Hicks was born on December 29, 1912, in Melbourne, Australia, and began her musical education at the conservatory there, studying composition with Fritz Hart.[30] From 1929 to 1931 she studied at the Melba Conservatory, and in 1931, at age nineteen, she won an open scholarship to the Royal College of Music in London. There for the next five years she studied composition with Ralph Vaughan Williams, piano with Arthur Benjamin, and conducting with Constant Lambert and Malcolm Sargent. In 1936 she won another traveling scholarship for further studies, in Vienna with composer Egon Wellesz and in Paris with Nadia Boulanger. In 1938 Glanville-Hicks achieved her first big success when Sir Adrian Boult conducted her *Choral Suite* at the International Society of Contemporary Music Festival in London, the first time Australia was represented at the festival.

About 1940 Glanville-Hicks moved to the United States, where she remained for the next twenty years, composing many of her major works, becoming active in the cause of contemporary music, and writing extensively. She directed the Composers Forum concert series, which featured new works, and she was hired by Virgil Thomson as a music critic for the *New York Herald Tribune* from 1948 to 1958. Her reviews and articles also appeared in *Musical Quarterly* and other journals. During this period, she became an American citizen with a permanent residence in New York, but she also found time to travel widely, to Morocco, Greece, Italy, Jamaica. Her interest in Near Eastern and North African music, early awakened, developed further through these trips and began to be reflected in her own compositions. Her travels were assisted by two Guggenheim fellowships, in 1956 and 1957, a Fulbright grant in 1957–58 for research in Greek music, and a Rockefeller grant in 1961 for travel and research in the Middle and Far East.

Glanville-Hicks's earliest compositions, produced between 1932 and 1945, included an opera, three ballets, a flute concerto, piano concerto, sinfonia, cantata, and many chamber works, but she later withdrew nearly all of these. Instrumental works she composed in America include her *Concertino da Camera* (1945) for flute, clarinet, bassoon, and piano; Harp Sonata (1950); Sonata for piano and percussion (1951); *Three Gymnopedie* (1953) for string orchestra with solo instruments; *Sinfonia da Pacifica* (1953) for chamber orchestra; *Letters from Morocco* (1952), a set of songs for tenor and orchestra, given their premiere by conductor Leopold Stokowski; *Etruscan Concerto* (1956) for piano and orchestra; and *Concerto Romantico* (1957) for viola and orchestra. In these and in her ballets, film scores, and vocal works, Glanville-Hicks increasingly made explicit her idea that melody and rhythm are the quintessential elements of music and that harmony should have but a minor role, as it always has had in non-Western and ancient music. Rejecting atonality, neoclassicism, and serial techniques, she developed what she called a new kind of melody-rhythm structure.

Though her reputation as a composer had been building steadily over the years, she was not really considered fully established until she wrote her first full-length opera, *The Transposed Heads.* It was commissioned by the Louisville Opera—apparently the first opera commission awarded to a woman composer—was composed in 1953, and produced on April 4, 1954, by the Kentucky Opera Company and Louisville Symphony Orchestra. It was later recorded, and it was performed again in New York in 1958 at the Phoenix Theater. With a libretto by Thomas Mann based on his novel of the same name, the opera is in six scenes, all set in India, and the music, which includes elements of Hindu melodies and rhythms, is, according to composer George Antheil, among Glanville-Hicks's finest works.[31]

Immediately afterward Glanville-Hicks was commissioned to write several ballet scores, beginning with *The Masque of the Wild Man* (1958) and *Triad* (1958). She also wrote another opera, the one-act *Glittering Gate,* composed in 1956 and first performed in New York in 1959. Intended as a comic half-hour "curtain raiser" to precede another opera, it was performed together with Lou Harrison's *Rapunzel.* It is scored for tenor, baritone, chamber orchestra, and tape.

In 1961 Glanville-Hicks moved to Greece, and the following year she produced her next full-length opera, *Nausicaa,* with a libretto after Robert Graves's novel, *Homer's Daughter.* It was first performed in the ancient Herod Atticus theater, at the base of the Acropolis, on August 19, 1961. The production was recorded and broadcast four days later in the United States, and excerpts later were released on a commercial recording. Again using folk music, this time from various parts of Greece and enhanced with appropriate orchestration, this opera embodied the composer's theory that melody and rhythm are the all-important elements of music.

Sappho, commissioned by the San Francisco Opera in 1963, also drew on Greek material. English novelist Lawrence Durrell contributed the libretto. Glanville-Hicks's other important works include the three ballets *Saul and the Witch of Endor, Tragic Celebration (Jephtha's Daughter),* and *Season in Hell.* As Virgil Thomson said, Glanville-Hicks "made for herself out of elements from India, North Africa, and Greece a musical idiom that has proved useful in ballet, and surprisingly so for English-language opera."[32] In 1967 Glanville-Hicks underwent surgery for a brain tumor, and although she recovered she composed little after that. In 1975 she returned to Australia at the invitation of the Australian Music Centre to set up an Asian music studies program, which proved highly successful. She also began to explore new ways of uniting heard and seen elements. Among the products of this investigation was a 1978 exhibit called *Seven Sculptures/Compositions,* for which seven composers, including Glanville-Hicks, each wrote a work relating specifically to a different sculpture by Pamela Boden. In the exhibit each piece is individually lighted and revolving while its related composition plays from a tape.[33] Her piece, entitled *Girondelle for Giraffes,* was her last composition. She died in 1990.

The other woman to break ground for women opera composers was Thea Musgrave.[34] Her *Voice of Ariadne* was the first opera by a woman performed by a major New York company since the Met put on Ethel Smyth's *Der Wald* in 1903. Musgrave was born on May 27, 1928, near Edinburgh, Scotland, and though interested in music throughout her childhood, she originally planned a career in medicine. First enrolled as a premedical student at the University of Edinburgh, she switched to music after a couple of years. She studied for four years in Paris with Nadia Boulanger and scored her first success with *Cantata for a Summer's Day,* for chamber ensemble, narrator, and small chorus, performed at the Edinburgh Festival in 1955. Other important early works are the ballet suite *A Tale for Thieves* (1953), *Triptych* for tenor and orchestra (1959), and her first full-length opera, *Decision* (1964–65), which was performed several times at Sadler's Wells. Still earlier, in 1955, she had written a chamber opera, *The Abbot of Drimmock.* Musgrave also wrote a considerable amount of chamber music—two piano sonatas, a violin sonata, a string quartet[35]—and from 1959 to 1965 lectured on music at London University.

In the 1960s Musgrave developed an instrumental style she called "dramatic-abstract," in which certain instruments become dramatis personae but the music remains abstract because there is no program. She composed three chamber concertos, nos. 1, 2, and 3, from 1962 to 1966, and Concerto for Orchestra (1967), in which she began to use devices such as not only setting the instrument in opposition to the orchestra, as in the classic concerto, but having the solo instrument woo some of the others to its side. In the Concerto for Orchestra the first clarinet rises, physically and musically, to challenge the conductor's authority and incites the other players to join the rebellion. In the Clarinet Concerto (1968), the soloist moves about from one section of the orchestra to another, playing with each in turn, and sometimes attracting subsidiary soloists to form a concertante, a group of soloists, in dialogue with the rest of the orchestra. In her Viola Concerto, commissioned by the BBC and written for her husband, violist Peter Mark, she carried this device further. The solo viola enlists the orchestral violas, and they rise from their seats to join the soloist's cause, and then almost overwhelm him. And in her Horn Concerto (1971), at one point the four orchestral horn players surround the soloist and engage him or her in a kind of parodistic battle, and at another point the soloist summons horn calls from the horn players placed in different parts of the hall.

Increasingly, however, Musgrave devoted herself to theater music. Her first full-length ballet, *Beauty and the Beast,* performed by the Scottish Theater Ballet at Sadler's Wells in 1969, was a great success. In it she used taped music for the first time. She followed it in 1969 with *Soliloquy* for guitar and tape.

In 1970 Musgrave and her husband came to the United States, both to teach at the University of California at Santa Barbara. Her compositions, still largely unknown in America, now began to be performed more widely, and she herself began to conduct them occasionally. She later said she had begun to conduct quite by chance, after only two lessons, when *Beauty and the Beast* was to be put on in Edinburgh for a special Christmas production and the conductor could not be there. "They said I should do it," she told an interviewer, "and I said that's crazy . . . but I did it. It was jumping in at the deep end but it was a challenge and I enjoyed it. One thing is in my favor. I do know the music, and that helps."[36] In 1977 she conducted the Philadelphia Orchestra in a concert including her Concerto for Orchestra, but then said she would conduct only her own works. Indeed, she preferred to be involved only in their premieres, in effect establishing how she wanted the performance to go and then relinquishing the baton to others.

Musgrave herself conducted the New York City Opera production of her *Voice of Ariadne* in 1977. Based on a short story by Henry James and dedicated to Benjamin Britten, the three-act chamber opera had been premiered in 1974 by the English Opera Group at Britten's Aldeburgh Festival. Essentially a romantic ghost story, it portrays a husband who is temporarily seduced by the voice of a statue of Ariadne, which only he can hear, but who then is made to realize that his wife is his only true love. The score requires no chorus and can be performed by a small orchestra of thirteen instruments. The voice of Ariadne, along with sounds suggesting the sea and other effects, is supplied on prerecorded tape. The New York audience gave the opera and its composer a standing ovation, and most reviewers were enthusiastic. They praised Musgrave's excellent setting of English to music and her clever combination of tape and aleatory elements (in which the performers make certain choices). Critic Andrew Porter pointed out the composer's skillful planning, with a well-balanced sequence of solos, duets, and ensembles. Stylistically, too, Musgrave paralleled the events of the story, moving from diatonic to troubled atonal harmonies as the characters' emotions change from clear to confused.[37] But one critic believed the opera fell short, mainly because it has no real melody in which singers can let themselves loose.[38] The composer herself did not agree; to her, lyricism and the idiomatic handling of the voice were of basic importance, and she held that "there's even a motif for the word 'Ariadne' that people will go away singing by the end of the evening."[39]

In fall of 1977 Musgrave returned to Edinburgh to conduct the premiere of her next full-length opera, *Mary, Queen of Scots*. In three acts, with a libretto by the composer, it chronicles the seven years from Mary's return to Scotland in 1561 to her flight to England in 1568, forced by her half-brother, James Stewart, Earl of Moray. Performed several more times in Britain, the opera was given its American premiere six months later by the Virginia Opera Company, with her husband, Peter Mark, conducting, and it was enthusiastically received:

It is an interesting, affecting, and important work, successful on many counts: as a poetic drama, as a presentation of characters and conflicts, as a study of history, as a long stretch of imaginative and excellently written music, and as a music drama in which words, sounds, spectacle, and action conspire to stir a listener's mind and emotions. In short, it succeeds as a show, as a score, and as that fusion of both which creates good opera.[40]

But the same critic who had not liked *Ariadne* again complained that, although the dramatic qualities and setting of the language here were admirable, "the opera, as a whole, just misses, mostly because of its lack of sustained melodic flow—a fatal defect in a score that attempts to be melodic throughout."[41] The disagreement of critics, however, did not diminish Musgrave's achievement. None would deny that she had written an important work, whether or not they personally liked it, and that she merited serious attention. Musgrave herself simply said, "Opera, with its combination of elements—theatrical, dramatic—is a fascinating challenge."[42]

Soon afterward, in 1979, she wrote what was to be her most frequently performed work, *A Christmas Carol.* There followed *Harriet, the Woman Called Moses* (1985), based on the life of Harriet Tubman and her exploits on the Underground Railroad. This work uses authentic folk songs and spirituals in telling of Tubman's escape from slavery. Works of the 1990s include Concerto for marimba and orchestra; *Journey through a Japanese Landscape* (1994); a bass clarinet concerto entitled *Autumn Sonata* (1994); an oboe concerto entitled *Helios* (1995); and the two-act opera *Simón Bolívar* (1995), to her own libretto. Of the last Patrick J. Smith wrote in *Opera News,* "Thea Musgrave's strongest work . . . this historical fantasy not only shows her to be an accomplished musical dramatist . . . but demonstrates that she now knows how to shape a libretto with sureness and power." Still later works include *Phoenix Rising* (1998) for orchestra, and *Three Women—Queen, Slave, Mistress,* premiered by the Women's Philharmonic in San Francisco in 1999.

In addition to composition, Musgrave continued to conduct her own works, directing the Philadelphia Orchestra, New York City Opera, San Diego and San Francisco symphony orchestras, St. Paul Chamber Orchestra, and Royal Philharmonic, among others.

Other women were writing operas during the 1970s. One who achieved some local success was Margaret Garwood.[43] She received a grant from the National Endowment for the Arts for her one-act opera, *The Nightingale and the Rose,* first performed in Pennsylvania in 1973 and receiving its New York premiere in December 1978. Born in 1927 in New Jersey and trained at the Philadelphia Musical Academy, from which she received a master's degree, Garwood taught piano for many years and began composing about 1960. At first she wrote chiefly songs. Her cycle *lovesongs,* a setting of six poems by e. e.

cummings, was performed at New York's Carnegie Recital Hall in 1964. Three ballets entitled *Aesop's Fables* (1970), commissioned by Young Audiences, were widely performed in the Philadelphia schools. In 1965 Garwood began work on her first opera, the one-act *The Trojan Women,* which was performed by the Pennsylvania Opera Company in 1967. Her third opera, *Rappaccini's Daughter,* in two acts and based on Nathaniel Hawthorne's tale, was premiered in 1983. Her fourth opera, *Joringel and the Songflower* (1990), in seven scenes, is billed as "an opera for young people" and scored for soprano, mezzo-soprano, tenor, baritone, and dancer-mime. In 1998 she finished *if there are any heavens,* for chorus, English horn, and string orchestra. Garwood's music is lyrical and accessible. She writes her own opera librettos, saying that often the music itself suggests the words.

Another composer who writes all her own librettos is Nancy Van de Vate, who wrote six operas between 1986 and 1999, in addition to a good deal of choral and instrumental music. For many years Van de Vate pursued a dual career, teaching and composing. In 1974 she added still another facet, founding the League of Women Composers, which she headed for a number of years, in order to help other women develop their talents and find more recognition.

Van de Vate was born on December 30, 1930, in Plainfield, New Jersey.[44] She began her undergraduate work at the Eastman School of Music as a piano major, studying with Cecile Genhart, but decided to complete it at Wellesley College, where she majored in theory and got her bachelor's degree in 1952. She went on to get a master's and eventually a doctorate in composition, writing Concerto for piano and orchestra (1968) as her doctoral dissertation. In 1957 Van de Vate moved to the South. She taught piano privately from 1957 to 1963 and then began to teach on the college level, first at the University of Mississippi and then at Memphis State University from 1964 to 1966. Meanwhile she had become a member and officer of the Southeastern Composers' League. In 1968 she moved to Knoxville, Tennessee, where she taught at Knoxville College and Maryville College and played viola in the Knoxville Symphony Orchestra. In 1975 she joined the faculty of the University of Hawaii. For some years she lived in Jakarta, Indonesia, and in 1985 she moved permanently to Vienna, Austria. She became an Austrian citizen but retained her American citizenship as well. In 1990 she and her husband, Clyde Smith, founded Vienna Modern Masters, a nonprofit recording company making CDs of contemporary music, much of it by women composers.

Van de Vate's compositions, numbering about 130 by 1999, include many chamber works and some songs, as well as choral and orchestral pieces. Notable among her early works are her Sonata for viola and piano (1964); *Six Short Pieces* (1969) for solo viola; Quintet for brass (1974), which won first place in the Delius Composition Contest; String Trio no. 1 (1974); *Three Sound Pieces* (1973) for brass and percussion; and *Concertpiece* (1976) for cello and small orchestra. After her move to Vienna, Van de Vate wrote such instrumental works as the orchestral *Chernobyl* (1987), about the nuclear disaster in the former Soviet Union; *Katyn* (1989) for chorus and orchestra, in homage to the Poles who died in a massacre in 1939; *A Peacock Southeast Flew: Concerto for Pipa and Orchestra* (1997), showing the influence of her years in Asia; the theater piece *Cocaine Lil,* for jazz singers with percussion; and operas in both German and English. Among her operas, the one-act *In the Shadow of the Glen* (1994) has a libretto based on J. M. Synge's play, and the four-act *All Quiet on the Western Front* (1998), and the German version *Im Westen nichts Neues* (1999), is based on Erich Maria Remarque's famous novel about World War I.

The most successful American woman opera composer of the 1990s was Libby Larsen.[45] Born in 1950 in Delaware but raised in Minneapolis, Minnesota, she received bachelor's, master's, and doctoral degrees at the University of Minnesota, where her principal teachers were Dominick Argento, Eric Stokes, and Paul Fetler. She has written not only operas and theater pieces, but numerous orchestral works, a great deal of both sacred and secular choral music, chamber music, and songs. She was cofounder of the Minnesota Composers' Forum, an advocacy group linking communities with composers and performers that evolved into the American Composers Forum. She was composer-in-residence for a number of groups and colleges, and has won many awards. Important orchestral works are Symphony no. 3: *Lyric* (1992) and *String Symphony* no. 4. Notable among her instrumental solo and chamber works are *Aubade* for solo flute, premiered by Eugenia Zukerman; *Four on the Floor* (1983) for piano, violin, cello, and bass, a very fast short piece that reflects her love for boogie-woogie; *Slang* (1994) for clarinet, violin, and piano; and *Holy Roller* (1997) for saxophone and piano. Outstanding vocal works include the song cycles *Songs from Letters* (1989), a setting of letters from Calamity Jane to her daughter, and *Sonnets from the Portuguese* (1991) a setting of Elizabeth Barrett Browning's poems that was featured on the Grammy Award winning CD *The Art of Arleen Auger* (the soprano commissioned this work). Larsen's operas include *Frankenstein: The Modern Prometheus* (1990), which featured giant projection screens and scrims hanging in the hall, invitations to "see what the monster saw," and *Eric Hermannson's Soul* (1998), based on the story by Willa Cather. According to Larsen, "Opera is . . . a form that lets us dwell deeply on a complex emotion for a long period of time. Opera really is the only vocal form that still allows us to do that. . . . To me opera is theater, and the best theater comes from the collaboration of passions [between librettist and composer]."[46]

Some composers best known for their use of experimental contemporary idioms also tried their hand at opera, among them Lucia Dlugoszewski *(The Heidi Songs),* Beth Anderson *(Queen Christina),* Shulamit Ran *(Between Two Worlds,* based on *The Dybbuk),* Meredith Monk *(Atlas),* and Anne LeBaron *(The E & O Line).* Some of them combine electronics with live performance. Their work is discussed in subsequent chapters.[47]

9

CONTEMPORARY AND
POSTMODERN IDIOMS—
AFTER 1950

*I*N THE SECOND HALF of the twentieth century composers began to work
with new modes of musical expression. Technical developments, notably
the perfection and increasing sophistication of electronic equipment and of
computers, enabled the creation of new kinds of sound. Pure electronic music,
in which all sounds are generated by machinery and recorded on tape, attracted
some composers; they are discussed in Chapter 10. Increasingly, however, such
material was combined with vocal and instrumental performance, both taped
and live. In some instances new instruments were devised. In others, instruments and human voices were used in new ways; for example, a pianist might
be required not only to play the keyboard but to pluck or otherwise manipulate the piano's strings, with or without the aid of mallets or other implements.
Sometimes performers were told to choose the portion of a composition they
would play, or in what order they would play its sections, or they were asked
to improvise. Composers used pitches lying between the conventional half-
tones of the chromatic scale—quarter tones and other microtones. Melodies
were broken into fragments. Contrasting rhythms were made to overlap or
were used simultaneously. Members of instrumental ensembles were physically separated into groups and subgroups. As might be expected, every one of
these techniques and styles has attracted both women and men composers.
And in the latter decades of the 1900s, some women rebelled against extreme
experimentalism and returned to more lyrical tonal music, although they
sometimes combined it with newer elements and techniques.

If composition is a difficult field in which to succeed, creating music in
new ways is harder yet. As Janet Baker-Carr put it:

> The eye delights in new sensation. Not so the ear, which seeks patterns
> and is grateful for repetition. If in hearing a new piece the ear does not
> recognize a familiar structure or pattern, the listener is prevented from
> participating and responding and so is unable to find the significance or
> meaning of the whole. . . . Only as the patterns and relationships become

familiar does the music itself become evocative and significant. This is why most people go to concerts to hear a beautiful performance of music that they know.[1]

Relatively few people are willing to experiment, and that is true of performers and conductors as well as audiences. Some composers, to be sure, were less radical. They continued to use the human voice and traditional instruments, although not always in conventional fashion.

Marga Richter was born on October 21, 1926, in Reedsburg, Wisconsin.[2] She received her bachelor's and master's degrees from the Juilliard School of Music in New York, where she studied composition with William Bergsma and Vincent Persichetti and piano with Rosalyn Tureck. Although at first intending to become a concert pianist, she soon turned to composition. Among her first published works were Clarinet Sonata, first played in New York in 1948, and *Two Short Suites for Young Pianists* (1947). Her three-movement Piano Sonata, composed in 1953 but not performed until 1964, shows some typical features of her style: wide-ranging pitches, free use of tone clusters and other dissonances, and, in the third movement especially, a strong rhythmic drive, in which chordal passages alternate with running passages.

Notable among Richter's longer orchestral works are Concerto for piano, violas, cellos, and string basses, also called Piano Concerto no. 1, given its premiere in San Francisco in 1957, of which critic Alfred Frankenstein wrote, "I do not recall hearing a new piano concerto with such keen interest since the second concerto of Ravel was revealed."[3] In five short, strongly contrasting movements, the concerto was later recorded and was described by several critics as "virile" and "masculine."[4] Richter did not compose her second piano concerto for nearly twenty years. Entitled *Landscapes of the Mind I,* or Piano Concerto no. 2, and composed in 1974, it received its orchestral premiere with the Tucson Symphony in 1976. In contrast to the first concerto, it is scored for a full orchestra of strings and brass, plus electric guitar, electric bass guitar, and a number of unusual percussion instruments, including electric tamboura, two tomtoms, and Indian drums. It is divided into two sections. The second is based on an Indian raga but is treated at least partly in Western style; for example, it concludes with a climax of volume and tempo, rather than subsiding to a quiet ending in characteristic Indian style.[5] In succeeding years Richter wrote *Landscapes of the Mind II,* a moody, impressionistic piece for violin and piano, and *Landscapes of the Mind III,* a piano trio. The second in the series was written for Daniel Heifetz, who included it in his prize-winning Tchaikovsky Competition concert in Moscow. The "Landscapes" of the titles refer to Richter's response to two paintings by Georgia O'Keeffe, *Sky Above Clouds II* and *Pelvis I.*

An earlier important work is *Abyss* (1964), commissioned by the Harkness Ballet and performed by that troupe on five continents. It later became part of the repertory of the Joffrey, Boston, Pennsylvania, and other ballet companies and has been played as an orchestral suite. Particularly notable is its first section, an extended, very lyrical viola solo, accompanied by the muted strings of the rest of the orchestra.

Married to Alan Skelly and a longtime resident of Long Island, Richter in 1972 became a cofounder, with Herbert A. Deutsch, of the Long Island Composers Alliance. From 1966 to 1978 she was an annual recipient of the ASCAP Standard Award, and in 1977 she received a National Endowment for the Arts grant to write a concerto, which led to *Spectral Chimes/Enshrouded Hills,* finished in 1980. Inspired by Thomas Hardy's novel *Tess of the d'Urbervilles,* specifically the author's references to phantoms and bells and the setting among misty hills, the concerto is in a single movement based loosely on sonata-allegro form and scored for string, woodwind, and brass quintets with orchestra. In 1986 Richter visited Tibet, and inspired both by chanting monks and the magnificent landscape, she wrote *Quanri* (Snow Mountain) in 1988, a set of theme and twenty variations for cello and piano, which she called "a paean to the fortitude and resilience of the oppressed Tibetan people."[6] Hearing the recording of this work, a reviewer called it a "startling ritual drama . . . a tour de force for cello and piano employing 'chromatic alterations' of a Jokhang Temple chant."[7] Another wrote, "The work is highly romantic, and vacillates between action and contemplation . . . [listeners] can revel in its wonderful expression of various moods."[8]

Richter's important orchestral works of the 1980s are *Out of Shadows and Solitude* (1985) for full orchestra, and *Düsseldorf Concerto* (1982) for string orchestra, harp, and solo flute and viola. The latter was commissioned by the Düsseldorf Ensemble and quotes material from other composers—Gubaidulina, Beethoven, Schumann, Brahms—and a hymn sung by her opera-singer mother, "Open My Eyes That I May See." After a 1992 performance by the Women's Philharmonic, a reviewer called it the most distinguished composition of the evening, saying "a skillful handling of means resulted in a completely finished work, in no sense a pastiche but the endeavor of a serious artist and composer."[9]

Richter's work of the 1970s and 1980s displays a dramatic, emotionally charged chromaticism, with a strong rhythmic drive and occasionally a modal orientation. Her music of the 1990s is somewhat more tonal, with fewer angular lines and more subtle rhythms.[10] This later group includes *Into My Heart* (1991), a cycle of seven poems for mixed chorus and brass sextet, dedicated to the memory of her husband, who died in 1988; *Variations and Interludes on Themes from Monteverdi and Bach* (1992), a one-movement concerto for piano, violin, cello, and orchestra that, as the title suggests, quotes from the two composers; and the one-act opera *Riders to the Sea* (1996), based on John Synge's play and scored for soloists, flute or penny whistle, Celtic harp, concert accordion, Irish drum, and string quintet.

A contemporary of Richter's, Ruth Schonthal was born in Germany in 1924 and began composing at the age of 5.[11] The political situation caused her family to move, first to Sweden, where her first Piano Sonatina was published in 1940, and then to Mexico. There she had performances of two large orchestral works, *Six Preludes for Orchestra* and *Concerto Romantico* for piano and orchestra. In 1946 she met Paul Hindemith while he was touring Mexico and accepted his offer to study with him at Yale University. Schonthal was not attracted to serialism or the extreme modernism of John Cage but retained her own classic-romantic heritage, sometimes combining it with elements of Mexican folk music, aleatory components, (in which are decisions left to the performers), and minimalist techniques. Her music is mainly tonal, with dissonance used for dramatic effect. Her output includes three string quartets, numerous keyboard works, chamber music, two piano concertos, many songs, and a number of theater pieces. Among this last group, *Jocasta* (1996–97), premiered in New York in 1998, has a libretto that sets the Oedipus legend from Jocasta's viewpoint. The work combines spoken words, Sprechstimme, recitative, arias, choral speaking and singing, and music for dance. Her *Bird over Jerusalem* (1992) for flute, prepared piano, and taped Arab music incorporates allusions to and quotations from Jewish and Christian music as well as Arab lamentations. Other late works include *The Young Dead Soldiers* (1986), for mixed chorus and chamber orchestra; *Self-Portrait of the Artist as an Older Woman* (1991) for piano; and *Trompetengesänge* (1993), for medium voice, trumpet, violin, cello, piano, and snare drum.

Ursula Mamlok also incorporated new modes of expression. Mamlok was born in 1928 in Berlin where she began her first music studies in piano and theory with composer-musicologist Gustav Ernst.[12] After emigrating with her family to Ecuador in 1939, she sent some of her compositions to the Mannes College of Music in New York and in 1942 was awarded a full scholarship to study composition there with George Szell. From that time on she made her home in the United States. Later she also studied with Roger Sessions, Edward Steuermann, Stefan Wolpe, and Ralph Shapey, and earned both bachelor's and master's degrees at the Manhattan School of Music.

Mamlok composed principally songs and chamber music, although she did write a symphony and in 1976 she produced one large-scale work, Concerto for oboe and orchestra, which received its premiere at the University of Illinois in 1978. Mamlok's most frequently performed compositions include Variations for solo flute (1961), the trio *Stray Birds* (1963) for soprano, flute, and cello, and *Haiku Settings* (1967), for soprano and flute. *Stray Birds,* five short songs based on writings by the Hindu poet Rabindranath Tagore and dedicated to the late President John F. Kennedy, is constructed on a twelve-tone row but is more emotional than most such compositions. Voice and instruments both reflect the quality of birdsong. A similar effect is achieved in the five *Haiku Settings,* in which both flute and voice are made to sound like the songs of a rocking gull, a nightingale, and a sparrow, the trill of a tree frog, and the spatter of rain. In Sextet for flute, clarinet, bass clarinet, violin, double bass, and piano, commissioned and premiered by Parnassus in New York in 1977, a scheme of musical pitches and time relationships gives the work its shape. Mamlok herself summed up her style of composition: "My primary concern as a composer has been the consolidation of old and new techniques which best serve to express the work at hand." Her work in general incorporates the neoclassicism of her early works with serial techniques. She further said: "My own 'recipes' for using the twelve-tone system, which change from work to work, give me the harmonic structure I need for unified compositions. As far as form is concerned, I prefer simple closed forms (such as ABA) and their extensions."[13]

Mamlok received numerous commissions, awards, and grants, and from 1976 on she taught composition at the Manhattan School of Music. Among her later works is *Constellations* (1994) for orchestra, commissioned and premiered by the San Francisco Symphony. Others are *Der Andreas Garten* (1987) for mezzo-soprano, flute, and harp, written for the Jubal Trio; *Polarities* (1995) for flute, violin, cello, and piano; *Festive Sounds* (1996) for organ; and String Quartet no. 2 (1998). At the time of this writing Mamlok was working on a number of piano pieces.

Joyce Mekeel, born in 1931 in New Haven, Connecticut, studied at the Paris Conservatory from 1955 to 1957 and in 1960 received her master's degree from Yale University.[14] Her teachers included Nadia Boulanger and Earl Kim; an accomplished harpsichordist, she also studied with Ralph Kirkpatrick and Gustav Leonhardt. A number of her compositions are closely related to theater and ballet—for a time she worked with theater and dance companies—including scores for productions of Shakespeare's *Othello, Macbeth,*and *Richard III* and George Bernard Shaw's *Androcles and the Lion.* Always interested in dramatic presentation of text, Mekeel wrote a tape score for Gertrude Stein's *Yes Is for a Very Young Man* (1965).

Beginning about 1970 Mekeel started to pursue two other interests, anthropology, which took her on several fields trips to West Africa, and sculpture, which led to several shows. From 1964 to 1970 Mekeel taught at the New England Conservatory, and in 1970 she joined the faculty of Boston University, where she taught for almost two decades.

Although Mekeel wrote for ordinary instruments and the human voice, she frequently treated them in unusual ways. For example, *The Shape of Silence* (1969) for solo flute calls for the flutist to walk and to whisper as well as to blow and overblow the instrument. Her *Corridors of Dream* (1972), for mezzo-soprano, alto flute, clarinet, viola, cello, harp, and conductor (who also speaks and plays percussion instruments), uses a variety of German texts, some in the original and some in translation. The first words are spoken by the flutist, partly through the instrument, over a repeated accompaniment played by the harp. Then, in the first large section, the singer performs in the manner used in Japanese Noh plays, that is, a kind of rhythmic recitation. In another section, the conductor recites a marching song, accompanied by winds and harp, while the singer utters a frantically rapid speech accompanied by the strings. In *Serena* (1975), for mezzo-soprano, speaker, and piano, the singer performs a multilingual text while the speaker, in the background, declaims a poem, and the piano, fitted with cymbals and other devices on the strings, accompanies this dialogue. *Planh* (1975), for solo violin, presents a set of motifs that, in the space of thirteen minutes or so, exploit virtually all the sonorities of that instrument. In 1978 she wrote *Alarums and Excursions* for the Boston Musica Viva ensemble. Scored for mezzo-soprano, flute, clarinet, piano, violin, viola, cello, and percussion, it uses texts in six languages, has the instrumentalists as well as the conductor declaim and sing, and includes a section in which the soloist utters gibberish and gesticulates wildly. The music is less a direct setting of the texts than an evocation of their feeling and atmosphere, and the overall effect is highly dramatic. A later work for woodwind quintet, *An Insomnia of Owls,* written in 1984 and revised in 1985, summons up the sound of voices though it is entirely instrumental.

In the 1990s Mekeel suffered a series of strokes. She recovered enough to compose *Pantoum* (1991) for violin and piano, and her last composition, *Soliloquy* for solo cello (1997). Of the latter, a critic wrote, "A dramatic journey through double stops and conflict to a final unison . . . made a powerful effect. Mekeel's music drew on many sources but it was always hers alone."[15] She died in 1998.

Like Mekeel, Lucia Dlugoszewski also used instruments in unusual ways. A composer who became known principally for works written for dance, Dlugoszewski in 1960 became associated with the Erick Hawkins Dance Company. In addition, she produced compositions for films, plays, and the concert stage.

Dlugoszewski was born on June 16, 1931, in Detroit, Michigan.[16] Her parents were Polish-born, her father an engineer and her mother a painter. She was educated at Wayne State University, where she was a premedical student, majoring in science and philosophy. At the same time, she wrote poetry —her book, *A New Folder,* was published in 1969—and studied piano and composition at the Detroit Conservatory of Music. About 1950 she went to New York, where she studied at the Mannes College of Music and privately with concert pianist Grete Sultan, who introduced her to dancer-choreographer Erick Hawkins, whom she later married. She also studied composition with Felix Saltzer and Edgard Varèse; the latter in particular she considered an important influence, because she believed he was one of few who understood the profound relationship between science and music. Another important influence was the philosopher F. S. C. Northrop, who taught at Yale and with whom Dlugoszewski collaborated on a long article on esthetics.[17]

Dlugoszewski did not use synthesizers and other electronic equipment to generate sounds. Rather, she used traditional instruments in unconventional ways, and sometimes she invented new instruments. The most important of her inventions, produced in 1951, was a timbre piano, a piano that can be muted in a variety of ways and can be struck, plucked with plectra, or stroked with bows. For this instrument she wrote numerous works, among them *Archaic Timbre Piano Music* (1953–56), *Instants in Form and Movement* (1957), for timbre piano and chamber orchestra, and *Duende Quidditas* (1982–83), for timbre piano and bass trombone. In 1958 she created an "orchestra" of 100 new percussion instruments, including wood, glass, paper, metal, skin, plastic ladder harps, tangent rattles, unsheltered rattles, closed rattles, wave rattles, a quarter-tone gong, and square drums, on which the performer can change the pitch somewhat by playing in the corners; Dlugoszewski herself performed on these. Some compositions for this ensemble are *Suchness Concert* (1958–60), *Clear Places* (1958–61), *Geography of Noon* (1964), and the film score *A Zen in Ryoko-In* (1971).

At the same time, Dlugoszewski continued to write for conventional instruments and ensembles. One of her best-known works is *Space Is a Diamond* (1970) for solo trumpet, which Virgil Thomson described as "an eleven-minute trumpet solo unaccompanied that seems virtually to exhaust the technical possibilities of the instrument without becoming didactic."[18] In *Angels of the Utmost Heavens* (1976) for brass quintet, the virtuosic potentialities of the instruments are similarly exploited, and they "bleat and gurgle and flare and snort from the depths of their registers to their highest extremes."[19] In *Abyss and Caress* (1975), a fifteen-section work for a standard chamber ensemble of seventeen players, the piano is prepared with odd materials to create special sound effects, and the string players sometimes use glass and comb bows on their instruments. "The result," said one reviewer, "is quite unlike anything. A good many of the sounds are extreme, in pitch, timbre, and dynamics. They are common enough in contemporary music, it is true, but the composer has put them through a cycle of white-hot intensity."[20]

Given her long-standing interest in poetry, it is not surprising that Dlugoszewski composed a number of works including narration. She also wrote an opera in 1970, *The Heidi Songs,* with a libretto by poet John Ashbery. Dlugoszewski's work in the 1980s was hampered by the long illness of her mother. After her mother's death in 1988 she resumed performing and composing, both with Erick Hawkins and in concerts of her own music. She once said about her work, "Great musical artists should make us hear for the first time . . . [One strategy] of how to do this . . . involves 'thusness'; the Zen Buddhist poets called it 'suchness'; James Joyce called it 'quidditas.'" Later she embraced a concept she called "otherness," musically presenting something strange or surprising; thus her works include *Quidditas String Quartet* (1984) and *Radi-*

cal Otherness Concert (1991), for flute, clarinet, trumpet, trombone, violin, and bass. She died in 2000.

Joan Tower, trained as a pianist, not only specialized in composing chamber music but founded her own chamber ensemble, the Da Capo Players.[21] The five-member group, for which Tower was the pianist, along with flute, clarinet, violin, and cello, won the highly prestigious chamber music award of the Naumburg Foundation in 1973. The group specialized in contemporary music and gave, from the time it was founded in 1970, an annual series of concerts at Carnegie Recital Hall in New York. It also toured widely and commissioned many new works from composers. Tower remained its pianist for fifteen years. At the time of this writing they are in residence at Bard College, where Tower teaches and coaches.

"In an ideal musical world a composer has a friendly, creative, and ongoing working relationship with performers for whom she writes," Tower wrote for a 1985 recording of her chamber music. True to her words, she composed numerous pieces for the Da Capo members and has written concertos commissioned by flutist Carol Wincenc, pianist Ursula Oppens, clarinetist David Shifrin, and violinist Elmar Oliveira. From 1985 to 1995 she was composer-in-residence with the St. Louis Symphony, which commissioned *Silver Ladders* (1986), the work that earned Tower the exclusive Gravemeyer Award in 1990. It was later choreographed and performed as a ballet. In 1998 she was inducted into the American Academy of Arts and Letters, only the fifth woman composer so honored, following Miriam Gideon, Vivian Fine, Betsy Jolas, and Ellen Taaffe Zwilich. In that same year she began a three-year residency with the Orchestra of St. Luke's in New York.

Tower was born on September 6, 1938, in New Rochelle, New York, and spent much of her childhood in South America, where her father worked as a mining engineer. She was educated at Bennington College, and while winning a doctorate from Columbia University, she also taught at the Greenwich House Music School from 1961 to 1971 and at Columbia from 1964 to 1971. In 1972 she joined the faculty of Bard College.

In the early part of her career Tower was to some extent immersed in the strict serial music of the postwar era. Around 1970, upon hearing Olivier Messiaen's *Quartet for the End of Time,* she finally found her own voice and began to write in a simpler, more organic and spontaneous style. Her "breakaway piece," as she calls it, was *Black Topaz* (1976) for piano and small chamber ensemble. *Platinum Spirals* (1976), for solo violin and *Wings* (1981), for solo clarinet are among her most frequently played solo works. Both pieces reflect Tower's preoccupation with choreographed sound. *Platinum Spirals* was inspired by platinum's malleability, familiar to her through her father's career, and *Wings* calls up the image of a large bird flying high, barely gliding, or diving downwards at great speed. Between 1986 and 1993 Tower wrote a series of five pieces called *Fanfare for the Uncommon Woman,* some of them for brass

ensemble and others for trumpet quartet; they have been frequently performed. Other works of the 1990s include Concerto for Orchestra (1991);
Stepping Stones (1993), a ballet score for orchestra; *Très Lent: Hommage à Messiaen* (1994), for cello and piano, a tribute to the French composer who influenced her so strongly; *Night Fields* (1994), her first string quartet; *Ascent*
(1996), her first work for organ; and *Rapids,* a piano concerto written in 1998
for Ursula Oppens.

In 1983 Ellen Taaffe Zwilich became the first woman composer to receive
the Pulitzer Prize in music for her Symphony no. 1. Born in 1939 in Miami,
Florida, she received her master's degree from Florida State University, and
then moved to New York to study violin with Ivan Galamian. She also played
in the American Symphony Orchestra under Leopold Stokowski. In time she
went on to Juilliard, studied composition with Elliott Carter and Roger Sessions, and received a doctorate in composition.

She married Joseph Zwilich, a violinist, who inspired her earliest important works, both from 1974, String Quartet and Violin Sonata in Three Movements. They illustrate her idea that an entire composition—melody, harmony,
development—should grow out of the first few phrases.[22] These early works
are atonal and dissonant, with jagged melodies and complex structures. After
the death of her husband in 1979 Zwilich wrote more accessible music, with
more lyrical melodies and increasingly tonal harmonies. Nevertheless, they
still illustrate her notion of developing a single idea; thus, her Symphony no.
1 is an elaboration of the first fifteen measures. Zwilich's style has been called
neoclassical in its conciseness and neoromantic in its intensity.[23] Her orchestration is vivid, reflecting her own experience as an orchestral violinist, and
her writing for strings is virtuosic.[24] *Baker's Biographical Dictionary of Music
and Musicians* (8th edition, 1992) states: "There are not many composers in
the modern world who possess the lucky combination of writing music of sub-
stance and at the same time exercising an immediate appeal to mixed audiences. Zwilich offers this happy combination of purely technical excellence
and a distinct power of communication."

The bulk of Zwilich's output is instrumental, for orchestra or chamber
ensembles. To date her works include three symphonies; concertos for piano,
trombone, flute, oboe, violin and cello, bassoon, trumpet, and violin; a double
string quartet; a piano trio; and a clarinet quintet. Of the last she wrote,

> The artist-performer on the clarinet has control of such a wide range of
> color that I found myself sometimes using color as a primary musical ele-
> ment: for instance, in contrasting 'warm' and 'cold' sonorities; using dif-
> ferent degrees of vibrato; and 'orchestrating' in a manner that ranges from
> having the clarinet completely integrated into a string ensemble to hav-
> ing the strings imitate woodwind sounds; in any case, allowing the nature
> of strings and of the clarinet to influence one another.[25]

In many cases Zwilich composes with a specific performer in mind, and in the program notes to her first symphony, premiered in 1992 by the American Composer's Orchestra under Gunther Schuller, she wrote, "I think of a symphony as an homage to the artists who keep musical tradition alive. While of course a huge cast of characters participate . . . it is the performers whose dedication, craft, and artistry make it vital." Another frequently performed orchestral work of hers is the 1988 *Symbolon.*

The Pulitzer Prize brought Zwilich recognition and numerous commissions, enabling her to make her living entirely by composing. She also became the fourth woman composer to be elected to the Academy of Arts and Letters and in 1995 was named to the first Composer's Chair in the history of Carnegie Hall. She served as composer-in-residence with the New York Philharmonic for three seasons, from 1996 to 1999, and has donated an annual prize for a young woman composer. An interesting work is her *Images,* written to open the National Museum of Women in the Arts in Washington in 1987. Scored for two pianos and orchestra, it is in five movements, each of which alludes to a painting in the museum—by Alice Bailly, Suzanne Valadon, Alma Thomas, Elaine DeKooning, and Helen Frankenthaler. It does not mimic their gestures but rather weaves percussive, angular variations.[26]

The second woman composer to win the Pulitzer Prize was Shulamit Ran. Born on October 21, 1949, in Tel Aviv, Israel, she began her music studies there.[27] In 1963 she came to New York, where she had a full-tuition scholarship at the Mannes College of Music, and she studied composition with Norman Dello Joio and piano with Nadia Relsenberg. An excellent pianist, she had made her debut recital in Israel at the age of twelve, and her first orchestral composition was performed when she was only fourteen. Following her graduation from Mannes in 1967, she made a number of recital tours, including several in Europe. In the early 1970s she continued to perform in public, mostly her own piano works, but devoted herself increasingly to composition and then to teaching. In 1973 she joined the faculty of the University of Chicago at the invitation of Ralph Shapey, with whom she also studied. In 1990 she was appointed composer-in-residence with the Chicago Symphony.

Ran has written for solo instruments, various instrumental and vocal groupings, and full orchestra, and her music is often described as dramatic, passionate, and complex. The early works are increasingly technically demanding, dissonant, and atonal. Her first major composition was *Capriccio* (1963) for piano and orchestra, which was performed by the New York Philharmonic under Leonard Bernstein in 1963 as well as by other orchestras. Other orchestral works are Concert Piece for piano and orchestra, written in 1970 and revised in 1973; Concerto for Orchestra (1986); *Three Fantasy Movements* (1993) for cello and orchestra; and *Vessels of Courage and Hope* (1998) for orchestra. Ran's later works are more lyrical and accessible. It was her Symphony, commissioned by the Philadelphia Orchestra and written in 1989–90 that won the Pulitzer Prize in 1991.

Ran also has written a considerable number of chamber works and piano pieces. Typical of her style is *Ensembles for 17*, for soprano and sixteen instrumentalists, given its premiere in Chicago in 1975. A work in two movements, it interweaves the final speech from *Othello* ("Loved not wisely but too well") with strong instrumental writing, so that the winds, strings, piano, and percussion convey the mood of Othello's famous speech as much as the voice itself.[28] Other important chamber works are *O the Chimneys* (1969) for voice, chamber ensemble, and tape, performed a number of times and recorded; *Double Vision* (1976) for two quintets and piano; *Hyperbolae* (1977) for solo piano, which was performed by all participants in the Second Artur Rubinstein Piano Competition in Israel in 1977; *Chicago Skyline* (1990) for brass and percussion; and two string quartets (1984, 1989). Much of her music reflects her Middle Eastern heritage; for example, Ran herself describes *Mirage* (1990), for five players, as a mixture of an "incantational style of delivery," frequent heterophonic textures, and Middle-Eastern scales and ornamentations.[29] Her opera *Between Two Worlds (The Dybbuk)* has a libretto by Charles Kondek based on a classic of the Yiddish theater by Shloime Ansky. It was commissioned by the Lyric Opera of Chicago and performed there in 1997.

Netty Simons is a composer who largely turned away from traditional styles.[30] She took up aleatory music, in which elements of the music are determined by the performer rather than the composer, and graphic notation, in which the conventional musical staff is replaced by drawn indications of how a work is to be performed. Born in New York City on October 26, 1918, the youngest of five children, she began studying music at the age of six with her oldest sister, who was a pupil of Walter Damrosch. She then studied piano and composition at Manhattan's Third Street Music School and presented her first concert at the age of thirteen.

Always attracted to contemporary composers, such as Ernest Shelling and Henry Cowell, Simons became increasingly interested in composition and enrolled at New York University, where her teachers included Percy Grainger and Marion Bauer. In 1933 she interrupted her studies there to accept a one-year scholarship at Juilliard to study piano with Alexander Siloti. She then returned to New York University and for the next three years studied composition with Stefan Wolpe, who, she later said, was probably the greatest single influence on her. During these years, besides composing and performing, she presented music broadcasts over New York radio station WHN and taught, both privately and at the Third Street School. In 1936 she married Leon Simons, an inventor, and they had two children, a son and a daughter. In 1949 she began working with Wolpe again, and from 1965 to 1971 she wrote and produced radio broadcasts of new music for the New York municipal radio station WNYC and the University of Michigan station WUOM.

Simons's early compositions are characterized by an extreme economy of means and imaginative control of tone color. They are principally chamber works, among them her earliest published work, Duo for violin and cello (1939); String Quartet (1950); Quartet for flute and strings (1951); *Piano Work* (1952); *Night Sounds* (1953), for piano; and *Set of Poems for Children* (1949), for winds, strings, and narrator, originally composed for her own children. She also wrote two later works "for children": *Puddintame* (1972), for one or more players plus narrator, which sets a series of limericks interspersed with a short refrain and employs a graphic, color-coded notation, and *The Pied Piper of Hamelin* (1972), for narrator, flute, piano, and violin orchestra, setting Robert Browning's version of the folk legend.

Simons's *Too Late, The Bridge Is Closed* (1972), for strings, is devised for any number of players and can be performed as a theater piece or ballet. Its graphic score resembles a linear maze, with colored lines to indicate dynamics, articulation, and occasionally duration, and letters for the seven basic pitches. Although requiring careful study of the performance directions, this work gives the players considerable choice and leeway. Also notable are four aleatory works, *Design Groups I* (1966), for one to three percussion players; *Design Groups II* (1968), a duo for any combination of high- and low-pitched instruments; *Silver Thaw* (1969), for any combination of one to eight players; and *The Great Stream Silent Moves* (1974), for piano, harp, and percussion. Many of her compositions may be performed as theater pieces, using dancers and actors along with or instead of musicians. Simons died in 1994, and her tapes and scores are in the New York Public Library at Lincoln Center.

Still another area of experimentation has been that of microtonal music, that is, music using intervals smaller than a half-tone, with pitches that lie between the conventional notes of the chromatic scale. Though only specially tuned keyboard instruments can produce these notes, they are easily accessible on some wind and all stringed instruments. Tui St. George Tucker, born in California in 1924 and a resident of New York from 1945 to the 1980s, began experimenting with quarter tones in 1955.[31] A quarter tone lies exactly in the middle of a half-tone interval, for example, midway between C-natural and C-sharp, or C-sharp and D-natural. At first trained as a violinist, Tucker later became a virtuoso performer on the recorder, for which she wrote many of her works. Her first successful quarter-tone composition was *The Bullfinch Sonata* (1960) for solo recorder; she later devised a fingering chart for playing quarter tones on this instrument. Tucker also worked as a conductor, both choral and instrumental, but by the late 1970s she confined her conducting largely to her own compositions. Her works include two piano sonatas; *Little Pieces for Quarter-tone Piano* (1972); two string quartets (1958 and undated); a violin sonata (1958); many works for recorder, including solo, with voices, and with other instruments; *Lift Up Your Heads, Ye Mighty Gates,* for oboe, bassoon, and clarinet; *Vigil 1* (1985) and *Vigil 2* (1989), for microtonal organ;

and a considerable number of choral works and songs. Her variations on *My Melancholy Baby* (1984) applies a quarter-tone scale to Ernie Burnett's popular chromatic song, that is, the song is played simultaneously on two pianos tuned a quarter tone apart. Some of her later works, such as *Ave Verum* (1992), for piano, are written for conventionally tuned instruments.

A number of composers combined the use of acoustic and electronic instruments in their work. One of the earliest was Barbara Kolb, born on February 10, 1939, in Hartford, Connecticut.[32] Her father, music director of a local radio station, did not want her to become a professional musician. He did allow her to attend Hartt College of Music in Hartford and major in music education. In her second year there, however, she changed her major to clarinet, and when she decided to get a master's degree in composition, he refused to finance her studies. For several years Kolb played clarinet in the Hartford Symphony Orchestra. In 1964 she moved to New York and spent the next four years supporting herself as a music copyist. She had won a scholarship to Tanglewood in 1960 and returned there again in 1964 and 1968, studying composition with Gunther Schuller and Lukas Foss. In 1969 she became the first American woman to win the Prix de Rome, entitling her to a year's study at the American Academy in Rome, and she was allowed to renew it the following year. The year after that she won a Guggenheim Fellowship. In 1983–84 Kolb was composer-in-residence at the Institut de Recherche et Coordination Acoustique/Musique (IRCAM) in Paris.

One of relatively few contemporary composers—men or women—who managed to live on commissions and grants, Kolb became quite successful from the time she won first prize in the Mu Phi Epsilon contest of 1963 with her Duo for violin and viola. Much of her music was written on commission, most often for chamber ensembles, and each work she produced seemed to have a truly original flavor. With *Trobar Clus, to Lukas* (1970) for chamber ensemble, she scored her first major success at Tanglewood's Festival of Contemporary Music in 1970. Named for a poetic form used by the troubadours of Provence during the eleventh and twelve centuries, this work is a kind of rondeau in which repetition functions through the recurrence of different groups of instruments rather than of melodies or rhythms. *Three Place Settings* (1968), for narrator and chamber soloists, humorously sets three texts concerned with food, one from an elegant wine cookbook of 1936. *Solitaire* (1971), for piano and vibraphone, consists of two prerecorded tapes of piano and vibraphone that are combined into one tape against which a live pianist plays. The music is divided into ten sections that can be played in various sequences, and some of them quote parts of a Chopin prelude. *Spring, River, Flowers, Moon and Night* (1975), for two pianos and tape, was inspired by an eighth-century Chinese poem. The piano parts include both conventional playing and special effects played directly on the strings; the tape, providing a soft background, consists of both electronically generated sounds and recorded parts for lute, guitar, mandolin, vibraphone, chimes, and three voices. In *Soundings,* a work originally for chamber ensemble and later revised for full orchestra, the same musical elements are developed at varying speeds by different subsections of the orchestra, so that the texture grows denser and denser and the music in effect echoes itself. It was performed by the New York Philharmonic and the Boston Symphony orchestras in 1977 and 1978, respectively. *Appello* (1976), for piano, is highly organized, using a tone row, a series of pitches in fixed order, in both the melody and the harmonic structure. The specific tone row used in all four movements is taken from Book 1A of Pierre Boulez's *Structures.* Kolb's *Homage to Keith Jarrett and Gary Burton* (1977), for flute and vibraphone, is an extended duet that resembles the improvisatory interaction of the two jazz musicians on whose material it is based. *Chromatic Fantasy* (1983), for narrator, amplified alto flute, oboe, soprano saxophone, electric guitar, and vibraphone, sets a poem by Howard Stern. Distinguished by elements of jazz and the blending of instrumental tone colors, it presents first a condensation of the poem, then the whole poem, and finally extracts of phrases and ideas from the poem. *Millefoglie* (1984–85), for chamber orchestra and a computer-generated tape, interweaves harmonic and rhythmic layers of sound. Her later works include *Voyants* (1991) for piano and chamber orchestra; *All in Good Time,* premiered by the New York Philharmonic in 1994; and the string quartet *In Memory of David Huntley* (1994). In 1999 she was commissioned to write a marimba concerto for the Scottish percussion virtuoso Evelyn Glennie.

Sorrel Hays was born Doris Hays in 1941 in Memphis, Tennessee,[33] and in 1985, adopted the family name Sorrel for its pleasing sound. She began her career as a pianist, specializing in contemporary music, especially with the cluster piano music of Henry Cowell, and in 1973 began touring with a Buchla synthesizer. Her compositions integrate music with sculpture, film/video, dance, and actors in a variety of notated and improvised forms. In recent years she has focused on combinations of text collage and electronic sound with lyrical forms. She also uses acoustic instruments along with electronic ones, and merges microtonal with tonal elements.

In reviewing her compositions, Hays believes her work falls into four main areas of interest. One is music related to the South, including such works as *Southern Voices for Orchestra and Soprano* (1982); *Sunday Mornings* (1978) for piano; and the opera *The Glass Woman* (1989). Another area is experimental and multimedia works, including electroacoustical mixtures and nonsynchronous lyrical layerings or structured improvisation. *Sensevents* (1976) uses motorized sculptures Sorrel built as conductors for the orchestra musicians and dancers. *Rocking* (1983) for flute, violin, and viola, also fits in this arena. Still another area involves dramatic, lyrical vocal pieces that include text collage, as in *Something [to Do] Doing* (1984), for fifteen chanters and scat singer, and the opera *Mapping Venus* (1998). Her fourth focus has been activist works using voices in textual or sung lines, such as *Celebration of NO* (1984), *Bits* (1987), and *90's, A Calendar Bracelet* (1990). An activist for both contemporary music and women composers, Hays and fellow composer Beth Anderson started the first American lecture concert series on women's music in 1976 at the New School for Social Research. Until 1985 she also lobbied various music programs on behalf of women composers. In that year she sustained a serious injury and upon recovering decided to reduce her performing and touring and focus on composition.

Anne LeBaron, born in 1953, made her name as both a performer and a composer in virtually every contemporary genre and wrote both acoustic and electronic music.[34] Trained originally as a pianist, she took up the harp in college and developed extended performance techniques and electronic enhancements for the instrument. She performed with numerous improvising musicians, ranging from jazz artist Lionel Hampton to pianist Ursula Oppens, and wrote for and performed as a harpist with the LeBaron/Smith/Dixon Trio and the Anne LeBaron Quintet, the latter a jazz group blending the sounds of brass, harp, guitar, and percussion. Holder of a doctorate from Columbia, she studied with some of the most notable contemporary composers, among them Bulent Arel, Daria Semegen, Mauricio Kagel, György Ligeti, Chou Wen-chung, Jack Beeson, and Mario Davidovsky. She herself taught theory and composition at the State University of New York at Stony Brook, where she assisted in the electronic music studio, and at Columbia in classical and jazz courses. In 1996 she accepted an appointment at the University of Pittsburgh.

LeBaron's compositions include a music theater piece, *Concerto for Active Frogs* (1975) for saxophone, trombone, percussion, male solo voice, mixed chorus, and tape, which records a collage of field sounds of North American frogs; *Strange Attractors* (1987) for orchestra; *Noh Reflections* (1986) for string trio, influenced by her sojourn in Korea and studies of Korean traditional music; *The E & O Line* (1992), a blues opera; *Eurydice is Dead* (1983) for electronic tape alone; *Southern Ephemera* (1997), incorporating instruments built by microtonal innovator Harry Partch; and *Croak (The Last Frog)* (1997), a music theater work telling the story of the last frog on earth. Later works include *Sukey* (1998) for string quartet, narrator, and children's chorus; *Bodice Ripper* (1999) for electric harp, clarinet or bass clarinet, and tape; and *Vegetable Dreams: Nightmare* (1999), a setting of poems by Maggie Anderson for men's chorus.

A contemporary of LeBaron's, Tina Davidson composed largely tonal and lyrical works.[35] Born in Sweden in 1952, she grew up in the United States and studied piano and composition at Bennington College with Henry Brant, Vivian Fine, and Lionel Nowak. Her output includes works for orchestra, mixed instrumental and vocal ensembles and soloists, as well as works with prerecorded tape playback. *They Come Dancing,* for full orchestra, was premiered by the Women's Philharmonic in San Francisco in 1999, and her opera

Billy and Zelda was premiered by OperaDelaware in 1998. *The Selkie Boy,* for narrator and orchestra, was at the time of this writing scheduled for the Philadelphia Orchestra's 1999–2000 season. Long involved in community outreach programs of various kinds, Davidson was appointed to a three-year residency at the Fleisher Art Memorial in Philadelphia in 1998.

A number of composers have generally relied on acoustic instruments, but their styles range from the boldly experimental (Julia Wolfe) to the ultraconservative (Stefania de Kenessey). Julia Wolfe was born in 1958 in Philadelphia.[36] She has written music for symphony orchestras, theater, string quartets, and unconventional ensembles, such as a work for six pianos. Such influences as Beethoven, Louis Andriessen, with whom Wolfe studied at Princeton, rock group Led Zeppelin, and folk music can be heard in her own high-energy works, often written for amplified sounds. Her *Four Marys* (1991) for string quartet evokes the sound properties of an Appalachian dulcimer. *Window of Vulnerability,* written in 1991 for the American Composers Orchestra, is named for the military euphemism to justify arms expenditures. It musically echoes the rock genre in sheer volume as well as other respects. Her other works include *Arsenal of Democracy* (1993) for chamber ensemble, and *Steam* for flute, violin, electric organ, and instruments devised by Harry Partch. As co-director of the Bang on a Can Festival in New York, founded in 1987 to provide a venue for experimental composers who fit into no particular category or genre, Wolfe helped present hundreds of contemporary works.

In 1999 Melinda Wagner became the third woman composer to win the Pulitzer Prize for music, for her Concerto for flute, strings, and percussion.[37] It was composed for the fifteenth anniversary of the Westchester (New York) Philharmonic and was premiered in 1998 with music director Paul Lustig Dunkel playing the solo flute part. "My music is very narrative—it tells a story," Wagner told an interviewer. "I start with a germ of an idea, usually a melody or mood. It could be small, a sweeping scale of notes, or something angular and percussive." Born in 1957 in Philadelphia, Wagner received graduate degrees from the University of Chicago, where she studied with Shulamit Ran, and the University of Pennsylvania. Her orchestral, chamber, and vocal works have been performed by numerous American orchestras and chamber ensembles. Her *Wing and Prayer* (1996) is a one-movement work for piano, clarinet, cello, and percussion that falls into three sections. The first section opens with a quiet melody for solo cello, gradually joined by the piano, vibraphone, and chimes. The clarinet enters at the beginning of the second section, a fast and furious scherzo. The third part features an ostinato figure in the piano and a reappearance of the cello melody, now varied. The work ends with a sustained cello tone, surrounded by somber chords from the piano and chimes.

Jennifer Higdon, born in 1962, is not only a composer but a conductor and flutist.[38] With a doctorate in composition from the University of Pennsylvania, by the late 1990s she was receiving enough commissions for orchestral, chamber, and choral works to earn a living entirely from composition. She also continued to teach at the Curtis Institute of Music, a post she has held since 1993. Although most of her music is tonal, it is not necessarily traditional. Among her works is *Shine* (1995) for orchestra, described as the best new piece of the year by reviewer David Patrick Stearns, who said "it bubbles over with color, rhythm, high spirits and invention, often sounding like Bartók's Concerto for Orchestra at warp speed but with a personality of its own."[39] She performed her solo flute piece, *rapid.fire* (1997), in a Chamber Music of Lincoln Center Recital in New York. *Southern Grace* (1998), for chorus, is a recomposition of Appalachian folk melodies. In three of the movements fragments of the folk tunes appear; the others use the original words with completely different melody and harmony. The chamber piece *wissahickon poeTrees* (1998), for flute, clarinet, violin, cello, piano, and percussion, features individual movements that mark the seasons of Wisshahickon, a large park outside Philadelphia, interspersed with one-minute "clock" movements that denote the passage of time. The second half of the piece's title refers to a one-line poem Higdon wrote for this music and to the park's heavy forestation. In 1999 Higdon was awarded a $50,000 Fellowship in the Arts for music composition by the Pew Charitable Trusts.

Augusta Read Thomas, born in New York in 1964, has produced a number of big works that show off her strengths, which one reviewer described as boldness mixed with sophistication, energetic lyricism, and a somewhat Franco-American style of subtle and occasionally eerie coloring.[40] The same reviewer said of her Triple Concerto (1992), subtitled *Night's Midsummer Blaze,* "She confronts the trio of flute, viola, and harp, for which she writes exquisitely, with surprisingly vociferous music for symphony orchestra." Thomas studied at Northwestern University, Yale University (with Jacob Druckman), and the Royal Academy of Music. On the composition faculty of the Eastman School of Music, she has also served a three-year term, 1997–2000, as composer-in-residence for the Chicago Symphony. She has written mostly instrumental works but her chamber opera, *Ligeia* (1994), based on Edgar Allan Poe's short story, won the prestigious Orpheus Prize. Her compositions include a number of works for cello—*Spring Song* (1995), for solo cello, and three works for cello and orchestra, *Vigil, Chanson* (1997), and *Ritual of Incantations* (1999). Other works are *Spirit Musings* (1997), a violin concerto; *Orbital Beacons* (1998), a concerto for "re-seated" orchestra, commissioned by the Chicago Symphony, in which the players are positioned unconventionally; *Whites* for solo piano; a Mass for male voices (1997); and a solo organ work (1998) commissioned by the American Guild of Organists.

The ultraconservative of this generation is Stefania de Kenessey.[41] Born in Budapest in 1956, she began her musical studies there at a school founded by Zoltán Kodály. Her education continued at Yale and Princeton, where she earned a doctorate under Milton Babbitt. Her compositions are unabashedly consonant, triadic, and tonal, recalling nineteenth-century idioms. They include two one-act operas, *The Monster Bed* (1990), a comedy about the monster's fear of humans lurking in the dark, and *The Other Wise Man* (1996), about the fourth of the Magi. Also among her works are *Wintersong* (1995), a pastorale for orchestra; *Manned Flight* (1999), a concerto for flute and strings; *Jumping Jacks* (1991), for a cappella chorus; *Sunburst* (1993), for solo piano; and *Beating Down* (1995), a piano trio. At this writing she was working on commissions for several song cycles.

In the mid-1990s de Kenessey founded The Derriere Guard, an alliance of traditionalists among contemporary artists, architects, poets, and composers; its first festival took place in 1997. She said, "After a century of experimentation in all the arts, I firmly believe that the only way to actually go ahead is to use elements of the past, not because the past is perfect . . . but because the avoidance of the past is no longer interesting at the end of the 20th century."[42] De Kenessey has taught at New School University since 1980.

Without the perspective of time it is impossible to assess with any accuracy the lasting value of newer works. Contemporary music is, after all, not a finite body; it is being written at this very moment. But it is not the purpose of this book to pass judgment on what is great music, or even to decide whether a work is or is not music. Rather, it is to chronicle the very active participation of women in American music, in every genre.

1 0

ELECTRONIC MUSIC,
MIXED MEDIA, FILM,
PERFORMANCE ART

*F*OR THE WOMEN COMPOSERS working since the late 1970s, allegedly the social climate has been freer, and many—if not most—emphatically deny that they have encountered either more or different problems on account of their sex. At least one of them, however, suggested that composing music performed by machines rather than human musicians is especially attractive to women for two basic reasons. First, it enables a composer to take a musical idea through to a form in which it can be heard without having to persuade musicians, managers, and others that the music is worth performing; machines certainly are nonsexist, and so they are politically liberating for composers. And second, machines enable relatively fast, often instant, feedback for composers, who through them can hear their own compositions performed and so can learn from their own successes and failures.[1]

Of all the new styles and techniques developed since 1950, electronic music of various kinds has attracted many composers, some of whom had long been working in other styles. Among the women composers who turned to electronic forms, was Jean Eichelberger Ivey.[2] Born on July 3, 1923, in Washington, D.C., Ivey spent the first twenty years of her career teaching, giving piano concerts, and producing fairly conventional compositions, basically tonal and neoclassic, with a strong affinity for the styles of Bela Bartók and Maurice Ravel. In the early 1960s, however, she became interested first in twelve-tone music, which is based on a fixed order of all twelve pitches of the chromatic scale, and then in electronic music. In 1969 she founded the Electronic Music Studio at the Peabody Conservatory in Baltimore, and in 1972 she earned a doctorate in music from the University of Toronto, where she had specialized in electronic music. By the late 1970s she was concentrating less on pure electronic music and more on combining it with live performance, often in very dramatic ways.

Ivey's music studies began at the age of six, when she started taking piano lessons and composing. She went on to study at Trinity College and then received two master's degrees, one in 1946 in piano from the Peabody Con-

230

servatory and another in 1956 in composition from the Eastman School of Music. In the meantime she had been teaching part time at a number of schools in the Washington-Baltimore area and serving as organist in several churches. In the 1950s she toured as a pianist, appearing in Mexico, Europe, and the United States in recitals that often included some of her own compositions. She also gave lecture-demonstrations on teaching contemporary music for groups of piano teachers throughout the United States. In 1958 she married Frederick Maurice Ivey.

By the time she became interested in electronic music Ivey had worked in practically every medium of composition. She had written orchestral pieces for both full and small ensembles, songs and song cycles, choral anthems, a piano sonata, many shorter piano works including teaching pieces, chamber music, incidental music for plays, and film scores. One of her first and most radical departures from traditional music was *Pinball,* an impressionistic study of sounds composed entirely from the actual rattles, clicks, and bells of a pinball machine in operation. Produced at the Brandeis University Electronic Music Studio in 1965, this work is an example of musique concrète, that is, music made up of taped real-life sounds, such as street noises, thunder, the ocean, and so on, a concept developed by Pierre Schaeffer and other composers in France in the late 1940s. Ivey's work also served as the score for a film by Wayne Sourbeer, *Montage V: How to Play Pinball,* produced during the same year.

Ivey's next important electronic work was *Continuous Form* (1967), a composition of indeterminate length written for use during station breaks for television broadcasts and for use in another film by Sourbeer. This work has had literally thousands of performances over educational television stations, principally in New York and Boston. In Sourbeer's film, random, nonsynchronized excerpts of the music are used in such a way that no two performances are exactly alike.

By 1970 Ivey had decided to use the best of both worlds and combine taped music with live performance. Her first completed works of this nature, *Terminus,* for mezzo-soprano and tape, and *Three Songs of Night,* for soprano, five instruments, and tape, had their first performance at the Peabody Conservatory in spring of 1971. Ivey herself described the technical problems raised by this kind of composition:

> It combines all the problems of composing for live performers and the problems of pure tape composition, with some special problems raised by their interaction. . . . A pure tape composition is like a painting—one puts it together alone in the studio, drawing on all one's resources of equipment, imagination, and taste. Unlike traditional composition, where the composer hears his work only in his mind until, often much later, performers bring it to life, the tape studio offers ready access to

CHAPTER 10

sound. . . . Composing for live performers, on the other hand . . . requires
an intimate knowledge of how voices and instruments behave, how performers react to each other, to notation, and to the whole performance
situation, including the audience. . . . some unpredictability is inevitable;
each performance differs, grossly or subtly, from every other.[3]

Ivey considered unpredictability a drawback for live performance, not an
advantage. On the other hand, she acknowledged that pure tape music lacks
visual interest. Although visual elements can be supplied by lighting, the use of
film, or other means, she believed that the visual experience of watching a live
performer has more direct appeal. Moreover, a live performer can be inspired
by audience reaction to perform better, whereas a tape remains unaffected.

Though combining tape and live performance overcomes some of these
drawbacks, it raises still other problems. Synchronization between performer
and tape must be carefully planned; the tape cannot adjust to the performer.
The performer also cannot adjust unless he or she is sufficiently informed and
cued. A new set of problems relates to the equipment needed: playback equipment may differ, the engineers may not understand the composer's instructions, the balance between stereo channels or other amplifiers may vary, what
sounds loud in one hall may be too soft in another, and so on.

Ivey found all these difficulties challenging. Both *Terminus* and *Three
Songs of Night* were given numerous performances, and both were used in an
all-Ivey recording issued in 1974, along with *Aldebaran* (1972), for viola and
tape, and the earlier purely electronic *Cortege—for Charles Kent* (1969), the
first piece to be composed in the Peabody Conservatory Electronic Music Studio. Two important works combining live performance and tape followed:
Hera, Hung from the Sky (1973), for mezzo-soprano, winds, percussion, piano,
and tape, which had been commissioned by the Collegium Musicum of the
University of North Dakota—its first New York performance came in 1974—
and *Testament of Eve* (1976), a monodrama for mezzo-soprano, orchestra, and
tape, given its premiere by the Baltimore Symphony Orchestra in April, 1976.
The latter work, with a text by the composer, tells the story of Eve's rejection
of pleasure in preference to the Spartan quest for knowledge outside the Garden of Eden. The score is conceived as a debate between Lucifer, who appears
on tape as a disembodied voice accompanied by electronic sounds, and Eve,
personified by the live voice. The dialogue is vivid, accompanied by pictur-
esque and colorful electronic sounds and impressive climaxes, aided by the
two dozen percussion instruments called for in the orchestra. The vocal part
contains difficult intervals, timbre changes, and meters. Though Ivey originally had written the text nearly ten years earlier, she did not complete the
music until she was promised a performance by conductor Sergiu Comissiona,
and she specifically tailored the vocal part for soloist Elaine Bonazzi, who had
recorded two other Ivey works. Later Ivey returned to conventional forces in

such works as the chorus *Entreat Me Not to Leave Thee* (1985); *Short Symphony* (1988); and *Flying Colors* (1994), a brass fanfare. Ivey retired from the Peabody about 1998 and returned to New York City.

Also working with electronic music but far more conventional in approach than Ivey is Daria Semegen.[4] Born in Germany on June 27, 1946, Semegen came to America at the age of four, and by the age of six she had begun both studying piano and composing. Semegen was interested also in acting and theatrical production, but she nevertheless committed herself to music and for four years attended the Eastman School of Music. She studied composition with Robert Gauldin, Burrill Phillips, and Samuel Adler, receiving her bachelor's degree in 1968. She then won a one-year Fulbright scholarship to the Warsaw Conservatory, where she studied composition with Witold Lutoslawski. She also studied electronic music with Wlodzimierz Katotonski at Warsaw University. Subsequently she went to Yale to study composition and electronic music with composer Bulent Arel and theory with Alexander Goehr.

Semegen completed her master's degree in 1971 and that summer went to the Columbia-Princeton Electronic Music Center, where she worked for the next five years, studying and teaching. During that period she also worked for two years as sound engineer for the Boulton Collection of World Music, where she edited and technically supervised materials that were later released as recordings. In 1974 she was appointed to the faculty of the State University of New York at Stony Brook, where she was named assistant professor of music, associate director (later director) of the Electronic Music Studio, and designer of the university's professional recording project.

Semegen has made significant contributions to nonelectronic music as well, with such works as *Triptych* (1966) for orchestra, *Lieder auf der Flucht* (Songs During the Flight, 1967) for soprano and eight instruments, *Quattro* (1967) for flute and piano, *Three Pieces* (1968) for clarinet and piano, and *Study for 16 Strings* (1968). Later works are *Music for Violin and Piano* (1987) and *Vignette* (1998) for solo piano. A *Washington Post* reviewer described her nonelectronic music as having "a wide dramatic range from powerful sound images to subtly shifting timbral colors and sonorities."[5]

Semegen's electronic works include the film score *Out of Into* (1971), a collaboration with Bulent Arel for an animated film by Irving Kreisberg; *Electronic Composition* no. 1 (1971); and *Music for Dancers* (1977), which combines electronic music, dance, and lighting with computer technology. *Music for Dancers* was performed in New York in May 1977 and at a number of electronic music festivals throughout the United States in that year and the next. Later works include *Rhapsody* (1990) for Yamaha MIDI grand piano and *Arabesque* (1992) for two-channel tape. (MIDI stands for Musical Instrument Digital Interface; in the MIDI grand piano each of the eighty-eight keys is programmable for pitch, volume, timbre, touch, and attack.) Of her electronic music, a *New York Times* reviewer wrote, "Semegen avoids electronic cliché

through lighthearted inventiveness and shows an interesting sonic imagination at play."6 In addition to composing, Semegen leads an active career as a
teacher, with visiting professorships at numerous institutions. She is a leading
authority on electronic music.

Anna Rubin has written some music for conventional instruments and
voice but the bulk of her output is electroacoustic music for chamber ensembles, that is, conventional instruments and tape, sometimes combined with
video.7 Rubin was born in Ohio in 1946 and studied sociology before turning
to music as a graduate student. Among her works are the acoustic *Die Nacht:
Lament for Malcolm X* (1982) for soprano and ten instruments, which won
the Gaudeamus Foundation's first prize; *Hiding Faces, Open Faces* (1988) for
live viola, electronic soundtrack, and video by Myrna Schloss; and *Family Stories: Sophie, Sally* (1997) for flute, clarinet, and cello with tape, in collaboration
with Laurie Hollander. Rubin also has produced several computer-generated
works, such as *Stolen Treasure* (1991) and *Seachanges IV* (1995) for zheng, a
Chinese instrument, and computer-generated tape. In 1998 she joined the
faculty of Oberlin Conservatory of Music.

Alice Shields, born in 1943 in New York City, is one of the few contemporary composers who also have sung as a soloist with leading opera compa-
nies.8 A mezzo-soprano, she sang the traditional repertory—Verdi, Mozart,
Wagner, Strauss—in the 1970s with the New York City Opera and the Opera
Society of Washington, among others. In 1975 she received her doctorate in
composition from Columbia University, where she studied with Vladimir
Ussachevsky. From 1965 to 1996 she was employed at the Columbia-Princeton Electronic Music Center in various capacities, including associate director
and director of development, and at this writing she is artist-in-residence at the
Brooklyn College Center for Computer Music. Since 1990 she has been studying the classical vocal music of India, first South Indian and then North
Indian, which she has been performing as well. Shields often uses her own
voice as a sound source in her electronic works. Her early *Study for Voice and
Tape* (1968) uses her prerecorded singing voice synchronized with taped electronic sounds, created from a Buchla synthesizer, her own live voice, and a
shaken bell-tree.

Indian music influenced Shields's opera *Apocalypse* (1993), for soprano,
alto, and baritone soloists, chorus, and dancers, including both live and prerecorded electronic music. The libretto, by Shields, is based on Greek stories
of Dionysus, written in English, Irish, and Greek. *Mass for the Dead* (1992), for
soprano, mezzo-soprano or countertenor, and bass-baritone, chorus, dancers,
cello, bassoon, oboe, organ, and electronic music on tape, is a drama about a
ghost. It has a multilingual text—Latin from the Requiem Mass, Italian from
Monteverdi's *Orfeo,* English from the King James Bible, and Greek by the
composer. Shields also wrote several instrumental operas, notably *Odyssey*
(1970), which had its premiere by the Lake George Opera Company, where

she was an apprentice-composer and mezzo-soprano. In addition, Shields has written a considerable amount of instrumental and vocal chamber music, such as *Komachi at Sekidera* (1999), for singer, alto flute, and koto, to a text adapted from a Japanese Noh play about the poet Komachi. Her multimedia works include incidental music for Buchner's 1988 play *Woyzeck* (1988) and *Fragile Breakfast, It's Haunted Here,* and *Sparkling Brains,* three works written in 1995–96 for computer monitor playback, with poems in English and German and computer graphics by the composer.

Wendy Carlos was an early proponent of electronic music. Born in Rhode Island in 1939 as Walter Carlos, she underwent a sex-change operation and took the name Wendy. Classically trained in music and physics at Brown and Columbia universities, in the mid-1960s Carlos helped Robert Moog modify the Moog synthesizer. In 1968 Carlos made an enormously popular recording, *Switched-on Bach,* which sold over a million copies and popularized the synthesizer. Her own compositions were used in the score for Stanley Kubrick's 1971 film, *A Clockwork Orange.* During the next decade Carlos worked on creating electronic versions of orchestral sound, culminating in the score for Walt Disney's film *TRON* (1982), which established a continuous blend between symphony orchestra and digital and analog synthesizers. Her 1984 recording, *Digital Moonscapes,* introduced the "LSI Philharmonic Orchestra," a digital replica of orchestral timbres virtually indistinguishable from their acoustic instrumental counterparts. Turning to the use of a Macintosh computer and the latest MIDI technology, Carlos produced *Switched-on Bach 2000* (1992), a striking new recording of her early classic, with sharp ensemble interplay rivaling a well-rehearsed acoustic performance.

Two composers who have experimented with machine-generated sound in their compositions are Laurie Spiegel, who became known for her computer music, and Suzanne Ciani, who worked with analog synthesizers. Spiegel, born in 1945 in Chicago, studied at Shimer College (Illinois), Oxford University, the Juilliard School, and privately with composers Jacob Druckman and Vincent Persichetti. She learned to play a number of plucked stringed instruments, notably five-string banjo, folk and classical guitar, and Renaissance and baroque lute. In 1975 she received a master's degree from Brooklyn College. She taught at various schools and directed the computer music studio at New York University. From the mid-1980s on she worked as a freelance computer consultant to major corporations.[9]

At first Spiegel composed for classical guitar and other traditional instruments, but about 1970 she turned to electronic music, and about three years later she chose the greater control and compositional complexity made available by computers. In computer music a program replaces a score. In effect, a score is a set of instructions for turning musical ideas into sound. Rather than writing such instructions in conventional (or unconventional) notation for performers to carry out, a computer composer writes a program, a set of instructions for a computer involving anything from specific pitches to a general set of relationships or processes for composing them. The computer itself then can generate the sounds directly, or it can control equipment such as an analog synthesizer that in turn generates the sounds, or it can print out a score consisting of specific notes it may have helped compose by following certain general rules. A simple example of this last method would be a program instructing the computer to play or store in its memory a canon in four voices made from a single melody that the composer has input by typing, playing on a keyboard, or instructing the computer to create. The computer memory functions as traditional staff paper does, for storage, editing, and performance instructions, but unlike conventionally written music notation it permits tremendous flexibility in the arrangement of the musical information it stores.

In the late 1970s computer music was still most often tape-recorded, but as ever smaller and less expensive machinery was devised, live-performance use of computers became increasingly feasible. In addition to performing preprogrammed compositions, computers can be played live as other instruments are. They can be instructed before a performance as to the nature of the sounds to be produced, which the composer-performer may generate by means of keyboards, knobs, switches, or other input devices. The most recently developed and sophisticated computer systems at the time of this writing are capable of a process called digital synthesis in which the actual sound—or literally, the wave motion of the speaker cone that ultimately "performs" the sound—is computed. Such computers have sufficient speed and memory capacity to produce an entire composition in real time, that is, to produce and perform a composition at virtually the same time that the program for it is being fed into the computer. In 1978 such systems were still rare. More common were hybrid systems, which used analog oscillators to generate the wave forms of sounds, thereby having to compute larger parameters of sound—pitches, dynamics, and so on. Such hybrid systems were the first practical way of improvising or performing entire compositions on computers in real time.

For a number of her compositions Spiegel used a hybrid system called the GROOVE (for Generating Real-Time Operations on Voltage-controlled Equipment) system. Notable among these works are *The Orient Express* (1974), a work giving the illusion of continuous acceleration; *The Expanding Universe* (1975), a slow, continuous, but highly structured meditative piece; *Drums* (1975), a rhythmic study of xylophone-like sounds, reflecting her interest in African and Indian rhythms; and *Patchwork* (1976), a composition exploring the relationships among four short melodic motifs and four basic rhythmic patterns, manipulated in a contrapuntal fashion reminiscent of the baroque motet. One reviewer described *Patchwork* as "an extremely pretty and pleasing contrapuntal effort."[10] Because Spiegel's works were principally taped music, they often were performed in conjunction with film, dance, theater, and other visual productions. In the late 1970s Spiegel wrote numerous soundtracks for films and videos and collaborated with others on video projects. She experimented with computerized real-time synthesis of visual images, recorded on film, and explored the idea of visual music, dealing with counterpoint, tension and resolution, groups of elements, and the like.

From about 1980 on, Spiegel worked as a consultant to several major corporations and devised many computer innovations, expanding their compositional and performance capabilities. Her software for the Macintosh computer, MusicMouse (1985–86), was a major breakthrough in performance of real-time music that does not rely on an instrumental keyboard or on acoustic or sampled sounds. She called it "an instrument for computer-assisted improvisation," and it went far toward fulfilling Spiegel's aim of making it easy for even untrained people at home to express themselves in musical sound. It enables control of numerous compositional factors—tone color, melody, harmony, rhythm. Spiegel had never totally abandoned composing nonelectronic music, and she continued to do so in the 1980s and 1990s, producing mainly works for solo instrumentalists, such as *Fughetta* for piano (1982, revised in 1990), and *A Musette* (1990) for harpsichord, piano, or other keyboard.[11] Spiegel's electronic works from the 1970s are characterized by folk melodies and a minimalist style. By the 1990s such works as *Unseen Worlds* still are minimalist in their slow movement of pitches, but their tone is darker, featuring complex timbres, very slow momentum, and cathartic climaxes.[12]

Another leader in electronic music is Suzanne Ciani. A *New York Times* article from 1999 revealed, "Suzanne Ciani lives in seclusion . . . but her most famous piece of music is heard about 280 million times every day. In 1988, balancing commercial work with her career as a composer, she created what may be the world's best-known audio signature: the miniature chordal flourish that introduces every AT&T [telephone] call."[13] Ciani, born on June 4, 1946, began studying piano at the age of six.[14] She went to Wellesley College and then earned a master's degree in composition at the University of California at Berkeley. It was in California that she began to compose for and perform on a Buchla synthesizer, a voltage-controlled electronic instrument developed by Donald Buchla. Until the development of these small machines in the 1960s, made possible by the rapid development and widespread use of transistors, electronic music could be created only in tape studios on large, expensive equipment. The small voltage-controlled synthesizer in effect combines the separate components of the tape studio in a single cabinet. The different components, called modules, are electrically interconnected and manipulated so that they perform together. There are two fundamental kinds of module, those that generate basic electric signals—oscillators and noise generators—and those that process or modify the signal in some way—envelope generators, random voltage generators, ring modulators, and filters.[15] To perform on such a synthesizer, one must first set up a "patch" by interconnecting the modules in chosen configurations by means of patch cords, and then one plays the instrument by activating switches, turning knobs, sliding levers, and touching pressure-sensitive plates, which in a sense are like a keyboard but do not have the mechanical action of a conventional keyboard. The musical signal is sent out through loudspeakers, often in multiple channels to allow the performer to manipulate the movement of the sound in space.

Ciani's first encounter with the Buchla synthesizer was at a new electronic center at Mills College, where she could rent a studio with a synthesizer for a modest fee. Soon afterward she took a course in computer music at Stanford University with Max Mathews, and then she began to give concerts in Berkeley and elsewhere in the San Francisco area. In 1969 she got her first paying assignment, composing twenty-three ads for a department store. After graduating from Berkeley in 1970, she went to work in the Buchla factory, hoping to learn enough about the instrument so that she could build her own. Meanwhile, to earn enough to buy her own synthesizer, she composed scores for educational films, sound effects for commercials, and any other assignments that paid.

More and more interested in her own compositions and in live performance, Ciani in 1974 moved to New York. Although she continued to produce music for television and radio commercials and film scores, she also found more opportunities for concert performance. In 1977 she joined a rock band called New Age, in the belief that electronic music presented a unique opportunity to combine elements of serious music with the more widespread appeal of popular styles. Among Ciani's important works for the Buchla synthesizer are *Koddesh-Koddeshim* (1972), *New York, New York* (1974), *Lixiviation* (1974), and *New York II* (1975). Her most successful popular electronic arrangement was the one she made for the 1977 *Meco Star Wars* album, the popular disco version of the score from the motion picture *Star Wars.*

In New York Ciani formed the Ciani/Musica production company, which pioneered sound design for television. It produced award-winning commercials for General Electric, Coca-Cola, Pepsi, General Motors, and other major companies. From there she branched out to scoring such films as Lily Tomlin's *The Incredible Shrinking Woman* (1980), and *Mother Teresa* (1986). There followed a collection of self-produced instrumental albums that achieved enormous popularity: *Seven Waves* (1982), *The Velocity of Love* (1986), *Neverland* (1988), and *History of My Heart* (1989). During this period Ciani decided to concentrate on recording and performing and closed her production company. In 1992 she moved to California and returned to her classical roots and the conventional acoustic piano, leaving electronic music behind. Two years later, together with entertainment lawyer Joe Anderson, who soon became her husband, partner, and manager, she formed a new label, Seventh Wave, to release her own recordings and those of other artists they considered important. Their first effort, *Dream Suite* (1994), was Ciani's first CD with full orchestra. The next was *Pianissimo II,* a solo piano work. Although primarily a piano and synthesizer soloist, touring widely, Ciani in 1997 formed a band for live performance called Suzanne Ciani and the Wave, a classical and jazz group made up of reeds, bass, guitars, percussion, flute, violin, cello, and Ciani herself on piano and synthesizers. In the same year she was awarded a Lifetime Achievement Award by Women in Audio of the Audio Engineering Society, in recognition of her achievements in the fields of production, engineering, composition, and performance, and of her ongoing commitment to advance the role of women in music and in the audio engineering field in particular.

Priscilla McLean, born in 1942, began her career as an elementary school teacher.[16] In her early twenties, she decided to pursue her love of music and went to Indiana University. In the late 1960s she came under the influence of Iannis Xenakis, director for a time of the Electronic Music Studio, and his stress on texture over melody and rhythm gave her a new way of hearing music. She also met her husband there, composer Barton McLean, who became director of another electronic music studio, and from 1970 on electronic composition was McLean's primary interest. In 1983 the McLeans left academia and settled in upstate New York. In 1974 they had formed McLean Mix, a composing and performing duo of both taped and live electroacoustic music, with which they toured extensively in the United States and Europe. McLean's first live electronic composition was *Spectral I* (1972) for percussion and synthesizer. She sometimes incorporated nature sounds, as in *Beneath the Horizon I* (1978), for processed whale sounds and tuba quartet, and *Rainforest Images,* a 1992 recording. Her purely acoustic works include *Variations and Mosaics on a Theme of Stravinsky* (1967–75), for orchestra, and *Interplanes* (1970) for two pianos. Her works of the 1990s often incorporate video images of various kinds. Thus *Jambori Rimba* (1997) is a multimedia installation involving stereo tape, synthesizers, a "jungle wheel" with violin bow, ceramic pipes and mallets, processor microphone, native tribal tapes, video projections, multiple slides, and interactive video. A 1998 recording of this work involves voice, sawblade gongs, soprano recorder, clariflute, bowed bicycle wheel digital delays, and stereo tape.

Electronic music has obvious advantages as an accompaniment for staged presentations—for theater, dance, and film—since it requires only the presence of playback equipment, and its lack of visual interest is compensated by the stage performance. Among the electronic composers who became known for their compositions for theater and film was Pril Smiley.[17] Born on March 19, 1943, in Mohonk Lake, New York, she began composing electronic music in 1963 at the Columbia-Princeton Electronic Music Center. She eventually became an instructor there and then served as associate director for twenty-five years. From 1968 to 1974 she also served as electronic music consultant to the Lincoln Center Repertory Theatre in New York, and from time to time she worked as a freelance percussionist.

During her career at Columbia, Smiley composed more than forty scores for theater, film, and dance productions, including one free-style skiing ballet.

One of Smiley's first successful electronic works was *Eclipse* (1967), chosen as runner-up in the First International Electronic Music Competition at Dartmouth College in 1968. This work was composed for four separate tracks, to be performed as though the music was being played from all four corners of a room. All the elements of this work—rhythm, timbre, loudness, and duration of pitches—were very precisely determined. In her own description of the work, Smiley said:

> In many ways the structure of *Eclipse* is related to the use of timbre. There are basically two kinds of sounds in the piece: the low, sustained gong-like sounds (always either increasing or decreasing in loudness) and the short, more percussive sounds, which can be thought of as metallic, glassy, or wooden in character. These different kinds of timbres are usually used in contrast to one another, sometimes set end to end so that one kind of sound interrupts another, and sometimes dovetailed so that one timbre appears to emerge out of or from beneath another. Eighty-five percent of the sounds are electronic in origin; the non-electronic sounds are mainly pre-recorded percussion sounds—but subsequently electronically modified so that they are not always recognizable.[18]

Both *Eclipse* and another of Smiley's electronic works, *Kolyosa* (1970), were commercially recorded and performed many times. Also, both works were used by Vladimir Ussachevsky, a founder of electronic music, as part of his extensive lecture-demonstration tours throughout the United States. Smiley was awarded a grant from the National Endowment for the Arts in 1974 and a Guggenheim Fellowship for 1975–76. Smiley stopped composing in the mid-1980s but continued to teach composition. She finally left Columbia in 1995. A pioneer in electronic music when analog equipment was first used, she never became comfortable with the advances of digital technology, and decided to pursue other interests. Her final composition, *Forty-Three* (1984), has been performed throughout the United States as well as in Mexico, Amsterdam, Tokyo, Stockholm, Montreal, Madrid, and Bourges (France); it also is commercially recorded.[19]

Elizabeth Swados, who became known mainly for her innovative music theater, said, "Though there has been progress, woman composers are still greatly ignored in theatrical, classical, and jazz idioms . . . generally women are breaking through in the areas of opera and experimental performance by producing and conducting their own works."[20] Swados was born in 1951 and studied composition with Henry Brant at Bennington College. In the early 1970s she went to New York, where she worked with La Mama Experimental Theater Company. She has composed scores for plays, ranging from Greek tragedies to Shakespeare, notably *The Merchant of Venice.* Her first outstanding musical theater piece was *Runaways,* a 1978 plotless accumulation of songs and sketches, which were performed by nonprofessional street children. She also collaborated with Gary Trudeau on a musical based on his comic strip, *Doonesbury* (1983), and a satirical political revue poking fun at President Ronald Reagan, *Rap Master Ronnie* (1984). Her theater music is eclectic, drawing on various styles of popular music, but she also has written a song cycle, symphonic overture, and other works for orchestra.

The creation of film scores is another means for involving composers in production. Swados has composed a number of them, but relatively few American women film composers have been recognized. In the latter 1990s two British women received Oscars for their scores: Rachel Portman in 1996, for *Emma,* based on the Jane Austen novel, and Anne Dudley in 1997, for the comedy *The Full Monty.* However, one British-born longtime American resident and two American women have been overcoming what seem like overwhelming odds in this field—Angela Morley, Shirley Walker, and Laura Karpman.

Angela Morley, born in England in 1924, studied piano, saxophone, and clarinet, and after leaving school played woodwind instruments in a number of London bands and studio orchestras.[21] During this time she studied harmony, counterpoint, and composition with Hungarian composer Matyas Seiber and conducting with German conductor Walter Goehr. About 1950 she stopped performing and began her career as an arranger, composer, and conductor. In film music an arranger executes the technical mechanics of the score for which a composer may not have the time or facility, helping to decide what instruments will best serve the themes, and setting these conclusions down on paper. Some composers do all their own arranging, and others collaborate with an arranger. Morley was appointed musical director of Philips Records in 1953 and began to compose film scores in that year. She was nominated for two Oscars, for *The Little Prince* (1973), for which she arranged all the music and composed additional music, and for *The Slipper and the Rose* (1975), for which she not only arranged and composed but conducted. Soon after writing the score for *Watership Down* (1977), she moved to Los Angeles, and in the next fourteen years she composed eighty-five scores for television, as well as assisting other composers with their scores. Winner of three Emmy Awards for arranging, Morley arranged for such groups as the Boston Pops, London Symphony, Royal Philharmonic, and Pittsburgh Symphony orchestras, and artists such as Frederica von Stade, Rosemary Clooney, Plácido Domingo, and Itzhak Perlman.

Shirley Walker, composer, conductor, pianist, synthesist, and producer, was born in 1945 in California.[22] She began her musical career as a pianist, performing as a soloist with the San Francisco Symphony while still in high school. Her first big break as a synthesist came with Francis Ford Coppola's film *Apocalypse Now* (1979), and the same year she was co-composer, with Carmine Coppola, and orchestrator for his film *Black Stallion.* During the next two decades she worked on numerous television and feature films, as composer, orchestrator, or conductor, and sometimes all three. Outstanding among these was her score for the suspense thriller *Turbulence* (1996) and for the animated film *Batman: Mask of the Phantasm* (1993). She garnered a daytime Emmy Award as musical director on the television *Batman* series. She also orchestrated and conducted the music for the popular films *Days of Thunder* (1990) and *A League of Their Own* (1992), among others. As a film composer, Walker became known for creating an intense and penetrating musical backdrop that cleverly captures the futuristic, eerie, industrial, or fantastic feel of the story setting. She had a special facility for dark superhero scores, as seen by her prolific work for both Batman and several Superman films.

Laura Karpman, born in Los Angeles, won three Emmy awards for her music for *The Living Edens,* the public television nature documentary series.[23] Beginning her musical education with piano and voice, she studied at the University of Michigan under William Bolcom and Leslie Bassett and then earned a doctorate in composition from the Juilliard School, where her principal teacher was Milton Babbitt. As of this writing she has scored more than thirty feature films, plays, movies of the week, and television miniseries. Her film scores include *A Woman of Independent Means* (1996), *Blue Rodeo* (1997), *The Breakup* (1998), and *The Annihilation of Fish* (1999). In addition Karpman has composed a sizable amount of concert music, including orchestral, chamber, and vocal works.

A number of other women composers, especially those working with electronic music, also wrote film scores. Although it was not a major part of their output, Jean Eichelberger Ivey, Daria Semegen, Pril Smiley, Lucia Dlugoszewski, Meredith Monk and Laurie Anderson all wrote some film scores. In live performance as well, they composed music to be combined with special stage effects and special lighting, with film, and with dance, all considered integral parts of a performance. Such multimedia works and performance art engaged many women composers.

Meredith Monk is generally known as a performance artist.[24] Born in Peru in 1943 while her mother, a singer, was on tour, she became a singer, composer, and creator of music theater. She began composing for voice when she was very young, and later she studied voice, piano, and dance. In many of her works, in which she also performs, dance remains an important element, notably in *Turtle Dreams* (1983), a waltz for four solo voices and two electric organs; in the film a dancer also appears. Monk's compositions range from wordless pieces for solo voice, such as *Songs from the Hill* (1976), in which she exploits a large variety of vocal sounds—singing, whispering, breathing, chants, slides, glottal stops, yelping, chattering, gasping—to ensemble pieces involving several voices. In *Dolmen Music* (1979) the voices are those of three women and three men, and one of the men plays a cello, which is bowed or struck. Much earlier she had written *Juice* (1969), a theater cantata for eighty-five voices, eighty-five Jew's harps, and two violins. Works such as *Quarry* (1976) combine music, film, dance, and acting. Monk also produced a feature-length film score, *Book of Days* (1988), in which she reworked an earlier vocal composition into a work for ten violins, cello, shawm, synthesizer, hammered dulcimer, bagpipe, and hurdygurdy. Her *Atlas: An Opera in Three Parts,* for twenty-nine performers, was commissioned by the Houston Grand Opera and premiered there in 1991. *A Celebration Service* (1996), for sixteen-member chorus, dancers, keyboardist, and readers, was commissioned by the Union Theological Seminary for the national convention of the American Guild of Organists. It relies on her extended vocalese to set texts from a broad cross section of spiritual traditions: an Osage Indian initiation song, a Buddhist text, a Zen poem, a Sufi poem, a Chinese poem, a Hasidic saying. It also includes a section of audience participation in which audience members learn the canon from *Quarry*.[25]

A more broadly experimental figure is Laurie Anderson, who like Monk is generally described as a performance artist rather than as a composer.[26] Born in Chicago in 1947, Anderson was trained as a violinist and as a painter and sculptor. In the 1970s she became active in New York's downtown avant-garde scene and made her first performance work, *Automotive* (1972), a concert for car horns. She also began making instruments, mostly modifying the violin. In 1977 she created a tape-bow violin, which has a tape playback head on the bridge and a bow with prerecorded lengths of audio tape instead of hair; drawing the bow across the head, the performer activates the tape and can control the speed and direction of the playback. Her first major work was *Americans on the Move* (1979), later incorporated into *United States.* Called an opera, *United States* is a four-part multimedia event about transportation, politics, money, and love, lasting seven hours, and first given in its entirety in 1983. Most of her pieces are solo operas built up from stories that she recites or sings, often augmented with computer graphics and special electronic devices, such as contact microphones attached to her body. Beginning in the 1980s she also wrote for orchestra and dance, and from the mid-1980s on, film and television scores. She wrote and directed a full-length feature film, *Home of the Brave* (1986), and wrote the scores for *Swimming to Cambodia* (1987) and *Monster in a Box* (1991). Augmented by slide projections, film, video, and lighting effects, Anderson's performance art is often wryly humorous, for the central point is the text. She has said that her real subject is the spoken word. Her later works include two large multimedia productions, *Stories from the Nerve Bible* (1995) and *Songs and Stories from "Moby Dick"* (1999), the latter based on Melville's novel.

Another notable performance artist was Charlotte Moorman (1933–1991). A cellist, she studied with Leonard Rose at Juilliard and played in the Boccherini Chamber Players and American Symphony Orchestra. In 1964 she began a longtime collaboration with composer and video performance artist

Nam June Pai. Their works, sometimes using unconventional instruments and involving nudity, on-stage sex, and similar elements, became famous for their outrageousness. A particularly notorious performance involved playing her cello under water, with Moorman herself wrapped only in cellophane.

A champion of avant-garde vocal technique is singer and composer Joan La Barbara. Born in 1947 in Philadelphia, she studied voice with Helen Boatwright, Phyllis Curtin, and Marion Szekely-Freschi and composition at New York University. Active as a promoter and performer of new music, she calls in her own compositions for the extended vocal techniques she developed in performance. Among them are multiphonics, circular breathing, throat clicks, and a high-pitched flutter. From early works mainly for solo voice and taped pieces, La Barbara later wrote works using more instruments, as in *The Solar Wind* (1983), for amplified voice and eight instruments, tape, and percussion; a second version of this work uses sixteen amplified solo voices, flute, keyboard, and percussion. She has also composed a number of film scores. Her setting for voice with electronics for the animation of the signing alphabet for Children's Television Workshops/Sesame Street has been broadcast worldwide since 1977. *Urban Tropics* (1988) mingles the taped real-life sounds of musique concrète with voice and percussion. It was designed as a sound portrait of Miami, blending Latin flavors with local tropical fauna. La Barbara said of the work, "I used my voice as percussion and as melodic punctuation, adding Latin percussion (cowbell, maracas, guiro) alternating with sounds taped at the Parrot Jungle, the Monkey Jungle, and on the waterfront in Miami."27

Pauline Oliveros was from the start attracted to unconventional kinds of music, and she became one of the most versatile experimenters.28 Born on May 30, 1932, in Houston, Texas, she later recalled that as a young child she had enjoyed listening to her grandfather's crystal radio over earphones, and she used to tune her father's radio to the whistles and white noise between stations. She also remembered listening, in the 1940s, to popular radio programs for their sound effects—the squeaking door on *Inner Sanctum* and others. In 1952 Oliveros moved to San Francisco. She studied there with Robert Erickson and worked as a freelance musician, and then, beginning about 1957, she became involved with group improvisation. In 1961 she began to work at the San Francisco Tape Center, where she remained for five years; in 1966 she was appointed director of the Tape Music Center at Mills College, and the following year she began teaching electronic music at the University of California at San Diego, where she later became director of the Center for Music Experiment and remained until 1981. Later she set up the Pauline Oliveros Foundation in New York, which seeks to provide support for innovative artists.

Before she began to work with electronic music, Oliveros composed for conventional instruments, using no particular system or style. Group improvisation, in which an ensemble of musicians simply produces music as a group, as it occurs to them, made her feel free to write whatever she pleased—she once said, "I simply listened until I heard the next sound to write down."[29] Although the electronic generation of sounds fascinated her, she believed, like Jean Eichelberger Ivey, that pure tape music performances lacked visual interest. Consequently she began to experiment with using dancers, actors, live musicians, film, and lighting effects in combination with taped music. Also like Ivey, she became interested in musique concrète, and in this vein created a series of works for amplified boxes: *Applebox* (1964); *Applebox Double* (1965); *Applebox Orchestra* (1966); and *Applebox Orchestra with Bottle Chorus* (1970). At the same time she experimented with real-time tape compositions, that is, compositions of electronically generated sounds recorded as soon as they are produced, without being mixed with other sounds or otherwise altered through splicing the tape. Outstanding among her early works of this nature is her *I of IV*, written in 1966.

Another area that attracted Oliveros was sound sculpture, that is, the creation of sound-producing sculpture. Such devices produce, mix, and process sound and light at the same time. Notable among her works in this vein is *In Memoriam Nicola Testa, Cosmic Engineer* (1968), which was commissioned by the Merce Cunningham Dance Company and was widely performed. In it Oliveros, according to her colleague, composer Gordon Mumma, "has the performers conduct an acoustical analysis of the performance space. For the closing section the space is subjected to a sea of low-frequency sounds which establish physically imposing standing waves and structural resonances in the building itself."[30]

Still another experimental area in which Oliveros became involved was astro-bio-geo-physical applications of electronic music. With the development of ultrasensitive electronic equipment, many previously unknown natural activities (astrophysical, biophysical, or geophysical in nature) could be detected, and the sounds and lights they emitted could be recorded and used as part of a musical presentation. For example, in Oliveros's *Valentine* (1968), for four card players, the heartbeats of four persons playing a game of Hearts and the sounds of the card table they play on are amplified. Combined with these sounds is an amplified narration of a historical text on the making of playing cards, and a series of projected images (the Queen of Hearts changing to the Queen of Spades, and others). Oliveros said of this work:

> The interest of this piece depends greatly on the players' real involvement in the game of Hearts and their peripheral interest in the hearing of their own heartbeat bio-feedback loop while the game is in progress. If the players' interest is real, audience sensitivity should increase, and the players' heart rates should change significantly with various events during the game.[31]

Multimedia presentations—performances using more than one artistic medium, such as music, dance, film, acting, sculpture—continued to engage Oliveros in the late 1970s, a time when she was also increasingly devoting herself to meditation and Eastern philosophies such as Tibetan Buddhism. *Horse Sings from Cloud,* presented in New York in 1977, featured the composer herself sounding chords on an accordion and sustaining a particular note along each chord. The accordion part began with a single note and evolved into chords of increasing complexity, moving slightly up the scale, and the single note picked out from the chord often quivered slightly in pitch. Whether or not this presentation constituted music seems to have been questioned even by the composer, for at this time she told an interviewer that she had not been working with musical ideas for some time but on her "mode of consciousness."[32] Six months later she presented *Rose Moon,* a ritual choral work commissioned and performed by Neely Bruce's Wesleyan Singers, an experimental choral ensemble. The music consists not only of choral singing but the sounds of running feet, percussive choral chanting, solo singing, and verbalizing. Theater entered into the presentation as well. As *New York Times* reviewer John Rockwell described the performance:

> There is a circular space with a center point and a cross, forming a mandala. Around the outer circle are runners, who pass eight "cuers" per revolution, each of whom marks the runner's passage with a percussive stroke. The next inner circle is a procession of figures walking counterclockwise, led by Miss Oliveros, who shakes a "moon rattle" and passes it periodically to the cuers. The next circle is four groups of three figures who chant and enact theatrical tableaux representing the elements. And at the center, inside a black and white tentlike structure, Mr. Bruce and his wife stand nude and intone the names of the moon from all the known languages and make nonverbal sounds of an emotional origin.[33]

In addition, three "lunatics," including the designer and choreographer, express disorder by wandering at random through the pattern. These and such works as *Sonic Meditations* (1971–72), *The New Sound Meditations* (1989), and *Deep Listening Pieces* (1990) seek to cultivate an intense sonic awareness in the listener.[34]

In later works Oliveros returned to writing for conventional instruments, especially accordion, her main instrument as a performer, and for voice. In the late 1980s she tuned her accordion to just intonation. *Inside Outside Space* (1992), is scored for accordion and electronics, and also for instruments and voice. Her *Out of the Dark* (1998) is scored for chamber orchestra, and the score consists of a set of directions that the musicians, who surround the audience in a darkened hall, must memorize. Each player is assigned a partner, and the pair are instructed to play in response to each other in what seems to be improvisation but is limited by the well-planned instruction. For example, each musician must stop playing if the musician next to him or her begins to play. This allows one to hear brief points of music coming from numerous— in the premiere, nineteen—places in the dark hall.[35]

Other radical experiments attracted Annea Lockwood, whose *World Rhythms* (1976) consists of natural sounds from pulsars, earthquakes, volcanic activity, rivers, human breathing, and ocean waves, combined with the playing of a gong. Some would argue that this is not even music.

Born in New Zealand in 1939, Lockwood moved first to England and then to the United States in 1973. Originally involved with electronic music— she taught electronic composition at several colleges—Lockwood concentrated on using acoustic sounds and has worked with sound sculptures and environmental installations. Like Oliveros's works, many of her pieces display her interest in holistic trance, meditation, and non-Western music. Her compositions often use environmental sounds; for example, *Sound Map of the Hudson River* (1983), a sound installation, is part of a project to record all of the world's rivers. Her *Amazonia Dreaming* (1990) for solo snare drum is a graphically notated work in which vocal gestures are used to complement and imitate actions performed on the drum, using conventional drum sticks, rubber mallets, a plastic can lid, chopsticks, and four glass marbles.[36] A work for more conventional forces is her *Shapeshifter* (1996) for chamber orchestra.

Sound environments, entire settings into which the listener enters and is surrounded by sound from various sources, as well as by film, dance, sculpture, and the like, also attracted Beth Anderson.[37] She was born on January 3, 1950, and grew up in Kentucky. After two years as a piano major at the University of Kentucky, she moved to California and completed her bachelor's degree at the University of California at Davis. She then earned two master's degrees from Mills College, one in piano and another in composition. Throughout this time she performed and taught piano and voice. She regards John Cage and minimalist composer Terry Riley among her most influential teachers.

Anderson's earliest compositions were songs and piano works, but in California she began to work increasingly with tape, usually combining taped sounds with live instruments and voices. Among the important works she produced there were the opera *Queen Christina,* performed at Mills College in 1973, the oratorio *Joan,* produced in 1974, and two string quartets of 1973 entitled *Music for Charlemagne Palestine* and *I Am Uh Am I.* Also from this period dates her first sound environment, *Hallophone* (1973), for two saxophones, steel guitar, voice, tape, slides, and dancers. The following year she collaborated with sculptor Paul Cotton on *The Messiah Is Come,* described as a "human sculpture with internal and external sound sources."

As much concerned with verbal ideas as with musical ones, Anderson found novel ways of combining the two. For example, a series of compositions she described as "text-sound pieces" are actually poems: *Torero Piece*

(1973), *Ode* (1975), *The People Rumble Louder* (1975), and *I Can't Stand It* (1976). But as one reviewer said, "In the most musical of these works, practically everything that makes music music—a coherent pitch vocabulary, patterned rhythms—was present."[38] Another writer defines text-sound as the use of words and syllables to make a percussive kind of music, similar to rap.[39]

Anderson also was active in encouraging other experimental composers. In 1973 she became coeditor and publisher of *Ear Magazine,* a musical and literary journal that included new music, poetry, drawings, and photographs. Two years later she moved to New York, where she continued publishing an East Coast edition of *Ear.* In 1976, together with composer Doris (now Sorrel) Hays, she organized an eleven-week course at the New School in New York called "Meet the Woman Composer," in which the works of eighteen contemporary women were performed and discussed.

In the 1980s Anderson returned to a more traditional neoromantic style, emphasizing lyrical melodies reminiscent of folk music and occasionally quoting from earlier music, especially hymns. Since 1985 she has been composing mostly "swales" for various instrumental combinations. A swale is a meadow or marsh where there is a rich diversity of plant life, and Anderson uses the term to mean a musical collage of newly composed material. Among them are *Pennyroyal Swale* (1995), *Rosemary Swale* (1986), and *January Swale* (1998), all for string quartet; *Minnesota Swale* (1994) for orchestra; and *Rhode Island Swale* (1999) for harpsichord or piano solo. Her other works include a piano concerto, choral pieces, band music, music for theater, musical comedy, an operetta, and many songs. She still teaches piano as well.

Practically all composers in any medium, including the most experimental, originally began by playing an instrument. And, as we will see in the next chapter, many women remained instrumentalists.

11

TODAY'S ORCHESTRAS, CONDUCTORS, AND INSTRUMENTALISTS

There are very few areas today within the musical world in which a woman need apologize for her sex. The time has long passed when a woman appearing as a concert soloist—pianist, violinist, singer—required special treatment as a kind of curiosity. The orchestral ranks are now open to her in all but a very few ensembles. . . . There are many reasons these days for not going into music as a career, but being female is not one of them.

Alan Rich, *Careers and Opportunities in Music,* 1964

T HE OLDEST of the top six American orchestras is the New York Philharmonic, founded as the Philharmonic Society of New York in 1842. By 1847 it allowed women to be associate members, which entitled them to attend rehearsals. Some of these associate members were professional musicians, but the majority were nonprofessionals who simply liked music or, in some cases, merely professed to. By the mid-1850s most of the associate members were women, and it was their fund-raising and publicity efforts that kept the society going. They did not, however, go so far as to run the organization. Women did not sit on the society's board until the 1920s, their way paved first by two wealthy and socially prominent women, Mrs. Edward Henry Harriman and then Mrs. Vincent Astor.[1] The first regular woman *player* in the New York Philharmonic, with a full season's contract, was Orin O'Brien, a double bassist hired in 1966. In earlier years the society had used women harpists, but not on a regular contractual basis.[2] The Symphony Society of New York, founded in 1878 and merged with the New York Philharmonic in 1928, had a regular woman harpist as early as 1891; at this time it was one of the country's four major orchestras, the others being the Philharmonic, the Chicago Orchestra, and the Boston Symphony.[3]

Although it took 124 years to admit a woman, the New York Philharmonic was only slightly slower than the nation's other major orchestras. Soon afterward it added a few more women, cellist Evangeline Benedetti in 1967 and seven others by 1976. By 1999 it had far more women, including assistant concertmaster Sheryl Staples, principal bassoon Judith LeClair,[4] principal viola Cynthia Phelps, and associate principal viola Rebecca Young. Phelps and Young have been called the best pair of violists of any orchestra in the country, if not the world.[5] The Boston Symphony, founded in 1881, hired its first woman, bassoonist Ann C. de Guichard, in 1945, and the Philadelphia Orchestra, founded in 1900, hired harpist Edna Philipps in 1930. She was followed by Marilyn Costello, principal harp from 1946 to 1992.

During World War II competent instrumentalists were much in demand, and by 1945 many women had found openings in formerly closed ranks. The conductor of the Chicago Woman's Symphony, for example, reported that by January 1945 two dozen of its players had found paying orchestral jobs, some of them as first chair in a leading orchestra, including principal horn in the Chicago Symphony, principal cello in Houston and New Orleans, and others.[6] Indeed in 1944 trombonist Betty Glover, newly graduated from the Cincinnati Conservatory of Music, was hired as principal trombone by the Kansas City Symphony.[7] An outstanding artist, Glover survived for years, but for most women these jobs ended after the war when the men returned home.

Why? Apart from the old prejudices against women instrumentalists discussed in Chapters 2, 3, and 5, there were other reasons. The dim view taken by some conductors was certainly one. In 1916 Josef Stransky, conductor of the New York Symphony, said he would not object to women in orchestras but they would have to be "better players than the men who apply for the same positions."[8] Nearly thirty years later Sir Thomas Beecham, commenting testily on the increasing numbers of women musicians, said, "I do not like, and never will, the association of men and women in orchestras and other instrumental combinations. . . . As a member of the orchestra once said to me, 'If she is attractive I can't play with her and if she is not I won't.'"[9]

Not all the prejudice was so straightforward. In 1933, for example, British composer Ethel Smyth pointed out that the BBC Orchestra, the only one of several London orchestras to hire women in appreciable numbers—twenty in 1931[10]—had never seen fit to hire a woman cellist.[11] In America Leopold Stokowski declared as early as 1916 that not hiring women constituted a terrible waste of "splendid power," but he himself did not engage one until 1930, and the first nonharpist, cellist Elsa Hilger, only in 1936. His reign over the Philadelphia Orchestra, however, had been undisputed since 1912. He later vindicated himself, for the American Symphony Orchestra, which he founded in 1962, from the beginning included many women and many blacks and members of other minority groups.

Other reasons for not hiring women were put forward. Women could not rehearse regularly because of their duties at home. It was difficult for them to travel, and when they did there were no appropriate facilities for them.[12] Even in the late 1970s this was occasionally true; on tour the women members of the Boston and New York orchestras sometimes found no dressing room or no toilet facilities. Oddly enough these handicaps had long been overcome by the managers of opera, theater, and ballet companies, where women were essential to the performance. Orchestral music can, of course, be performed entirely by men; operas, plays, and ballets rarely are.

Yet another excuse was offered by Helen Thompson, who after twenty-five years with the American Symphony Orchestra League became manager of the New York Philharmonic. Thompson maintained that fewer women auditioned for orchestra jobs, and therefore fewer were accepted. Perhaps many felt that there was no point in trying.

It was not only men who kept women out of orchestras. Music critic Alan Rich reported that in 1944, at a Boston Symphony fund-raising meeting attended largely by women, the president said that if not enough money was raised the orchestra would have to reduce both the number of players and the length of its season, as well as "lower its standards" by hiring women players; allegedly the last alternative was greeted with a "horrified gasp."[13] Nevertheless, only eight years later the Boston Symphony hired its third permanent woman player, and at the head of a section at that. She was Doriot Anthony Dwyer, the orchestra's principal flute, who remained in that position until 1990.

How had Dwyer managed to overcome the barrier? By dint of great talent and extremely hard work. A great-grandniece of feminist Susan B. Anthony, Dwyer preferred to play down her sex. "It's a rough life being a musician, whether you are a man or a woman. Period!" she said. Dwyer was born in 1922 in Streator, Illinois.[14] She began to study flute at age eight with her mother, Edith Maurer Anthony, a professional flutist who had toured the Chautauqua circuit and played under Ethel Leginska in Chicago but had abandoned her performing career with marriage and the arrival of four children. All four children learned to play an instrument, but only Doriot, the third, became a professional musician. As a child, Dwyer had to listen to weekly broadcasts of symphony orchestras and of the Metropolitan Opera, but it was not until she heard Rossini's Overture to *William Tell* performed at a Chicago concert that she really decided to become a professional flutist. After four years in the high school band and another four years at the Eastman School of Music, where she studied with Joseph Mariano and graduated in 1943, Dwyer obtained her first paying job with the National Symphony in Washington, D.C., under Hans Kindler. One of few conductors at that time who was sympathetic to women players, Kindler hired Dwyer as second flute, a post she held from 1943 to 1945. Meanwhile she commuted to Philadelphia for regular lessons with William Kincaid of the Philadelphia Orchestra, one of the world's greatest flutists.

In 1945 Dwyer left Washington for New York, and faced with a half-year residence period then required to join the New York union, she attended Columbia University for a semester. After joining the union, she took a number of touring engagements. She then went to the Los Angeles Philharmonic, where she played second flute for six years. She also taught at Pomona College during this time. Summers she played at the Hollywood Bowl under various conductors, including Bruno Walter, who gave her her first chance as principal flute. Elsewhere she was not even allowed to audition for first chair. In 1952 Dwyer learned that Georges Laurent, the Boston Symphony's principal flute, was retiring, and decided to apply for an audition there. She always signed her letters "Miss Doriot Anthony" so that her unusual first name would not be mistaken for a man's, and frequently she would get no answer at all. But Boston decided to give her a hearing.

She prepared rigorously for two months, practicing until late at night. She memorized everything she planned to play: a Mozart sonata, a Bach partita, Ravel's *Daphnis et Chloe,* and numerous shorter works. She would play a perfect audition, and then if she still did not get the job she would abandon orchestral work and seek a solo or chamber music career. Several other women had been invited to apply for the Boston job, and they all were heard on a single midsummer day at Tanglewood. Dwyer played for Laurent, for concertmaster Richard Burgin, and for conductor Charles Munch. Her hard work paid off, because she got the job.

It was a post she had wanted badly, and she continued to work hard at it, constantly trying to improve. During these years she married, had a daughter, and was divorced. She taught at the New England Conservatory, and then at Boston University and the Berkshire Music Center at Tanglewood, but she tried to restrict her teaching commitments so she could continue to practice and perform, both with the orchestra and in solo recitals and guest engagements with other ensembles. Her appointment originally had made headlines, but in 1976 she declared, "Now the controversy I caused is forgotten." Not entirely. In the late 1970s still very few women were principal players in major American orchestras, though by 1977 Boston had one other, Marylou Speaker (later Churchill) leading the second-violin section. In fact Boston had a total of eleven women—strings, harp, and flute, but still no brass or percussion— and ninety-two men.[15] In 1980 Ann Hobson Pilot, who had become the first African-American member of the orchestra in 1969, was named principal harp and remains so at this writing.

In 1999 the Boston Symphony had twenty-five women, all strings except for two flutes, seventy men players, and six vacancies.[16] In general women string players are better represented in the major orchestras. The Minnesota Orchestra had a woman concertmaster, Jorja Fleezanis, as did the Atlanta Symphony, Cecilia Arzewski, two of the few women to occupy this chair in an important American ensemble.[17] However, merely being accepted into an orchestra may not mean the end of one's difficulties. Sexual harassment exists in the musical workplace as well as elsewhere, ranging from offensive remarks and behavior by male colleagues and conductors to more serious problems. One violinist who played in a large southwestern orchestra had ongoing difficulties with the conductor, who persisted in inappropriate touching and vulgar comments. She was not unique. All the women in the orchestra hate him, she said. Verbal protests had no effect and two of the women have consulted attorneys.[18] In 1996 composer William Osborne wrote that five major U.S. orchestras—Philadelphia, St. Louis, Pittsburgh, Chicago, and Boston—had ongoing or recently settled gender-related lawsuits. In the case of Philadelphia, the suit was settled but the woman was removed from the orchestra; in St. Louis the man was removed.[19] Discrimination may be more subtle, too. Timpanist Mary Koss was playing backstage for a Chicago Symphony recording with conductor Claudio Abbado who, when he saw who was performing, complained from that point on that she was not playing loudly enough. When she did what he asked, despite believing the volume was excessive, the engineer's red light went on, signaling that she was indeed too loud.[20]

Employment discrimination on the basis of sex alone is illegal, and the powerful American musicians union denies its existence entirely, but the union's role in this respect does not seem to have been an active one. American musicians' unions date from Civil War days. One of the first was the Boston Musicians Union, founded in 1863, which admitted as full members all musicians living in or near Boston who were able to pay $10 plus an initiation fee; or, for $2 a musician could become an associate nonvoting member. Further, members had to be able—that is, not infirm—to pursue music as a profession and be under the age of forty-five. The union had another category, the honorary member, for which the requirements were simpler: anyone who donated $100 or more to the Relief Fund was an honorary member. The Relief Fund was in fact the basic purpose of the early unions—to help support musicians out of work for prolonged periods. Although the constitution of the Boston union referred to members as "he," nowhere did it explicitly specify the sex of members.

By the turn of the century this and other local musicians' unions had been absorbed or replaced by the much larger Mutual Musical Protective Union. Originally chartered in 1864, it became affiliated in July 1903 with the American Federation of Labor, which required that it admit women, and from that time on it always included some women members. The first women to join what is today called the American Federation of Musicians were harpists from the New York Metropolitan Opera; by mid-1904, thirty-one women had joined the union, which had a total of about 4500 members. Each member had to pay a $100 initiation fee and take an examination of musical ability; only two or three applicants failed to pass. Ten of the new women members belonged to the Ladies Elite Orchestra of the Atlantic Garten.

The admission of women to the union was controversial enough to rouse public interest, and therefore the *Musical Standard* decided to collect the "Opinions of Some New York Leaders on Women as Orchestral Players," which it published in its issue of April 2, 1904. Most of the opinions printed were unfavorable. Gustave Kerker, musical director at the Casino, felt women and men should not play together: "Neither sex will benefit from such an arrangement," he said, "*except in the matter of wages*" (author's italics). Although women were ideally suited to play the harp, Kerker said, nature never intended them to play winds or brass. They lack the lip and lung power to hold notes and therefore play out of tune. They do not look pretty playing brass. Also, women cannot be depended on to work hard, rehearse regularly, or meet similar requirements. William Furst, music director of the Belasco Theater, agreed that as harpists women were desirable but as wind players they were impossible. In the same *Musical Standard* article, he said they cannot compete with men, and they cannot learn to read music easily. Occasionally you hear a good female violinist or cornetist, but "as a rule the fair sex is too fond of fancy playing to be of actual value to a serious musical organization." In contrast, Nahan Franko, concertmaster of the Metropolitan Opera and brother of violinist Jeanne Franko, said that union membership would encourage women to become musicians and he would hire any he found capable. He did not expect to find any for some years to come, but he predicted that in ten years, "we shall see mixed orchestras in theaters and opera houses."

The only wholly positive opinion in the article was expressed by Charles Eschert, who, as director of the Atlantic Garten orchestra, described in Chapter 5, had considerable personal experience with women players. He maintained that only lack of opportunity kept women out of metropolitan orchestras. Said he:

> They would fill the positions quite as well as men. They are hard workers, they are punctual, they keep their minds on the work at hand, and ought really to receive higher salaries than men who do fill similar positions, since women are considered an attraction outside their musical powers. The outcome of this latest advancement for women will be the formation of many mixed orchestras.

Joining the union was a big step. In 1917 the only major American orchestra not yet unionized was the Boston Symphony, which held out until 1942. Almost all theater orchestras—one of the biggest sources of employment—were unionized, as were many orchestras playing in cafés, hotels, restaurants, movie theaters, and dance halls.[21] However, despite predictions of "mixed" orchestras in the near future, very little happened in this direction. In the spring of 1938—thirty-five years after women were first admitted to the union—the Committee for the Recognition of Women in the Music Profession was formed to promote the granting of full employment opportunities to women instrumentalists. On May 18 of that year, 150 women members of Musicians Local 802, the New York local, met to discuss their problems.[22] Not much appears to have come of this meeting, but union or no union, women musicians still faced greater odds against being hired than men. In 1999 the Musicians Union had somewhere between 103,000 and 110,000 members, of whom 19,232 were women—a little under 20 percent.[23]

Just what were the economic stakes? In 1911 violinist Maud Powell said that the average orchestral player earned $2000 a year, but really good wind players, who were in short supply, might make anywhere from $35 to $75 per week.[24] In October 1925 *Etude* reported on violinists' salaries. The Chicago Civic Opera paid string players $119 per week plus rehearsal fees for an average of $155 per week for a twenty-two week season, or more than $3000 per season. Symphony players received similar pay. A violinist in a first-class hotel dance orchestra earned $90 per week, whereas in jazz orchestras the pay was $100 to $150 per week. As for teaching, a violinist could expect $1.50 to $2 per lesson in smaller towns, but up to $5 in large cities. A concert engagement, on the other hand, might yield anywhere from $50 to $1000.[25] The difference in pay between a symphony job and private teaching was, therefore, considerable, and fortunate indeed were those women who were hired.

They added up to little more than a handful. Cleveland hired four women in 1923, San Francisco five in 1925, Minneapolis a few the same year. Baltimore hired five women string players in 1937. The lesser orchestras were more open. For example, the Civic Orchestra of Chicago, founded in 1918, included twenty-four women by 1921, one of them a clarinetist;[26] during the same time the much richer Chicago Symphony had only a single woman harpist, and not every year, either. Wind players had a harder time yet. Although in 1937 conductor Otto Klemperer engaged twenty-year-old Ellen Stone as first horn for the Pittsburgh Symphony, this was an isolated case among major orchestras.

Leona May Smith, born in 1916, was the foremost woman trumpeter of this period. She was featured as a soloist at Radio City Music Hall and worked with both Fred Waring's Pennsylvanians and the Goldman Band, two of the nation's leading popular ensembles. Yes, she said in 1938, there is a future for women musicians, but they must somehow overcome the common critic's attitude: "This is a commendable performance, considering the player is a woman." The best steady income for a woman musician, Smith concluded, was teaching.[27] Though Smith played first trumpet with the National Orchestral Association, performed with the Chautauqua Symphony, and won a number of awards, she devoted most of her time in succeeding years to teaching brass instruments to high school students. In 1973 she moved to Plymouth, Massachusetts, and became involved in local church and cultural affairs, as well as managing a rest home for elderly women. Well into her eighties at this writing, she is still playing, teaching, and working on a method book for trumpet students.

There were, of course, many other prominent women brass players in the mid-1900s, as there had been in the nineteenth century. (See Chapter 5 for more about women's brass bands and brass players in jazz.) Dorothy Miriam

Ziegler (1922–1972) was hired as principal trombone by the St. Louis Symphony in 1947, but she soon turned to working as a vocal coach and opera conductor.[28] Although she continued to play trombone, her main work was with such organizations as the St. Louis Grand Opera Guild, Indiana University Opera Theater, and University of Miami Opera Theater.

Nancy Taylor was the first woman to play trumpet in the U.S. Marine Band, and Jan Z Duga in 1983 became the first woman to play tuba in the U.S. Air Force Band. Women tuba players have had an especially difficult time getting jobs. African-American tuba player Velvet M. Brown, former director of bands at Boston University, from which she holds a master's degree, played and taught for years in the Boston area but then moved to teach at Bowling Green State University. Betty S. Glover, bass trombone and tenor tuba player, who had played with the Kansas City orchestra, performed with the Cincinnati Symphony Orchestra and Opera from 1952 to 1985 and retired to France in 1992 after forty years with the Cincinnati Conservatory. At this writing, Catherine Compton in the Detroit Symphony appears to be the only woman tubist in a major orchestra.

Some women brass players turn toward academia. Tubist Constance J. Weldon played at various times with the Boston Pops, North Carolina Symphony, Amsterdam Concertgebouw, and Kansas City Philharmonic, but spent most of her career teaching and coaching at the University of Miami. Trumpeter Barbara Butler, who played with numerous major orchestras, then went to teach at the Eastman School of Music and later at Northwestern University School of Music. She and her trumpeter husband, Charles Geyer, also played in the Eastman Brass Quintet and with Music of the Baroque, a Chicago-based chorus and orchestra, and at the Grand Tetons Music Festival. Others, like trombonist Monique Buzzarté and horn player Katherine Canfield, remain freelancers in large cities. Both Buzzarté and Canfield are in the New York area, and they, too must sometimes bring charges for harassment. And some, like Carole Dawn Reinhart, Abbie Conant, and Julia Studebaker, move to employment in Europe. Studebaker joined the Royal Concertgebouw of Amsterdam as principal horn in the 1970s, a rare achievement at that time.

The underlying reason for job discrimination in any field is economic. The difference between a major and a lesser orchestra is also purely economic. Indeed, in 1979 America's 1400 orchestras were classified on just that basis— by the size of the annual budget, the minimum annual salary, the length of the season, and the number of players employed. According to this system of classification, the smallest were the college and community orchestras, about 1000 in all, with budgets under $50,000. Then came the urban orchestras, with $50,000 to $100,000 budgets, and the metropolitan orchestras, with $100,000 to $500,000. None of these could afford to pay players very much, nowhere near a living wage. Consequently fewer men accepted jobs in them, and more women were willing to settle for them. Finally, there are regional orchestras, with $500,000 to $1.5 million, and at the top, thirty-one major orchestras with budgets over $1.5 million, which provide a full season's employment. In 1978 eleven of the major orchestras worked the year round. Clearly these were the most desirable employers. The New York Philharmonic, for example, which in 1976 paid a minimum of $23,000 per year for a fifty-two-week year, including a forty-nine-day paid vacation, might have as many as 100 highly qualified players show up to audition for a single opening.[29]

By 1999 the budget figures had changed. The American Symphony Orchestra League now classed the nation's 1200 orchestras according to their total expenses:[30]

Group 1 (top 25 U.S. orchestras)	$10,900,001 or higher
Group 2	$4,000,001–10,900,000
Group 3	$2,050,001–4,000,000
Group 4	$1,350,001–2,050,000
Group 5	$725,001–1,350,000
Group 6	$300,001–725,000
Group 7	$50,001–300,000
Group 8	$50,000 or less

Of the six U.S. orchestras with a fifty-two-week year and a 1998–99 budget exceeding $30 million, the minimum annual salary paid was $84,500 in Boston; $85,020 in Chicago; $82,680 in Los Angeles; $85,540 in New York; $85,330 in Philadelphia; and $82,020 in San Francisco. The thirteen other major orchestras with a full year's employment had lower budgets and, in most cases, somewhat lower minimum salaries. The average annual salaries of regional orchestras, those in Group 2, with shorter seasons, were roughly one-fourth to one-third of salaries for the top six.[31]

Music is rarely a lucrative profession. For every diva or conductor who makes a fortune, there are thousands of musicians who cannot find employment at all. According to the 1960 census, musicians and music teachers earned an average of $4757 per year versus a median of $6778 for all professions; this was only $7 more than the average experienced male laborer over the age of fourteen. Of forty-nine professional groups, musicians and music teachers ranked fortieth in national income. Between 1940 and 1960, when American production workers in manufacturing raised their earnings by 150 percent, orchestral players' earnings rose only 80 percent. Strenuous concerted efforts, both by the musicians union and the International Conference of Symphony and Opera Musicians, greatly improved earnings between 1963 and 1971, the average annual salary rising from $4147 to $9893 in that period,[32] but by and large musicians were only beginning to keep up with the overall rate of inflation. Two decades later, according to the 1990 census, musicians and composers who were "full-time year-round workers" earned a mean of $29,951 and art, drama, and music teachers earned $34,422 compared to $30,377 for all occupations. Thus musicians' earnings had just barely outpaced inflation by 1.3 percent a year.[33]

Though accurate statistics are hard to come by, it is estimated that about half the players in urban and community orchestras—who are either not paid at all or only on a per concert basis—are women. According to the American Symphony Orchestra League's report on women in symphony orchestras, published in *Symphony News* in April 1976, orchestras with the highest budgets, longest seasons, and most generous salaries tend to have the fewest women players, and on the average, the best of the major orchestras had fewer than 10 percent women players.[34] According to a more recent study, published in 1995, women players make up about 25 percent of major U.S. orchestras and 36 percent of all U.S. orchestras.[35] (For the 1998–99 percentages of women in thirteen orchestras with budgets over $10 million, see the Appendix.) Another article gives slightly different figures, holding that in 1995 nearly half America's orchestra players were women. Specifically, it found orchestras with budgets under $1.3 million to be more than half women, and among the nation's twenty-five largest orchestras the article found women players at around 30 percent.[36]

The 1976 *Symphony News* article also stated that the use of blind auditions—in which applicants are hidden from the judges by a screen—greatly increased the number of women hired. In 1976 one-third of all major orchestras used a screen for preliminary auditions, and three orchestras—all with a high percentage of women players—used a screen in their final auditions. Needless to say, this system also could be expected to help black, Asian, or other minority-group musicians of either sex. On the other hand, the screen is often removed when it comes down to a few finalists, or when the conductor or an orchestra committee has final say, and sexism may again be operative. In the 1998–99 season, although all the forty-seven largest orchestras reported that they hold *preliminary* auditions behind screens, only about a dozen do so for *final* auditions.[37]

In 1974 *New York Times* critic Donal Henahan described the new auditioning system adopted by the Metropolitan Opera. Weeks before preliminary auditions, notice of a vacancy was sent to the players' committee, a group selected by the orchestra to act as its representative, and ads were placed in the union periodical and perhaps also in other media. Test music was sent to candidates in advance of their preliminary audition. For the final audition, judges sat scattered about the hall to discourage conversation among themselves, and the candidates played behind black cloth screens. The candidates were forbidden to speak or to tune up from behind the screen, to avoid the possibility of using prearranged signals that would reveal their identity to the judges. Each judge had one vote, and the panel of judges was made up of conductors and first-chair players, as well as any members of the relevant orchestra section who wanted to participate. Henahan, who attended one such audition, pointed out that the system was not as "blind" as it sounded. Judges did chatter among themselves, and the black curtain screening the candidates was not quite opaque, so that the outlines of the players were discernible. The results for this orchestra at least, were not markedly favorable to women: in 1977 the Metropolitan Opera had ninety-seven players, ten of them women. These figures changed over the next two decades, however, possibly because of music director James Levine. In 1999 the Met orchestra had thirty-six women, including three brass players—all French horn—and fifty-nine men.

Traditionally, each orchestra has its own system for filling vacancies. For many years the decision was wholly up to the principal first violinist, or concertmaster, second in power only to the conductor. Some orchestras were ruled entirely by their conductors, whereas others had a small group of musicians, usually longtime members of the orchestra, who chose any candidate they liked. Thus, if an applicant was a favorite student of a player who in turn was a favorite of the orchestra management, the audition might be a mere formality.

Until the mid-1960s vacancies were rarely publicized. Word of mouth was the only form of advertising, and jobs often were filled before any outsider even knew they were available. As a result, some sections were filled entirely by the pupils of the first-chair player. Unfair as this system might seem, it often yielded superior results. Most of the first-class musicians of a good orchestra, like other musicians, do some teaching, but they tend to be quite selective with their pupils; moreover, the most talented students flock to such players. Consequently their pupils generally are of a very high caliber. Beginning in the early 1960s, however, pressure from minority groups, government agencies, civil rights organizations, and the newly founded International Conference of Symphony and Opera Musicians forced orchestras to convert to a system of selection that had at least more semblance of fairness. Now all openings are publicly advertised, applicants initially audition behind a screen, and the music director's right to intervene in the auditioning process has been constrained.

In recent decades players who believed themselves discriminated against occasionally instituted legal action. In 1969 two black musicians charged that the New York Philharmonic hired substitutes and extra musicians on the basis of cronyism, and that many of those hired were pupils of orchestra members. Further, they pointed out, only one New York Philharmonic player was black, indicating that blacks were discriminated against in the hiring of permanent members as well as freelancers. The New York City Human Rights Commission upheld their charge of cronyism but dismissed allegations of discrimination against these two musicians because, it ruled, discrimination in matters regarding artistic judgment is too difficult to prove.

A dramatic and highly publicized case of discrimination was that of Elayne Jones, who sued the San Francisco Symphony for denying her tenure. Jones, a timpanist, became the only black woman to occupy a first chair in a major

American orchestra when she joined the San Francisco Symphony in 1972. She had been professionally active for nearly twenty-five years, most notably at the New York City Opera and in the American Symphony Orchestra. She was recommended for the San Francisco opening by Seiji Ozawa, the orchestra's newly appointed music director. In May 1974 the players' committee, which under the San Francisco Symphony's union contract was the most powerful such committee in the nation, voted to deny tenure to Jones and one other player, a male Japanese bassoonist, Ryohei Nakagawa. Conductor Ozawa formally dissociated himself from this decision, saying he wanted to keep both players. The union charged coercion, and a poll of the entire orchestra upheld the committee's vote, but both players were invited to reaudition for another trial appointment. Nakagawa took the opportunity and failed the audition; Jones refused and instead brought suit. Reinstated for one year, she agreed the following summer to withdraw the suit if a new vote could be taken by a new committee. That vote was taken in late August 1975, and Jones again was denied tenure. Further, this time Ozawa publicly agreed with the committee decision. And again the legal outcome was indecisive. Because "artistic judgment" was involved, it could not be determined if Jones was actually incompetent, or if she was a victim of discrimination, or if, perhaps, she had become a pawn in a battle for power between Ozawa and the orchestra.[38] In any event, she left the San Francisco Symphony but continued to play with the San Francisco Opera Orchestra.

The situation is not unique to San Francisco, or to the United States. American trombonist Abbie Conant, in worldwide demand as a recitalist, soloist, and performance artist, was appointed principal trombone of the Munich Philharmonic in 1980, and in 1982 the music director tried to remove her from the position, apparently for no reason other than that she is a woman. Conant spent the next ten years fighting to retain both the position and its salary, engaging in numerous lawsuits. When she finally won and promptly left for the Trossingen Conservatory, to become the first and only woman professor of trombone in Germany, she was replaced in the orchestra by a seventeen-year-old man with no orchestral experience.

Woodwind players at least appear to have had a somewhat easier time. The Pittsburgh Symphony, for example, hired Nancy Goeres as principal bassoon in 1984 and Cynthia Koledo DeAlmeida as principal oboe in 1991. But brass players continue to have problems. The first woman trombonist to be hired by the New York Philharmonic was Lisa Albrecht, appointed in 1996 as assistant principal. She joined an elite minority: Susan Slaughter, principal trumpet of the St. Louis Symphony; Rebecca Bower Cherian, former coprincipal trombone of the Pittsburgh Symphony; Heather Buchman, principal trombone of the San Diego Symphony; Julie Landsman, principal French horn with the Metropolitan Opera; and Gail Williams, associate principal French horn with the Chicago Symphony. Cherian's situation at Pittsburgh was not trouble-free. Hired in 1989, she was at first denied tenure, and then, when it was granted, was still assigned to play second trombone most of the time.[39]

Perhaps the most highly respected and best established woman brass player of recent times is trumpeter Susan Slaughter.[40] She joined the St. Louis Symphony Orchestra in 1969 and three years later became the first woman ever to be named principal trumpet of a major symphony orchestra. A graduate of Indiana University, Slaughter had previously spent two years as principal trumpet of the Toledo Symphony. A frequent soloist with both St. Louis and other ensembles, Slaughter in 1991 founded the International Women's Brass Conference, an organization dedicated to providing opportunities and recognition for women brass musicians. Its first conference was held in St. Louis in 1993 and for the first time brought together women brass players from all over the world. According to its mission statement, "The IWBC exists to provide opportunities that will educate, develop, support and inspire all women brass musicians who desire to pursue professional careers in music." This first conference also honored three "pioneers in brass"—jazz trombonist Melba Liston, trumpeter Leona May Smith, and trombonist Betty Glover. It also gave rise to a seventeen-piece all-women's brass ensemble, the Monarch Brass, which went on tour and included such notable players as Julie Landsman, principal horn from the Metropolitan Opera; trumpeters Slaughter, Carole Dawn Reinhart, and Marie Speziale; trombonist Lynn Mostoller from the Tulsa Philharmonic; Ava Ordman, principal trombone from the Grand Rapids Symphony; and tubist Velvet Brown. The second IWBC took place in 1997 and honored tuba player Constance Weldon, trumpeter Jane Sager, who played in the International Sweethearts of Rhythm, and trumpeter Clora Bryant, whose jazz career included playing with Duke Ellington, Louie Armstrong, and numerous others. The third conference was scheduled for 2000 in Cincinnati. Meanwhile, Marie Speziale, associate principal trumpet with the Cincinnati Symphony from 1964 until her retirement in 1996, the first woman trumpeter hired by a major orchestra and longtime teacher at the Cincinnati Conservatory, replaced Susan Slaughter as president of the IWBC in 1998.

In earlier decades, frustrated ambitions prompted some women to found their own orchestras. Among them was Mrs. Davenport Engberg, who started an orchestra and turned over its management to her husband while she concentrated on training its musicians and conducting it. Engberg founded her orchestra in 1911 in Bellingham, Washington, a city of 30,000, and by 1916 it had eighty performers, about half of them women. Engberg began her career as a violinist, and appeared as soloist with several West Coast orchestras. She claimed that only a violinist could become a conductor because only a violinist could understand the all-important string sections, and only a teacher of violin would have enough students to supply the string sections. She herself gave individual lessons to any section members who needed help. In May 1917

Etude published her article, "How to Start a Local Symphony Orchestra," and described her as the only "lady conductor" of a symphony orchestra in the world.

Her article includes a detailed description of the orchestra's budget. The principal initial expense was the purchase of new instruments: six violas, four cellos, two double basses, and percussion instruments. Music was purchased for a total of about $9000, and the YMCA auditorium was hired for weekly rehearsals for $1 per week. A theater rented for a concert cost $140. After six years, the orchestra still had no oboist or bassoonist. Other instruments played these parts during rehearsals, and players were imported for concerts for fees of $60 to $100. The local musicians' union was paid $5 per player, or approximately $125.

Over the years these costs rose, but the orchestra managed to survive without special help until the fifth season, when a wealthy local music lover put up $500 to cover the accumulated deficit. Until then Engberg's husband, a pharmacist, donated his services as manager and those of his store's stenographer. At the beginning of the sixth season a proper board was formed. It is not reported how many concerts were given each season, but works such as Schubert's "Unfinished" Symphony, Beethoven's Overture to *Egmont,* and the Prelude to Wagner's *Lohengrin* are mentioned as part of programs.

In the 1930s at least two women founded urban orchestras that they themselves conducted and which have survived past 1999. One was Bertha Roth Walburn Clark, who founded the Knoxville (Tennessee) Orchestra, a fifty-piece ensemble. The other was Grace Kleinhenn Thompson Edmister, who in 1932 founded the Albuquerque Civic Symphony, now called the New Mexico Symphony Orchestra.

Bertha Roth was born on December 8, 1882, in Ohio and graduated from the Cincinnati College of Music in 1902 as an accomplished violinist.[41] She married Jamie Walburn and bore two children, Elsa Walburn Stong, who became a pianist, and Lenore Walburn Bryan, a cellist. About 1910 she moved to Knoxville, Tennessee, and soon became active in the city's musical life. She taught violin and voice, coached local opera groups, and founded the Ladies String Quartet. In 1923 she put together the Philharmonic Orchestra, which, however, foundered for lack of funds. In 1925 she tried again and organized the Walburn-Clark Little Symphony (several years after Walburn died, she had married flutist-cellist Harold Clark), an ensemble of twenty to twenty-five members.

At first the programs were few in number and modest in content. By March 3, 1927, however, the orchestra presented Mozart's Symphony no. 39 in celebration of its new name, the Knoxville Symphony Orchestra. The name change was devised to win more financial support. Some years later, in 1935, the orchestra was officially chartered by the State of Tennessee and Bertha Clark, still its conductor, for the first time began to be paid for her services. A symphony society to establish a firmer financial base was organized in October 1941, and the first concert under its aegis was given on December 7, 1941, the day the Japanese attacked Pearl Harbor.

During the war years Clark continued to maintain her orchestra, performing regularly throughout the state, even at the camp for conscientious objectors at Gatlinburg. After the war, on April 9, 1946, she made her farewell appearance as conductor, although she and her husband continued to play in the orchestra until 1962. Lamar Stringfield took over as conductor and established a pops series, which won the orchestra a huge following. In 1947 he was replaced by David Van Vactor, who served as music director and conductor until 1972. Under his tenure the orchestra grew to a standard full size—eighty-five to one hundred players, many of them faculty members of the University of Tennessee. In 1974 Bertha Clark died. By then the orchestra was under Arpad Jou, who in 1977 was replaced by Zoltan Rosynai. A regional orchestra today, its budget is more than $3 million per year, and it has a thirty-five-week season.

Grace Kleinhenn was born on August 2, 1890, near Defiance, Ohio, and began her music studies with local teachers.[42] At age nine she began studying at Defiance College and continued there until she received her bachelor's degree in 1908. Later she studied at the American Conservatory in Chicago and the Juilliard School in New York. She began teaching piano at the age of fifteen and continued for a number of years. In 1912 she married Lewis B. Thompson, a choir director and cellist; they had two children, Robert and Marilyn. In 1918, Grace Thompson was stricken with tuberculosis, and in a desperate effort to save her life she was taken to New Mexico, where the desert air was thought to benefit lung disease. She eventually recovered, and in 1923 she began to teach piano and theory at the University of New Mexico. She founded its department of public school music education, and in 1925 she was made head of the university's entire music department. During these years, she became interested in the music and dance of the local Indian tribes and the early Spanish settlers, transcribing some of it. From these endeavors grew a four-day pageant, *The First American,* produced not only in Albuquerque, where it was performed annually for some years, but also in a shorter form in New York and Ohio.

In October 1932 some members of the Rotary Club of Albuquerque decided to provide their city with a civic orchestra, an idea long entertained by a number of local musicians. Pointing to the success of similar organizations in Tulsa and Tucson, the Rotarians decided to establish an orchestra of thirty-five to fifty players, primarily local, and charge a very low admission to concerts—twenty-five cents at the outset—in order to make good music available to everyone. The cost would be underwritten by patrons from local businesses and professionals. The committee then asked Grace Thompson, as head of the university music department, and William Kunkel, a fine flutist also teaching at the university, to form the orchestra. Thompson, who by now had considerable experience conducting the student orchestra, was appointed conductor, and Kunkel assistant conductor. Kunkel had been principal flute in John Philip Sousa's band for four years, was a band instructor in the army during World War I, and had played with the Cincinnati Symphony as well.

The new civic orchestra gave its first concert in the university gymnasium on November 30, 1932. Including the conductor's husband in the cello section and their daughter Marilyn as harpist, there were fifty-eight players, forty-three of them men. A number of the players had considerable experience; the rest were students and amateurs. Concertmaster Mrs. John D. Clark had studied with Jacques Hoffman in Boston, had played for four years in the second Orchestral Club of Boston under Georges Longy, and was one of the leading violin teachers in Albuquerque. Guy Eaglesfield, principal double bass, came from Tucson, where he was an orchestra and band instructor. Cornetist A. J. Schminke had played in Victor Herbert's orchestra for many years and in many theater orchestras. Myrlin Payne, violinist, was formerly with the Pittsburgh Symphony and had conducted community orchestras and bands in Kansas.

At its first concert the orchestra played to an audience of 2000, presenting both classical and semiclassical works. They played Schubert's Overture to *Rosamunde,* Mozart's "Jupiter" Symphony, portions of Bizet's *L'Arlésienne Suite* no. 2, Strauss's waltz *The Blue Danube,* and, assisted by New York baritone Robert Castle, who was spending the winter in New Mexico, arias from Gounod's *Faust* and Verdi's *Masked Ball.* The concert was a resounding success, and three more were presented during that first season. The following summer Grace Thompson went to the Juilliard School to study orchestral arranging and conducting with Julius Schmid. Thompson and the Albuquerque orchestra continued to present four or five concerts a year, holding the admission price to twenty-five cents with the costs underwritten by the city's businesses. The number of players grew to about seventy, and guest artists were regularly imported. In addition to regular programs, the orchestra played on various special occasions, such as the dedication of the first 50,000-kilowatt radio station in Albuquerque and for the centenary of the San Pedro Mine in 1940, where they played underground, inside the mine.

In 1941 Grace Thompson appeared for the first time as piano soloist with the orchestra, performing Constant Lambert's *Rio Grande* for piano, orchestra, and chorus. By then her marriage to Thompson had ended, and the following year she married William R. Edmister, an Ohio businessman, and moved with him to Columbus. She left a healthy organization behind her. William Kunkel took over as conductor for one season, and then was succeeded by several other conductors. Edmister remained in Columbus until 1959, for most of that time teaching at St. Mary's of the Springs College. She visited Albuquerque a number of times and occasionally conducted one of the orchestra's performances. After her husband's death she moved to New York to live with her sister, but in 1970 she decided to return to Albuquerque, where she continued to help the orchestra, now renamed the Albuquerque Symphony. In 1972 its conductor, Yoshima Takeda, invited her to be guest conductor at the orchestra's fortieth anniversary concert—she led the ensemble in Schubert's Overture to *Rosamunde,* with which she had opened the first concert. In 1975 she became one of six New Mexicans receiving the first Governor's Award for achievement in the arts, and the following year she received the highest honor of her alma mater, the Pilgrims' Medal of Defiance College, following only six other graduates so honored, including President Dwight D. Eisenhower. In 1978 her friends honored her on the sixtieth anniversary of her arrival in New Mexico in 1918, on a stretcher and given three months to live. She was always grateful to New Mexico and said that one major reason for establishing the orchestra was that "I wanted to give something to that part of the country that had given me my health." She died in 1983, at the age of 93.

The New Mexico Symphony Orchestra grew still more, at first becoming a metropolitan orchestra and at this writing a regional orchestra. From an initial budget of $500 in 1932, it expanded to $75,000 in 1970 and $450,000 by 1977. For the 1999–2000 season it had a budget of $2,865,800 for sixty-three concerts in Albuquerque, twenty-one on tour in New Mexico, and ninety-six ensemble programs in schools. The estimated annual audience has grown to 125,000.

Another field that has engaged women since the second half of the nineteenth century is orchestra management. The American Symphony Orchestra League cites as the first woman manager of a major orchestra Anna Millar, who ran Theodore Thomas's Chicago Orchestra from 1893 to 1897, setting up all its engagements as well as making travel, transportation, and billeting arrangements.[43] But she was not the first. Norma Knüpfel, born in Detroit in 1858, went to California as a child and there married a wine merchant, H. J. A. Stuhr. She organized charity concerts, in both Los Angeles and San Francisco, and later directed a three-year series of concerts of the San Francisco orchestra. She was widowed, remarried, and widowed again. She then took up directing the foreign tours of the Leipzig Philharmonic, which still engaged her in April 1901. In the fall of 1901 she settled as an independent manager with offices in New York and Leipzig.

Another nineteenth-century manager was May Valentine, the manager and conductor of a touring opera company. Still another was May Beegle, born in 1887, who organized the Pittsburgh Orchestra Association in order to bring touring orchestras to Pittsburgh; in 1923 she also started a concert series there. Lenore Armsby founded the San Francisco Symphony in 1909 and managed it for some years thereafter. Adella Prentiss Hughes organized the Cleveland Orchestra in 1918 and ran it until 1933. Mrs. L. A. Irish managed the Los Angeles Philharmonic during the 1930s and 1940s. Later women managers include Ruth O. Seufrert of the Kansas City Philharmonic, Helen Black of the Denver Symphony, Mrs. Hugh McCreery of the Seattle Symphony, Helen Thompson of the New York Philharmonic, Cathy French of the New Jersey Symphony, and Joan Briccetti of the St. Louis Symphony.

Many women managers are associated with orchestras that have low budgets and short seasons, but that is hardly true of Deborah Borda, who started with the New York Philharmonic in 1987 and became executive director in 1991. Borda was trained as a violist at the New England Conservatory and the Royal College of Music. She began her administrative career with Boston's Handel and Haydn Society, after being a member of the viola section. She then held top administrative posts with the Minnesota, Detroit, St. Paul Chamber, and San Francisco orchestras. In New York, in her efforts to broaden the Philharmonic's audiences, she instituted Rush Hour and Casual Saturdays concerts, Conductor Debut Week, Composer Week, Children's Promenades, and a preconcert lecture series. Like other administrators, top orchestra executives work with boards of directors who may have old-fashioned ideas about the role of women; however, Borda's competence, dedication, and professionalism have far outweighed such concerns. In 1999, after nine seasons with the orchestra, she announced her departure to become vice president and managing director of the Los Angeles Philharmonic.[44]

Two women were intimately involved with the management of the Chicago Lyric Opera. Singer Carol Fox (1926–1981) cofounded the Lyric Theatre of Chicago in 1954, using mainly Italian artists, including Maria Callas in her U.S. debut. Two years later Fox took over complete control and renamed the company the Lyric Opera of Chicago. Ardis Krainik (1929–1997) worked for Fox from the beginning and sang with the company in the 1950s. After Fox's death, Krainik took over as general manager and later became general director.

A notable opera director of more recent times is Pamela Rosenberg. Born in California in 1945, she was appointed general director of the San Francisco Opera beginning in 2001, the first woman named to head a major American opera house. Until then Rosenberg had made her career in Europe. After graduating from the University of California at Berkeley, in 1966 she went to study at Bayreuth and then at the Guildhall School of Music and Drama in London. From 1977 to 1987 she worked as artistic administrator and assistant director of the Frankfurt Opera, and in 1990 she began a ten-year tenure as joint general director of the Stuttgart Opera, the first American to head a major European company. In San Francisco Rosenberg was expected to bear out her reputation for an innovative and adventurous theatrical style.

Another outstanding woman manager was Judith Arron. Formerly manager of the Cincinnati Symphony, she was general manager and artistic director of New York's Carnegie Hall from 1986 until her untimely death from cancer in 1998. Not only did she oversee the hall's renovation and construction of new performance space, but she instituted a series of professional training workshops led by renowned musicians: Robert Shaw for choral music, Isaac

Stern for chamber music, Marilyn Horne for vocal performance, and others. She also established a composer's chair, occupied for several seasons by Ellen Taaffe Zwilich, expanded the hall's educational activities, and installed the Carnegie Hall Jazz Band. Arron was widely regarded as having completely transformed the institution.[45]

In the concert management field in the 1960s and 1970s, approximately one-third of managers were women. Interestingly, slightly fewer than one-third of newspaper music critics were women at that time.[46] One of the most innovative concert managers was Susan Wadsworth, whose Young Concert Artists, founded in 1961, concentrated on presenting little-known young musicians in informal concerts in order to bridge the gap between their conservatory and full-fledged concert careers. Among the musicians she helped get started were Pinchas Zukerman, Murray Perahia, Anthony Newman, the Tokyo String Quartet, and Ani Kavafian.[47] Other artist managers of note are Ann Colbert, Edna Landau, and Thea Dispeker.

Not many American orchestras have women conductors. Even in the late 1970s the majority of women who aspired to conducting resigned themselves to choral work or to low-budget orchestras. One entirely self-taught woman began, in the 1960s, to hire a New York hall from time to time, paying musicians to play under her baton and charging no admission. Considered a recluse and an eccentric, Charlotte Bergen originally began in music as a cellist and gave two well-received recitals in Town Hall.[48] She was educated privately and later said, "I spent 35 years of my life in a little room on the third floor, playing the cello." Her father died in 1936 and thereafter she remained at home, caring for her mother until her death. By then she had gone into the dairy business on the family estate in Bernardsville, New Jersey, building a barn, buying cows, and putting in a pasteurizing plant. The enterprise was successful, but music continued to attract Bergen, and she became increasingly interested in conducting. She began by forming a choir in the local church. Then for a time she hired Town Hall in New York once a year for a performance of Monteverdi's *Orfeo*. About 1970 she began to rent Carnegie Hall at least once a season, and by the 1976–77 season she was presenting four concerts a year there. By then Bergen, who was born in 1898, was well into her seventies. At one concert she put on Beethoven's *Missa Solemnis*, of which a reviewer wrote, "Miss Bergen's unfussy approach worked best in the more stable stretches, which sometimes accumulated real power."[49] Another program, devoted to Mozart, presented the "Jupiter" Symphony and a piano concerto with Malcolm Frager as soloist; the orchestra was made up of members of the American Symphony Orchestra. "It's the fulfillment of my life," Bergen told, an interviewer. "I consider what I'm doing [to be] inviting people to listen to what we're playing. . . . To me, music is too precious to sell. I respect people who have to sell music to make a living . . . but it happens that I don't have to. And so, why should I?" She died in 1982, at the age of eighty-four, but she left behind the Frank and Lydia Bergen Foundation, which continued to fund free concerts at Carnegie Hall.

With all respect, it is doubtful that Bergen could in fact have made a living in this way, for few women have succeeded as orchestral conductors. Several had brief flurries of success in Europe in the 1930s. Ruth Kemper, an American, joined the faculty of the Salzburg Conservatory in 1930 and in April 1931 conducted a regular orchestral concert in Vienna, which included Brahms's First Symphony, a Chopin concerto, and MacDowell's *Indian Suite*.[50] In the same year another American, Carmen Studer, led the Vienna Symphony in a concert that included Abram Chasins's piano concerto, with the composer as soloist.[51] Married to the eminent conductor Felix Weingartner, Studer in 1933 became the first woman to conduct a major orchestra in France.[52] But as leaders of male orchestras these women represented exceptions, along with Antonia Brico, Ethel Leginska, and Nadia Boulanger, who were discussed earlier in this book.

Choral conducting was somewhat more open to women. In 1926 Margarete Dessoff (1874–1944), a German choral conductor who first came to the United States in 1923, led the Schola Cantorum, becoming the first woman to conduct a major New York choral concert.[53] In New York she founded both a women's chorus and a mixed chorus, which in 1929 merged and became the Dessoff Choirs, a long-lived ensemble. She also led other groups, as well as teaching and coaching. But in 1936 an automobile accident cut short her career, and soon afterward she retired.

A pioneer among women choral conductors was Eva Jessye (1895–1992), the first black woman to win international distinction in this field.[54] She first studied in her native Kansas and later in New York with Will Marion Cook and music theorist Percy Goetschius, then becomimg a music teacher. In 1922 she moved to New York and by 1926 was appearing regularly with her singers, the Original Dixie Jubilee Singers (later the Eva Jessye Choir), on radio programs such as the *Major Bowes Family Radio Hour*. She soon was being commissioned to organize ensembles and quartets to sing on radio programs in New York and London. In 1933 she was choral director for Virgil Thomson's acclaimed opera, *Four Saints in Three Acts*, and in 1935 George Gershwin chose her as choral director for *Porgy and Bess*. Jessye also composed several folk oratorios, *Paradise Lost and Regained, The Life of Christ in Negro Spirituals*, and *The Chronicle of Job*, which she conducted. During the same era, the 1930s, composer Gena Branscombe became a highly respected choral conductor and founded her own women's chorus, the Branscombe Choral.

In the Midwest, Mary Willing Megley became the first woman to conduct the Toledo Music Festival in 1924, leading a fifty-piece orchestra and a chorus of 385.[55] By about 1919 she had become the regular conductor of the Toledo Choral Society, which throughout the 1920s she led in annual concerts of Handel's *Messiah*, assisted by members of the Detroit Symphony Orchestra.[56]

Blanche Honegger Moyse, a violinist who turned to choral conducting of J. S. Bach's works, was born in 1909 in Geneva, Switzerland.[57] She began violin studies at the age of eight and soon began studies with the great German violinist Adolph Busch. After her debut at age sixteen she moved to Paris, where she continued her musical education, studying with Georges Enesco, Wanda Landowska, and Andres Segovia. Before World War II she moved in with the family of Marcel Moyse, the preeminent flutist of that time, and then married his son Louis, a concert pianist. Shortly afterward the three formed the Moyse Trio, which won many awards.

After the war, the trio were invited by Adolph Busch and Rudolf Serkin to come to southern Vermont and establish a music department at the fledgling Marlboro College. In 1949 they, together with Adolph and Hermann Busch and Rudolf Serkin, founded the Marlboro Music Festival. At the same time Blanche Moyse set up the music department at Marlboro College and served as its chair for the next twenty-five years. In 1951 she also established the Marlboro Music Center, to foster a variety of performance and music education programs. Still its artistic director as of this writing, Moyse plays an active role in the center's programs, which include the Blanche Moyse Chorale, a select chorus, as well as a music school with 400 students, a chamber series, and an orchestra for the area's amateur musicians.

After a bow-arm ailment forced Moyse's retirement as a violinist in 1966, she dedicated the majority of her time to the study and performance of the choral works of J. S. Bach. In 1969 the New England Bach Festival was born, with Moyse conducting her first St. Matthew Passion. At age seventy-eight she made her Carnegie Hall debut in what the *New York Times* reviewer called "an absolutely glorious rendition of Bach's Christmas Oratorio."[58] In 1989 she conducted the St. Matthew Passion at Carnegie Hall to wide acclaim, and in 1999 she planned to celebrate her ninetieth birthday with a repeat performance of the work.

A conductor of the next generation was Margaret Hillis, who founded the Chicago Symphony Chorus and went on to conduct both choral and orchestral programs.[59] Hillis was born in 1921 in Kokomo, Indiana, started piano lessons at the age of five, and by age eight knew she wanted to conduct. She studied a number of orchestral and band instruments in high school, playing baritone horn in the band and later double bass in the orchestra at Indiana University. She also made her conducting debut in high school as assistant conductor of the school orchestra. Although she said that orchestral conducting was her first love, there were no opportunities in this field for women in the 1950s, and her teachers discouraged her from pursuing it. After earning her bachelor's degree in composition at Indiana, she went to the Juilliard School to study choral conducting with Robert Shaw and Julius Herford, and later became assistant conductor of Shaw's Collegiate Chorale. In 1950 she organized the Tanglewood Alumni Chorus and presented it in a full series of concerts in New York. The group soon became known as the American Concert Choir and Orchestra and gave a series of concerts and recordings. It concentrated on performing choral works with a small orchestra, a repertory that large ensembles usually ignore entirely. In 1958 the group was invited by the U.S. State Department to represent the nation at the Brussels World Fair.

In 1957 Fritz Reiner, music director of the Chicago Symphony, asked Hillis to organize a permanent chorus worthy of regular performances with the symphony. Made up mostly of professional singers joined by some devoted, talented, and unpaid amateurs, the chorus began to perform in the 1957–58 season and in its first decade appeared in more than 100 regular subscription concerts, as well as performing with the orchestra on tour in New York and elsewhere. Meanwhile Hillis also taught at the Union Theological Seminary and Juilliard School, founded the American Choral Foundation, and worked at various times as a conductor and choral director with the American Opera Society, New York City Opera, Santa Fe Opera, and Cleveland Orchestra Chorus. In 1962, after twelve years of residence in New York, she moved back to the Midwest.

Inevitably Hillis's involvement with training choruses for choral orchestral performances led her back to orchestral conducting. In 1976 she became the first woman to conduct a regular Chicago Symphony subscription concert, leading the world premiere of Alan Stout's Passion for chorus, soloists, and orchestra. By then she had often conducted the Chicago orchestra for special occasions and in pops concerts, and had substituted for regular conductor Rafael Kubelik in 1972 for performances of Handel's *Jephtha.* In 1977 she made headlines when she stepped in at the last minute to replace ailing conductor Georg Solti and conducted the Chicago Symphony in a New York performance of Mahler's very long and difficult Symphony no. 8. The work is nicknamed "Symphony of a Thousand" because it uses such large forces: enlarged orchestra, double chorus, eight soloists, and a children's chorus. Hillis's performance was widely praised. During the 1970s she also worked as resident conductor of the Chicago Civic Orchestra and finally got an orchestra of her own, the Elgin (Illinois) Symphony Orchestra, a community orchestra that she led from 1971 to 1985. She also accepted an increasing number of guest-conducting assignments and served as professor of conducting and head of the choral department at Northwestern University. "There's only one woman I know who could never be a symphony conductor," Hillis told the *New York Times* in 1979, "and that's the Venus de Milo."[60] She died in 1998.

A contemporary of Hillis's who confined herself entirely to choral conducting, was Lorna Cooke de Varon, who in 1978 celebrated her thirtieth anniversary as director of choruses at the New England Conservatory of Music.[61] Born about 1922 in Illinois, she moved with her parents to Rhode Island at the age of fifteen, and remained in the Boston area from the time she went to Wellesley College. While a student at Wellesley, she studied theory and harmony with Nadia Boulanger, as well as voice, piano, and organ with other teachers. She went on to get a master's degree from Radcliffe College, where she studied choral conducting with G. Wallace Woodworth. She then became assistant professor of music at Bryn Mawr College and conducted the chorus there. In 1947 she joined the faculty of the New England Conservatory and a year later became its director of choruses. She also spent two summers studying choral conducting with Robert Shaw at Tanglewood, and in 1953 she joined the Tanglewood faculty, with which she spent a number of summers; she was in charge of the Tanglewood Festival Chorus, and she taught choral conducting to many students. At the conservatory, her 135-voice chorus, founded in 1950, sang and recorded with the Boston Symphony Orchestra and premiered the works of contemporary composers such as Irving Fine, Daniel Pinkham, and Donald Martino. From the late 1960s on it began to tour abroad as well, making several tours of Europe, an exchange tour to the Soviet Union, and in 1978 a tour of Israel. "Working with student singers has great frustrations and rewards," she told an interviewer in 1978. "My one regret about my career is that I never founded an adult chorus." With young singers, she pointed out, one must be careful at any sign of fatigue lest their voices be injured, but because many works are new to them there is a rewarding freshness and excitement to their performances. De Varon retired from the New England Conservatory in 1988 but continued to teach and conduct at the Longy School of Music in Cambridge, Massachusetts, and elsewhere.

Another fine choral conductor was Iva Dee Hiatt (1919–1980).[62] Born in Indiana and educated at the University of California, Berkeley, she studied with Ernest Bloch, Roger Sessions, and Manfred Bukofzer. She then taught in California and founded the Berkeley Chamber Singers, which Darius Milhaud called "one of the finest small groups I have ever heard." Moving to Smith College in 1948, Hiatt was the first choral conductor and the first woman to conduct a work for chorus and orchestra at Tanglewood, with which she was associated for many years. She also was music director of the Cambridge Society for Early Music from 1965 to 1977. Hiatt conducted in Europe, the Middle East, and South America, and her singers and instrumentalists performed at festivals throughout Europe. At Smith Hiatt was professor and director of choral music for thirty-one years. During her last years she suffered from Lou Gehrig's disease (amyotrophic lateral sclerosis) and eventually conducted the chorus from a wheelchair.

One of Hiatt's outstanding pupils was Amy Kaiser.[63] Born in New York in 1945, she was a graduate of Smith College and was invited back to conduct its freshman glee club in 1971, the first of her numerous choral conducting posts. Also holding a master's degree in musicology from Columbia University, Kaiser worked in the New York area for a period of about twenty years. She was music director of the Mannes Chamber Singers, also called the 92nd Street

Chorale, from 1978 to 1995 and the Dessoff Choirs from 1983 to 1995. She was also director of choral music at Mannes College of Music and part of the choral conducting faculty of the Manhattan School of Music. In 1995 she was named director of the St. Louis Symphony chorus. She also has served as guest conductor for numerous orchestras and the Metropolitan Opera Guild. When asked if she would really prefer to have an orchestra of her own, Kaiser said her first love had been vocal music, both choral and operatic. Originally wanting to be a singer, she had studied voice for seven years, but after seeing Eve Queler conduct an opera and after working with Iva Dee Hiatt and Lorna Cooke de Varon at Tanglewood, she realized a woman could conduct, and she never turned back. Her most important teachers, she now says, were Hiatt and John Nelson at the Aspen Music Festival.

Judith Clurman, born in 1953, is the founder and music director of the New York Concert Singers, a professional chorus, and the Judith Clurman Chorale, a volunteer symphonic chorus performing with orchestras in New York City.[64] Educated at Oberlin College and the Juilliard School, where she serves on the conducting faculty, she frequently prepares choruses for such orchestras as the New York Philharmonic, the Orchestra of St. Luke's, and the American Composers Orchestra, as well as preparing ensembles for opera. Clurman is a tireless proponent of American music and has commissioned choral works by William Bolcom, David Diamond, Libby Larsen, Stephen Sondheim, Paul McKibbins, and Augusta Read Thomas. Reviews of her work have been extremely good. For example,

> For the director of a new ensemble, two tasks would seem to be paramount: getting the group to sound polished and cohesive quickly, and establishing a repertory persona. Judith Clurman has succeeded in both those mandates with the New York Concert Singers. In the opening concert of its fourth season . . . the group sang with ravishing smoothness and warmth and with complete flexibility in dynamics and coloration.[65]

Another woman making her name in choral conducting was Karen P. Thomas.[66] Born in 1957, she holds advanced degrees from Cornish College and the University of Washington. In 1987 she became artistic director and conductor of the Seattle Pro Musica, which under her tutelage grew from a small ensemble to a sixty-voice semiprofessional chorus and professional orchestra. She also served as director of music for University Unitarian Church in Seattle, supervising a comprehensive music program. In 1996 she won the ASCAP–Chorus America Award for adventuresome programming of contemporary music. Also a composer, Thomas has written *Coyote's Tail* (1991), a one-act children's opera; *When Night Came* (1994, revised 1996) for clarinet and chamber orchestra; a brass quintet, string quartet, and saxophone quartet; works for brass ensemble and mixed chamber ensemble; and numerous choral works, among them *Four Lewis Carroll Songs* (1989) and *Three Medieval Lyrics* (1993). As she explains, "I enjoy the solitary creative part of composing and the very public process involved in conducting. I find they inform each other."[67]

In orchestral conducting a small number of women were establishing themselves in the 1960s and 1970s, mostly with smaller orchestras.[68] Beatrice Brown (1917–1997), a violist who studied conducting with Serge Koussevitsky, Leopold Stokowski, and Hermann Scherchen, became one of the first women to hold a permanent conducting post when she took over the Scranton (Pennsylvania) Philharmonic in 1962. In that same year she received the following reply from a manager whom she had asked to handle her career:

> For reasons unknown to us, we have never been able to interest managements [of orchestras] in women conductors. There seems to be no logical reason for this, but the situation exists, nevertheless. We are perfectly certain that many women conductors are far superior to the males but since we have had no luck at all in handling women conductors, it seems useless to encourage you to have any kind of a career with us.[69]

Brown continued as music director with the Scranton orchestra for a decade, and then took over the Ridgefield (Connecticut) Symphonette, later renamed the Ridgefield Symphony Orchestra. In the twenty-six years she led the orchestra as conductor and musical director, it grew from a small community orchestra to an organization of seventy-six professional musicians with a $100,000 annual budget.

Carolyn Hills was an orchestral conductor of the same era. She did postgraduate study in conducting at the International Academy Mozarteum in Salzburg, where she was the only woman and the only American. She founded the New York Music Society, became head of the United Nations International School in New York, and became music director of the Livingston (New Jersey) Symphony Orchestra.

All these women seemed to agree that orchestral conducting is an extremely difficult and competitive field for anyone, considering the combination of skills, talent, and personality it requires, the limited number of conducting posts available, and the straitened finances of many—perhaps most —American orchestras. But most of them also felt that it was at least twice as difficult for women to succeed in this traditionally male-dominated profession. Even so, some headway was made. In May 1978 the Juilliard School received a $3 million grant to endow a training program for young American conductors. Four to six musicians were to be chosen annually by audition, and, it was specifically stated, female candidates would be welcome. In the summer of 1978, one of the five fellowships for studying conducting at the Berkshire Music Center at Tanglewood—among the most sought-after fellowships in the world of music—was given, for the first time in a dozen years, to a woman, organist Patricia Handy of Baltimore. Of the six conducting fellows at Tanglewood in 1999, four were American and none was a woman.

Three other conductors who began their careers in the 1970s were active in California in the late 1990s. Joyce Johnson Hamilton, born in 1938 in Nebraska, began her career with the Omaha Symphony.[70] An excellent trumpeter, she became principal trumpet of the Oregon Symphony and then served as assistant principal in the San Francisco Symphony for the 1968–69 season. This was a time of the earliest screened auditions, but for two sets of auditions conductor Josef Krips refused to decide among any of the finalists, of whom she was one. In the third set of auditions Johnson was accepted, but only for one year. She then went on to study early music and conducting at Stanford University and in the early 1970s became assistant conductor of the Oakland (California) Symphony Orchestra. There she was responsible for conducting rehearsals, youth and pop concerts, and one regular subscription concert each season. She also founded and conducted the Sinfonia of Northern California, a chamber orchestra specializing in seventeenth- and eighteenth-century music. After four years with Oakland, she spent the next four as conductor and principal trumpet of the San Jose Symphony. From 1980 to 1989 she conducted the Napa Valley Symphony, a small but fully professional orchestra, as well as the Diablo Symphony, a volunteer group of sixty to seventy players who present eight programs a year. At this writing she retains only the Diablo post, guest-conducts periodically, performs as a soloist, principally on baroque trumpet, serves as an adjunct professor of trumpet at Stanford, and teaches privately.

Frances Steiner, born in 1937 in Portland, Oregon, began her career as a cellist.[71] Her teachers included Gregor Piatigorsky, Rudolf Serkin, Eugene Istomin, Alexander Schneider, and Leonard Rose. After graduating from the Curtis Institute of Music she studied composition with Walter Piston and Randall Thompson at Harvard, and conducting and composition with Nadia Boulanger in France. In 1974 she became music director of the Chamber Orchestra of the South Bay, a professional chamber orchestra, and in 1977 she became music director of the Carson-Dominguez Hills Symphony, a combined university-community orchestra that focuses not only on standard orchestral works but also on the compositions of African-American and women composers. Steiner also teaches conducting at California State University, Dominguez Hills. In addition, she has guest-conducted numerous North American and Latin American ensembles.

In 1999 Kate Tamarkin was named music director of the Monterey County Symphony Association, the first time in its fifty-four years that the ensemble was headed by a woman.[72] Born in 1955 in Newport Beach, California, Tamarkin studied at Chapman College, Northwestern University, and holds a doctorate from the Peabody Conservatory. Tamarkin was a conducting fellow at the Los Angeles Philharmonic, where she conducted at the Hollywood Bowl, and in 1988, as part of the American conductor program with

Leonard Bernstein, she conducted the Chicago Symphony. In that same year she was a conducting fellow at Tanglewood. She went on to conduct the Vermont Symphony Orchestra for eight years, building it into a stable ensemble. During those years she served also as associate conductor of the Dallas Symphony, from 1989 to 1994, and music director of the East Texas Symphony Orchestra.

Another orchestral conductor who became known in the late 1970s was Victoria Bond.[73] She was the first woman admitted to Juilliard as a doctoral candidate in conducting, receiving her degree in 1977. Born on May 6, 1949, Bond began composing music at the age of five. She attended the Mannes School of Music in New York and received her bachelor's degree at the University of Southern California, where she studied composition with Ingolf Dahl. She then returned to New York and the Juilliard School, where she studied composition with Roger Sessions and conducting with Sixten Ehrling, in 1977 becoming the first woman to earn a doctoral degree in orchestral conducting. Initially she was interested chiefly in conducting performances of her own works, but she soon found herself pursuing it for its own sake. At Juilliard she became conductor of the Juilliard Repertory Orchestra, as well as assistant conductor of the Contemporary Music Ensemble and the Juilliard Orchestra. Meanwhile she also continued to compose, producing songs, orchestra works, and chamber music. In 1977 she was commissioned by the Pennsylvania Ballet to compose a full-length work to open their season, *Equinox.*

Unlike some older women conductors, Bond believed that conducting was indeed open to anyone with enough talent. In an article published in 1976, in which women musicians were asked to offer advice, she said:

> I would encourage anyone, man or woman, who is interested in conducting to pursue it. It is a long road, since there are many skills which must be mastered before you even hope to stand before an orchestra, but it is tremendously rewarding. . . . In the beginning no one believed that I would "make it" and assumed that I would quit because it was a field that just wasn't open to women, but I think that I can safely say now that I have proved to them that they were wrong. It can be done, and I know because I am doing it.[74]

On May 6, 1978, Bond made an important appearance as conductor with the Pittsburgh Symphony Orchestra, and a few months later she was appointed conducting assistant of that orchestra and music director of the Pittsburgh Youth Symphony. She also served as music director of the New Amsterdam Symphony Orchestra in New York City. From 1986 to 1995 she served as music director of the Roanoke (Virginia) Symphony Orchestra and from 1989 to 1995 as artistic director of Opera Roanoke. Thereafter she divided her time between composing and conducting. Her first opera, *Travels,* based on *Gulli-*

ver's Travels, premiered in 1995. She also produced numerous chamber works and orchestral music.

Through the 1980s and 1990s the situation for women orchestral conductors improved somewhat. In 1999 there still were no women music directors among the twenty-five orchestras with the highest budget, although several had employed women assistant conductors. Among the fifty orchestras with the next highest budget, five had women music directors, but three of those were employing the same woman, JoAnn Falletta.[75] In 1998 Simone Young conducted the New York Philharmonic in two concerts; she was only the third woman on their podium to conduct a regular-season concert, after Sarah Caldwell and Gisèle Ben-Dor. British-born Iona Brown led the Los Angeles Chamber Orchestra, and was its concertmaster, but her career remained principally in Britain, where she directed the Academy of St. Martin-in-the-Fields. Catherine Comet, born in France in 1944, studied at the Paris Conservatory and with Nadia Boulanger, as well as obtaining a master's degree in conducting at Juilliard. After a number of posts in France, she became director of conducting studies at the University of Wisconsin. Comet then served as associate conductor of the St. Louis Symphony from 1981 to 1984 and the Baltimore Symphony from 1984 to 1986, as music director of the American Symphony Orchestra in New York from 1989 to 1992, and music director of the Grand Rapids Symphony from 1986 to 1997. In addition, Comet appeared as guest conductor with most leading North American orchestras as well as in Europe and the Far East. American Rachel Worby worked in New York in the 1970s but then moved to West Virginia, where she became music director of the Wheeling Symphony. In the 1990s she also commuted to New York where she was music director and conductor of Carnegie Hall's education program.

By the late 1990s at least four other women conductors were making a name for themselves—JoAnn Falletta, Marin Alsop, Gisèle Ben-Dor, and Anne Manson. JoAnn Falletta was born in 1954 and began her musical education with guitar lessons, because her family's apartment had no room for a piano. She went on to obtain a doctorate at the Juilliard School of Music, where she studied with Jorge Mester. In 1985 she won first prize in the Stokowski Conducting Competition and received the Toscanini Conductors Award. For more than a decade she served as music director of the Women's Philharmonic in San Francisco and conducted the Long Beach (California) Symphony Orchestra, Denver Chamber Orchestra, Virginia Symphony, and Queens (New York) Philharmonic. In 1999 Falletta was appointed artistic director of the Buffalo Symphony, as well as continuing with the Long Beach and Virginia symphony orchestras.

Marin Alsop, a native of New York, attended Yale and the Juilliard School of Music. In 1984 she founded the New York-based Concordia Orchestra, which has the specific aim of combining the classical repertory with twentieth-century American works and jazz. In 1988 and 1989 she was a conducting fellow at Tanglewood, where she studied under Leonard Bernstein, Seiji Ozawa, and Gustav Meier. In 1989 she won the Koussevitsky Conducting Prize, and in 1993 she became principal conductor of the Colorado Symphony Orchestra, and two years later its music director. Also beginning in 1996 she was appointed to the Creative Conductor Chair of the St. Louis Symphony, and consequently had to give up her six-year-old posts as music director of the Long Island Philharmonic and Eugene (Oregon) Symphony. She continued to serve as music director of the Cabrillo Festival in California. Alsop also appeared as guest conductor with many leading American orchestras, and in January 2000, in celebration of the new millennium, she conducted the London Symphony Orchestra. An avid jazz violinist, Alsop founded and led the jazz group String Fever.

Gisèle Ben-Dor, born in 1955 in Uruguay, began piano lessons at age four and was already conducting her school's choir at age twelve. In 1972 she and her family moved to Israel, where she earned bachelor's and master's degrees from Tel Aviv University, majoring in conducting. In 1982 she received a second master's degree in conducting from Yale's School of Music. That December she made her professional debut with the Israel Philharmonic in Stravinsky's *Rite of Spring,* when she was nine months pregnant. Other conducting engagements in Israel followed, as well as conducting fellowships with the Los Angeles Philharmonic Institute and at Tanglewood. In 1991 she became music director of the Pro Arte Chamber Orchestra in Cambridge, Massachusetts, and the Annapolis (Maryland) Symphony, and in 1994 she also became music director of the Santa Barbara Symphony. In December 1993, when Kurt Masur of the New York Philharmonic came down with the flu, Ben-Dor conducted the orchestra without rehearsal and on one day's notice. She was then invited to conduct four Philharmonic concerts in Central Park in 1995.[76] She repeated her feat with the New York Philharmonic in 1999, this time as a last-minute replacement for Daniele Gatti. The *New York Times* responded, "If Ms. Ben-Dor had merely survived in a work as complex as the Mahler [Symphony no. 4] under the circumstances, she would have done well; she did more, making the interpretation on some small level her own. She has this trick down pat."[77] Busy with many guest-conducting assignments, in 1998 she gave up the Annapolis post and in 1999 she ended her work with Pro Arte Chamber Orchestra, deciding to spend more time with her two sons.

Born in 1961 in Boston, Anne Manson became the first woman ever to conduct at the Salzburg Festival, where she led a performance of *Boris Godunov* to wide public and critical acclaim. A graduate of Harvard, she trained at King's College London and the Royal College of Music on a Marshall scholarship and subsequently became a fellow in conducting at the Royal Northern College of Music. From 1988 to 1997 she founded and served as music director of the London-based Mecklenburgh Opera, where she became known for her adventurous programming of twentieth-century works. In addition, she was guest conductor with numerous symphony orchestras and opera companies in Europe and America. In 1998 she was appointed music director of the Kansas City Symphony Orchestra.

A conductor closely associated with programming music by women composers, Nan Washburn was a cofounder of the Women's Philharmonic and served as its artistic director from 1980 to 1990. She was the winner of thirteen ASCAP awards for adventuresome programming, having worked with such important composers as Ned Rorem, Libby Larsen, Ellen Taaffe Zwilich, Joan Tower, Chen Yi, Hilary Tann, Katherine Hoover, and Lou Harrison. Born in 1954, Washburn worked as a professional flutist for a number of years and began her conducting studies in 1984. She has served as music director and conductor of the Camellia Orchestra in Sacramento, Orchestra Sonoma (California), and Channel Islands Symphony Orchestra, and as resident conductor of the American Jazz Theater in Oakland. In 1999 she was named conductor of the Plymouth (Michigan) Symphony and the West Hollywood Orchestra.

During the second half of the 1900s, the situation for black women conductors improved only slightly. Margaret Harris (1943–2000) made her debut as a pianist in 1946 at the age of three—she played fourteen classical selections before a church audience in Chicago—and performed as soloist with the Chicago Symphony at age ten. She pursued her musical education at Curtis and Juilliard, and appeared for some years as a soloist in Europe and the United States. She also was the first black woman music director to conduct a major Broadway show—*Hair* in 1968—which brought her nationwide recognition. She was also the first to have guest-conducted more than ten major American orchestras, including a 1972 appearance with the Los Angeles Philharmonic in the premiere of her own piano concerto. Her other compositions include two ballets, the opera *King David,* and another piano concerto. Harris never acquired a permanent conducting post with a major orchestra. Rather, she spread her talents among theater and ballet companies, opera productions, choral coaching, lecturing, and consulting.

Another African-American conductor, Kay George Roberts, born in 1950, was the first woman to receive a doctorate in orchestral conducting from Yale University School of Music, and she held conducting posts with a number of smaller orchestras. Beginning her musical studies as a violinist, she made her conducting debut with the Nashville Symphony Orchestra in 1976 and went on to numerous university and guest-conducting assignments. She spent the 1989–90 season in Germany, where she founded a new professional chamber group, Ensemble Americana. She conducts the Black Music Repertory Ensemble of Chicago, which performs classical music by African-American composers from the 1800s to the present. A professor of music at University of Massachusetts, Lowell, she also is music director of a chamber orchestra, String Currents, that promotes music by American composers. Despite all these activities, she, too, has not found a permanent post with an established professional ensemble.

A form of affirmative action seems to be called for. In 1999 a project called the National Women Conductors Initiative, conceived by the Women's Philharmonic of San Francisco, planned to use a $1 million donation to the orchestra to help develop and assist thirty young women conductors, in the form of mentoring and financial aid. Falletta, Tamarkin, Alsop and Ben-Dor all are on the project's steering committee.

For those instrumentalists who choose solo careers rather than orchestral jobs the path is also rough, for both men and women. At least one such woman, pianist Susan Starr, maintained that there is active prejudice against women, whether they are soloists or orchestra players. Starr herself, after graduating from the Curtis Institute in 1961, auditioned before a top manager of musicians. He was very impressed with her and said, "If only you were a man I'd sign you in a minute."[78] She was able to obtain a manager only after winning several competitions, a bronze medal in the First International Mitropoulos Competition in New York and second prize in the renowned Tchaikovsky Competition in Moscow in 1962—she was one of twelve finalists in Moscow, half of them women. But pianists and string players are discussed at length in Chapters 2 and 3. What about some of the other instruments?

In the late 1970s a small number of performers, mostly women in their thirties, seemed to be succeeding in solo careers, augmented by work in chamber ensembles and other activities. Paula Robison, flutist of the Orpheus Trio, was in the late 1970s one of the most successful solo flute recitalists of either sex.[79] Born in 1941 in Nashville, Tennessee, and raised in Los Angeles, she began piano studies at an early age. At age eleven she was given a flute, which she later said she knew at once would be her instrument. She played all through high school, in student orchestras and little recitals. She attended the University of Southern California and then was heard by flutist Julius Baker, who persuaded her to study with him at Juilliard. Accepted as a scholarship student, she stayed at Juilliard for four years, graduating in 1963. Soon afterward she married cellist Robert Sylvester. Robison studied with the great French flutist Marcel Moyse, and then went to Marlboro. In 1964 she was a prizewinner in the Munich Flute Competition, and two years later, in 1966, she won first prize at the Geneva International Competition, the first American ever to win this honor. Even so, she had doubts about succeeding as a soloist, but she later said, "I could have done the safe thing and joined an orchestra. If I had done that, mine wouldn't have been such a rocky road. But I took the risk."

For a time Robison played some solo recitals with pianist Samuel Sanders, and then she and Sylvester formed a chamber group with violist Scott Nickrenz, his pianist wife Joanna, and violinist Donald Wellenstein. The Nickrenz and Sylvester marriages both dissolved, and in 1971 Robison was remarried, to Nickrenz. In 1970 the Chamber Music Society of Lincoln Center had been formed and its director, Charles Wadsworth, invited Robison to be one of its eleven resident artists. In 1999 she was still with the society, as well as giving numerous solo recitals, appearing with orchestras and music festivals, and recording and teaching. For ten years she served as codirector of chamber music at the Spoleto Festival. With a lively interest in expanding the repertory for her instrument, she has commissioned works for flute and orchestra from Leon Kirchner, Toru Takemitsu, Oliver Knussen, and other contemporary composers.

Two other flutists have carved out outstanding careers. Eugenia Zukerman, born in 1944 in Cambridge, Massachusetts, studied at Juilliard with Julius Baker. Since 1975 she has been appearing throughout the world with orchestras, in solo and duo recitals, and with chamber music ensembles. For sixteen years she has performed three yearly concerts with keyboardist Anthony Newman in a lecture-performance series in New York. In 1998 she became artistic director of the Vail Valley Music Festival in Colorado. In addition, since 1980 she has been profiling artists as arts correspondent for *CBS Sunday Morning,* she has published two novels, and she and her sister have coauthored a nonfiction book.

Flutist Carol Wincenc, born in 1949 in Buffalo, New York, studied at Oberlin, the Manhattan School of Music, and Juilliard, where she has taught since 1989. Winner of first prize in the Naumburg Solo Flute Competition in 1978, she has appeared as a soloist with major orchestras around the world and premiered works written for her by prominent contemporary composers, among them Christopher Rouse, Joan Tower, Tobias Picker, and Henryk Górecki. Also in demand as a chamber musician, Wincenc has collaborated with prominent string quartets and in 1997 joined the New York Woodwind Quintet, in residence at Juilliard. She also performs regularly with Nancy Allen, principal harp of the Metropolitan Opera.

Summarizing the work of instrumental soloists, Carole Dawn Reinhart, an American woman trumpeter who toured widely in the 1960s and 1970s, stated three main qualifications for success: excellent training, a great deal of varied performing experience, and a "strong desire, almost-to-obsession" to succeed. Musicianship, she believed, is also important, but it can be developed through training and experience. As for innate talent, Reinhart said it is generally overrated, the individual work required far exceeding any natural ability. And finally she added: "As a woman trumpeter I have the advantage of being a novelty and often have been used for this purpose. It's much more difficult to be taken seriously. That can only be accomplished through performing not *as well* but *better* than men."[80] Reinhart herself moved to Europe, and, based in Vienna, performs, has taught at the Hochschule für Musik since 1983, plays in the Carole Reinhart Trio, and conducts clinics in her instrument.

Unfortunately, an honest statement like Reinhart's can be—and often has been—dismissed as an excuse, equivalent to saying that if a woman really played as well as this or that man, she would have an equal chance of getting his job. Because musical ability is to some extent a matter of subjective judgment, such arguments are difficult to counter, and it is for this reason that many women musicians are reluctant to admit that they face job discrimination. It is simply too hard to prove, and they fear that if they admit lack of success, it will be blamed on their inferior ability. Yet when more than half of all music students are female, and more than half of all American women are in the labor force, surely something other than lack of ability must be keeping the representation of women in the top echelons of professional music down to 10 or 15 percent.

1 2

TEACHING MUSIC

When we come to the regular music-lessons of the children, we see that this is nearly all done by women, and rightly so, because this is woman's sphere. Probably if parents were asked why they engaged a lady teacher in preference to a man, the general answer would be that it was cheaper.

Unfortunately this is true, but it is not just. Work of equal merit should receive equal compensation, regardless of sex. But, in truth, pay is not the determining factor in this case. Women teach children because they are better fitted for the work than men. They are in closer touch with childhood, and can therefore work along the line of the child's sympathies. . . . Of course, some of our women teachers will work with more advanced students, but that is a work which men can do equally well—in some cases, perhaps, better.

Daniel Batchellor, *Etude*, September 1901

*T*ODAY, at the start of the twenty-first century, nearly all full-time classical musicians teach, either privately or at one or more schools, conservatories, or universities. Much the same is true for composers; practically none could make a decent living from composition alone. As composer Nancy Van de Vate pointed out, colleges and universities are the patrons of modern times, and teaching positions are the principal means of financial support for contemporary composers.[1] Composer Shulamit Ran agreed; earn whatever credentials you need to get a good teaching position, she advised, for you cannot earn enough to live from composition alone.[2]

It is as teachers that women musicians have been most visible. Women began to teach music in America in the eighteenth century, or perhaps even earlier. Though the masters of the singing schools were invariably men, private music teachers frequently were women, as is evident from the advertisements carried in eighteenth-century newspapers and journals. Elisabeth von Hagen and Sophia Hewitt, discussed earlier in this book, both advertised themselves as music teachers in the early 1800s. Moreover, music was part of the curriculum at many of the private schools for girls at this time. For example, at Mme

Addiks's Female Academy at 97 Chestnut Street in Philadelphia, "music either on the piano or harp" was offered.[3]

The practice of holding musical conventions, where music teachers met annually and exchanged information, was begun by Lowell Mason in Boston in the late 1820s and was well established by the late 1830s. And women participated along with men; the 1838 meeting was attended by ninety-six men and forty-two women.[4] The teaching of music, by then widespread in the Boston public schools as well as in private schools, was not confined to the East Coast. By 1856 San Francisco had a Mrs. G. Waldo teaching music, along with twenty-three men teachers, and two years later the city boasted seven women teachers and thirteen men.[5]

By the mid-nineteenth century full-scale conservatories of music were being established, among them the Chicago Conservatory and Peabody Institute of Music, both founded in 1857; the New England Conservatory, Chicago Musical College, and Cincinnati Conservatory, all founded in 1867; and the Philadelphia Conservatory, founded in 1877.[6] Smaller, shorter-lived institutions had preceded them; for example, a Miss Wieth opened a music school in Chicago in 1838.[7] And finally, universities began to offer music courses—Harvard in 1862, Northwestern in 1865, and Oberlin in 1867, though Oberlin already had established a chair of sacred music in 1835.[8] Fanny Raymond Ritter (c.1845–1891), salon musician, singer, pianist, organist, and writer, started teaching music in 1860 at Ohio Female College, and well-known critic John Sullivan Dwight praised her for extending the horizon of her students and for her recognition that mere lesson-giving is not sufficient to ensure a pupil's progress.[9]

Though no exact figures are available, it seems safe to assume that for every woman who taught in a music school of some kind there were at least a half-dozen who taught privately, in their own homes or their pupils' homes. Teaching, especially teaching of the young, was considered both respectable and appropriate for a woman, and an occupation she could pursue part time without neglecting her family obligations. Moreover, since music was considered one of the social graces, along with embroidery and French, it was particularly appropriate for a woman teacher. Women were considered patient and sympathetic, important qualities for a teacher. On the other hand, women teachers often did not regard their work as a permanent or serious occupation, and even when they taught primarily to earn their livelihood, their qualifications were sometimes very minimal. Then, as today, there was no objective standard to separate the good from the indifferent or poor teacher. In part because of this lack of standards and in part owing to traditional sex stereotypes, teaching music tended to have low status. As Belle Squire pointed out in *Etude* in 1907, if music teaching was genteel enough for women, then the man who taught was showing that he lacked something. Music teaching did indeed become a predominantly female occupation. It is estimated that in 1870, 60 percent of all music teachers were women;[10] by 1909 *Etude* believed that figure to be 75 to 80 percent.[11]

Although the figures for private teachers are inexact, the record for the conservatories is better preserved, and indeed, a number of conservatories were founded and directed by women in the second half of the nineteenth century. Among these were the Hershey School of Musical Art, founded in Chicago around 1876 by singer and voice teacher Sara B. Hershey, later the wife of Clarence Eddy;[12] the National Conservatory of Music of America in New York, founded in 1885 by Jeannette Thurber; and, perhaps most important, the Cincinnati Conservatory of Music, founded in 1867 by Clara Baur and directed, after her death, by her niece, Bertha Baur.

Cincinnati, with its large German population, had had music schools for some time and became a music center very early. About 1830 Mr. and Mrs. W. Nixon founded the Musical Seminary; Mr. Nixon wrote *A Guide to Instruction on the Pianoforte* in 1834, and young ladies attending the seminary were taught theory, in addition to voice and piano.[13] The Cincinnati Conservatory, however, was a much more ambitious undertaking.[14] Clara Baur (1835–1912), a native of Stuttgart, Germany, wanted to establish a music school modeled after the great European conservatories. She herself had studied piano and theory at the Stuttgart Music School and began to teach piano while in Cincinnati on an extended visit to her brother Theodore, who had settled there. During this visit, she also studied voice with Caroline Rivé, mother of pianist Julia Rivé-King. Deciding to establish a music school in Cincinnati, Baur returned to Europe about 1858 to study the teaching methods at her old school in Germany and at schools in Paris. She returned to America and in 1867 began her school in a few rooms rented from the Misses Nourse's School for Young Ladies.

From the first Baur established separate departments and hired both European and American musicians for her faculty. The teachers and students presented frequent concerts, and the school also included a teacher-training course —so-called normal training—to prepare students for teaching. A children's department, for teaching youngsters after school hours, was opened in 1870. Cincinnati was one of the first conservatories to set up a residence for women students, and it was one of the first to conduct a special summer school, for both local students and those coming a considerable distance. Drama, literature, and languages were taught, as well as harmony, counterpoint, composition, voice, church music, and the various instruments. The school even had a placement bureau to help its graduates find jobs. By 1902 more than 1000 students were enrolled, and the faculty numbered more than fifty. Among the artists who often visited the conservatory were Lilli Lehmann, Franz Kneisel, Leopold Stokowski, and Enrico Caruso, who called it his "little home."

Clara Baur's niece, Bertha Baur (1858–1940), originally intended to become a physician, but in June 1876, immediately after graduation from high school, she came to visit her aunt. Somehow she was persuaded to give up her original ambition and stay on as her aunt's assistant, which she remained for more than thirty-five years. Allegedly she also was persuaded to remain unmarried, for the sake of the family and the school. When Clara died, she bequeathed the school and its directorship to Bertha, and in her able hands it continued to prosper. The instrumental departments were expanded, and players from the Cincinnati Symphony frequently came to teach their respective instruments. The opera department grew as well, with entire productions being mounted. In 1930 Bertha Baur retired from active management of the conservatory and presented it as a gift to the City of Cincinnati through the Institute of Fine Arts.

In 1878 Cincinnati had acquired a second school, the Cincinnati College of Music. Its directorship was offered to Theodore Thomas, by then well on his way to becoming one of the most respected musicians in the country. He accepted and gave the school a solid start, establishing an orchestra, quartet, and chorus, but he felt the school was too commercially oriented—it accepted anyone as a pupil, for any length of time—and after two years he resigned.[15] The college survived and thrived, and after decades of rivalry it merged, in 1955, with the conservatory.

Jeannette Thurber's National Conservatory of Music in America was an outstanding institution for musical preparation. At its height in the 1890s it had a faculty of international renown, including pianist Adele Margulies and singer Eleanor Everest Freer. It attracted Antonin Dvořák to New York—he served as its director from 1892 to 1895—and it set up a course of study that became a basis for the curriculum of music institutions a century later. Neither race nor gender limited student enrollment; African-Americans and women were not only admitted but encouraged. A wealthy woman who had studied at the Paris Conservatory, Thurber (1850–1946) underwrote numerous other musical undertakings and founded the American Opera Company in 1885 to perform standard repertory in English translation, but the opera closed down after two seasons. In the early 1900s the school declined, partly because of competition—the Institute of Musical Art, which later became Juilliard, was founded in 1904—and partly because Thurber's efforts to obtain a federal endowment and make it a national institution failed. It survived, however, until 1930.[16]

Several other women founded music schools or departments. May Garretson Evans, a music critic for the *Baltimore Sun,* wanted the Peabody Institute to organize a preparatory department to teach music after regular school hours to children enrolled elsewhere. She prepared a detailed plan for such a department, but, since nothing came of it, she and her sister opened a school of their own in 1894. It proved so successful that in 1899 their school was merged with the Peabody and became its preparatory department. Evans herself headed the department until 1929, when she retired.[17] Yet another important conservatory, and free to students, was the Curtis Institute of Music in Philadelphia, founded in 1924 by Mary Louise Curtis Bok (1876–1970), who presided over it until her death.

In order to make musical training more accessible to African-Americans, who were barred from many other schools, a number of conservatories were established by African-American women.[18] Chief among them was the Washington Conservatory of Music and School of Expression, founded in Washington, D.C., in 1903 by Harriet Gibbs Marshall (1869–1941). The first black person to graduate from Oberlin as a piano major, Marshall established a school that attracted students from the North, South, and Midwest and employed highly competent teachers. It also offered an annual concert series that presented artists of national stature. The school survived until 1960, mainly through the contributions of both black and white philanthropists.

The Manhattan School of Music in New York was founded by Janet Daniels Schenck in 1917, and she served as its director until 1956. A graduate of the New York School of Social Work and the American Institute of Applied Music, Schenck had studied music abroad as well; the pianist Harold Bauer was among her teachers. She taught on a volunteer basis at a settlement house in New York's Upper East Side until World War I, when all but essential community services were discontinued to fund the war effort. Rather than disappoint the 100 or so students who studied at the settlement house, she set about to organize a school of music and in 1917 founded the Neighborhood Music School. In 1918 Schenck persuaded Bauer and cellist Pablo Casals to become the first members of the school's Artist Auxiliary Board, and she engaged a talented faculty. In 1938 the school, which by then attracted students from the entire metropolitan area, changed its name to the Manhattan School of Music, and today it is a full-sized conservatory, granting degrees up to the doctorate level. Schenck died in 1976, at the age of ninety-three.

Another New York musical institution, the Henry Street Settlement Music School, owes much of its success to Grace Harriet Spofford (1887–1974).[19] A graduate of Smith College and the Peabody Conservatory, from which she held diplomas in both piano and organ, Spofford taught at Peabody from 1914 to 1924 and then served as dean of the Curtis Institute in Philadelphia until 1931. In 1935 she became director of the Henry Street Settlement Music School. Its advisory board included Aaron Copland, George Gershwin, and Jascha Heifetz, among others. A year after Spofford's arrival, she persuaded Copland, whom she had appointed to the composition faculty, to write a new work for the children at the school, one that would be suitable for performance by students without sacrificing musical standards. The result was his *Second Hurricane,* a play opera that was directed by Orson Welles and numbered Joseph Cotten in the cast. After her retirement from the school in 1952, Spofford became active in numerous international organizations promoting music education and remained so until her death.[20]

Perhaps best known of all these women music educators was Angela Diller (1877–1968), born in Brooklyn and educated at Columbia University, where she studied with Edward MacDowell and Percy Goetschius, and in Germany.[21] From 1899 to 1916 she headed the theory department of New York's Music School Settlement, and then was in charge of music education for five years at the David Marines School (later the Marines College of Music). In 1921 she and another teacher at Marines, Elizabeth Quaile (1874–1951), founded their own school, the Diller-Quaile School of Music, which is still in existence at this writing. The two women also collaborated on a famous piano-teaching series, the Diller-Quaile books, which, likewise, are still in use. Diller alone also wrote several books on theory and harmony.

The majority of students in the conservatories were girls. In 1888, for example, the New England Conservatory graduates were: in piano, twenty-five women, three men; in voice, twenty-nine women, three men; and in organ, four women, three men. This disproportion was said to be even more marked in western, meaning midwestern, schools of music.[22] In 1902 the same conservatory graduated fifty-six women and twelve men. Like the Cincinnati Conservatory, it had a residence for out-of-town women students; an ad in the *Musical Herald* of March 1886 announced that the New England Conservatory's new home on Franklin Square had "elegant accommodations for 500 lady students."

At this writing women students continue to outnumber men in most American conservatories. In 1964 it was estimated that women constituted about 60 percent of the total.[23] Three decades later the figures were only slightly different. In 1996–97 at Juilliard women constituted 53 percent; Manhattan School of Music, 57 percent; Mannes School of Music, 59 percent; New England Conservatory of Music, 54 percent. A notable exception was the Berklee School of Music in Boston, known for its jazz program, where women made up less than 20 percent of the student body.[24]

At the Cincinnati Conservatory the men teachers outnumbered the women considerably, but this was not so at the Detroit Institute of Music, founded in 1894, where women teachers outnumbered men eight to five. There, the teachers were, for piano, four women; violin, one woman, one man; viola, one man; cello, harmony, and composition, one man; normal classes, in music education, one woman; and ensemble classes, one woman, two men.

Women may have outnumbered men as music teachers in the 1890s, but nonetheless they took a back seat in the affairs of the Music Teachers National Association (MTNA), which held its first annual meeting in 1877. However, women often did play a more prominent role in the local chapters. The fourth annual meeting of the MTNA, held in Buffalo in the summer of 1880, did not include a single woman's name in either its very detailed program or its list of officers. In contrast, at the annual meeting of the Music Teachers State Association of Indiana, held in Franklin in June 1880, the program included a presentation entitled "How to Keep Pupils Interested" by piano teacher Miss R. R. Ebright and another on what music teachers should know and teach by Mrs. W. E. Bates of the Columbus (Indiana) Conservatory.[25]

In 1884 the MTNA, in an attempt to set standards for music teachers, established an American College of Musicians, which was to certify teachers on the basis of examinations. The committee for this college, made up of the leading music teachers in the association, included four women: pianist Amy Fay; two prominent midwestern voice teachers, Clara Brinkerhoff and Sara Hershey Eddy; and a New York voice teacher, Mme L. Cappiani (originally Luisa Kapp-Young), who served as the only woman examiner for the college. Through the 1890s the MTNA continued to be run by men, even though most of its members were women. In the local associations, however, women often held office, and the programs of the national conventions occasionally included a woman performer or two, notably pianist Fannie Bloomfield-Zeisler, who appeared a number of times.

In 1897 the MTNA added a "Woman's Department," directed by Florence Clinton Sutro (1865–1906). Sutro, a former pupil of William Mason and Dudley Buck, was an excellent pianist and a composer. A woman of talent and means who had long been active in local music clubs, she married Theodore Sutro, a prominent New York lawyer, in 1884. In 1895 she published a book entitled *Women in Music and Law*. For the MTNA annual convention held in New York in June 1897, Sutro set up a program of papers and compositions by music club women. At the end of this program a meeting was held, and she was elected president of a temporary federation of these musical societies and was urged to form a permanent federation of all clubs in the United States devoted to music.[26]

Local music clubs had sprung up all over America during the second half of the nineteenth century. They served a number of purposes. For those women who loved music but could not, for one reason or another, attempt a professional career, the club was a rewarding outlet. At the very least it fulfilled a social function. For music teachers and other professionals in small towns and rural areas, the club provided performance opportunities and a chance to work with other musicians, amateur and professional. And the clubs played a role in their communities, for not only did they present concerts by members but they raised money to buy instruments and import singers and instrumentalists, sometimes entire orchestras. Last but by no means least, the clubs were educational for their members. A whole series of meetings would be devoted to the study of a single composer's works, a single musical form, or a period of music history—subjects not universally taught in rural or even urban nineteenth-century America. Members were encouraged to perform and to compose, and their compositions were performed. In her book Florence Sutro declared that America had several thousand women composers; in large part they were members of music clubs. The role of the clubs and the National Federation of Music Clubs are discussed more fully in Chapter 13.

Although music clubs and teachers' organizations can raise standards and educate popular taste, it is on an individual basis that a music teacher can have the greatest impact. Few teachers had more impact than a Russian-born pianist who taught at the Juilliard School for a half-century. She was Rosina Lhévinne (1880–1976), a child prodigy who had studied at the Moscow Conservatory and won its Gold Medal in 1898.[27] That same year she married Josef Lhévinne and immediately stopped playing in public, aside from occasional appearances in two-piano performances with her husband, until after his death. In the meantime she devoted herself to furthering his career as a concert pianist and to assisting him with his students. At the outbreak of World War I the Lhévinnes were living in Berlin, and after the war they emigrated to the United States. They both joined the faculty of the Institute of Musical Art (later the Juilliard School). Actually, it was Josef Lhévinne who had a separate contract with the school, but she always took over his students during his frequent tours, and after he died, in 1944, she was asked to stay.

Lhévinne always maintained that it was her husband who was the great musician and the great teacher. Though they sometimes disagreed on various fine points, even in front of a pupil, they usually conducted their arguments in Russian and presented a united front in English. When he died, Rosina Lhévinne resolved to carry on what she regarded as "his tradition," but she became a brilliant success on her own. Her most renowned pupil was Van Cliburn, who won the Tchaikovsky Competition in 1958, the first American ever to do so. Her other famous pupils included John Browning, Daniel Pollack, Misha Dichter, Olegna Fuschi, David Bar-Illan, and Garrick Ohlsson. In addition to these well-known pianists, hundreds of others benefited from her untiring devotion to bring out the best in her pupils.

Lhévinne's approach to music was very open-minded. Rather than insisting on particular techniques or interpretations, she emphasized beautiful tone. She tried to pass on the great romantic tradition of nineteenth-century piano playing, as represented by Anton Rubinstein, Sergei Rachmaninoff, and Josef Hofmann, all of whom she had known personally. She also resumed, after 1945, her own career as a performer, appearing as soloist in several concertos at the Aspen Music Festival, beginning in 1956, and more often in chamber music concerts, especially for about a decade with the then newly formed Juilliard Quartet. In 1961, at the age of eighty-one, she appeared with the New York Philharmonic, playing the difficult Chopin Concerto in E minor. Many of her pupils came to hear this performance, some fearing that their beloved teacher might have overreached herself; but she played beautifully, demonstrating that she could still practice what she taught. Lhévinne continued to teach well into her nineties. When she died at age ninety-six, Peter Mennin, then president of Juilliard, said, "She was quite simply one of the greatest teachers of this century. With her passing, a whole concept of teaching and performing goes with her."

There were, of course, others. Russian-born Nadia Reisenberg (1904–1983), a pianist whose technique had been praised by Rachmaninoff, and who had been a frequent soloist with major orchestras in Europe and America, taught from 1922 at the Curtis Institute, Juilliard, Mannes College of Music, and Queens College (New York). Her pupils included Richard Goode and Myun-Whun Chung. Pianist Adele Marcus (1906–1995) studied with Josef Lhévinne at Juilliard and served as his assistant for seven years. She played with most of the major American orchestras and gave many recitals. But teaching was the center of her career. She taught at Juilliard from 1954 to 1990 and gave master classes all over the world. Especially known for her classes at the Aspen Festival, in 1980 she established her own summer piano festival in Norway. Her pupils included Byron Janis and Horacio Gutierrez, among others.

The most celebrated American-born violin teacher of her time and the first woman to take a place among history's great violin teachers is Dorothy DeLay. Born in 1917 in Medicine Lodge, Kansas, she began violin studies at age four, attended Oberlin College, graduated from Michigan State University with a major in music, and earned her artist's diploma from the Juilliard Graduate School of Music in 1941. Although she continued to perform after marrying Edward Newhouse in 1941, she realized that a concert career was not for her and in 1946, after bearing two children, she began to teach at Juilliard. There she became Ivan Galamian's assistant for two decades, but in 1970 she struck out on her own. At Juilliard, at the University of Cincinnati College-Conservatory of Music, and summers at the Aspen Music School she taught violinists of every caliber from every continent, concentrating on training soloists with the goal of a concert career. Among her many honors are the 1994 National Medal of the Arts and honorary doctorates from Oberlin, Columbia University, Michigan State University, and University of Colorado. Unlike the classical approach of Leopold Auer or Galamian, who insisted on their own interpretations and styles, DeLay's emphasis, in addition to technical command, was on helping students find their own distinctive artistic voices. Among her star pupils were Itzhak Perlman, Shlomo Mintz, Midori, Nadja Salerno-Sonnenberg, and Sarah Chang.

A European-born musician who devoted herself to the survival of the works of her composer-husband after his death, and who also found a new teaching career late in life, was Vally Weigl.[28] Born in Austria in 1894, she studied musicology at the University of Vienna with Guido Adler, piano with Richard Robert, and composition with Karl Weigl, whom she later married. After completing her studies, she began to teach as Robert's assistant and at the University's Musicological Institute. Summers she worked with visiting students who came to the Salzburg Festival. She also performed, usually together with her husband in chamber and piano duo recitals.

In 1938 the Weigls and their young son moved to New York, where they continued to compose and perform. Karl Weigl died in 1949, and his widow took up the task of collecting and disseminating his music. Around this time a serious fall, resulting in orthopedic surgery and a long recovery period, turned her to a new career. At midlife she enrolled at Columbia University and in 1953 earned a master's degree in music therapy, rehabilitation through the use of music for patients with physical and emotional illnesses. Weigl did her on-the-job training at Columbia Presbyterian Psychiatric Institute, and at the same time taught at the American Theater Wing. She then worked for ten years at New York Medical College, where she became chief music therapist and inaugurated a dance therapy department. She also lectured widely in Europe and America, taught for fourteen years at Roosevelt Cerebral Palsy School, and directed research projects concerned with psychiatric patients and residents of a nursing home. In 1975 she was engaged to teach at the New School for Social Research in New York.

Throughout these years Weigl went on composing, principally choral works, chamber music, and songs. Her compositions, which have been widely performed and published, include the clarinet trio *New England Suite* (1954); the song cycle *Nature Moods* (1956), for soprano, clarinet or flute, and violin; *Requiem for Allison* (1971), for soprano and string quartet, a brief work in memory of a student shot by the National Guard at Kent State University in 1970; and *The People, Yes!* (1976), a chamber cantata setting poems by Carl Sandburg. She died in 1982.

Becoming a world-famous teacher, like Lhévinne or DeLay, or mastering a specialty such as music therapy, like Weigl, is not in everyone's grasp. At the top of the pecking order for music teachers is the institution of higher learning, the college or university that grants degrees up to a doctorate, or the top-flight conservatory such as Juilliard, New England, Eastman, Peabody, and Curtis. In these composers and performers alike find a reliable income and assured professional status. And there are fringe benefits, too. The academic institution provides access to experienced performers and opportunities for recitals where new music can be introduced to more tolerant audiences than the average symphony subscription audience. Moreover, an academic affiliation makes it easier for composers to obtain grants and fellowships. Indeed, some awards are administered exclusively through an institution.

Though these institutions in the 1970s still enrolled more women students than men, their faculties were predominantly male. In an article concerning the status of men and women engaged in teaching music on the college level, Adrienne Fried Block, herself a professor of music, indicated that the disparity between the number of women trained and the number of women employed was enormous.[29] Though women earned 55 percent of all bachelor's degrees in music, 48 percent of all master's degrees, and 16 percent of all doctorates, they made up only 21 percent of music faculties on the college level.

Moreover, those women who did get such appointments tended to cluster about the lower academic ranks, such as lecturer and instructor, rather than associate or full professor. The ratio of men to women hired was about four to one, but the ratio of men to women full professors was nine to one.

Besides rank, there is still another pecking order in college and university teaching. Teaching composition and conducting have far more status than teaching piano or school music education, that is, preparing teachers to teach music. The former two were still virtually exclusively male preserves in the 1970s; the latter were considered relatively appropriate for women. Even within those enclaves where more women were employed, the men held the higher ranks. Thus, although 32 percent of all music education faculties were women, women held only 18 percent of the full professorships in this field; similarly, though 49 percent of all piano faculties were women, only 12 percent of the full professors of piano were women. Less than 5 percent of all conducting appointments were held by women, and only 4 percent of all composition teachers were women. In 1975 a total of sixty-seven women held college-level teaching positions in composition in the United States.

In 1975 teacher and composer Nancy Van de Vate described the position of women in academic music, meaning those in college and university music departments, as a "well-documented disaster." Unless a musician lived in a large metropolitan area, she pointed out, the university offered practically the only avenue for development and opportunities for performance. Although federal law prohibited the arbitrary exclusion of women from college music departments, its provisions were not being enforced. It was time that these conditions change, Van de Vate said, and that women themselves become more assertive in their work and that the musical profession become more receptive to them.[30] In 1976, asked to advise young women who were considering a career in composition, Van de Vate was very specific:

> Young women entering the field should obtain as much formal training as possible in rigorous programs. Later they should go to professional meetings and meet their colleagues; enter composition contests, especially those using anonymous entries; perform their works if necessary; write articles for professional periodicals; in other words, use the same means as their male colleagues do to capture public attention.[31]

The situation did not change much during the 1980s and 1990s. Many institutions were creating part-time status for almost all applied music and ensemble direction, with only music history and theory taught by full-timers. Moreover, part-timers, paid hourly rates, generally do not receive such benefits as health care. Gender disparity was present in many if not most schools, but was especially blatant at Boston's Berklee School of Music, where a former faculty member, trumpeter Susan Fleet, filed a gender-bias suit. In 1996–97,

18 percent of faculty were women; of 150 full-time, salaried faculty members, only nine were women.[32] Promotion and salary increases are similar issues. In at least one case a California university kept promising a lecturer she would get job security of some kind, if not tenure, but the promise was never fulfilled and she finally left for another tenure-track teaching post, necessitating a 3000-mile separation from her husband. And in another California university a long-time, highly respected full professor of composition was refused a normal merit increase in salary and resigned the following year.[33]

Nevertheless, a number of women composers have pursued successful academic careers. Among them were Marion Bauer, Louise Talma, and some composers of electronic music, which often requires elaborate technical facilities available only at an institution, such as Jean Eichelberger Ivey, Pril Smiley, Daria Semegen, and others. These women have been discussed in earlier chapters, but two other notable composer-teachers are Miriam Gideon and Vivian Fine.

In 1975 Miriam Gideon became the second woman composer to be elected to the American Academy and Institute of Arts and Letters; the first had been Louise Talma in 1973. The first public performance of a work by Gideon had taken place more than forty years earlier, in 1933. Since then her compositions have been performed in the United States, Europe, and Latin America, by leading orchestras, chamber ensembles, and soloists.

Gideon was born on October 23, 1906, in Greeley, Colorado.[34] She revealed her talent for music by the age of fourteen, and at that time went to live with a musician uncle, Henry Gideon, in Boston. She received her bachelor's degree from Boston University in 1926, with a major in piano, and soon afterward began to compose. Gideon then moved to New York, which became her permanent home. She studied piano with Hans Barth and composition privately with Lazare Saminsky from 1931 to 1934 and with Roger Sessions from 1935 to 1943. In 1944 she accepted her first faculty appointment at Brooklyn College, where she remained for ten years. Meanwhile she had enrolled at Columbia University, where she earned a master's degree in musicology in 1946. From 1947 to 1955 she added a second teaching job at City College of the City University of New York. She married Frederic Ewen of Brooklyn College's English department and later she said that because of her political views and association with Ewen, she was fired from Brooklyn College in 1954, during the years of the McCarthy hearings and anti-leftist feeling.[35] She then joined the faculty of the Jewish Theological Seminary of America, which awarded her a doctorate of sacred music composition in 1970. In 1971 she rejoined the faculty of City College, from which she retired in 1976. She also taught at the Manhattan School of Music from 1967 to 1991.[36]

Gideon's principal compositions are chamber music with and without voice, keyboard works, song cycles, and choral music, including two sacred services. She preferred to avoid any particular musical style or system—despite her long period of study with twelve-tone composer Roger Sessions she did not choose to write strictly serial music. When pressed, she described her style as "free atonality," but composer Eric Salzman called it "atonal expressionism."[37] In her vocal works, however, elements of synagogue services and traditional Judeo-Christian organ and choral music are present. For example, an early work of hers, *The Hound of Heaven* (1945), for baritone, oboe, and string trio, sets several lines of Francis Thompson's poem of the same name that concern profound experiences that mar, in order to make, the human being. Instrumental interludes are interspersed with the text, some phrases of which are repeated. The oboe is treated almost as a separate voice. The texture, composer George Perle wrote in a detailed analysis of this work, is strikingly personal, characterized by lightness, the sudden exposure of individual notes, and constantly shifting octave relationships. Repetition is used a great deal, but it is rarely exact, differing slightly in pitch, register, or some other element.[38]

It is interesting to compare this work with *Rhymes from the Hill* (1968), a song cycle for mezzo-soprano, clarinet, marimba, and cello, setting five poems from *Galgenlieder* (Gallows Songs) by the German poet Christian Morgenstern. Here the voice and chamber ensemble are made to express the ironic ideas and mood of the poems. Gideon herself described the songs in part:

> 1. Songs of the Gallows Gang. Nocturnal shrieks and sinister sounds of nature are heard in the clattering of the marimba and the wail of the clarinet. . . . 5. The Sigh—a tribute to love. Skating on the ice, the sigh becomes so overheated by amorous thought that the ice melts and he disappears. Tremolos on the marimba, grace notes on the clarinet, and glissandi on the cello are used to depict this ironic tragedy.[39]

A New York reviewer wrote of this work that it "is beautifully crafted and a success on its own unpretentious terms. The vocal lines are sensitive, the accompanimental colors glow, and all goes together splendidly."[40]

Always very careful in her setting of texts, Gideon carried this care even further in *Songs of Youth and Madness* (1977), for soprano and orchestra. In this setting of four poems by nineteenth-century Friedrich Hölderin, whose thwarted love for a married woman led him into insanity, Gideon alternated separate verses and entire poems between the English translation and the original German. The English and German versions of the text each have their own, often quite different, music, which adds another dimension to the whole. A later work is *Wing'd Hour* (1983), for voice and a chamber ensemble of flute, oboe, violin, cello, and vibraphone, composed in memory of a close friend. A setting of three poems by Dante Gabriel Rossetti, Christina Rossetti, and Walter De La Mare, it too uses instrumental interludes, but the harmonies are dissonant and the melody more angular. Gideon also wrote two earlier works for orchestra, *Lyric Piece* (1941), for string orchestra, and *Symphonia Brevis* (1954).

In 1969 she received the National Federation of Music Clubs award for her contribution to symphonic music. She died in 1996.

Gideon resisted the label "woman composer" and for a long time denied any difficulties she had owing to her gender. But in the mid-1970s she began to admit that there was a subtle discrimination against women, particularly on the part of award committees and juries.[41]

Gideon's contemporary, Vivian Fine, was born on September 28, 1913, in Chicago, Illinois.[42] She became known for her performances of contemporary piano music—she gave many lecture-recitals on "new" music—and for her compositions, including a number for dance, as well as for her teaching. Besides extensive private teaching, she was on the faculties of New York University (1945–48); State University of New York at Potsdam (1951); Connecticut College School of Dance (1963–64); and Bennington College (1964–88).

Fine began to study piano at the age of five and soon obtained a scholarship to study at the Chicago Musical College. From 1925 to 1931 she attended the American Conservatory, studying piano with Djane Lavoie Herz, harmony and composition with Ruth Crawford, and counterpoint with Adolf Weidig. She was only twelve when she began, and after six months or so Crawford asked her to write a piece. Fine later said, "It had never occurred to me to write music before. I wrote it and could see that she liked it. I became so intrigued with composition that I have never stopped since then."[43] She always regarded Crawford as having had an important place in her development, not only as a role model—for she was the first woman composer Fine encountered—but for a time, at least, as a specific influence on her style. One of Fine's earliest works, *Four Pieces for Two Flutes,* shows her mastery of dissonant counterpoint,[44] and indeed all her compositions until about 1937 were totally atonal. Crawford also introduced her to Henry Cowell, who later published some of Fine's works in his *New Music.*

In 1931 Fine left Chicago for New York, where she studied piano with Abby Whiteside and composition with Roger Sessions. In 1935 she married Benjamin Karp, a sculptor who later taught at New York University; they had two daughters, but Fine never stopped composing, even when her children were young. In 1937 Fine wrote her first ballet score, *The Race of Life,* for Doris Humphrey, a humorous piece based on a series of drawings by James Thurber. There followed *Opus 51* (1938), for Charles Weidman and his dance company, and then two ballets for Hanya Holm, *Tragic Exodus* (1939) and *They Too Are Exiles* (1939). Later Humphrey wrote about Fine: "She has an uncanny sense of what to choose as sound and that *sine qua non* for dance composers, a complete understanding of body rhythm and dramatic timing."[45] With the completion of *Alcestis* (1960), commissioned by Martha Graham, and *My Son, My Enemy* (1965), written for José Limón and his company, Fine had written at least one work for each of the leading dance companies in America over a period of two decades. Several of the ballets were later arranged into independent orchestral works, notably *The Race of Life* and *Alcestis.*

When she first began to write ballets, from 1937 to the mid-1940s, Fine's style became less dissonant, and tonality became evident from time to time. From 1945 on, however, she returned to an almost completely atonal style. Many of her compositions reveal her finely tuned sense of humor. For example, in 1956 she took an article from the gardening column of the *New York Times* and set it for soprano, tenor, flute, violin, clarinet, cello, and harp. Entitled *A Guide to the Life Expectancy of a Rose,* this work sets the text in such a way—through exaggerated stresses on unstressed syllables and similar devices—that the down-to-earth seriousness of lines such as, "There are no tables of life expectancy, and it is impossible to quote any real statistics as to the longevity of a rosebush," is transformed into high comedy.[46]

Enormously prolific despite a continued heavy teaching schedule, Fine wrote songs and chamber works, choral and orchestral pieces. Notable among her compositions are *Paean on the Sound "I"* (1969), for brass ensemble, women's chorus, and narrator, which has been recorded; *Two Neruda Poems* (1971), for voice and piano; Missa Brevis (1972), for four cellos and taped voice; Concerto for piano, strings, and percussion (1972); and two works celebrating the feminist cause, *Meeting for Equal Rights, 1866* (1976), for orchestra, chorus, soloists, and narrator, and *The Women in the Garden* (1977), a chamber opera for five soloists and nine instruments, written with the assistance of a grant from the National Endowment for the Arts.

Two Neruda Poems, Missa Brevis, and a piano concerto were performed in an all-Fine program in New York on April 15, 1973, prompting Donal Henahan of the *New York Times* to write:

> The 10-part mass was full of melismatic slides, microtones, and other currently popular devices but it left an impression of distant times and cool cathedrals. The composer also gave the first performance of her Concerto for Piano, Strings and Percussion (1972), in which she functioned as a one-woman band. Although heavily in debt to Cowell, Ives, and Cage, the Concerto was absorbing in its aural sensitivity and its tongue-in-cheek manner (a parody, perhaps, but of whom?). . . . The Neruda songs made a delicious pair, "La tortuga" crawling along in hushed beauty and "Oda al piano" closing the concert with a witty melodrama. The singer silenced the pianist (Miss Fine) by gently closing the lid, removing the music, and, finally, dropping the key covering. The final chord was played woodenly but expressively by Miss Fine, a marvelous straight-woman.[47]

Succeeding years brought a number of all-Fine programs, principally at universities and colleges throughout the country.

Meeting for Equal Rights, 1866, a setting of nineteenth-century American writings on the subject of women, was first performed in April 1976 by the Oratorio Society of New York at Cooper Union. The score again shows Fine's sense of humor: Horace Greeley's sententious statement that a woman's place is in the home is set to music more than faintly reminiscent of Brahms's famous *Lullaby,* and the male chorus shouting that women should be "Obedient, meek, patient, forgiving, gentle, and loving" is set to insipidly sentimental music. The opera *The Women in the Garden,* first performed in San Francisco in 1978, sets writings of Emily Dickinson, Isadora Duncan, Gertrude Stein, and Virginia Woolf. *After the Tradition* (1988) commissioned and premiered by the Bay Area Women's Philharmonic in honor of the composer's seventy-fifth birthday, alludes to her Jewish origins; the first movement is a Kaddish.[48] Her last major work was *The Memoirs of Uliana Rooney* (1994), a multimedia opera that follows a woman composer through the decades of the twentieth century. The work is partly autobiographical, but also alludes to Ruth Crawford and to singer-composer Alma Mahler. Fine died in 2000, at the age of eighty-six.

To Fine, teaching and composing were inextricably entwined in the 1970s. "All my composer friends teach," she said, "and there is a great deal of musical activity going on in the universities. I enjoy teaching immensely. My only reservation is that I put so much energy into it that I don't leave enough for my composing."[49]

This indeed is the pitfall for all composer-teachers, and one that Dorothy James was unable to avoid.[50] In fact, she described herself as an "occasional composer,"[51] in that most of her works had been written for high school and college performances, some being commissioned for specific occasions. James was born on December 1, 1901, in Chicago, and she taught theory, literature, and composition at Eastern Michigan University from 1927, when it was Michigan State Normal College, until 1968; the school awarded her an honorary doctorate in 1971.

Like Fine, James attended the Chicago Musical College and the American Conservatory where she studied composition with Louis Gruenberg and counterpoint with Adolf Weidig, and obtained both her bachelor's and master's degrees. Later she also studied with Howard Hanson at the Eastman School of Music, Healy Willan at Toronto, and Ernst Krenek at the University of Michigan. Her works include *Three Symphonic Fragments* (1931), for orchestra, first performed in 1931 by the Rochester Philharmonic. It is dedicated to Marian MacDowell, and James eventually spent four summers at the MacDowell Colony. Others are *Paola and Francesca* (1930–34), a three-act opera, and many choral works, including two for children's chorus, *The Jumblies* (1935) and *Paul Bunyan* (1938). Songs, chamber music, and keyboard works round out her output. James continued to be active after her retirement from the university, producing *Motif* (1970) for organ and oboe and *Patterns* (1977) for solo harp. She died in 1982.

Another woman who combined teaching with composition and wrote many works for school performance was Emma Lou Diemer.[52] Born on November 24, 1927, in Kansas City, Missouri, she received her bachelor's and master's degrees in composition from Yale and her doctorate from the Eastman School of Music. She studied composition with Richard Donovan, Paul Hindemith, Bernard Rogers, Howard Hanson, Roger Sessions, and Ernest Toch; she also studied piano with Wiktor Labunski and organ with David Craighead.

After several years as a composer-in-residence and consultant in the Washington-Baltimore area, Diemer taught theory and composition at the University of Maryland from 1965 to 1970, and then joined the faculty of the University of California at Santa Barbara, where she taught until 1991. At the same time, from the age of thirteen on, she served as organist in various churches, and since 1984 has been organist at the First Presbyterian Church in Santa Barbara. Meanwhile she continued to combine teaching and composition as well as performing on organ, piano, harpsichord, and synthesizer. She has received numerous awards, including a 1980 National Endowment for the Arts fellowship in electronic music, and was named American Guild of Organists Composer of the Year in 1995.

Diemer's compositions, which numbered some 500 by 1999, include works for orchestra and band, chamber ensemble, organ, piano, chorus, solo songs, and song cycles. Among them are symphonies, concertos for piano, flute, harpsichord, marimba, trumpet, and organ, and overtures. Among her best known earlier works are *Youth Overture* (1959), *Symphony Antique* (1960), and *Festival Overture* (1961), all for orchestra; *Three Madrigals* (1960), for mixed chorus with piano or organ; and *Dance, Dance My Heart* (1967), for mixed chorus, organ, and percussion. Known for her well-crafted, effective style, Diemer in the 1970s began to experiment with newer modes of expression, including some electronic and computer music. In this vein are her Trio for flute, oboe, harpsichord, and tape (1973), and Quartet for flute, viola, cello, harpsichord, and tape (1974). Outstanding among her works of the 1990s are *Concerto in One Movement for Marimba* (1990), *Concerto in One Movement for Piano* (1991), *Santa Barbara Overture* (1996), the song cycle *Seven Somewhat Silly Songs* (1997), and *Psalms for Flute and Organ or Piano* (1998). In addition, she wrote dozens of compositions for mixed chorus.

Many other composer-teachers might be mentioned, from Ethel Glenn Hier (1889–1971), charter member of the Society of American Women Composers and longtime teacher of piano and composition in Cincinnati and then New York, to young women just beginning their careers at the time of Hier's death. Esther Williamson Ballou (1915–1973) began by accompanying and composing for modern dance and had a distinguished teaching career from 1943 until her death. She taught at the Juilliard School, Catholic University, and then American University in Washington, D.C.

Claire Polin (1926–1995) pursued a multifaceted career as a flutist, composer, and musicologist.[53] She began her studies early, and at age ten she had written her first symphony, even though she did not know how to score it. She continued studies at the Philadelphia Conservatory with Vincent Persichetti, at Tanglewood with Lukas Foss and Aaron Copland, and at Juilliard with Roger Sessions. She also studied flute with William Kincaid and after his death published a five-volume flute method series based on notes he had left. In 1962 she joined the faculty of Rutgers University and taught there until her retirement in 1991. Her music developed from atonalism through serialism, and as she traveled she began to incorporate such elements as Eastern scales, Welsh folk material, medieval chant, and microtones. She produced numerous works for flute or harp, many chamber works, among them three string quartets and a brass quintet, as well as three symphonies and many songs.

Elaine Barkin, born in 1932, earned bachelor's, master's, and doctoral degrees and taught at various schools.[54] In 1974 she accepted an appointment with tenure at the University of California at Los Angeles and taught there for twenty years. From 1963 to 1985 she also served as associate editor of a distinguished journal, *Perspectives of New Music*, and frequently wrote about contemporary composers. She officially retired from UCLA in 1994, but continued teaching until 1997. Principally a composer of chamber music, her own works include String Quartet (1969), *Plus ça change* (1971) for strings and percussion, and *Sound Play* (1974), for solo violin. From the late 1970s on she composed numerous vocal pieces, including *Two Emily Dickinson Choruses* (1977) for mixed a cappella chorus, the chamber opera *De Amore* (1980), and several theater pieces. She also became interested in electronic music; *Anonymous Was a Woman* (1984) is a four-track tape collage for dancers. In 1988 she discovered Indonesian music, specifically gamelan, which is basically a percussion orchestra. She then started composing for gamelan, producing *Kotekan Jam* (1991), followed by *Gamelange* (1993), for harp and mixed gamelan, and *Lagu Kapal Kuning* (Song of the Yellow Boat, 1996), for Balinese gamelan.

Also known for her chamber compositions was Eleanor Cory, born in 1943 in Englewood, New Jersey.[55] She was educated at Sarah Lawrence College, Harvard University, the New England Conservatory, and Columbia, where she received her doctorate in composition in 1975. Her composition teachers included Chou Wen-Chung, Bulent Arel, and Charles Wuorinen. She taught at various colleges in the New York metropolitan area from 1971 on, served as associate editor of *Contemporary Music Newsletter* from 1972 to 1977, and in 1978 was appointed to the faculty of Yale University to teach theory and composition. Her compositions, mostly instrumental, include *Combinations* (1974), for piano; *Tempi* (1971), for clarinet and tape; Trio (1973) for clarinet (bass clarinet), cello, and piano; *Epithalamium* (1973), for solo flute; Trio (1977) for flute, oboe, and piano; and *Counterbrass* (1978), for

French horn, trumpet, trombone, piano, and percussion. Of *Designs* for viola, cello, and piano (1979), a three-section work in which each instrument is introduced in a solo capacity, composer Betty Beath said, "These solos are expressive, simple, and contrast with the technical demands of the *tutti* passages. It is a work of unpredictability and complexity in which various influences rise, are noted, then finally merge in an ending which seeks reconciliation."[56] Cory's later works are *Profiles* (1983), for clarinet, cello, and piano; *Hemispheres* (1989), for cello and piano; *Foreign Echoes* (1995), for orchestra; *Play within a Play* (1996), for solo piano, which contrasts modal and atonal harmonies; and *Visions* (1998), for flute, clarinet, French horn, violin, viola, and cello.

Judith Lang Zaimont, born in 1945 in Memphis, Tennessee, was educated in New York, at the Juilliard School, Queens College, the Long Island Institute for Music, and Columbia University.[57] She also studied privately for a year with André Jolivet in Paris. After seven years of appearances as a duo-pianist with her sister Doris, throughout the United States and on radio and television, in 1967 she became resident composer and accompanist for the Great Neck (Long Island) Choral Society. In 1970 she began to teach as well, first at New York City Community College, then at Queens College, Peabody Conservatory of Music, and Adelphi University. Since 1992 she has been professor of composition at the University of Minnesota School of Music. She also frequently appeared as a guest lecturer on twentieth-century composition before various music teachers' groups, and during the 1980s and 1990s was composer-in-residence at a number of institutions. Zaimont also was editor-in-chief of the three-volume *Musical Woman: An International Perspective*, for which she received the Pauline Alderman Prize in international musicology.

Zaimont's early compositions were principally songs, choral works, and piano pieces. Notable among them are *Sacred Service for the Sabbath Evening* (1976), for baritone solo, chorus, and orchestra, and *Greyed Sonnets* (1975), five songs for soprano and piano to texts by women poets, which a *New York Times* reviewer described as "strongly emotional, suiting the texts, yet carefully constructed."[58] A third significant work is *Songs of Innocence* (1974), for soprano, tenor, flute, cello, and harp, commissioned by the Gregg Smith Singers. Of her vocal works, with texts ranging from the French symbolist poets to Native American materials, one writer said she uses complex rythms and meters (polymeters, rapid meter and tempo changes, off-beat rhythms) and traditional tertiary harmony (based on thirds), polytonality or atonality, depending on the nature of the text.[59] By about 1980 Zaimont was working principally on commissioned compositions, among them a wind quintet, a string quartet for the Primavera String Quartet, and *Songs for Soprano and Harp* for the New York State Music Teachers Association. Among her later works are *Hidden Heritage* (1987), a four-movement "dance symphony" for five players. It was inspired by eight paintings by African-American artists and incorporates elements of jazz.

Her *Doubles* (1993), for oboe and piano, Zaimont describes as a piece about all issues of twoness—two people, double notes, the double nature of the oboe and the double reed.[60] She also wrote Symphony no. 1 (1995), *Hesitation Rag* (1996) for piano, and a piano sonata (1999).

Two other composer-teachers, both born in 1949, have followed somewhat different career paths. Maria Niederberger was born in Davos, Switzerland, to a farming family.[61] She studied violin from an early age, and after high school and a music education course, she taught music in a Zurich school. She married an American and in 1975 moved with their two children to California. Her undergraduate education at University of California, Davis, steered her back to the violin and to composition. She next moved across the country to pursue doctoral studies at Brandeis University, receiving a doctorate in music theory and composition in 1991. She then joined the faculty of her undergraduate alma mater as lecturer in music, to date the first and only woman composer employed there. In 1999 she accepted an appointment at Eastern Tennessee State University. She has received several awards and commissions, including some from her native Switzerland.

Niederberger's compositions are influenced by her early background in baroque and classical music as well as by her principal composition teachers, Martin Boykan, Donald Martino, and Arthur Berger. She herself says, "I write atonal works for the most part. . . . I like counterpoint and subtle rhythmic and dynamic changes. On rare occasions I write tonal works, mainly for choirs. I was trained in twelve-tone techniques and worked in that style."[62] Her early twelve-tone works include *Daedalum* (1984) for solo cello and Piano Quintet (1989–90). Her tonal works include *Six Choral Songs* (1995–96) and *Remember: A Lament* (1999), a setting of a Christina Rossetti poem for alto voice or French horn, violin, and cello. Her most recent atonal work as of this writing is her three-movement, contrapuntal Concerto for oboe and instrumental ensemble (1999–2000), in which, rather than assuming dominance or virtuosity, the oboe in effect plays with the other instruments (flute, clarinet, horn, harp, and strings).

Judith Shatin, flutist and composer, is a graduate of Douglass College and holds a master's degree from Juilliard and a doctorate from Princeton.[63] Upon receiving her doctorate she joined the faculty of the University of Virginia and has remained there. She now is professor and chair of the music department and directs the Virginia Center for Computer Music, which she founded in 1987. Shatin has received numerous awards and commissions. She also has worked on behalf of her fellow women composers. From 1989 to 1993, following two terms as a board member, she served as president of American Women Composers, and from 1994 to 1998 she served on the board of the American Composers Alliance.

Shatin's interest in electronic and computer music dates from her student days, but not until the 1980s, with the development of MIDI (Musical Instrument Digital Interface) and more sophisticated personal computers, was she attracted to working with electronic and computer-generated sound. Her works include some for tape alone, notably *Music for Emergence* (1988), but in the 1990s she preferred to combine acoustic and electronic forces, either with taped electronic playback or live electronics. Examples of these include *Four Songs for Treble Chorus and Tape* (1993), *Elijah's Chariot* (1995–96), for string quartet and electronic playback, and *Sea of Reeds* (1997), for clarinet and live electronics. A particularly interesting work is the 1994 folk oratorio *COAL,* for chorus, an Appalachian band of banjo, fiddle, guitar, dulcimer, and two Appalachian singers, and synthesizer and tape. In this piece electronics are used mainly as transitions; between sections the sound of pickaxes striking coal is heard leaping from left and right speakers, and at one point those sounds are converted via computer to a banjo-like sound.[64] Shatin also composed a considerable body of works for acoustic instruments, both solo and chamber music, and for choirs. Among them are *Fantasy on St. Cecilia* (1996) for piano solo, *Songs of War and Peace* (1998), for mixed chorus and piano, and in progress at the time of this writing *Ockeghem Variations* for wind quintet and piano. A chamber music theater piece, *Houdini: Memories of a Conjurer,* premiered in Portsmouth, New Hampshire, on January 22, 2000.

Women composers and instrumentalists who teach are more apt to introduce their pupils to the works of other women composers and to performances by women musicians. But according to composer Libby Larsen, we still have a long way to go. As she said in a 1999 interview:

> The kids are still taught that Beethoven is the best composer who ever lived. And the canon of composer's names that they're still being given already sets the thing in motion, because they're all men. . . . Then you move into instruments . . . and the boys are headed towards brass and percussion; the girls are steered toward flutes, clarinets, a little percussion, and maybe one or two saxophones. . . . Then they'll head into their school orchestras where the compositional canon is overwhelmingly male again.[65]

1 3

ANGELS AND ADVOCATES

*T*HE PRINCIPAL ROLE women played in American orchestras for 100 years or so, and one they have not yet relinquished, was as patronesses and supporters. Very early on the New York Philharmonic instituted the practice of "Public Rehearsals." Held on Friday afternoon before each concert, these rehearsals, which until about 1870 were genuine practice sessions with halts for corrections, gave regular subscribers a chance to hear any work twice in a short period of time and so to know it better. Moreover, it enabled ladies to attend performances without a gentleman escort, which in those days was not possible for an evening performance.[1]

Over the years the "symphonic ladies," as they were called, made themselves indispensable. Not only did they raise money to support their orchestras, but they provided a strong and active community base through their concern with music education, the promotion of ticket sales, and the generation of publicity. Shortly after the United States entered into World War II, the symphonic ladies' activities were more formally organized and expanded through the founding of the American Symphony Orchestra League, which in 1944 discovered a dynamic leader in Helen M. Thompson.[2] Ironically, just as women acquired the opportunity to play in American orchestras as replacements for men in the armed services during World War II, it was their supportive role that was enlarged and formalized. Indeed, in 1976 an entire book, *Music Angels: A Thousand Years of Patronage,* was published about women's support of music.[3]

The events of the Chicago World's Columbian Exposition of 1893 included an eight-session assembly of women's music clubs from all over the United States. Out of this grew a movement to organize the clubs nationally.[4] Rose Fay Thomas, wife of conductor Theodore Thomas and sister of Amy Fay, had long been active in the Musicians Club of Women in Chicago, which was founded in 1875 and at this writing still exists, the oldest such organization. Thomas favored the formation of a national body, but somehow ill feeling sprang up between her and Florence Sutro, another leader among the

303

women's music clubs. Their disagreement was aired through a number of letters printed in national music journals, and although this gave the music-clubs
movement publicity, it portrayed it in the light of a petty squabble. In the end,
Thomas had enough supporters so that her candidate, Mrs. Edwin T. Uhl,
was elected president of the new national federation in 1898.

Nevertheless, the National Federation of Music Clubs grew and continues
to function at the start of the twenty-first century as a strong supporter of
women musicians and composers. Fanny Morris Smith, writing in *Etude* of
July 1909, chronicled some of the federation's activities. It offered a bureau of
reciprocity, which published a list of members of all clubs in the federation
who were willing to give recitals for either expenses only or a small fee. It had
a program exchange, which made available to all clubs a well-prepared scheme
of programs. It also offered a plan of study with programs covering various
aspects of music. It kept a circulating library of scores and had a well-tested
constitution and bylaws prepared to help organize new clubs. In addition, in
1907 the federation inaugurated a competition for American composers, offering cash prizes in three categories of composition.

In succeeding years these activities were considerably expanded. By 1999
the federation had an estimated 200,000 members in 690 Senior Music Clubs
and 5239 Junior Music Clubs. Its members were professional and amateur
musicians, singers, composers, dancers, performing artists, arts and music educators, students, and music benefactors. The federation discovers, fosters, and
supports talented musicians of all ages with 135 competitions and awards in
voice, instrumental music, and composition. It gives $10,000 for each of four
biennial Young Artist Awards and a $10,000 award for duopianists, which
include two years of performance bookings for winners. It enrolls more than
150,000 young musicians annually in state Junior Festivals, assists hundreds of
youngsters to attend summer music camps, and offers musical therapy programs in hospitals, nursing homes, and prisons. It is an active promoter of
American music, sponsoring the Parade of American Music, an annual festival.
It issues several publications, the most important of which is *Music Clubs Magazine,* and it sponsors a national music week each year. And finally, to help
American women musicians specifically, it sponsored a Decade of Women
from 1975 to 1985, chaired by composer Julia Smith, which helped promote
performances of works by American women composers.

From the late 1800s on the local music clubs within the federation played
a major role. They developed concert series and brought soloists, orchestras,
and music festivals to their communities. They not only contributed money
but they enlisted subscribers and raised funds for these activities. The Cincinnati Symphony, founded in 1894, was established and managed largely by a
group of women from the city's Ladies Musical Club. The first president of the
symphony's board, who served from 1894 to 1900, was club member Helen
Herron Taft, wife of future President William Howard Taft. She was suc-

ceeded by Bettie Fleischmann Holmes, who prior to her resignation in 1913 "recommended that the increased demands of managing the orchestra called for delegating more responsibility to men, so that women's work load could be reduced."[5]

African-American women had a club movement as well, which was consolidated with the founding of the National Association of Colored Women in 1896.[6] One important group was the Treble Club in Washington, D.C. Founded in 1897 and made up of professional women musicians and music teachers, it encouraged young musicians and presented annual concerts concentrating on the music of black composers. Its founder, Mamie Hilyer, also went on to found the Coleridge-Taylor Choral Society, named for Samuel Coleridge-Taylor, a greatly admired black British conductor and composer. The group of 160 to 200 singers was extremely well received and attracted white as well as black audiences. Another important figure in Washington at this time was Mary L. Europe, organist and choir director of the Lincoln Memorial Congregational Church. Europe was also a pianist, giving recitals and accompanying the Coleridge-Taylor Choral Society.

Another important music patron whose work was an outgrowth of her activity in several well-known women's clubs was Elizabeth Sprague Coolidge (1864–1953).[7] She was a pianist—she played the Schumann concerto at the 1893 World's Columbian Exposition with the Chicago Symphony—and, later, a composer. After suffering a series of family tragedies and deaths that left her with a large fortune, her first act of patronage was to give $100,000 to the Chicago Symphony to establish a pension fund as a memorial to her father. The gift was repeated a year later. In 1917, she began her career as a patron of chamber music by establishing the Berkshire Quartet, setting up the Berkshire Festival of Chamber Music, and inaugurating the Berkshire Festival Competition for the composition of chamber music. (Readers will recall that Rebecca Clarke's Viola Sonata narrowly lost this competition in 1919.) The quartet was formed by a Chicago Symphony violinist and three colleagues who appealed to Coolidge for help. Upon hearing them she immediately offered them a contract, stipulating that if they required a pianist she would play with them, and moved them to New York. That summer she also set about building a festival hall on her son Sprague's land in the Berkshires near Pittsfield, Massachusetts. Her first chamber music festival there took place in August 1918.

Within the next few years Coolidge decided that the continuation of her work would require institutional support, and having become friends with Carl Engel, chief of the music division of the Library of Congress, she contributed funds for building an auditorium for chamber music there. It required an act of Congress to be implemented, but it was accomplished, and a Library of Congress Chamber Music Festival was established. It was there that the Coolidge Prize was awarded to such composers as Aaron Copland, for *Appalachian Spring*, Igor Stravinsky, and Samuel Barber. In succeeding years Coolidge set up programs to bring good music and musicians to colleges, universities, and libraries, free of charge; commissioned new works; underwrote festivals in numerous European cities and, during World War II, in Mexico City, San Juan, and Honolulu; assisted projects of contemporary music and early opera; and funded musicological research. Also, from 1916 on she was a major contributor to the MacDowell Colony and became a close friend of Marian MacDowell's.

Coolidge was not the only wealthy woman to contribute to music and musicians, although unlike some others she was a well-trained musician and exercised considerable control over her contributions. Eleanor Robson Belmont, wife of industrialist August Belmont, founded the Metropolitan Opera Guild, which raises the funds to mount expensive new productions and publish its program book and its magazine, *Opera News.* Anne Macomber Gannett, wife of newspaper publisher Guy Patterson Gannett, was a board member and president of the National Federation of Music Clubs. She helped found the Berkshire Music Center at Tanglewood and served on the Metropolitan Opera Guild. Martha Baird Rockefeller, wife of John D. Rockefeller Jr. and at one time a professional pianist, established the fund named for her, which between 1962 and 1982 made more than 2000 grants to performers, composers, musicologists, and musical organizations. Betty Freeman, based in California, made multiple individual grants to avant-garde composers such as John Cage, John Adams, Steve Reich, Mel Powell, and others.

Apart from individual gifts such as Freeman's, a principal means of funding musical composition are commissions, grants, fellowships, or after the fact, awards and prizes. Composers who teach in order to support themselves are nearly always pressed for time to compose. A grant or fellowship can release them from teaching hours; a commission guarantees payment and performance for a work that would otherwise be composed on speculation, as it were. The award of a prize confers prestige, status, and publicity, both on the composer and on the institution where he or she is employed.

In the mid-1970s Carol Neuls-Bates conducted a study of four foundations that give grants in music—the John Simon Guggenheim Memorial Foundation, the National Endowment for the Humanities, the American Council of Learned Societies, and the Martha Baird Rockefeller Fund for Music. The results of her study, presented before the annual meeting of the College Music Society in February 1975 and later published, showed what had long been suspected: a much smaller percentage of women than men received foundation support.[8]

A study of awards and prizes reveals a similar pattern. Indeed, some have been openly restricted to men. In 1916 the Sinfonia, a Boston musical society, announced its fourth annual prize competition for a choral work with orchestra: "The composer must be a male and an American citizen who has received the major part of his musical education in America."[9] The Pulitzer Prize in music, awarded since 1943, was not given to a woman until Ellen Taaffe Zwilich in 1983. Two more women, Shulamit Ran and Melinda Wagner, have won it in the years up to this writing.

American women composers have yet another strike against them—the fact that they are American. European music continues to be highly valued in the United States and still makes up the bulk of programs of serious music. (Similarly, there is a tendency to fill conductors' openings in major orchestras with European men.) Periodically movements and organizations have been formed to combat this tendency and help American composers obtain at least a hearing. In the mid-1970s, when considerable public attention was focused on America's bicentennial, a number of companies and institutions attempted to celebrate American artistic achievement. Two commercial record companies undertook historical surveys of American music. The two-record *Nonesuch Treasury of Americana* (Nonesuch H7-14) included an assortment of serious and popular music; not one woman composer was represented. The other, much more ambitious series, *A Recorded Anthology of American Music* (New World Records; forty-three records by September 1978), represented only two women—Amy Beach with her Violin Sonata and Ruth Crawford with *Three Songs*. The impression given clearly was that there *were* no other American women composers.

There have been notable exceptions to the prevailing pattern. The various prizes of the National Federation of Music Clubs have frequently gone to women composers. Also, the fellowships offered by the MacDowell Colony have been awarded to an extraordinary number of women composers. Of the composers and musicians discussed in this book, several dozen have been MacDowell Colony Fellows, and eight of them spent five or more summers there (Marion Bauer, Amy Beach, Mabel Daniels, Ethel Glenn Hier, Mary Howe, Dika Newlin, Julia Perry, and Louise Talma).[10] To these women the MacDowell Colony gave a space and time they could devote entirely to work without thought of other obligations. And many did highly productive work there.

The MacDowell Colony was officially established in 1908 by Marian Nevins MacDowell (1857–1956), a fine pianist and widow of composer Edward MacDowell.[11] She carried out her husband's wish that their farm in Peterborough, New Hampshire, become a haven of tranquillity for other artists, as it had been for him. Two dozen studios were constructed in remote parts of the expansive property—as of 1999 there are 400 acres—and to augment the memorial fund supporting the colony and ensure its continued existence, Marian MacDowell carried on vigorous fund-raising for many years. Every winter she toured America, giving concerts of her husband's works, speaking in public of his life and his ambition to create a working place not only for composers but for poets, painters, sculptors, novelists, and playwrights. In this way she raised 80 to 90 percent of the colony's financial support during its early years. And every summer she personally supervised the building of roads and construction of eventually more than forty houses and cabins.

Each MacDowell Fellow receives room and board in one of several central buildings and the exclusive use of a private studio equipped for his or her art. The average length of stay is two months. Some studios are equipped with heat, enabling their use during the winter. None is within sight or sound of another, and phone messages are delivered only in emergencies. Lunch and firewood are delivered daily, so an artist may work uninterrupted all day long. In MacDowell's time, fellows were selected largely on the basis of her personal judgment, though she did have an official admissions committee. Since the early 1950s, however, applications have been reviewed by the Composers Admissions Committee made up of composers, teachers, and critics, who rank all applicants on the basis of works they submit. Submissions must include at least one work in a larger form, such as a string quartet, sonata, or orchestral work.

A similar but less well-known working community for artists and writers is Yaddo, a 400-acre estate near Saratoga Springs, New York. An artistic center during the lifetime of its original owners, Mr. and Mrs. Spencer Trask, it was later set aside under the direction of the Yaddo Corporation. Like the MacDowell Colony, it offers room, board, and studio space for periods averaging a month or two. During the 1930s and early 1940s Yaddo became known in the musical world especially because it sponsored an annual festival of contemporary American music, in order to give young composers a chance to hear their works performed. Yaddo, too, has fostered numerous women composers.

A totally different form of advocacy, if it can be called that at all, was exercised by Sophie Hutchinson Drinker (1888–1967). She and her husband, well-to-do and well-educated amateur musicians, believed that music is a soulful, spiritual experience for amateurs. To that end they held weekly singing parties for invited guests at their suburban Philadelphia home to perform choral music of the Drinkers' selection. Seemingly they did not include any works by women composers. In 1932 Sophie joined a small women's amateur chorus, the Montgomery Singers, and they met at her home for about fifteen years. In the end she was inspired to do research on women and music, and in 1948 her book, *Music and Women: The Story of Women in Their Relation to Music,* was published, the first and largest effort of its kind since the early 1900s. It is a curious work, combining her version of feminism with some genuine historical research.

As in other fields where women were long excluded or, if allowed entrance, were not taken seriously, in music one elusive but nonetheless real difficulty they faced was their exclusion from the "old boy network," which functions to perpetuate the status quo. Instrumental teachers (male) help their students (male) to get orchestra jobs; professors (male) tell their students (male) of competitions they might enter, fellowships that are available, teaching jobs in their own departments or other universities; conductors (male) select programs of new works (by men). Because these are usually quite informal procedures, they are difficult to pin down, let alone combat. However, one measure women have taken in fields such as business management is to organize their own cooperative network, which is precisely what women composers began to do in the mid-1970s. Nancy Van de Vate was among the first to recognize the need for an organization whereby composers could exchange information and perhaps also act collectively, and in 1974 she founded the League of Women Composers (renamed in 1979 as the International League of Women Composers). Its aims were to obtain more commissions, recordings, and orchestral performances for women composers, to ensure that state and federal tax revenues were not allocated exclusively to men composers, and to obtain more foundation support for women.

In 1976 a second organization was founded by Tommie Ewert Carl, who recruited Judith Lang Zaimont as vice-president. First named Female Composers of America and then renamed American Women Composers, it issued an ambitious statement of purposes and goals that included serving as a business organization to assist women composers in the areas of live performance, publication, and recording, sponsoring specific performances of new works, and holding annual workshops. Among the first steps the new organization took was to set itself up as a publisher of new music and as a recording agent. Yet another such group was founded in 1979 by Jeannie Poole, the International Congress on Women in Music, to promote an international exchange of information, form an organizational basis for conferences, and recognize outstanding women in music. In 1995 the three groups merged to form the International Alliance for Women in Music (IAWM) in order to pursue their common purpose, to be a strong, effective, high-profile advocate on behalf of all women in music, including not only composers but performers and musicologists. Through its journal, membership directory, library of members' scores, international congresses, and promotion of concerts, broadcasts, competitions, and educational programs, it aimed to provide cooperation and networking opportunities for all women musicians. In 1999 the Eleventh International Congress on Women in Music met in London, with keynote speaker Nicola LeFanu, principal founder of the British Women in Music. A joint venture with the like-minded organization Feminist Theory and Music, the four-day congress featured compositions by women composers ranging from the twelfth-century Hildegard von Bingen to women born in the second half of the 1900s, including ones from Asia, Australia, Europe, and the Americas.

The large-scale networking provided by IAWM is one form of helpful affirmative action, as is the work of the International Women's Brass Conference, founded in 1991 by trumpeter Susan Slaughter. Still more practical advocacy is undertaken by companies that specialize in publishing or recording music by women composers. Chief among these are Clara Lyle Boone's

Arsis Press, Sylvia Glickman's Hildegard Press, and Marnie Hall's Leonarda recording label.

Clara Lyle Boone, a grandniece of Daniel Boone, taught school, composed music, and ran for congress in Kentucky.[12] By 1974 she had saved enough money to launch Arsis Press, the first company dedicated to publishing the chamber and sacred choral music of living women composers. Her own composition, *Meditation,* was the first work she published. In the next twenty-five years, some forty composers were listed in the company's catalog. Born in Kentucky in 1928, Boone studied composition with Walter Piston at Harvard and published her first works under the male pseudonym of Lyle de Bohun. Boone takes a close interest in Arsis composers, attending performances of their works and promoting them. She secures copyrights and negotiates contracts, hires printers and deals with distributors, and pays twice the standard industry royalty rate, 20 percent instead of 10.

Pianist-composer Sylvia Glickman, trained at Juilliard and the Royal Academy of Music in London, is active as a teacher, researcher, and music editor as well as a performer and composer.[13] In 1988 she founded the Hildegard Publishing Company, named for the German composer Hildegard von Bingen, which publishes modern editions of historic music and music by contemporary women. As of 1999 more than 100 composers are represented. Glickman is the coeditor of a twelve-volume series, *Women Composers,* which contains the musical scores of women composers from the ninth to the twentieth century. The first five volumes became available in 1999. Several other companies publish music by women, but to date none has been as ambitious as Arsis and Hildegard.

Marnie Hall, a violinist who played with the Kansas City Philharmonic (now Symphony), American Symphony Orchestra, and New Jersey Symphony, among others, founded an all-women's string quartet, the Vieuxtemps, in 1972.[14] Responding to questions about playing music by women, in 1975 she produced a two-record set, *Women's Work,* on her own Gemini Hall label, featuring 300 years of music by eighteen European women composers. It received enormous publicity and in 1977 she formed a nonprofit company called Leonarda Records. Efforts to obtain funding took time, but even after grants came that supported the company, Hall could not pay herself and had to continue to work as a violinist. Between 1979 and 1985 Leonarda issued twenty-four LPs, nearly all of them first recordings of works. Although a few modern and contemporary men composers have been recorded by Leonarda, nearly all the music is by women. In the mid-1980s CDs supplanted LPs, and because Hall still was not able to earn a living from the enterprise she became a recording engineer. From 1993 on she herself produced nearly a dozen CDs. Hall's methods of music selection vary, but usually a performer sends a tape of the repertory and proposes a list of suitable pieces from which Hall makes the final selection. Sometimes composers propose works and find other composers to share a CD. It is necessary for the artists to find some kind of funding. Since Leonarda is nonprofit, it can apply for grants on behalf of artists, but very few are available for recordings. It clearly is a difficult business, but Leonarda is making a major advocative contribution.

The principal pitfall for efforts of advancement is that they combat discrimination by instituting a kind of separatism and thereby perpetuate the very image that most women composers and performers reject outright, that is, their identification as "women musicians" and not simply "musicians." However, until society has changed enough so that women have a truly equal chance for achievement in all traditionally male-dominated areas—medicine, engineering, and business, as well as music—such advocacy may represent a necessary temporary compromise. True, the closing decades of the 1900s saw significant improvements for women musicians. Some resulted from the gradually changing social and economic climate, for by 2000 a very large proportion of the female population worked outside the home. Other advances were the result of vigorous activism. Thus, in 1999 the efforts of musicologist Liane Curtis paid off and the Metropolitan Dictrict Commission of Boston agreed to inscribe the name of Amy Beach on the walls of the Hatch Shell, where Boston Pops summer concerts take place. To date it had borne the names of eighty-seven male composers—among them Bach, Beethoven, Gershwin, Sousa, Loeffler, and just one living American, John Williams. Some might regard adding Amy Beach as a trivial step, but it was a step in the right direction.

WOMEN MUSICIANS IN THIRTEEN MAJOR U.S. ORCHESTRAS

*T*HESE ARE organizations with a fifty-two-week season and budgets over $10 million for the 1998–99 season. Figures come from a survey by the American Symphony Orchestra League and from direct orchestra responses to the author's queries.

Orchestra	Total musicians	Women musicians	Percentage women	Women principals
Baltimore Symphony	96	30	31%	2
Boston Symphony	101[b]	25	25%	2
Chicago Symphony	110	27	25%	0
Cleveland Orchestra	106	25	23%	2
Detroit Symphony	94	22	23%	3
Los Angeles Philharmonic	108	34	31%	6
Minnesota Orchestra	95	29	31%	3[c]
National Symphony	100	32	32%	3
New York Philharmonic[a]	107	36	29%	4[e]
Philadelphia Orchestra	103	19	18%	2
Pittsburgh Symphony	101	32	32%	7[d]
San Francisco Symphony	105	39	37%	2[e]
St. Louis Symphony	95	36	38%	4

[a] Figures for 1999–2000 season.

[b] Includes six vacancies.

[c] Includes a co-held principal position.

[d] Includes woman concertmaster.

[e] Includes one acting principal.

NOTES

CHAPTER 1. THE FIRST FLOWERING—
AT THE ORGAN

1. John Cotton's tract is entitled "Singing of Psalms a Gospel ordinance, or a Treatise wherein are handled these four particulars. I. Touching the duty itself. II. Touching the matter to be sung. III. Touching the singers. IV. Touching the manner of singing." It is quoted by F. L. Ritter, *Music in America.*

2. Letter to Josiah Flynt, March 27, 1661, in Massachusetts Historical Society Collection, 1st series, VI (1799), p. 106.

3. The Reverend Thomas Walter published *Grounds and Rules of Musick explained* in 1721 and is quoted in *History of the Handel and Haydn Society,* vol. 1, p. 19.

4. McKay and Crawford, *William Billings of Boston,* p. 37.

5. Krueger, *The Musical Heritage of the United States,* pp. 17–18.

6. *Euterpiad,* April 15, 1820. The practice of excluding women persisted for years. F. L. Ritter, writing in the 1880s, said that most of the many amateur vocal societies then in existence, about three-fourths of them German-American, excluded women. New York's Liederkranz Society, founded in 1847, began to admit women in 1856, two years after a splinter group had withdrawn and formed the all-male Arion Society. Milwaukee's Musikverein, founded in 1849 and among the most influential of these groups, consisted of a male chorus, an orchestra, and a mixed chorus that performed only on special occasions. A rare exception was the Musical Fund Society of Philadelphia, founded in 1820, which included all of that city's prominent musicians and music patrons and resolved only "that no female professional members be admitted without a written certificate from some lady of established character in this city" (Campbell, *Old Philadelphia Music,* p. 192).

7. John Tufts's collection of church music of c. 1714, the Reverend Thomas Walter's collection of 1721, and Thomas Bailey's collection of 1769.

8. F. L. Ritter, *Music in America,* p. 238.

9. The organ originally was purchased for the Brattle Street Church, which, however, refused to install it. The instrument then was offered to King's Chapel. An Englishman, Edward Eustace, was hired as organist at a salary of twenty pounds per year.

10. Ochse, *The History of the Organ in the United States,* p. 14.

11. *History of the Handel and Haydn Society,* vol. 1, pp. 27–28.

12. F. L. Ritter, *Music in America,* p. 103.

13. Quoted by Brooks, *Olden-Time Music,* p. 100. Elisabeth von Hagen, her husband, and her children performed in New York as early as 1789; they moved to
Boston in 1796.

14. P. E. Paige, "Musical Organizations in Boston: 1830–1850," p. 34.

15. Loesser, *Men, Women, and Pianos,* p. 449. Wrighten was the daughter of English
actress-singer Mary Ann Pownall. At this concert she, her sister, and their mother
also sang, and her four-year-old brother Felix appeared as well. Another early
pianist was a Mrs. Sully, who performed in Charleston in 1794 and 1795 and in
Boston on September 13, 1796. See also Sonneck, *Early Concert-Life in America,
1731–1800,* pp. 29, 31, 227ff, 305.

16. Her death, however, is recorded in the State of Maine Archives. She died on
August 31, 1846, in Portland, at the age of forty-six.

17. The second born, John Hill Hewitt (1801–1890) ran away from home, became
interested in music while at West Point, studied law for a time, and eventually
composed some 300 songs, as well as an oratorio; from 1828 on he lived principally in Baltimore. The second son, James Lang Hewitt (1807–1853), became a
music publisher in Boston, as did the third son, Horatio Nelson Hewitt. The
youngest son, George Washington Hewitt, entered a disastrous publishing venture in Philadelphia and later settled in Burlington, New Jersey, where he composed many piano pieces and taught; his mother spent her last years with him.
Sophia's sister Eliza Hewitt became a music teacher and eventually also went to
live with brother George. John's oldest son, Horatio Dawes Hewitt, became a
musician and composer and wrote some comic operas; he died in 1894. George's
son, Hobart Doane Hewitt (1852–1932), taught piano and violin in Burlington
and was for a number of years associated with the Philadelphia publishing firm of
Theodore Presser, which published many of his compositions. See also Howard,
"The Hewitt Family in American Music."

18. Quoted by F. L. Ritter, *Music in America,* p. 121.

19. Lowens, *Music and Musicians in Early America,* p. 201. Though it was customary
for established local musicians, of whom Graupner was an undisputed leader, to
assist newcomers, Graupner's name is conspicuously absent among the assisting
artists at Hewitt's concerts, nor were tickets to these events sold at his music store.
Further, at an important concert in which Graupner led the orchestra and the
highly regarded organist George K. Jackson played selections from Handel's
works, the phrase "Mr. Hewitt has declined" was printed on the program.

20. H. E. Johnson, *Musical Interludes in Boston, 1795–1830,* pp. 84, 99. The solo part
of this concerto by the German pianist-composer Daniel Steibelt (1765–1823)
was rivaled in popularity only by Franz Kotzwara's *Battle of Prague.*

21. Parker, *Musical Biography, Or Sketches of the Lives and Writings of Eminent Musical Characters,* pp. 193–196.

22. Wolverton, "Keyboard Music and Musicians in the Colonies and United States
of America Before 1830."

23. Virginia Larkin Redway, *Music Directory of Early New York City.* New York: New
York Public Library, 1941. See also Howard, "The Hewitt Family in American
Music."

24. The same advertisement appeared in the June 3, 1820, issue of *Euterpiad,* which
was the leading music periodical in Boston at that time.

25. *Euterpiad,* April 8, 1820.

26. H. E. Johnson, *Musical Interludes in Boston, 1795–1830,* pp. 107, 144. Loesser, *Men, Women, and Pianos,* p. 466, says only that Sophia *may* have given this performance and says nothing about her later playing of works by Beethoven.

27. *Euterpiad,* June 10, 1820. In the same ad, which was repeated on June 17, June 24, and July 1, Mrs. Hewitt, presumably Sophia's mother, announced her intention of opening an academy of the French language for young ladies as soon as she could form a class of eight to ten scholars, and also offered private lessons at ladies' houses or at her own. Further, a young man—probably one of Sophia's brothers, perhaps James, then aged thirteen—also got into the ad: "A smart active lad who writes a good hand and understands arithmetic wants a situation in a store apply as above."

28. *History of the Handel and Haydn Society,* vol. 1, pp. 76–77.

29. H. E. Johnson, *Musical Interludes in Boston, 1795–1830,* p. 140.

30. H. E. Johnson, *Musical Interludes in Boston, 1795–1830,* pp. 18–19.

31. *Euterpiad,* May 11, 1822.

32. *Euterpiad,* May 25, 1822.

33. *Columbian Centinel,* August 14, 1822.

34. Parker, *Euterpiad,* May 11, 1822.

35. Edwards, *Music and Musicians of Maine,* pp. 26ff.

36. Edwards, *Music and Musicians of Maine,* p. 58.

37. Edwards, *Music and Musicians of Maine,* p. 58.

38. Brooks, *Olden-Time Music,* pp. 179–181.

39. Howard, *Our American Music,* p. 86. However, Wolverton, "Keyboard Music and Musicians," says he died August 1, 1827, in Boston.

40. Unsigned article from the *Providence Journal* reprinted in *Dwight's Journal of Music,* April 16, 1859, p. 20.

41. *History of the Handel and Haydn Society,* vol. 1, p. 98.

42. P. E. Paige, "Musical Organizations in Boston: 1830–1850," p. 54. Lowell Mason (1792–1872), conductor, composer, and educator, became famous as an innovator in public-school music education and the training of music teachers. In Boston he directed several church choirs and became superintendent of music in the public schools.

43. *History of the Handel and Haydn Society,* vol. 1, p. 101.

44. *History of the Handel and Haydn Society,* vol. 1, pp. 102ff.

45. *History of the Handel and Haydn Society,* vol. 1, p. 116. The society eventually did give him a raise to $75 per quarter in January 1834 but continued to have problems with Zeuner, who proved to be very hard to get along with. In April 1834 the society's president actually resigned on account of a quarrel with the organist. Moreover, the society accepted his resignation, realizing it would be easier to replace a president than a competent organist who also composed. Indeed, the society's very next concert, on May 18, 1834, featured, in addition to the customary oratorio selections, an organ concerto, duet, cavatina, and recitative and aria—all composed by Zeuner. Bad temper notwithstanding, in 1838 Zeuner was elected president of the society, but after nine months he resigned, and later he moved to Philadelphia, where he committed suicide in 1857.

46. Edwards, *Music and Musicians of Maine,* p. 261.

47. *History of the Handel and Haydn Society,* vol. 1, p. 105.

48. *Eastern Argus,* July 15, 1833, and August 2, 1833.

49. P. E. Paige, "Musical Organizations in Boston: 1830–1850," p. 426.

50. *History of the Handel and Haydn Society,* vol. 1, pp. 141ff.

51. H. E. Johnson, *Hallelujah, amen!,* pp. 68–69.

52. *Dwight's Journal of Music,* April 15, 1859. Presumably his death was assumed because no one in Boston had heard from him for some years.

53. A dramatic account of her decline appears in *History of Music in San Francisco,* vol. 2, p. 116. An accompanying photograph shows she had dark eyes and brows, an oval face with delicate, birdlike features, and a slightly aquiline nose. She wore her dark hair parted in the center, flat on top and puffed out at the sides.

54. Newspaper clipping, source unidentified, Boston Public Library, Music Division.

55. *Folio,* October 17, 1885.

56. *Folio,* January 1869.

57. *Musical Record,* October 1878.

58. James M. Tracy, in *Folio,* 1888. She did not play every Saturday at the Music Hall, but about once every three weeks. The Arlington Street Church records list her as organist and show that she was paid from 1865 through 1867. In 1979 this venerable Boston church hired the second woman organist in its 250-year history, Joyce Painter.

59. Penny, *The Employments of Women,* pp. 76–77.

60. Mary Chappell Fisher, "Women as Concert Organists," and Everett E. Truette, "Women as Organists," *Etude,* September 1901.

61. Ellinwood, *The History of American Church Music,* pp. 202, 232–233.

62. Morin, *The Worcester Music Festival,* p. 34.

63. *Musical Herald,* May 1886, p. 147.

64. John Rockwell, *New York Times,* May 4, 1976.

65. *Oregonian,* May 17, 1998.

66. Information about Marilyn Mason comes from letters and e-mail in 1998 and 1999, and the University of Michigan Music Department.

67. Information about Papadakos comes from e-mail from her, November 1999.

68. Marie MacConnell, quoted by Mary Chappell Fisher, *Etude,* July 1909, p. 484.

CHAPTER 2. THE "LADY VIOLINISTS"
AND OTHER STRING PLAYERS

1. Joseph Singer in *Musical Register,* reprinted in *Musical Record,* November 26, 1881.

2. *Dwight's Journal of Music,* June 9, 1877.

3. *Boston Evening Transcript,* May 9, 1877.

4. A child prodigy who lived from 1839 to 1911, Normann-Neruda was considered the first truly great woman violinist and the only woman ever to become the most famous member of a musical family—she originally performed together with her father, brother Franz, and sister Amalie. She came to the United States only once, in 1899.

5. Reprinted in *Freund's Weekly: A Review of Music and Drama,* May 22, 1884. *Musical Record* of June 1884, p. 6, said, "More than five hundred ladies are studying the violin in Boston, while many others are proficient soloists."

6. Lahee, *Famous Violinists in America,* p. 300. The fever had also spread across the Atlantic. *Etude* of December 1894 reported that of 2000 female pupils at the London Guildhall School of Music, 300 were studying the violin.

7. Fisher, *Musical Prodigies: Masters at an Early Age,* pp. 175–176.

8. *Etude,* September 1901.

9. F. L. Ritter, *Music in America,* p. 140.

10. P. E. Paige, "Musical Organizations in Boston: 1830–1850," p. 76.

11. Richard Dyer, *Boston Globe,* June 25, 1977.

12. Information about Lehwalder comes mainly from her interview with Raymond Ericson, *New York Times,* September 9, 1977, and from a review by Peter G. Davis, *New York Times,* September 11, 1977.

13. Information about Allen comes from e-mail and clippings sent in 1999 from the harpist herself.

14. *Musical Gazette,* April 26, 1847, p. 54.

15. For information about Urso up to about 1873 I have relied on Barnard, *Camilla: A Tale of a Violin.*

16. *Dwight's Journal of Music,* February 14, 1863.

17. *Dwight's Journal of Music,*March 2, 1867.

18. *Dwight's Journal of Music,*March 16, 1867.

19. *Dexter Smith's Musical, Literary, Dramatic and Art Paper,* September 1874.

20. *Dwight's Journal of Music,* January 7, 1869. She was among the first violinists to perform this work in America.

21. *Dwight's Journal of Music,* December 12, 1874.

22. *Etude,* November, 1891.

23. Morin, *The Worcester Music Festival,* pp. 2–3. The Worcester County Music Association was formed in 1852 as an outgrowth of the musical "conventions" begun in the late 1820s by music teachers meeting to exchange information. In 1858 it began to present annual festival concerts in which large works were performed and to which notable artists were invited from all over the world. The festivals remained an important event in American music up to the beginning of World War II.

24. Morin, *The Worcester Music Festival,* p. 23.

25. Morin, *The Worcester Music Festival,* p. 28.

26. Morin, *The Worcester Music Festival,* p. 35.

27. *Dexter Smith's Musical, Literary, Dramatic and Art Paper,* January 1874, p. 7.

28. The Concerts Classiques were reported in *Dwight's Journal of Music.* The September 1874 issue of *Dexter Smith's* prefaces an interview with Urso by the following: "We found the brave little lady almost fully recovered from the effects of the ugly accident, which is still fresh in the minds of the public, and which but for her heroism and presence of mind, would probably have proved fatal."

29. *Musical Record,* June 21, 1879.

30. *Musical Herald,* July 1880.

31. *Musical Record,* December 1884.

32. *Freund's Weekly,* June 1891.

33. *Musical Herald,* April 1893.

34. *Folio,* September 1883, p. 325.

35. *Etude,* January 1891.

36. *Musical Record,* November 1891.

37. Tick, "Why Have There Been No Great Women Composers, or Notes on the Score of Sexual Aesthetics?" First printed in *International Musician* of July 1975, Tick's paper, in manuscript, came into the hands of musicologist Susan Kagan and was reprinted in *Signs,* vol. 2, no. 3, Spring 1977, pp. 731–34.

38. Letter to *Musical Courier,* March 1898.

39. *Etude,* September, 1901.

40. Adella Prentiss, in *Musical Record,* June 1900.

41. *Dwight's Journal of Music,* April 7, 1860.

42. Morin, *The Worcester Music Festival,* p. 29.

43. *Dwight's Journal of Music,* March 2, 1878.

44. Quoted by Morin, *The Worcester Music Festival,* pp. 42–43.

45. *Musical Record,* April 12, 1879, p. 20.

46. Maria Milanollo (1832–1848) was a superb performer but died too soon to fulfill her early promise. Teresa Milanollo (c. 1827–1904) was so affected by her sister's death that she retired for a time but eventually resumed her career. She did not, however, play in public after her marriage in 1857 to a French army officer named Parmentier. She composed an Ave Maria for men's voices, *Grande Fantasie* for piano, and a number of works for violin.

47. *Musical Record,* June 28, 1879, p. 194.

48. Powell's only rival on the international circuit was an Italian, Teresina Tua (1867–1955), who married and retired several times, taught at the Milan Conservatory, and eventually entered a convent.

49. Information about Powell comes from Lahee, *Famous Violinists in America,* and other standard sources, and from Shaffer and Greenwood, *Maud Powell: Pioneer American Violinist.* Their book is based on documents, photos, letters, and memorabilia concerning Powell amassed through a longtime search by Neva Garner Greenwood (1906–1986), to which Shaffer added her own research and wrote the book at Greenwood's request.

50. Thomas, *A Musical Autobiography,* vol. 2.

51. *Etude,* September 1901.

52. *Musical Herald,* April 1887, p. 112.

53. *Folio,* November 1890, p. 398.

54. Finck, *My Adventures in the Golden Age of Music,* p. 313.

55. *Musical Record,* March 1898, p. 95.

56. George Lehmann, head of the violin column, *Etude,* January 1907.

57. *Etude,* November 1918. Also F. H. Martens in *Dictionary of American Biography,* vol. 15, pp. 149–50.

58. Reprinted in *Ladies' Home Journal,* February 1896.

59. *Etude,* July and August 1909.

60. Quoted in Shaffer and Greenwood, *Maud Powell: Pioneer American Violinist,* p. 101.

61. According to Neva Garner Greenwood, who spoke with family members and checked contemporary newspaper reports, Powell prided herself on not disappointing audiences by canceling. She had been advised to rest but insisted on finishing her tour.

62. So it was reported in the press. However, at some time the violin was either owned or borrowed by the French violinist Renée Chemet, and in October 1925 Turner sold it, stating its history along with the bill of sale. Somehow it fell into the hands of Henry Ford and presently is in the Ford collection at Greenfield Village, Dearborn, Michigan.

63. Sidney Homer, *My Wife and I,* p. 28.

64. *Musical Herald,* August 1882. Her most recent translation, in 1882, had been of Brahms's *Nänie.*

65. *Folio,* February 1877.
66. Arthur M. Abell, "The Arma Senkrah Tragedy," *Musical Courier,* October 17, 1900, p. 33.
67. Mary Park Clements, a longtime friend of Jackson's in her later years, said in a letter to me, June 24, 1978, that Jackson was born February 20, 1874. Jackson's scrapbooks and other papers were left to the Maryland Historical Society and Library of Congress.
68. *Musical Record,* January 1900.
69. Philip Hart, *Orpheus in the New World,* p. 36.
70. Information about Clarke comes from Liane Curtis, *The Musical Times,* May 1996, pp. 15–21, and from *Musical Quarterly,* Fall 1997, vol. 81, no. 3, pp. 393–429.
71. Information about Mukle comes from Shaffer and Greenwood, *Maud Powell: Pioneer American Violinist.*
72. *Freund's Weekly,* October 1885.
73. *Folio,* April 1888.
74. W. S. B. Mathews, in *Etude,* February 1897, lists the Musical College, Chicago Conservatory, Gottschalk School, Metropolitan Conservatory, and American Conservatory. In addition, the Spiering, Listermann, and (new) Chicago Symphony quartets were raising the profile of chamber music. In 1912 it was estimated that New York City was home to at least 2000 teachers of the violin and other non-keyboard instruments, and they had some 20,000 pupils.
75. Mr. and Mrs. Adolf Hahn, violinists who played together and as soloists, both began their studies at the Cincinnati College of Music and were married in 1898. Their repertory for joint performances included the Bach and Mozart double concertos and many arrangements of works made especially for them *(Musical Record,* August 1, 1899, p. 364).
76. *Musical Record,* February 1890.
77. M. P. French, *Kathleen Parlow: A Portrait.* The author, Maida Parlow French, was a cousin of the violinist. Parlow taught at Mills College, in California. In 1938 Parlow was in the South Mountain Quartet in Pittsfield, Massachusetts, and she worked for Elizabeth Sprague Coolidge for about six years. She returned to Canada in 1941, and also taught at the Toronto Conservatory.
78. Obituary by Eleanor Blau, *New York Times,* April 27, 1983.
79. *Etude,* December 1917, announced a great demand for girl violinists to play in orchestras, for vaudeville, and in concerts, and good violinists had no trouble getting jobs. Presumably they, like World War II's Rosie the Riveter, were laid off when the men returned home.
80. Winn's statement appeared in "Music and Matrimony," *Musical Record,* December 1900.
81. Quoted in *Women in Music,* vol. 2, no. 8, June 1937.
82. Fisher, p. 177.
83. *Etude,* May 1921. See also note 62.
84. Ross Parmenter in the *New York Times,* as reported in Parmenter's *Times* obituary, January 11, 1999.
85. Donal Henahan, *New York Times,* February 9, 1976.
86. *New York Times,* March 5, 1998.
87. Most of the information about Phillips comes from her.
88. *Instrumentalist,* March 1975.

89. *BBC Music Magazine,* 1993.
90. January 4, 1998.
91. Information about Isbin comes from her web page and an interview with Richard Dyer, *Boston Globe,* February 14, 1999.

CHAPTER 3. SEATED AT THE KEYBOARD

1. Quoted by Loesser, *Men, Women, and Pianos,* p. 509.
2. Brooks, *Olden-Time Music,* p. 99. Another early performer was nine-year-old Lucy Moller, who appeared with her father, John Christopher Moller, in Philadelphia in 1792 and 1793.
3. Loesser, *Men, Women, and Pianos,* p. 449.
4. Loesser, *Men, Women, and Pianos,* p. 453. Brooks, *Olden-Time Music,* p. 100, quotes von Hagen's ad from the *Columbian Centinel,* 1799. Her composition is mentioned in Clark, *The Dawning of American Keyboard Music.*
5. Loesser, *Men, Women, and Pianos,* pp. 472ff.
6. P. E. Paige, "Musical Organizations in Boston: 1830–1850," p. 347. A small book of unknown authorship, *A Biographical Sketch of Jane Sloman the Celebrated Pianiste* (Boston: Dutton and Wentworth, 1841) gives a little more information about her childhood.
7. Pincherle, *The World of the Virtuoso,* p. 23.
8. Most of the biographical information about Carreño comes from Milinowski, *Teresa Carreño, "By the Grace of God,"* and Chapin, *Giants of the Keyboard,* pp. 138–46.
9. This was the single most famous work of Philadelphia composer Septimus Winner (1827–1902), who often wrote under the pseudonym Alice Hawthorne, a rare—perhaps unique—example of a male composer taking a woman's name for the purpose of publication. The reverse was much more common (see Claghorne, *The Mocking Bird*). However, James Weldon Johnson wrote in 1930 in "Negro Songmakers" (in Patterson, *The Negro in Music and Art*) that Winner originally heard the tune from Richard Milburn, a black barber, guitarist, and whistler who worked on Lombard Street in Philadelphia and used to perform it in public. The title page of the original publication, by Winner and Shuster in 1855, said "Melody by Richard Milburn, written and arranged by Alice Hawthorne," but in the 1856 edition, published by Lee and Walker, Milburn's name did not appear.
10. Teresa Carreño, "Individuality in Piano Playing," *Etude,* 1909, p. 805.
11. Milinowski, *Teresa Carreño, "By the Grace of God,"* and Chapin, *Giants of the Keyboard,* agree. Further, *Freund's,* April 10, 1884, quotes Carreño herself from an article of hers in the *Chicago News.*
12. The biographical details in the preceding paragraphs come from Milinowski, *Teresa Carreño, "By the Grace of God."*
13. The program also included the "Appassionata" Sonata by Beethoven, a prelude, a polonaise, and a tarentelle by Chopin, an impromptu by Schubert, and shorter works by Mendelssohn, Rubinstein, and Schumann, among others (Mathews, *A Hundred Years of Music in America,* pp. 116–17).
14. James Huneker in *Etude,* January 1888, p. 2.
15. Charles Wolff in *Musical Record,* May 1891, p. 3.
16. Carreño, *Possibilities of Tone Color by Artistic Use of Pedals.* Like many musicians,

however, she was less successful in teaching her own children, though at least two of them were undeniably gifted. Teresita Tagliapietra made her debut as a pianist in 1901, but although talented, she proved too undisciplined for a successful concert career. Giovanni Tagliapietra Jr. became an opera singer, but he, too, proved too temperamental and undisciplined to fulfill his early promise. Eugenia and Hertha appear not to have tried to play professionally; both eventually married Germans and remained in Germany.

17. Quoted by Lahee, *Famous Pianists in America,* pp. 302–13.

18. *Musical Record,* December, 1900, p. 523.

19. *Etude,* August 1917.

20. Ruth Payne Burgess, "Reminiscences of Teresa Carreño," *Etude,* November 1930.

21. Egbertina Remy, "Teresa Carreño as Teacher," *The Associated Music Teacher League,* November 1951, p. 3.

22. The statement appeared in an editorial in *Freund's,* May 16, 1885.

23. *Dwight's Journal of Music,* May 15, 1875; July 1876; April 14, 1877; September 1, 1877.

24. There are several brief accounts of her early life and career. I have relied, among others, on those of J. M. Green, *Musical Biographies,* pp. 145–46; F. O. Jones, *Handbook Of American Music and Musicians,* pp. 145–46; Lahee, *Famous Pianists,* pp. 318–21; and Wier, *The Piano: Its History, Makers, Players, and Music,* p. 406.

25. Mathews, *A Hundred Years of Music in America,* p. 116.

26. *Dwight's Journal of Music,* April 14, 1877, p. 5.

27. *Dwight's Journal of Music,* October 27, 1877, p. 117.

28. *Musical Record,* February 8, 1879, p. 290, letter to the editor from "G."

29. *Dwight's Journal of Music,* April 26, 1879. Such transcriptions were common practice throughout the nineteenth century. Beethoven himself transcribed his Violin Concerto for piano, and as late as 1918 or so one of the most popular piano recital pieces was Ernest Hutcheson's transcription of the *Ride of the Valkyrie* from Wagner's *Ring,* preserved in a legendary recording by Olga Samaroff.

30. *Musical Herald,* August 1883, p. 212.

31. *Etude,* January 1888.

32. Raymond Morin, *The Worcester Music Festival,* p. 47.

33. *Folio,* June 1881.

34. *Etude,* May 1899, p. 134.

35. Loesser, *Men, Women, and Pianos,* p. 539.

36. Annette Essipoff (1851–1914), a Russian, was a pupil of Leschetizky's and also was married to him for a time. A brilliant virtuoso, she toured Europe and America, and then returned to Russia to teach at the St. Petersburg Conservatory. Prokofiev was one of her pupils.

37. *Freund's,* November 15, 1883.

38. *Freund's,* March 1885. A. L., or Amelia Lewis, was the pen name of Amelia Louise Freund, mother of publisher Harry E. Freund and one of the wittiest, most outspoken reviewers of this period.

39. *Etude,* April 1887, p. 51.

40. *Etude,* December 1894.

41. Leschetizky was the most renowned piano teacher of his time. The pianist Harold Bauer, in his autobiography *(Harold Bauer, His Book,* p. 135) tells of dining at

Leschetizky's home in Vienna just after a large class had met. As the young women were leaving, Leschetizky looked at them and said, "Just think! Some fellow must be found for each one of these girls, and his sole reason for existence will be to nullify their studies and ruin their careers."

42. Francis Williams in *Freund's,* July 12, 1890.

43. *Freund's,* January 3, 1891.

44. Bauer, *Harold Bauer, His Book,* p. 87, says that the artist was greeted with yells, catcalls, and the like. She began to play and was forced to stop. Charles Lamoureux, the conductor, then announced to the audience that the performance would proceed, so they might as well stop making noise and listen to what they had paid to hear, but some of the rumpus continued.

45. *Etude,* February 1896. Actually, her repertory was even larger. Between 1891 and 1924, when she appeared almost annually with the Chicago Symphony, she played in addition concertos by Grieg, Henselt, Moszkowski, Mendelssohn, Liszt, Mozart, and Tchaikovsky.

46. "Fannie Bloomfield Zeisler," *Dictionary of American Biography,* pp. 647–48.

47. *Etude,* November 1929.

48. *Etude,* December 1908.

49. *Etude,* August 1909.

50. *Etude,* April 1910.

51. Information on Amy Fay comes largely from Mathews, *A Hundred Years of Music in America,* and McCarthy, *Amy Fay: America's Notable Woman of Music,* a full-scale biography including correspondence, writing, and programs, as well as the testimony of contemporaries concerning Fay's life.

52. *Dwight's Journal of Music,* March 3, 1877.

53. Susan Andrews Rice, *Etude,* May 1891, p. 91.

54. Fay, *Music Study in Germany,* p. 168.

55. Biographical details for Aus der Ohe come from Lahee, *Famous Pianists;* Wier, *The Piano: Its History, Makers, Players, and Music;* and *Baker's Biographical Dictionary of Music and Musicians.*

56. *Freund's,* February 1889.

57. *Etude,* January, 1888.

58. *Musical Herald,* February 1888, p. 44.

59. *Etude,* January 1925.

60. Much of the biographical detail about Samaroff comes from her autobiography, *An American Musician's Story,* and from Kline, *Olga Samaroff Stokowski: An American Virtuoso.*

61. Milinowski, *Teresa Carreño, "By the Grace of God,"* p. 308.

62. *Etude,* January 1917.

63. For information about Tureck I have relied heavily on an unsigned article in the *New Yorker,* October 10, 1977, pp. 36–38.

64. Allan Kozinn, *New York Times,* October 9, 1977.

65. *Boston Globe,* March 25, 1999.

66. Cazort and Hobson, *Born to Play: The Life and Career of Hazel Harrison.*

67. Wier, *The Piano: Its History, Makers, Players, and Music,* p. 398.

68. *History of Music in San Francisco,* vol. 5, pp. 80–87; the two quotations appear on p. 83 and p. 87.

69. Menuhin, *Unfinished Journey,* pp. 319–20.

70. Slenczynska and Biancolli, *Forbidden Childhood.*

71. Fisher, *Musical Prodigies: Masters at an Early Age,* pp. 73ff, and Talalay, *Composition in Black and White: The Life of Philippa Schuyler.*
72. *New York Times,* October 27, 1998.
73. Information about McDermott comes from her web page.
74. Information about Shapiro comes from e-mail and telephone communication, 1999.

CHAPTER 4. THE FIRST "LADY COMPOSERS"

1. Several groups of composers were active in eighteenth-century America, but they were isolated from the mainstream. The most important were two German-speaking religious groups in Pennsylvania, the Cloister at Ephrata, and the Moravians of Bethlehem, Lititz, and Nazareth, who composed hymns and other sacred music in the prevailing European idioms of their forebears. A branch of Moravians who composed also moved to North Carolina, settling in Salem, now Winston-Salem.
2. L. C. Elson, *The History of American Music,* pp. 293–94.
3. Newman wrote for London's *Musical Times,* and is quoted in *Etude,* August 1910.
4. Leigh K. Scruggs, "Creative Women in Music," p. 8.
5. *Musical Record,* February 1896.
6. H. R. Hawed in *Music and Morals,* quoted in the *Musical Herald,* October 1884, p. 247.
7. Leo R. Lewis in *Music,* July 1896.
8. These arguments were still alive in February 1973, when *High Fidelity/Musical America* published two articles under the title "Why Haven't Women Become Great Composers?" pp. 46–52. In one article, Grace Rubin-Rabson said women did not have "the ultimate creative spark"; in the other, Judith Rosen said they had been too long squelched by men.
9. Bloomfield-Zeisler, "Women in Music."
10. *Musical Record,* November 11, 1882, p. 113.
11. Tick, "Women as Professional Musicians in the United States, 1870–1900," pp. 115ff.
12. *Etude,* September 1901, p. 312, gives a long list of works by women who produced many kinds of music, but only their songs are listed.
13. L. C. Elson, *Woman in Music,* pp. 293–94, said that Carl Reinecke, longtime director of the Leipzig Conservatory, believed there is a point beyond which women cannot progress, in both performance and composition, and composers Johan Svendsen of Norway and Niels Gade of the Copenhagen Conservatory expressed similar views.
14. Many women published under masculine pseudonyms or simply used initials. Among them were Dame Ethel Smyth (1858–1944), whose Mass was published under the name E. M. Smyth; Helen Guy Rhodes (1858–1936), who used the pseudonym Guy d'Hardelot; Augusta Holmès (1847–1903), whose early songs were published under the name Hermann Zenta; and Carrie Williams Krogmann (1863–1943) of Boston, who wrote more than 1000 semiclassical works under various names, including Paul Ducelle, Karl Kleber, and Victor Hope.
15. Sonneck, *A Bibliography of Early Secular American Music.*
16. The best source for these early composers is Tick, *American Women Composers before 1870.*

17. Cheney, *The American Singing Book,* p. 103. According to Ebel, *Women Composers,* she married a man named Torry.
18. Browne later married a man named Garrett and moved to Washington, D.C. By 1875 she had written some 200 works, including fantasies, waltzes, and songs. See Moore, *Complete Encyclopedia of Music,* p. 22.
19. *Musical Review,* vol. 1, no. 11, 1838, p. 120.
20. Tick, *American Women Composers before 1870;* also, Ebel, *Women Composers,* p. 69.
21. Biographical information about Amy Beach comes from standard works such as Chase, *America's Music,* p. 378; Howard, *Our American Music,* pp. 319–23; Reis, *Composers in America,* 1st ed., p. 21; L. C. Elson, *The History of American Music,* pp. 294ff; and Wier, *The Piano: Its History, Makers, Players, and Music.* Of special interest are the articles by Jenkins, "Mrs. H. H. A. Beach," in the *Dictionary of American Biography,* Supplement 3, pp. 41–43, and by Tuthill, "Mrs. H. H. A. Beach," in *Musical Quarterly,* as well as an unpublished Ph.D. dissertation by Merrill, "Mrs. H. H. A. Beach: Her Life and Music." Block, *Amy Beach, Passionate Victorian,* published in 1998, is a comprehensive biography.
22. *Folio,* April 1875, p. 123.
23. *Musical Herald,* December 1887, p. 382.
24. *Musical Herald,* December 1888, p. 352.
25. *Musical Herald,* May 1891, p. 93.
26. *Musical Herald,* December 1891, p. 35.
27. *Musical Courier,* May 10, 1893, p. 14.
28. *Musical Herald,* August 1893, p. 206.
29. Hughes, *Contemporary American Composers,* pp. 426–27.
30. Block, *Amy Beach, Passionate Victorian,* p. 83.
31. Before Beach's symphony, Alice Mary Smith (1839–1884), an English composer, had written a symphony as well as four orchestral overtures, five cantatas, a clarinet concerto, and many smaller works. Louise Farrenc (1804–1875) of France wrote mostly keyboard and chamber music but also produced three symphonies and two overtures. Augusta Holmès (1847–1903), also French, wrote several large orchestral works but no symphony as such.
32. Merrill, "Mrs. H. H. A. Beach: Her Life and Music," p. 121.
33. Even feminists like Fanny Morris Smith (*Etude,* March 1901) expressed this conventional wisdom.
34. Elson, *The History of American Music,* p. 295. Merrill, "Mrs. H. H. A. Beach: Her Life and Music," p. 29, also regards it as the best of her instrumental works.
35. Tick, "Women as Professional Musicians," p. 114, says just about all music by women was praised or blamed on the basis of masculine and feminine characteristics, but my research has not found this to be totally true.
36. March 1897.
37. *Musical Record,* May 1, 1899, p. 230.
38. W. T. Upton, *Art-Song in America,* p. 304.
39. Mary Louise Boehm, jacket notes on Turnabout recording QTV-S 34665, May 1976.
40. Tuthill, "Mrs. H. H. A. Beach," p. 304; also Merrill, "Mrs. H. H. A. Beach: Her Life and Music," p. 17.
41. *Etude,* February 1904, p. 51.
42. Andrew Porter, *New Yorker,* November 24, 1975, p. 154, and Allan Kozinn, *New*

York Times, September 22, 1998. The work was performed in 1998 by the Chamber Music Society of Lincoln Center.

43. The list first appeared in the *Los Angeles Examiner,* June 28, 1915, and was reprinted in the *Musical Courier,* July 7, 1915. A year later, in an article on piano Beach wrote for *Etude,* October 1916, she repeated the same dictum for pianists, that is, technique is a vital basis for expressive playing.

44. Morin, *The Worcester Music Festival,* p. 135.

45. *Etude,* January 1915, p. 14.

46. The Piano Trio was performed in 1974 at Boston's Gardner Museum in an all-Beach program and again in New York in 1976 in a program of American music by the Bergson Trio. Reviewing the latter, Patrick J. Smith in the *New York Times,* April 5, 1976, described the work as "far from negligible in its forthrightly direct rhapsodics, although now and then it exudes a whiff of the palm-leafed salon." He was probably referring to the unabashedly late-romantic last movement. The middle movement, Lento espressivo, includes a highly original, playful, almost Ivesian treatment of motifs from children's songs.

47. In 1927 the members of the society included, among others, Gena Branscombe, Mabel Daniels, Marion Bauer, Ulric Cole, Ethel Glenn Hier, Mabel Wood Hill, Mary Howe, Mary Turner Salter, Lily Strickland, and Harriet Ware.

48. Merrill, "Mrs. H. H. A. Beach: Her Life and Music," p. 54.

49. Jenkins, "Mrs. H. H. A. Beach."

50. Howard, *Our American Music,* p. 322.

51. *Musical Leader,* May 25, 1940, p. 9.

52. Ellinwood, *The History of American Church Music,* pp. 221–22. Lang played the piano from an early age, studied in Europe with Satter, Jaell, and Liszt, and made his debut at the age of fifteen in a Mendelssohn Quintette Club concert. In 1862 he organized several concerts in which he conducted a large orchestra, soloists, and a chorus. He was organist at the Old South Church and South Congregational Church before going to Kings Chapel, and he was among the organists who gave recitals in the 1860s at the Boston Music Hall, as was Lillian Frohock. His last public appearance was at Boston's Symphony Hall on February 12, 1909, when he took part in a 100-year memorial service for Abraham Lincoln. See also Ryan, *Recollections of an Old Musician,* pp. 85–86.

53. Mrs. Crosby Adams, "Musical Creative Work Among Women," *Music,* January 1896, p. 170.

54. Hughes, *Contemporary American Composers,* p. 434.

55. *Musical Herald,* January 1891, p. 10.

56. *Musical Herald,* May 1893, p. 157.

57. *Boston Herald,* January 11, 1917.

58. Hughes, *Contemporary American Composers,* p. 435.

59. The principal sources for information about Hood are Elson, *The History of American Music,* p. 306, and J. M. Green, *Musical Biographies,* p. 388.

60. An excellent biographical account of Daniels is in Goss, *Modern Music Makers,* pp. 61–69. Daniels's personal papers, including correspondence, programs, and scores, are in the Schlesinger Library Manuscript Section, Radcliffe College, Cambridge, Massachusetts.

61. Mabel Daniels in *The Christian Science Monitor,* April 22, 1961.

62. In addition to Elson, *The History of American Music,* pp. 307–8, the biographical information about Hopekirk comes from Hall and Tetlow, *Helen Hopekirk.*

63. *Musical Herald,* April 1891, p. 67.
64. *Etude,* September 1901, p. 318.
65. A short biography of Lewing appears in the *Musical Record,* March 1900, p. 144.
66. Information about Rogers comes from her autobiography, *Clara Kathleen Rogers, The Story of Two Lives: Home, Friends, and Travel,* published in 1932.
67. *Musical Herald,* January 1883, p. 24.
68. Rogers, *Clara Kathleen Rogers, The Story of Two Lives,* p. 81.
69. W. T. Upton, *Art-Song in America,* p. 110.
70. A book about Mary Salter, *In Memoriam,* author unknown (but probably her husband), was privately published in 1939; a copy is in the New York Public Library Music Division.
71. Harris, "Women Composers of Religious Music."
72. Ellinwood, *The History of American Church Music.*
73. E. M. Smith, *Woman in Sacred Song.*
74. Tick, "Women as Professional Musicians," p. 105, says that the percentage of women in the New York Manuscript Society, a professional composers' organization, doubled between 1892 and 1898. In 1899 the name was changed to the Society of American Musicians and Composers, and all the newly appointed officers and directors were men (*Musical Age,* June 1, 1899, p. 7).
75. *Freund's Weekly,* June 26, 1886, p. 6.
76. The composers represented, in addition to Amy Beach, were Julia Rivé-King, Mrs. J. T. Draper, Eleanor Smith, Nellie Bangs Skelton, Gertrude Griswold, Helen Hopekirk, Marie Antoinette, and Cécile Chaminade (*Musical Courier,* May 31, 1893, p. 16).
77. *Freund's Weekly,* January 1896.
78. This information is based on performance lists appearing in F. L. Ritter, *Music in America,* pp. 362–67; M. A. De Wolfe Howe, *The Boston Symphony Orchestra 1881–1931,* appendix Q; H. E. Johnson, *Symphony Hall, Boston,* appendix; Huneker, *The Philharmonic and Its Seventy-fifth Anniversary: A Retrospect,* pp. 49–130; Erskine, *The Philharmonic Society,* pp. 66–168; and Shanet, *Philharmonic, A History of New York's Orchestra,* pp. 496–738.
79. *High Fidelity/Musical America,* June 1975, p. 21. The others were Elizabeth Lutyens (English) and Grazyna Bacewicz (Polish).
80. Atlanta, Boston, Chicago, Cleveland, Dallas, Detroit, Los Angeles, Philadelphia, St. Louis, Utah, and the National Symphony Orchestra listed no works by women. Deon Nielsen Price, *IAWM Journal,* vol. 4, no. 1, Winter 1998, p. 21.

CHAPTER 5. APARTHEID—
THE ALL-WOMEN'S ORCHESTRAS

1. Otis, *The Chicago Symphony Orchestra,* appendixes listing orchestra personnel to 1924.
2. Drinker, *Music and Women,* pp. 106–7, 178ff.
3. Drinker, *Music and Women,* pp. 5, 8, 9.
4. Burns, "The Distaff'd Composers."
5. See *Women in Music,* vol. 1, no. 3, September 1935. Burney wrote, "It was really curious to see, as well as to hear, every part of this excellent concert performed by femáles, violins, tenors, bases, harpsichords, and double bass."

6. Hanslick in *Neue Freie Presse* of Vienna, quoted in *Dwight's Journal of Music,* April 10, 1880, and in the *Musical Record,* March 27, 1880, p. 395.

7. *Musical Record,* April 17, 1880, letter from George B. Nind, Iowa.

8. *Musical Record,* March 1889.

9. Advertisement in the *Musical Record,* April 1897.

10. *Dexter Smith's Musical, Literary, Dramatic and Art Paper,* December 1873, p. 165.

11. *Dexter Smith's,* March 1874.

12. *Dexter Smith's,* March 1876. Arbuckle (1828–1883), virtuoso cornetist and band-master, published a cornet method book.

13. *Musical Record,* December 1879, p. 206.

14. *Folio,* 1880, 1881, 1882.

15. *Musical Herald,* May 1885.

16. *Freund's Weekly,* August 22, 1885. Levy was a famous male brass virtuoso.

17. *Musical Record,* October 1889.

18. *Musical Herald,* March 1890.

19. *Musical Record,* March 1900. Some thirty-five years earlier Alphonse Sax, inventor of the saxophone, had written a treatise claiming that playing wind instruments was highly beneficial for the lungs and women should be encouraged to do so in women's orchestras (*Gymnastique des Poumons,* Paris, 1865).

20. *Musical America,* February 26, 1910, p. 15. At the start of the twenty-first century women saxophonists are rarely hired by major American orchestras, although in jazz they have won more acceptance, and only since the late 1980s have they begun to attain university positions in important schools of music and conservatories. According to Carolyn J. Bryan, professor at Georgia Southern University, Kandace Brooks of the University of Florida was the first woman president of the North American Saxophone Alliance, and Jean Lansing was the first woman to earn a doctor of music degree in saxophone performance at Indiana University.

21. *Musical Record,* June 13, 1882, p. 538.

22. *Folio,* June 1888.

23. *Etude,* August 1901.

24. *Musical Bulletin,* June 1871, p. 125.

25. *Metronome,* October 1871, p. 55.

26. *Dexter Smith's Musical, Literary, Dramatic and Art Paper,* June 1873.

27. Tick, "Women as Professional Musicians in the United States 1870–1900," p. 100.

28. Tick, "Women as Professional Musicians in the United States 1870–1900," pp. 100–101.

29. *Musical Record,* October 21, 1882, p. 43.

30. *Musical Record,* December 16, 1882, p. 205.

31. *Musical Record,* August 1884, p. 4.

32. "Opinions of New York Leaders on Women as Orchestral Players," *Musical Standard,* April 2, 1904.

33. *Freund's Weekly,* March 5, 1889.

34. *Musical Herald,* March 1885 and January 1886.

35. *Musical Herald,* February 1890.

36. *Folio,* February 1888, p. 10.

37. *Folio,* May 1888, p. 176. Osgood was also an Eichberg pupil, and this ensemble survived for several seasons. It played at the Plattsburgh (New York) Music Fes-

tival in May 1889 (reported in *Freund's Weekly,* June 1889) and in 1891 appeared at the YMCA Hall in Brooklyn, New York (Tick, "Women as Professional Musicians," p. 101).

38. *Freund's Weekly,* September 30, 1896, p. 6.
39. *Musical Record,* March 1900, p. 137.
40. Information about the Fadettes comes principally from *Women in Music,* February 1936, and Naylor, *The Anthology of the Fadettes.*
41. *Freund's Weekly,* September 30, 1896. p. 6.
42. Reported in the *Christian Science Monitor,* June 3, 1952.
43. Tick, "Women as Professional Musicians," pp. 103–4.
44. *Women in Music,* vol. 1, no. 7, March 1936. The other five women's orchestras were the Philadelphia Women's Orchestra with sixty members, Orchestrette Classique of New York with twenty-four, Portland Women's Symphony with thirty-five, New York Women's Symphony with eighty-five, and Women's Little Symphony of Cleveland with forty-three.
45. The principal sources of information about these organizations are contemporary music journals and all the issues of *Women in Music.* A summary appears in Petrides, "Women in Orchestras."
46. *Etude,* April 1916.
47. *Etude,* June 1925, p. 383.
48. *Etude,* August 1925, p. 591.
49. Beatrice Brown of the Ridgefield (Connecticut) Symphonette, quoted by Jepson, "American Women in Conducting."
50. H. E. Johnson, *Hallelujah, amen!,* p. 113.
51. Boston Public Library scrapbook, Boston Music Hall.
52. Fay, *Music Study in Germany,* p. 117.
53. Biographical information about Leginska comes chiefly from the clipping files of the New York and Boston public libraries, and the history of the Boston Women's Symphony from a clipping file in the Boston Public Library.
54. *Musical Courier,* July 1919.
55. Biographical material about Brico comes chiefly from a clipping file in the New York Public Library, an article in *Current Biography* (September 1948), and articles in the *New York Times* (September 15 and 19, 1974; May 19, 1975; March 4, 1977), *Boston Globe* (February 8, 1976), and *Opera News* (February 14, 1976, p. 14).
56. *New York World Telegram,* February 5, 1937.
57. *Current Biography,* September 1948, p. 10.
58. *Women in Music,* June 1937, reported that as of April 1, 1937, the WPA Music Project included 2253 female musicians and had featured some of them as guest conductors with major orchestras.
59. A more complete listing is found in Carol Neuls-Bates, "Women's Orchestras in the United States, 1925–1945," in Bowers and Tick, *Women Making Music,* pp. 351ff.
60. This information was provided by letter and telephone from Joan Ferst, long-time concertmaster of the Cleveland Women's Orchestra and project manager in 1999.
61. Information about this orchestra comes principally from *Women in Music,* the periodical edited by Petrides. Groh, *Evening the Score,* reprints all the issues and intersperses explanatory remarks and more about Petrides's own history.

62. *New York Herald Tribune,* October 16, 1940.
63. This information comes from the Boston Public Library clipping file on the Boston Women's Symphony.
64. One of the most extraordinary women's orchestras was that of the Birkenau concentration camp at Auschwitz. Created in 1944 and functioning for about one year, it was conducted by Alma Rosé, a niece of Gustav Mahler's, and included a bizarre assortment of players: ten violins, one flute, reed pipes, two accordions, three guitars, five mandolins, drums, and cymbals. The forty-nine women engaged in playing and copying music for this ensemble in large part owed their lives to it, for they were given a heated room and blankets, though no extra food, and were released from the arduous physical labor required of ordinary inmates. This remarkable story is told in two books: *Playing for Time* (Judith Landry, trans., New York: Atheneum, 1977) by a member of the ensemble, Fania Fénelon (1909–1983), and *Alma Rosé: Vienna to Auschwitz,* by Richard Newman with Karen Kirtley (Portland, Oregon: Amadeus Press, 2000).
65. Some had done so for a long time. The Civic Orchestra of Chicago already had twenty-four women—one clarinet and the others string players—during the 1921–22 season.
64. Information provided by the Columbus Women's Orchestra.
65. Information provided by the Women Composers Orchestra of Baltimore.
66. Information provided by the Women's Philharmonic.
67. Most of the information here relies on Michael J. Budds, in Pendle, *Women and Music,* and Dahl, *Stormy Weather.*
68. Tucker, "Female Big Bands, Male Mass Audiences."
69. Tucker, "Female Big Bands, Male Mass Audiences," p. 87.
70. Gourse, *Madame Jazz,* p. 224.
71. *Time,* February 13, 1989, p. 41.
72. Gourse, *Madame Jazz,* p. 14.

CHAPTER 6. AMERICAN COMPOSERS
IN EUROPEAN IDIOMS

1. Biographical information about Mary Howe comes largely from Goss, *Modern Music Makers,* Howe's autobiography, *Jottings,* and from Howe's friend Anne Hull, who supplied information in conversations and correspondence of 1977 and 1978, and from Howe's son Calderon in a telephone conversation of 1978. Information about programs comes from Mary Howe's papers, including programs, reviews, letters, and so on, preserved on microfilm in the New York Public Library Music Division.
2. M. Howe, *Jottings,* p. 89.
3. M. Howe, *Jottings,* p. 89.
4. Emilie Bauer in *Musical Leader,* October 15, 1925.
5. M. Howe, *Jottings,* p. 89.
6. This last piece, *Canción romanesco,* was written in what Mary Howe called "an access of musical spleen" *(Jottings,* p. 85). She had entered a number of competitions without results. Finally one year the League of American Pen-Women's Music Division offered a prize for a chamber work to be played at the big dinner or lunch of their convention. "Imagine," wrote Howe, "five hundred women

lunching and trying to make them swallow chamber music. I thought violently to myself, 'I bet I can write a piece that's sobbing and sloppy enough to win that prize, serve them right!'" So she wrote *Canción romanesco* and it won. "I was really ashamed," she said, but went on to say it had since been played beautifully by several string quartets, so maybe "it had or has its uses."

7. Interview published in the *Washington Post,* December 26, 1952, p. 25.

8. Ray C. B. Brown, *Washington Post,* April 16, 1939.

9. Reviews from *Music Clubs Magazine* and *Musical America,* quoted in M. Howe, *Jottings,* p. 170.

10. Interview published in the *Washington Post,* December 26, 1952, p. 25.

11. For biographical information about Marion Bauer I have relied chiefly on Reis, *Composers in America;* Goss, *Modern Music Makers;* Bazelon, "Woman with a Symphony"; Ewen, *American Composers Today,* pp. 20–22; an interview with her friend of thirty years, Harrison Potter, on June 20, 1978; and letters from two of her former students, J. Vincent Higginson and composer Julia Smith.

12. Emilie Frances Bauer also was born in Walla Walla, Washington. She studied with Miguel Espinosa and at the Paris Conservatory, and then taught piano and voice in Portland, Oregon. She went east about 1896, teaching and writing in Boston for a time, and then moved to New York. From 1902 to 1903 she edited a women's page in *Etude.* For many years she also wrote for the *Musical Leader, Concert Goer,* and other periodicals, as well as publishing her own compositions under the pseudonym Francesco Nogero.

13. Stewart, "The Solo Piano Music of Marion Bauer."

14. W. T. Upton, *Art-Song in America,* p. 145.

15. E. M. Hisama, *Gendering Musical Modernism: The Music of Ruth Crawford, Marion Bauer, and Miriam Gideon,* chap. 6.

16. The other board members, in addition to chairman Copland, were Douglas Moore, Elie Siegmeister, Quincy Porter, Roy Harris, Wallingford Riegger, Virgil Thomson, Roger Sessions, Goddard Lieberson, and Bernard Wagenaar, according to J. Smith, *Aaron Copland,* p. 181.

17. *New York Times,* May 9, 1951.

18. Bazelon, "Woman with a Symphony," p. 6.

19. For biographical and critical information about Ruth Crawford Seeger I have relied heavily on an excellent unpublished doctoral dissertation by Mary Matilda Gaume, "Ruth Crawford Seeger: Her Life and Works." Gaume, born in 1910, taught music and musicology for many years and did exhaustive research for her dissertation, studying all Crawford's scores in the Library of Congress and contacting Charles Seeger and many musicians who had known her well. In 1997 her work was superseded by Judith Tick's excellent biography, *Ruth Crawford Seeger,* which corrected earlier errors and provides a searching analysis of the compositions.

20. The Violin Sonata, played at least once in New York and in Chicago, was later destroyed by Crawford.

21. Although Gaume believed it is significant that almost all Crawford's chamber works are entitled "Suite," the Delos recording of this work calls it *Two Movements for Chamber Orchestra.*

22. Cowell, *American Composers on American Music,* p. 119.

23. Gaume, "Ruth Crawford Seeger," p. 19.

24. Gaume, "Ruth Crawford Seeger," p. 178.

25. Robert P. Morgan, record jacket notes, Nonesuch H-71280.
26. *Musical America,* December 15, 1953.
27. Kendall, *The Tender Tyrant: Nadia Boulanger.*
28. Aaron Copland, *Our New Music: Leading Composers in Europe and America,* pp. 217–19. New York: McGraw-Hill Book Co., 1941.
29. Interview with Richard Dyer, *Boston Globe,* July 24, 1978.
30. Kendall, *The Tender Tyrant,* pp. 90–91.
31. Quoted in Kendall, *The Tender Tyrant,* p. 77.
32. For biographical information about Louise Talma I have relied on Goss, *Modern Music Makers,* pp. 383–91; a biographical questionnaire she filled out for the American Music Center, New York; and a curriculum vitae she sent to me in 1978.
33. *New York Times,* May 5, 1946.
34. According to Virgil Thomson, writing in 1962; quoted by Kendall, *The Tender Tyrant,* p. 69.
35. Berger, "Stravinsky and the Younger American Composers."
36. Interview with Raymond Ericson, *New York Times,* February 4, 1977.
37. Barkin, "Louise Talma: 'The Tolling Bell.'"
38. Donal Henahan, *New York Times,* March 18, 1976.
39. Joseph Horowitz, *New York Times,* February 7, 1977.
40. On February 28, 1978, at Christ and St. Stephens Church, New York.
41. Donal Henahan, *New York Times,* March 2, 1978.
42. Biographical information about Dika Newlin comes from my correspondence of 1978 with the composer herself; *New Jersey Music and Arts,* May 1953, pp. 9–10; and Wolff, "Dika Newlin."
43. Wolff, "Dika Newlin."
44. Wolff, "Dika Newlin."
45. Newlin's letter to me, February 2, 1978.
46. Biographical information about Elinor Remick Warren is based on the composer's own brochure, which lists her published works, and her letter to me, February 20, 1978.
47. Quoted from the record jacket, Composers Recordings Inc., CRI 172.
48. *Musical America,* June 1975, p. 21.
49. Information about Katherine Hoover comes from a 1999 letter and clippings from the composer herself.
50. Interview with David Futrelle, *Chicago Tribune,* September 30, 1997.
51. Interview with Futrelle, *Chicago Tribune,* September 30, 1997.

CHAPTER 7. GRASS ROOTS—
COMPOSERS IN AMERICAN IDIOMS

1. Chase, *America's Music,* p. 209.
2. Southern, *Readings in Black American Music,* p. 139.
3. Quoted in Southern, *The Music of Black Americans,* 1st ed., p. 200.
4. For basic information about these women I have relied on Chase, *America's Music,* pp. 405–6; Howard, *Our American Music: A Comprehensive History;* and *Baker's Biographical Dictionary.*
5. Reported in *Etude,* August 1893.
6. M. S. Green, "Consider These Creators," p. 11.

7. Southern, *The Music of Black Americans,* 3rd ed., p. 428, and Doris Evans Mc-
   Ginty, "'As Large as She Can Make It'—The Role of Black Women Activists in
   Music, 1880–1945," chapter 7 in Locke and Barr, *Cultivating Music.*

8. For biographical information about Julia Smith I have relied on the following:
   Vinton, *Dictionary of Contemporary Music,* pp. 687–88; Howard, *Our American
   Music,* p. 569; Craig, "Julia Smith: Composer and Ambassadress of U.S. Music";
   program notes by the composer for Columbia University concert, November 7,
   1976.

9. From Julia Smith's letter to me, December 30, 1975, written shortly after her
   husband's death.

10. Smith, *Aaron Copland,* p. 10.

11. From program notes by Smith for the Decade of International Women concert,
    November 7, 1976, at Columbia University's McMillin Theatre, New York City.

12. *New York Herald Tribune,* May 15, 1950, quoted in Howard, *Our American
    Music.*

13. From Smith's letter to me.

14. Biographical material for Radie Britain is from Reis, *Composers in America,* 1st ed.,
    pp. 51–52; Goss, *Modern Music Makers: Contemporary American Composers,* pp.
    347ff; and a letter from Britain to me, April 27, 1978.

15. From Frederick Douglass, *My Bondage and My Freedom,* 1855, quoted by South-
    ern, *Readings in Black American Music,* pp. 83ff.

16. According to Eileen Southern in her excellent book, *The Music of Black Americans,*
    the greater body of the blacks' social music—work songs, play songs, dance songs,
    story songs, songs of social comment, satirical songs, field hollers, and street cries
    —was largely ignored. Spirituals were an amalgamation of many elements—the
    psalmody of the early American churches, later Protestant hymnody, Anglo-
    Saxon ballads, and even French band music. They were sung during actual wor-
    ship services in church, for funerals and other sorrowful occasions, and for shouts,
    a kind of religious dance in which the dancers moved in a circle using a kind of
    rhythmic shuffling step with a jerking, hitching motion, accompanied by a group
    of singers who also provided percussion accompaniment by clapping their hands
    or hitting their knees or thighs.

17. Zora Neale Hurston, "Spirituals and Neo-spirituals," in Patterson, *The Negro in
    Music and Art,* pp. 15–17.

18. Southern, *The Music of Black Americans,* 1st ed., p. 213.

19. Southern, *The Music of Black Americans,* 1st ed., pp. 100–4.

20. Most biographical information about Florence Price is from M. D. Green, "A
    Study of the Lives and Works of Five Black Women Composers," and Yuhasz,
    "Black Composers and Their Piano Music." A full-scale biography of Price by Rae
    Linda Brown is in production at the time of this writing.

21. Margaret Bonds, "A Reminiscence," in Patterson, *The Negro in Music and Art,* pp.
    190–93.

22. For biographical information about Margaret Bonds I have relied on her "Rem-
    iniscence," in Patterson, *The Negro in Music and Art;* on M. D. Green, "A Study
    of the Lives and Works of Five Black Women Composers "; and on Yuhasz,
    "Black Composers and Their Piano Music."

23. Bonds, "A Reminiscence," in Patterson, *The Negro in Music and Art.*

24. M. D. Green, "A Study of the Lives and Works of Five Black Women Com-
    posers," p. 143.

25. Roach, *Black American Music: Past and Present,* p. 113.
26. Bonds, "A Reminiscence," in Patterson, *The Negro in Music and Art,* p. 192.
27. For information about Julia Perry I have relied on M. D. Green, "A Study of the Lives and Works of Five Black Women Composers"; Southern, *Music of Black Americans;* Howard, *Our American Music,* p. 613; and a letter from Perry to me, April 24, 1978.
28. M. D. Green, "A Study of the Lives and Works of Five Black Women Composers," pp. 195–213.
29. M. D. Green, "A Study of the Lives and Works of Five Black Women Composers," pp. 255–85.
30. J. Michele Edwards, in Pendle, *Women and Music: A History,* pp. 212–14.
31. Published in *American Music,* Summer 1986, p. 202.
32. Walker-Hill, *Black Women Composers;* also an e-mail from her daughter, Janis Rozena Peri, August 21, 1999.
33. V. Taylor, *Art Songs and Spirituals.*
34. Information about Alice Parker comes principally from program notes, a letter written by the composer to me in May 1978, the composer's web site, and the newsletter of Melodious Accord.
35. Newsletter of Melodious Accord, June 1999, vol. 14, no. 3.
36. For information about Gena Branscombe I have relied on Goss, *Modern Music Makers,* pp. 82–90; Reis, *Composers in America,* 1st ed., pp. 47–48; Howard, *Our American Music,* p. 634; "Showcase" (no author), *Music Clubs Magazine,* Special Issue, 1962; and Elkins-Marlow, "Gena Branscombe: American Composer and Conductor."
37. Goss, *Modern Music Makers,* p. 87.
38. "Showcase," *Music Clubs Magazine,* Special Issue, 1962, p. 9.
39. "Showcase," *Music Clubs Magazine,* Special Issue, 1962, p. 9.
40. Max Morath, "May Aufderheide and the Ragtime Women," in Hasse, *Ragtime: Its History, Composers, and Music.*
41. Most of the information on black women jazz composers comes from Plackson, *American Women in Jazz.*
42. Dahl, *Stormy Weather,* p. 117.
43. Dahl, *Stormy Weather,* p. 25.
44. Dahl, *Stormy Weather,* p. 61.
45. Dahl, *Stormy Weather,* p. 66.
46. *Downbeat* interview of 1957, quoted by Dahl, *Stormy Weather,* p. 67.
47. Interview with Bob Blumenthal, *Boston Globe,* November 6, 1998.
48. Information from Plackson, *American Women in Jazz,* and Dahl, *Stormy Weather.*
49. Information about Liston comes from Gourse, *Madame Jazz,* and an obituary by Peter Watrous, *New York Times,* April 30, 1999.
50. Information about León comes from a review by Walter Aaron Clark in *American Music,* Fall 1997, vol. 15, no. 3, pp. 421–22, and from Handy, *Black Conductors,* pp. 315–320.
51. Information about Chen Yi comes from the composer's web site and the Women's Philharmonic.
52. *IAWM Journal,* vol. 4, no. 1, Winter 1998, p. 46.
53. Information about Lam Bun-Ching comes from the composer's web site and the Women's Philharmonic.

CHAPTER 8. OPERA COMPOSERS
AND CONDUCTORS

1. Hipsher, *American Opera and Its Composers,* pp. 321–22.
2. For information about Eleanor Everest Freer I have relied on Hipsher, *American Opera,* pp. 183–89; Freer, *Recollections and Reflections of an American Composer;* and Foster, *Eleanor Everest Freer—Patriot and Her Colleagues.*
3. Hipsher, *American Opera,* pp. 353–55.
4. Hipsher, *American Opera,* pp. 256–58, and *Etude,* May 1928.
5. *Musical America,* July 17, 1909.
6. *Etude,* April 1916.
7. *Musical America,* July 24, 1909; Barnes, *American Women in Creative Music,* pp. 9, 10; program notes, *Sacramento Souvenir* (Music and Art), 1907.
8. Information about Mary Carr Moore comes from Howard, *Our American Music,* from contemporary papers and journals, and from Smith and Richardson, *Mary Carr Moore, American Composer,* a full-scale biography.
9. Grandval is listed in *Baker's Biographical Dictionary.* See also *Etude,* July 1909, p. 446.
10. *Baker's Biographical Dictionary,* and Goldin, *The Music Merchants,* p. 110.
11. Information about Emma Steiner has been exceptionally difficult to obtain. A pamphlet edited by Margaret I. MacDonald, *The Greatest Battles Ever Fought Are the Silent Ones Fought by Women,* published on March 17, 1918, is the only source of biographical information I could locate, but it conflicts in some details with paragraphs published in various music journals, notably the *Musical Record,* January 1897, p. 2; *Folio,* March 1891, p. 90; *Etude,* March 1897; *Women in Music,* November 1935; Petrides, "Women in Orchestras," in *Etude,* July 1938; and the *New York Times* obituary, February 27, 1929.
12. *Freund's Weekly,* August 29, 1891.
13. *Freund's Weekly,* February 12, 1896.
14. *Etude,* March 1897.
15. Andrew Porter, *New Yorker,* January 26, 1970, p. 90.
16. Information on Caldwell is largely based on Donal Henahan, "Prodigious Sarah," *New York Times Magazine,* October 5, 1975, and Robert Jones, "Walking into the Fire," *Opera News,* February 14, 1976.
17. Richard Dyer, *New York Times,* January 11, 1976.
18. Interview with Raymond Ericson, *New York Times,* January 7, 1977.
19. Interview with Raymond Ericson, *New York Times,* January 7, 1977, and Walker, *Women Today: Ten Profiles,* pp. 75–89.
20. Joseph Horowitz, *New York Times,* April 24, 1978.
21. Interview with Raymond Ericson, *New York Times,* January 7, 1977.
22. Walker, *Women Today: Ten Profiles,* pp. 87–88.
23. Anthony Tommasini, *New York Times,* April 19, 1999.
24. Biographical information about Judith Somogi comes from Allen Hughes, *New York Times,* March 15, 1974; Raymond Ericson, *New York Times,* May 8, 1977; and a press release from Herbert Barrett Management, New York, April 12, 1977.
25. *New York Times,* June 4, 1977.
26. Quoted by Jepson, "American Women in Conducting," p. 18.
27. Ericson, *New York Times,* May 8, 1977.

28. Biographical information on Masiello is from Deborah Seabury, "La Maestra," *Opera News,* February 14, 1976.

29. Deborah Seabury, "La Maestra," *Opera News,* February 14, 1976.

30. Material about Glanville-Hicks comes from a 1969 brochure from Broadcast Music, Inc., New York; Howard, *Our American Music,* p. 566; and correspondence from the composer herself in 1978.

31. George Antheil, "Peggy Glanville-Hicks," *American Composers Alliance Bulletin,* vol. 4, no. 1, 1954.

32. Thomson, *American Music Since 1910,* p. 12.

33. Glanville-Hicks described the exhibit in a letter to me, June 1, 1978.

34. Information about Musgrave comes from Bradshaw, "Thea Musgrave"; Shirley Fleming, *New York Times,* September 25, 1977; Andrew Porter, *New Yorker,* November 24, 1975; and *Time,* October 10, 1977, p. 72.

35. Searle and Laton, *Twentieth Century Composers,* vol. 3.

36. Quoted by Shirley Fleming, *New York Times,* September 25, 1977.

37. Andrew Porter, *New Yorker,* October 24, 1977.

38. Harold C. Schonberg, *New York Times,* October 2, 1977.

39. Quoted by Shirley Fleming, *New York Times,* September 25, 1977.

40. Andrew Porter, *New Yorker,* May 1, 1978.

41. Harold C. Schonberg, *New York Times,* March 31, 1978.

42. *Opera News,* February 14, 1976.

43. Information about Garwood comes from her correspondence, 1978, 1999.

44. Information about Van de Vate comes from correspondence from the composer, 1976–99.

45. Information about Larsen comes from correspondence from the composer, 1999.

46. Interview with Susan Chastain, *IAWM Journal,* vol. 2, no. 1, February 1996.

47. Composers of opera discussed in other chapters because they are notable principally for work in other forms are Amy Beach (Chapter 4); Ethel Leginska (Chapter 5); Louise Talma (Chapter 6); Julia Perry, Julia Smith, Radie Britain, Evelyn LaRue Pittman, Lena Johnson McLin, Zenobia Powell Perry, Betty Jackson King, Dorothy Rudd Moore, Alice Parker, Carla Bley, Tania León, and Lam Bun-Ching (Chapter 7); Marga Richter, Lucia Dlugoszewski, Shulamit Ran, Sorrel Hays, Stefania de Kenessey, Tina Davidson, and Augusta Read Thomas (Chapter 9); Alice Shields, Meredith Monk, Laurie Anderson, and Beth Anderson (Chapter 10); Miriam Gideon, Vivian Fine, Dorothy James, and Emma Lou Diemer (Chapter 11).

CHAPTER 9. CONTEMPORARY AND POSTMODERN IDIOMS—AFTER 1950

1. Baker-Carr, *Evening at Symphony,* p. 141.

2. Information about Richter comes from correspondence and phone conversations from the composer herself, 1978, 1999.

3. *San Francisco Chronicle,* December 12, 1957.

4. Unsigned review, *Long Player,* May 1958, and Oliver Daniel, *Saturday Review,* December 26, 1959.

5. R. L. Cherry, *Tucson Tonight,* May 25, 1976, reprinted in part in *High Fidelity/ Musical America,* July 1976.

6. Jacket notes of Leonarda CD LE 337, 1992.
7. Michael Redmond, *Newark Star-Ledger,* May 26, 1995.
8. Jocelyn Mackey, *Pan Pipes,* Summer, 1997.
9. Basil DePinto, *The Montclarion,* February 11, 1992.
10. Letter from Richter to me, June 1999.
11. Information about Schonthal comes from correspondence and a brochure from her German publisher, Furore Verlag.
12. Biographical information about Mamlok comes from correspondence from the composer herself, 1978 and 1999, and from Broadcast Music, Inc., *The Many Worlds of Music,* Issue 4, 1977, p. 31.
13. Mamlok in interview with David L. Sills, *ILWC Journal,* October 1993, p. 7.
14. Biographical information about Mekeel comes from record jacket notes, Delos 25405, *Premiere Performances by Boston Musica Viva,* and from correspondence with the composer herself, 1978.
15. Richard Dyer, *Boston Globe,* October 17, 1998.
16. Biographical material about Dlugoszewski comes from Vinton, *Dictionary of Contemporary Music,* pp. 185–87; Thomson, *American Music Since 1910,* p. 139; Broadcast Music, Inc., *The Many Worlds of Music,* Issue 4, 1977, p. 17; and Gagne, *Soundpieces 2: Interviews with American Composers,* pp. 55ff.
17. Published in *Main Currents,* 1971.
18. Thomson, *American Music Since 1910,* p. 139.
19. George Gelles, *New York Times,* April 11, 1976.
20. Raymond Ericson, *New York Times,* December 10, 1975.
21. Gagne, *Soundpieces 2: Interviews with American Composers,* p. 66.
22. Information from Zwilich herself.
23. Robert Schwarz, *Norton/Grove Dictionary of Women Composers.*
24. Robert Schwarz, *New York Times,* March 22, 1998.
25. Jacket notes, Delos recording, 1997.
26. James R. Oestreich, *New York Times,* March 3, 1999.
27. Information about Ran comes from *The Instrumentalist,* December 1976; curriculum vitae at American Music Center, New York, and University of Chicago; and a letter from the composer to me, July 9, 1978.
28. *High Fidelity/Musical America,* July 1975, p. MA-29.
29. Quoted by Cynthia Folio, *IAWM Journal,* vol. 3, no. 2, June 1997, p. 34.
30. Biographical information about Simons comes mainly from correspondence with her, 1977–78, and from Broadcast Music, Inc., *The Many Worlds of Music,* Issue 4, 1977, pp. 43, 46.
31. Information about Tucker comes from correspondence with the composer, 1977–78, and telephone conversation, 1999.
32. Biographical information about Kolb comes from interviews with Donal Henahan, *New York Times,* November 17, 1976, and Richard Dyer, *Boston Globe,* February 18, 1978; jacket notes of Turnabout TVS 34487 and Desto 7143; Vinton, *Dictionary of Contemporary Music;* and Boosey and Hawkes brochure.
33. Information about Hays comes from correspondence with the composer, 1999.
34. Information about LeBaron comes from the composer's web site and from Gagne, *Soundpieces 2,* pp. 155–74.
35. Information about Davidson comes from correspondence with the composer, 1999.
36. Information about Wolfe comes from the composer's web page.

37. Information about Wagner comes from the composer's publisher, G. Schirmer, 1999.
38. Information about Higdon comes from correspondence with the composer, 1999.
39. *USA Today,* December 30, 1996.
40. Paul Griffiths, *New York Times,* February 28, 1999.
41. Information about de Kenessey comes from correspondence and telephone conversations with the composer, 1998, 1999.
42. Interview with David Futrelle, *Chicago Tribune,* September 30, 1997.

CHAPTER 10. ELECTRONIC MUSIC, MIXED MEDIA, FILM, PERFORMANCE ART

1. Letter from Laurie Spiegel to me, August 30, 1978.
2. Information about Ivey comes from correspondence with the composer herself, 1977–78, and from Joseph McLellan, *Washington Post,* November 10, 1974; Sam di Bonaventura, Baltimore Symphony Orchestra, program notes for *Testament of Eve,* April 21–22, 1976; and Jean Eichelberger Ivey, "Observations by Composers," in Schwartz, *Electronic Music: A Listener's Guide,* pp. 230–33.
3. Ivey in Schwartz, *Electronic Music,* p. 231.
4. Biographical information about Semegen comes principally from correspondence with the composer, 1977–78 and 1999, and from Broadcast Music, Inc., *The Many Worlds of Music,* Issue 4, 1977, pp. 41–42.
5. Joan Reinthaler, *Washington Post,* January 31, 1988.
6. Edward Rothstein, *New York Times,* May 3, 1992.
7. Information about Rubin comes from correspondence with the composer, 1999.
8. Information about Shields comes from correspondence with the composer, 1999.
9. Information about Spiegel comes from correspondence with the composer, 1999.
10. John Rockwell, *New York Times,* September 19, 1976.
11. Cole Gagne, *Soundpieces 2: Interviews with American Composers,* pp. 297–332.
12. Kyle Gann, liner notes for *Unseen Worlds,* CD, Aesthetic Engineering, 1994.
13. Philip Nobel, *New York Times,* April 29, 1999.
14. Information about Ciani comes from correspondence with the composer, 1978 and 1999, and an interview with Helen Epstein, *New York Times,* June 21, 1974.
15. Joel Chadabe in Appleton and Perera, *The Development and Practice of Electronic Music,* pp. 139–40, 143.
16. Information about McLean comes from correspondence with the composer, 1998, 1999.
17. Information about Smiley comes from correspondence and telephone conversation with the composer herself, 1978, 1999.
18. Record jacket notes, *Electronic Music,* vol. 4, Turnabout TV 34301.
19. From my telephone conversation with Smiley, July 11, 1999.
20. Swados, *Listening Out Loud: Becoming a Composer,* pp. 181–2.
21. Information about Morley comes from correspondence with the composer, 1999.
22. Information about Walker comes from correspondence with the composer, 1999.
23. Information about Karpman comes from correspondence with the composer, 1999.
24. Information about Monk comes from Jowett, *Meredith Monk,* and Duckworth, *Talking Music,* pp. 345–67.

25. Debra Cash, *Boston Globe,* April 16, 1999.

26. Information about Laurie Anderson comes from Duckworth, *Talking Music,* pp. 368–85.

27. Liner notes for *Urban Tropics* on the CD *Sound Paintings,* Lovely Music, Ltd., CD 3001, 1991.

28. Information about Oliveros comes principally from a biography by Barney Childs in Vinton, *Dictionary of Contemporary Music;* Pauline Oliveros, "Observations by Composers," in Schwartz, *Electronic Music,* pp. 246–49; John Rockwell, *New York Times,* September 23, 1977 and March 26, 1978; Gunden, *The Music of Pauline Oliveros;* and a little from Cole Gagne's *Soundpieces 2,* pp. 209ff.

29. Quoted by Barney Childs in Vinton, *Dictionary of Contemporary Music,* p. 530.

30. Gordon Mumma, in Appleton and Perera, *The Development and Practice of Electronic Music,* pp. 329–30.

31. Pauline Oliveros, "Observations by Composers," in Schwartz, *Electronic Music,* p. 248.

32. John Rockwell, *New York Times,* Sept. 23, 1977.

33. John Rockwell, *New York Times,* March 26, 1978.

34. Smith and Smith, *New Voices,* p. 285.

35. William Osborne, *IAWM Journal,* vol. 5, no. 1, Winter 1999.

36. Daniel C. Adams, "Women Composers and the Noble Snare," *ILWC Journal,* October 1992, pp. 1–2.

37. Information about Beth Anderson comes from correspondence with the composer, 1977–78, 1999.

38. Robert Palmer, *New York Times,* May 16, 1978.

39. Michael Sahl, *IAWM Journal,* vol. 3, no. 3, Fall 1997, p. 11.

CHAPTER 11. TODAY'S ORCHESTRAS, CONDUCTORS, AND INSTRUMENTALISTS

1. Shanet, *Philharmonic: A History of New York's Orchestra,* pp. 107–8.

2. Shanet, *Philharmonic: A History of New York's Orchestra,* p. 347.

3. *Musical Herald,* November 1891.

4. LeClair joined the orchestra in 1981 at age twenty-three and by 1999 had made more than forty solo appearances with it, including in *The Five Trees* in 1995, a bassoon concerto written for her by John Williams.

5. James R. Oestreich, *New York Times,* April 25, 1999. Tomoko Masur, wife of music director Kurt Masur, commissioned the renowned Russian composer Sofia Gubaidulina to write a concerto for two violas for them, and they premiered the work, *Two Paths,* with the New York Philharmonic in 1999.

6. Jerzy Bojanowsky, "Championing the Woman Orchestral Player," *Musical Courier,* January 15, 1945. Hope Stoddard in "Fine Musicianship Knows No Sex," *Independent Woman,* November 1947, said women had broken into eighteen major orchestras: sixty-six violins; twelve violas; twenty-one cellos; seven double basses; four piccolos; seven flutes; four oboes; one English horn; five bassoons; three French horns; two trombones; two percussionists; twenty-one harps. But she contended that most think a woman must play better than a man to get the same job.

7. Elicia Hill, "A Tribute to Betty Glover," *ITA Journal* [International Trombone Association], Spring 1986, pp. 12–15. Glover held the job for four years, then became principal bass trombone with the Cincinnati Symphony and taught at the Cincinnati Conservatory.

8. *Etude,* February 1916.

9. Beecham, "The Position of Women." He also maintained that "there are no women composers, never have been, and possibly never will be."

10. *Etude,* April 1931.

11. Ethel Smyth, *Female Pipings in Eden,* pp. 10–11.

12. Drinker, *Music and Women,* p. 239.

13. Rich, *Careers and Opportunities in Music,* p. 129. Fisher agrees in *Musical Prodigies: Masters at an Early Age,* p. 176.

14. Information about Dwyer comes principally from *Opera News,* February 14, 1976; an interview with Richard Dyer, *Boston Globe,* January 15, 1978; *Christian Science Monitor,* October 7, 1952; and Helen Epstein, "Notes from the Orchestra Pit," *MS,* March 1977.

15. In 1979, there were still eleven women and ninety-five men. The Appendix indicates the numbers increased after that.

16. Boston Symphony archivist, telephone call, July 20, 1999. In 2000 Marylou Speaker Churchill resigned after thirty years with the orchestra, leaving only one woman principal.

17. *New York Times,* February 3, 1998, and Atlanta Symphony Orchestra roster, July 23, 1999.

18. Told to me privately; I am protecting the source's name.

19. *IAWM Journal,* October 1996, p. 9.

20. Reported by Susan Fleet, trumpeter and teacher, formerly at Berklee School of Music.

21. *Etude,* April, 1917.

22. *Women in Music,* June 1, 1938.

23. The figures come from the American Federation of Musicians and are approximate because the number varies depending on the dues status of members.

24. Powell, "The Violinist."

25. It is interesting to compare this with figures released by the American Federation of Musicians for 1967. The average annual salary for a member of a major symphony was $6900 for thirty-seven weeks; in a small ensemble, up to $200 per concert; in a dance band, $60 to $300 per week.

26. Otis, *The Chicago Symphony Orchestra: Its Growth and Development 1891–1924,* p. 351.

27. L. M. Smith, "Is There a Career for Women Musicians?"

28. Fleet, "Dorothy Miriam Ziegler," pp. 1543–44.

29. *New York Times,* December 21, 1975, p. 36, and December 19, 1976.

30. These figures come from Jeffrey Ostergren, Information Resources Assistant, American Symphony Orchestra League, July 21, 1999.

31. Figures supplied by the American Federation of Musicians.

32. Hart, *Orpheus in the New World,* pp. 110, 115–16.

33. Statistics and calculation from John M. Ammer, economist, Federal Reserve Board of Governors.

34. A summary published in *Music Journal,* January 1972, gave the following figures: New York Philharmonic, 3 women, 103 men; Philadelphia Orchestra, 9

women, 99 men; Boston Symphony Orchestra, 8 women, 93 men; Chicago Symphony, 4 women, 100 men; Cleveland Orchestra, 14 women, 94 men.

35. Julia Allmendiger and J. Richard Hackman, "The More, the Better? A Four-Nation Study of the Inclusion of Women in Symphony Orchestras," *Social Forces,* vol. 7, no. 2, December 1995, pp. 23–40. The other nations studied were the United Kingdom, Germany, and Austria.

36. Melinda Whiting, *Symphony,* vol. 50, no. 4, July/August 1999.

37. From *Wage Scales and Conditions in Symphony Orchestras, 1998–99,* published by the American Federation of Musicians.

38. Information about the Elayne Jones case comes from the following sources: *New York Times,* August 2, 1974, and August 27, 1975; Richard Dyer, *Boston Globe,* September 21, 1975; Helen Epstein, "Notes from the Orchestra Pit," *MS,* March 1977.

39. Monique Buzzarté, *IAWM Journal,* February 1996.

40. Information comes from correspondence and telephone conversation with Slaughter herself, 1999.

41. Information on Clark comes from material put together by Katherine D. Moore from Clark's and her own files and sent to me June 24, 1979. Moore was a pupil of Clark's, played in the orchestra from 1927 to 1972, and wrote much of its publicity.

42. Information about Kleinhenn (later Thompson and still later Edmister) comes from a letter from her to me, March 8, 1978; a telephone interview with me, February 14, 1978; and clippings from contemporary New Mexico papers *(Albuquerque Advance, Albuquerque Journal, New Mexico State Tribune)* and the Ohio *Defiance Crescent News.*

43. *Freund's Weekly,* May 13, 1896.

44. Elaine Fine, "A Look at Changing Attitudes Toward Women in Orchestras," *Signature,* vol. 1, no. 4, Spring/Summer 1996, p. 13; Ralph Blumenthal, *New York Times,* September 30, 1999.

45. James R. Oestreich, *New York Times,* January 17, 1999.

46. Bowen, "Women in Music: Their Fair Share," p. MA-20.

47. Helen Epstein, "Selling Tomorrow's Big Names Today," *New York Times,* February 15, 1976.

48. Information about Bergen comes mainly from an interview with Joseph Horowitz, *New York Times,* January 14, 1977.

49. Joseph Horowitz, *New York Times,* November 8, 1976.

50. *Etude,* April 1931.

51. *Etude,* October 1931.

52. *Etude,* April 1933.

53. *Etude,* March 1927.

54. Southern, *The Music of Black Americans,* 3rd ed., pp. 422–3.

55. *Etude,* July 1924.

56. *Etude,* February 1972.

57. Information about Moyse is from Brattleboro Music Center, Marianne Shaughnessy, Administrator, July 1999.

58. Michael Kimmelman, *New York Times,* December 24, 1987.

59. Information about Hillis comes from the 1978 Program Notes of the Chicago Symphony Orchestra; *Pan Pipes,* May 1976, p. 22; *Time,* August 2, 1976; and articles by Donal Henahan and Raymond Ericson, *New York Times,* November 2, 1977.

60. Alan Kozinn, *New York Times* obituary, February 6, 1998.
61. Interview with Richard Dyer, *Boston Globe,* March 28, 1978.
62. Information about Hiatt is from her obituary, *Daily Hampshire Gazette,* January 7, 1980.
63. Information about Kaiser comes from an interview with me, July 13, 1999.
64. Information about Clurman comes from correspondence with her, 1999.
65. Alan Kozinn, *New York Times,* October 15, 1991.
66. Information about Thomas comes from correspondence with her, 1999.
67. In *IAWM Journal,* Fall 1998, p. 31.
68. For much of the information in the succeeding paragraphs on Harris, Steiner, and Brown, I have relied on Jepson, "American Women in Conducting."
69. Quoted by Jepson, "American Women in Conducting," p. 14.
70. Information about Hamilton is from her interview with me, June 2, 1999.
71. Additional information about Steiner is from correspondence with her, 1999.
72. Information about Tamarkin comes from her web page.
73. Information about Bond comes mainly from *International Musician,* vol. 74, no. 1, July 1975; Herbert Kupferberg, "Women of the Baton—The New Music Masters," *Parade,* May 14, 1978; and from correspondence with Bond herself, 1978, 1999.
74. "Career Alternatives in Music: Some Advice from Outstanding Women Musicians," *Instrumentalist,* December 1976, p. 34.
75. Mike Antonucci, *San Jose Mercury,* January 17, 1999, based on information from the American Symphony Orhestra League.
76. Debbie Rittner, *The Cambridge Current,* November 22–December 6, 1996.
77. James R. Oestreich, *New York Times,* March 11, 1999.
78. Starr, "The Prejudice Against Women."
79. For Robison I have relied on an interview with John Gruen, *New York Times,* January 9, 1977, and the biography issued by her manager, Kazuko Hillyer International, Inc., June 1977.
80. *Instrumentalist,* December 1976, p. 37.

CHAPTER 12. TEACHING MUSIC

1. Van de Vate, "Every Good Boy (Composer) Does Fine."
2. In answer to my questionnaire, July 1978.
3. According to an ad in *Daily Aurora,* quoted by Gerson, *Music in Philadelphia,* p. 366.
4. F. L. Ritter, *Music in America,* pp. 261ff.
5. *History of Music in San Francisco,* vol. 1, p. 196.
6. Krueger, *The Musical Heritage of the United States,* pp. 24–25.
7. Keefer, *Music Angels: A Hundred Years of Patronage,* pp. 166–67.
8. Krueger, *The Musical Heritage of the United States,* p. 25.
9. *Dwight's Journal,* July 7, 1860, quoted by Petra Meyer Frasier, *Sonneck Society for American Music Bulletin,* vol. 24, no. 1, Spring 1998, p. 1.
10. Tick, "Women as Professional Musicians in the United States, 1870–1900," p. 97.
11. *Etude,* August 1909.
12. F. O. Jones, *Handbook of American Music and Musicians,* p. 32.

13. Loesser, *Men, Women, and Pianos,* p. 478.
14. For information about Clara and Bertha Baur and their school, I have relied on Bertha Baur, "The Cincinnati Conservatory of Music," *Musical Observer,* May 1913, and Board, *Bertha Baur: A Woman of Note.*
15. Thomas, *A Musical Autobiography,* pp. 80, 180.
16. Emanuel Rubin, "Jeannette Meyers Thurber and the National Conservatory of Music," *American Music* vol. 8, Fall 1990, pp. 294–325.
17. *Women in Music,* vol. 5, no. 4, April 1940.
18. Doris Evans McGinty, "'As Large as She Can Make It'—The Role of Black Women Activists in Music, 1800–1945," chapter 7 in Locke and Barr, *Cultivating Music in America.*
19. Information about Schenck and Spofford comes from files in the Sophia Smith Women's History Archive at Smith College.
20. S. Margaret William McCarthy, in *IAWM Journal,* February 1996.
21. Wier, *The Piano, Its History, Makers, Players, and Music.*
22. *Etude,* November 1888, p. 166.
23. Ward, *Careers in Music,* p. 111.
24. These figures were assembled by Susan Fleet and conveyed to me through correspondence, 1999.
25. *Musical Herald,* June 1880, p. 143.
26. *Musical Age,* March 17, 1898.
27. Raymond Ericson, *New York Times,* November 11, 1976; Harold C. Schonberg, *New York Times,* November 11 and 21, 1976; and Wallace, *A Century of Music-Making: The Lives of Josef and Rosina Lhévinne.*
28. Information about Weigl comes principally from correspondence with the composer herself, 1978.
29. Block, "The Woman Musician on Campus: Hiring and Promotion Patterns."
30. Van de Vate, "Notes from a Bearded Lady: The American Woman Composer."
31. *Instrumentalist,* December 1976, pp. 36–37. Van de Vate herself eventually left academe; see Chapter 8 for more on her career.
32. Correspondence with Susan Fleet, 1999. Of 337 faculty members, sixty, or 18 percent, were women; of 150 full-time faculty, only nine were women. No women and eleven men were in the bass performance department; one woman, Susan Fleet, and four men were in the brass department. Only in the voice department did women outnumber men: thirteen women, but only three full time, compared to three men, all full time.
33. Names are omitted to protect these women's privacy.
34. Biographical information about Gideon comes chiefly from correspondence with the composer, 1978, and from Broadcast Music, Inc., *The Many Worlds of Music,* Issue 4, 1977.
35. Linda Ardito, "Miriam Gideon, A Memorial Tribute," *Perspectives of New Music* 34/2, Summer 1996, p. 208; quoted by Ellie Hisama, "(Re)discovering Miriam Gideon," *ISAM Newsletter,* vol. 27, no. 2, Spring 1998.
36. Ellie Hisama, "(Re)discovering Miriam Gideon," *ISAM Newsletter,* vol. 27, no. 2, Spring 1998.
37. Liner notes, *Miriam Gideon Retrospective,* New World Records, NW 80393-2.
38. Perle, "The Music of Miriam Gideon."
39. Record jacket, Composers Recordings, Inc., CRI SD 286.
40. Allen Hughes, *New York Times,* December 18, 1975.

41. Quoted by Ellie Hisama, "(Re)discovering Miriam Gideon," *ISAM Newsletter,* vol. 27, no. 2, Spring 1998.
42. Biographical information about Fine comes principally from correspondence with the composer, 1978.
43. Interview with Joan McKinney, *Oakland Tribune,* April 2, 1975.
44. Riegger, "The Music of Vivian Fine," p. 2.
45. Doris Humphrey, "Music for an American Dance," *American Composers Alliance Bulletin,* vol. 8, no. 1, 1958, p. 5.
46. Riegger, "The Music of Vivian Fine," pp. 2–3.
47. *New York Times,* April 17, 1973.
48. J. Michele Edwards in Pendle, *Women and Music: A History,* pp. 218–19.
49. Interview with Joan McKinney, *Oakland Tribune,* April 2, 1975.
50. Information about James comes principally from correspondence with the composer, 1977–78.
51. Letter from James to me, January 27, 1978.
52. Information about Diemer comes from correspondence with the composer, 1978, 1999.
53. Information about Polin comes from an obituary by Daniel Webster, *Philadelphia Inquirer,* December 8, 1995.
54. Information about Barkin comes from correspondence with the composer, 1978, 1999.
55. Information about Cory comes from correspondence with the composer, 1978, 1999.
56. In *IAWM Journal,* vol. 1, no. 2, October 1995, p. 37.
57. Information about Zaimont comes from correspondence with the composer, 1978, 1999.
58. Raymond Ericson, *New York Times,* November 20, 1975.
59. Linda Ostrander, *ILWC Journal,* June 1994, p. 41.
60. From an interview in *Fanfare,* vol. 19, no. 5, May/June 1996, p. 34.
61. Information about Niederberger comes from correspondence with the composer, 1999.
62. Letter from Niederberger to me, June 11, 1999.
63. Information about Shatin comes from correspondence with the composer, 1999.
64. Anna Larson, *ILWC Journal,* October 1994.
65. Interview with Richard Kessler, "In the First Person," *NewMusicBox,* February 1999. http://www.newmusicbox.org/archive/firstperson/larsen/index.html.

CHAPTER 13. ANGELS AND ADVOCATES

1. F. L. Ritter, *Music in America,* p. 277.
2. Hart, *Orpheus in the New World,* pp. 120–21.
3. Lubov Keefer, *Music Angels: A Thousand Years of Patronage.*
4. Sablosky, *American Music,* pp. 105–6.
5. Linda Whitesitt, "Women as 'Keepers of Culture,'" chapter 2 in Locke and Barr, *Cultivating Music in America.*
6. For information about black women's clubs I have relied on Doris Evans McGinty, "'As Large as She Can Make It'—The Role of Black Women Activists in Music, 1880–1945," chapter 7 in Locke and Barr, *Cultivating Music in America.*

7. Cyrilla Barr,"A Style of Her Own," chapter 6 in Locke and Barr, *Cultivating Music in America.* Barr also has written a complete biography of Coolidge, *Elizabeth Sprague Coolidge, American Patron of Music.*

8. Carol Neuls-Bates, "Foundation Support for Women in Music," *The Status of Women in College Music: Preliminary Study,* College Music Society Report no. 1, 1976.

9. *Etude,* May 1916.

10. The attendance record is held by Mabel Daniels, who was there twenty-four times between 1914 and 1947. The others of the twenty-six were Ballou, Emilie Frances Bauer, Branscombe, Britain, Cory, Crawford, Diller, Garwood, Gideon, James, Kolb, Mekeel, Polin, Semegen, Tower, Tureck, Weigl, and Zaimont. Since 1978 forty women composers have been fellows there, including Barkin, Parker, Shatin, and (again) Kolb and Talma. The source is the MacDowell Colony's unpublished list of fellows.

11. Information comes from the colony's 1978 brochure and from R. W. Brown, "Mrs. MacDowell and Her Colony."

12. Gayle Worland, "Clara Lyle Boone, Pioneer in Music Publishing," *IAWM Journal,* vol. 3, no. 2, June 1997, pp.16–18.

13. Information about Glickman comes from correspondence with her, 1999.

14. Information about Hall comes from correspondence with her, 1999.

BIBLIOGRAPHY

*I*N ADDITION to the books, articles, and dissertations listed in alphabetical order, I used the following clipping files, scrapbooks, and periodicals in the Boston Public Library, Music Division:

Boston, concert life in, 4 vols. in 9, 1896–.
Boston, music in, 1845–1914.
Boston, Nadia Boulanger in, 1938–39.
Boston Conservatory of Music, programs of faculty and pupils' recitals, 1870–80.
Boston Musical Education Society, 1840–56.
Boston Musical Fund Society, programs, 1847–55.
Boston Musicians Union, Constitution of the, 1863; rev. 1865.
Boston Orchestral Club, programs and reviews, 1885–91; 1899–1911.
Carnegie Hall, New York, programs, 1892–1929.
Eichberg, Julius, clippings, programs, music manuscripts, 1843–1894.
Leginska, Ethel, programs and reviews.
U.S. Secular Songsters, collection of music, to 1851.
Women's Symphony Society of Boston and Women's Symphony Orchestra, clippings and programs, 1939–42.
Yaddo, music at, clippings, 1932–46.

Boston Musical Gazette, 1838–46.
Boston Musical Times, 13 vols., 1860–70.
Dexter Smith's Musical, Literary, Dramatic and Art Paper, 14 vols., Boston, 1872–78.
Dwight's Journal of Music, 41 vols., Boston, 1853–1881.
Etude Music Magazine, 75 vols., Philadelphia, 1883–1957.
Euterpiad or Musical Intelligencer, 3 vols., Boston, 1820–1822.
Folio, 42 vols., Boston, 1869–1895.
Freund's Musical and Dramatic Times, 1875–1880; *Freund's Daily,* 1882,

1883; *Freund's Weekly: A Review of Music and Drama,* 1883–1891; *Freund's Musical Age,* 1893–1896; *Freund's Weekly,* July–November 1893; *Freund's Musical Weekly,* December 1893–January 1896. Numerous volumes all published in New York by Harry E. Freund.

Massachusetts Musical Journal (originally *Boston Musical Journal*), 1855–57.

Metronome, 3 vols., Boston, 1871–74.

Music, Chicago, 1891–1902.

Musical Age, 59 vols., New York, 1896–1908 (succeeeded *Freund's Musical Weekly*).

Musical America, New York, 1898–99; 1910–65 (succeeded *Music Trades;* after 1965 became *High Fidelity/Musical America*).

Musical Bulletin, 7 vols., New York, 1870–73.

Musical Courier, 164 vols., New York, 1880–1962.

Musical Gazette, Boston, 1847.

Musical Gazette, Boston, 1854–55.

Musical Herald, 14 vols., 1880–93.

Musical Record, 22 vols., Boston, 1878–1900.

Musical Record and Review, 3 vols., Boston, 1901–3.

Musical Review, 3 vols., New York, 1879–81.

Musical Review and Record of Musical Science, 2 vols., New York, 1938.

Music Review, 2 vols., Boston, 1898–1900.

Music Trades, New York, 1900–1911 (ed. John C. Freund).

Register of Deaths, vol. 4, p. 1218, State of Maine Archives.

Women in Music, New York, 1935–40.

Adams, Mrs. Crosby. "Musical Creative Work Among Women." *Music,* vol. 9, January 1896, p. 170.

"After God Comes Papa." *Stereo,* spring 1972.

Albuquerque, Ann. "Teresa Carreño: Pianist, Teacher and Composer." D.M.A. thesis, University of Cincinnati, 1988.

Aldrich, Richard. *Concert Life in New York 1902–23.* Edited by Harold Johnson. New York: G. P. Putnam's Sons, 1941.

Applebaum, Samuel, and Sada Applebaum. *The Way They Play.* Neptune City, New Jersey: Paganiniana Publications, 1972.

Appleton, Jon H., and Ronald C. Perera, eds. *The Development and Practice of Electronic Music.* Englewood Cliffs, New Jersey: Prentice-Hall, 1975.

Bachmann, Alberto. *An Encyclopedia of the Violin.* 1925. Reprint. New York: Da Capo Press, 1966.

Baker-Carr, Janet. *Evening at Symphony: A Portrait of the Boston Symphony Orchestra.* Boston: Houghton Mifflin, 1977.

Baker's Biographical Dictionary of Music and Musicians. 8th ed. Revised by Nicolas Slonimsky. New York: G. Schirmer, 1992.

Barkin, Elaine. "Louise Talma: 'The Tolling Bell.'" *Perspectives of New Music,* vol. 10, no. 2, Spring/Summer 1972, pp. 142–52.

Barnard, Charles. *Camilla: A Tale of a Violin.* Boston: Loring, 1874.

Barnes, Edwin N. C. *American Women in Creative Music.* Washington, D.C.: Music Education Publications, 1936.

Barr, Cyrilla. *Elizabeth Sprague Coolidge, American Patron of Music.* New York: Schirmer Books, 1998.

Bauer, Harold. *Harold Bauer, His Book.* New York: W. W. Norton, 1948.

Bauer, Marion. *Twentieth-Century Music.* New York: G. P. Putnam's Sons, 1947.

Bauer, Marion, and Ethel Peyser. *How Music Grew.* New York: G. P. Putnam's Sons, 1939.

Bazelon, Irwin A. "Woman with a Symphony." *Baton,* vol. 30, no. 3, March 1951, pp. 4–7.

Beckett, Wendy. *Peggy Glanville-Hicks.* Pymble, Australia: Angus and Robertson, 1992.

Beecham, Sir Thomas. "The Position of Women." In *Vogue's First Reader.* Garden City, New York: Halcyon House, 1944.

Berger, Arthur. *The American Composer Speaks.* Edited by Gilbert Chase. Baton Rouge: Louisiana State University Press, 1966.

———. "Stravinsky and the Younger American Composers." *The Score and I.M.A. Magazine,* no. 12, June 1955, p. 38.

Bingley, William. *Musical Biography.* 1834. Reprint. New York: Da Capo Press, 1971.

Block, Adrienne Fried. *Amy Beach, Passionate Victorian: The Life and Works of an American Composer 1867–1944.* New York: Oxford University Press, 1998.

———. "The Woman Musician on Campus: Hiring and Promotion Patterns." *High Fidelity/Musical America,* vol. 25, no. 6, June 1975, pp. MA-22–23.

Bloomfield-Zeisler, Fannie. "Women in Music." *American Art Journal,* vol. 58, no. 1, October 17, 1891, pp. 1–3.

Board, Helen. *Bertha Baur: A Woman of Note.* Philadelphia: Dorrance and Co., 1971.

Bojanowsky, Jerzy. "Championing the Woman Orchestral Player." *Musical Courier,* January 15, 1945.

Bond, Carrie Jacobs. "Music Composition as a Field for Women." *Musical Standard,* vol. 16, no. 342, October 23, 1920.

———. *The Roads of Melody.* New York: D. Appleton and Co., 1927.

Bortin, Virginia. *Elinor Remick Warren: Her Life and Her Music.* Metuchen, New Jersey: Scarecrow Press, 1987.

Bowen, Jean. "Women in Music: Their Fair Share." *High Fidelity/Musical America,* vol. 4, no. 8, August 1974.

Bowers, Jane and Judith Tick, eds. *Women Making Music: The Western Art Tradition, 1150–1950.* Urbana and Chicago: University of Illinois Press, 1986.

Bradshaw, Susan. "Thea Musgrave." *Musical Times,* vol. 104, no. 1450, December 1963, pp. 866–68.

Britain, Radie. *Ridin' Herd to Writing Symphonies: An Autobiography.* Lanham, Massachusetts: Scarecrow Press, 1996.

Brooks, Henry M. *Olden-Time Music: A Compilation from Newspapers and Books.* Boston: Ticknor and Co., 1888.

Brown, Cynthia Clark. "Emma Lou Diemer: Composer, Performer, Educator, Church Musician." Ph.D. dissertation, Southern Baptist Theological Seminary (Louisville), 1985.

Brown, Rae Linda. *The Heart of a Woman: The Life and Music of Florence B. Price.* Urbana: University of Illinois Press, forthcoming.

Brown, Rollo Walters. "Mrs. MacDowell and Her Colony." *Atlantic Monthly,* July 1949, pp. 42–46.

Bruce, Phyllis Ruth. "From Rags to Roses: The Life and Works of Carrie Jacobs-Bond, an American Composer." Master's thesis, Wesleyan University, 1980.

Burns, Don. "The Distaff'd Composers." *Music Journal,* vol. 32, no. 3, March 1974, pp. 16–17, 32–37.

Campbell, Jane. *Old Philadelphia Music.* Philadelphia: City Historical Society, 1926.

"Career Alternatives in Music: Some Advice from Outstanding Women Musicians." *The Instrumentalist,* vol. 31, December 1976, pp. 34ff.

Carreño, Teresa. *Possibilities of Tone Color by Artistic Use of Pedals.* Cincinnati: John Church Co., 1919.

Cazort, Jean E., and Constance Tibbs Hobson. *Born to Play: The Life and Career of Hazel Harrison.* Westport, Connecticut: Greenwood Press, 1983.

Chapin, Victor. *Giants of the Keyboard.* Philadelphia: J. B. Lippincott Co., 1967.

Chase, Gilbert. *America's Music.* 2d ed., rev. New York: McGraw-Hill, 1966.

———, ed. *The American Composer Speaks.* Baton Rouge: Louisiana State University Press, 1966.

Cheney, Simeon Pease. *The American Singing Book.* Boston: White, Smith and Co., 1879.

Claghorne, Charles Eugene. *The Mocking Bird: The Life and Diary of Its Author, Septimus Winner.* Philadelphia: The Magee Press, 1937.

Clark, J. Bunker. *The Dawning of American Keyboard Music.* Westport, Connecticut: Greenwood Press, 1988.

Cline, Judith. "Margaret Ruthven Lang, Her Life and Songs." Ph.D. dissertation, City University of New York, 1993.

Coolidge, Arlan R. "Maud Powell," *Notable American Women 1607–1950,* vol. 3, pp. 90–92. Cambridge, Massachusetts: Belknap Press of Harvard University Press, 1971.

Cowell, Henry, ed. *American Composers on American Music.* 1933; renewed 1961. New York: Frederick Ungar Publishing Co, 1961.

Craig, Mary. "Julia Smith: Composer and Ambassadress of U.S. Music." *Musical Courier,* July 1959, p. 7.

Crichton, Ronald, ed. *The Memoirs of Ethel Smyth.* New York: Viking Penguin, 1987.

Crothers, Stella Reid. "Women Composers of America." Biographical series in *Musical America,* vol. 10, nos. 4–26, 1909; vol. 11, nos. 1–22, 1910.

Dahl, Linda. *Stormy Weather: The Music and Lives of a Century of Jazzwomen.* New York: Pantheon Books, 1984.

———. *Morning Glory: A Biography of Mary Lou Williams.* New York: Pantheon Books, 2000.

Daniels, Mabel. *An American Girl in Munich (Impressions of a Music Student).* Boston: Little, Brown and Co., 1905.

Dart, Susan. *The Friday Club: The First Hundred Years, 1887–1987.* Chicago: Friday Club, 1987.

Dictionary of American Biography. 20 vols. Edited by Dumas Malone. New York: Charles Scribner's Sons, 1943.

———, Supplement 3. Edited by Edward T. James, 1973.

Drinker, Sophie Lewis. *Music and Women: The Story of Women in Their Relation to Music.* New York: Coward McCann, 1948.

Duckworth, William. *Talking Music: Conversations with John Cage, Philip Glass, Laurie Anderson, and Five Generations of American Experimental Composers.* New York: Schirmer Books, 1995.

Ebel, Otto. *Women Composers. A Biographical Handbook of Woman's Work in Music.* 3rd ed. Brooklyn: Chandler-Ebel Music Co., 1913.

Edwards, George Thornton. *Music and Musicians of Maine.* Portland: Southworth Press, 1928. Reprint. New York: AMS Press.

Eichberg, Julius. "Violin Techniqs." *Town and Country,* April 1879.

Elkins-Marlow, Laurine. "Gena Branscombe: American Composer and Conductor." Ph.D. dissertation, University of Texas at Austin, 1978.

Ellinwood, Leonard. *The History of American Church Music.* New York: Morehouse-Gorham Co., 1953.

Elson, Arthur. *Woman's Work in Music.* Boston: L. C. Page, 1904.

Elson, Louis C. *The History of American Music.* New York: Macmillan, 1904.

———. *Woman in Music.* New York: The University Society, 1918.

Erskine, John. *The Philharmonic Society of New York: Its First One Hundred Years.* New York: Macmillan, 1943.

Eversole, Sylvia. "Eleanor Everest Freer: Her Life and Music." Ph.D. dissertation, City University of New York, 1992.

Ewen, David. *American Composers Today.* New York: H. W. Wilson, 1949.

Fay, Amy. *Music Study in Germany.* Edited by Mrs. Fay Pierce. New York: Macmillan, 1880.

Finck, Henry T. *My Adventures in the Golden Age of Music.* New York and London: Funk and Wagnalls Co., 1926.

Fisher, Renée B. *Musical Prodigies: Masters at an Early Age.* New York: Association Press, 1973.

Fleet, Susan. "Dorothy Miriam Ziegler." In *Jewish Women in America.* New York: Routledge, 1997.

Foster, Agnes Greene. *Eleanor Everest Freer—Patriot and Her Colleagues.* Chicago: Musical Art Publishing Co., 1927.

Freer, Eleanor Everest. *Recollections and Reflections of an American Composer.* Self published, 1929.

French, Florence. *Music and Musicians in Chicago.* Chicago: F. F. French, 1899.

French, Maida Parlow. *Kathleen Parlow: A Portrait.* Toronto: Ryerson Press, 1967.

Gagne, Cole. *Soundpieces 2: Interviews with American Composers.* Metuchen, New Jersey: Scarecrow Press, 1993.

Gaume, Mary Matilda. "Ruth Crawford Seeger: Her Life and Works." Ph.D. dissertation, Indiana University, 1973.

Gerson, Robert A. *Music in Philadelphia.* Philadelphia: University of Pennsylvania Press, 1940.

Gilbert, Steven E. "'The Ultra-modern Idiom': A Survey of New Music." *Perspectives of New Music,* vol. 12, nos. 1 and 2, Fall/Winter 1973, Spring/Summer 1974.

Goetschius, Percy. *Mrs. H. H. A. Beach.* Boston: Arthur P. Schmidt, 1906.

Goldin, Milton. *The Music Merchants.* New York: Macmillan, 1969.

Goss, Madeleine. *Modern Music Makers: Contemporary American Composers.* New York: E. P. Dutton and Co., 1952.

Gourse, Leslie. *Madame Jazz: Contemporary Women Instrumentalists.* New York: Oxford University Press, 1995.

Graham, Shirley. "Spirituals to Symphonies." *Etude Music Magazine,* vol. 54, no. 11, November 1936, p. 691f.

Green, Janet M. *Musical Biographies.* 2 vols. Part of *American History and Encyclopedia of Music.* Edited by W. L. Hubbard. New York: Irving Square, 1908.

Green, Mildred Denby. "A Study of the Lives and Works of Five Black Women Composers in America." Ph.D. dissertation, University of Oklahoma, 1975.

Green, Miriam. "Women: From Silence to Song." *American Music Teacher,* September/October 1974.

Green, Miriam Stewart. "Consider These Creators." *American Music Teacher,* vol. 25, no. 3, January 1976, pp. 9–12.

Groh, Jan. *Evening the Score: Women in Music and the Legacy of Frédérique Petrides.* Fayetteville: University of Arkansas Press, 1991.

Gunden, Heidi von. *The Music of Pauline Oliveros.* Metuchen, New Jersey: Scarecrow Press, 1983.

Hall, Constance Huntington, and Helen Ingersoll Tetlow. *Helen Hopekirk.* Cambridge, Massachusetts: self published, 1954.

Hall, Jacob Henry. *Biography of Gospel Songs and Hymn Writers.* New York: Fleming H. Revell Co., 1914.

Hallman, Diana Ruth. "The Pianist Fannie Bloomfield-Zeisler in American Music and Society." Master's thesis, University of Maryland, 1983.

Handy, D. Antoinette. *Black Conductors.* Metuchen, New Jersey: Scarecrow Press, 1995.

———. *Black Women in American Bands and Orchestras.* Metuchen, New Jersey: Scarecrow Press, 1981.

———. *The International Sweethearts of Rhythm,* rev. ed. Metuchen, New Jersey: Scarecrow Press, 1998.

Harris, Clement Antrobus. "Women Composers of Religious Music." *Musical America,* December 25, 1939, p. 5.

Hart, Philip. *Orpheus in the New World.* New York: W. W. Norton, 1973.

Hasse, John Edward, ed. *Ragtime: Its History, Composers, and Music.* New York: Schirmer Books, 1985.

Hewitt, John Hill. *Shadows on the Wall, or Glimpses of the Past: A Retrospect of the Past Fifty Years.* Baltimore: Turnbull Brothers, 1877.

Hipsher, Edward Ellsworth. *American Opera and Its Composers.* Philadelphia: Theodore Presser, 1927.

Hisama, Ellie M. "Gender, Politics, and Modernist Music: Analyses of Five Compositions by Ruth Crawford and Marion Bauer." Ph.D. dissertation, City University of New York, 1996.

———. *Gendering Musical Modernism: The Music of Ruth Crawford, Marion Bauer, and Miriam Gideon.* New York: Cambridge University Press, forthcoming.

History of Music in San Francisco. 7 vols. San Francisco: United States Works Progress Administration, Northern California. 1939–42.

History of the Handel and Haydn Society, 2 vols. Vol. 1 edited by Charles C. Perkins and John Sullivan Dwight. Boston: Alfred Mudge and Son, 1883–93. Vol. 2 edited by William Frothingharn Bradbury. Boston: Handel and Haydn Society, 1911.

Hixon, Donald L., and Don Hennessee. *Women in Music: A Biobibliography.* Metuchen, New Jersey: Scarecrow Press, 1975.

Homer, Sidney. *My Wife and I.* New York: Macmillan, 1939.

Hood, George. *History of Music in New England with Biographical Sketches of Reformers and Psalmists.* Boston: Wilkin Carter and Co., 1846.

Howard, John Tasker. *Our American Music: A Comprehensive History.* 4th ed. New York: Thomas Y. Crowell, 1965.

———. "The Hewitt Family in American Music." *Musical Quarterly,* January 1931.

Howe, M. A. De Wolfe. *The Boston Symphony Orchestra 1881–1931.* Boston: Houghton Mifflin, 1931.

Howe, Mary. *Jottings.* Washington, D.C.: self published, 1959.

Hughes, Rupert. *Contemporary American Composers.* Boston: L. C. Page and Co., 1900.

Huneker, James Gibbons. *Overtones: A Book of Temperaments.* New York: Charles Scribner's Sons, 1904.

———. *The Philharmonic and It Seventy-fifth Anniversary: A Restropect.* N.p., n.d.

In Memoriam Mary Turner Salter. N.p., n.d.

Jepson, Barbara. "American Women in Conducting." *Feminist Art Journal,* Winter 1975–76, pp. 13–18.

Johnson, Harold Earle. *Hallelujah, amen! The Story of the Handel and Haydn Society of Boston.* Boston: Bruce Humphries, 1965.

———. *Musical Interludes in Boston, 1795–1830.* New York: Columbia University Press, 1943. Reprint. New York: AMS Press, 1967.

———. *Symphony Hall, Boston.* Boston: Little, Brown and Co., 1950.

Johnson, Tom. "Lucia Dlugoszewski." *High Fidelity/Musical America,* vol. 25, no. 6, June 1975, pp. MA-5–6.

Jones, F. O., ed. *Handbook of American Music and Musicians.* Canaseraga, New York: Jones, 1886.

Jones, John Robert Douglas. "The Choral Works of Undine Smith Moore: A Study of Her Life Work." Ed.D. dissertation, New York University, 1980.

Jowett, Deborah, ed. *Meredith Monk.* Baltimore: Johns Hopkins University Press, 1987.

Kagan, Susan. "Camilla Urso: A Nineteenth-Century Violinist's View." *Signs,* vol. 2, no. 3, Spring 1977, pp. 727–34.

Keefer, Lubov. *Music Angels: A Thousand Years of Patronage.* Baltimore: Sutherland Press, 1976.

Kendall, Alan. *The Tender Tyrant: Nadia Boulanger.* Wilton, Connecticut: Lyceum Books, 1976.

Kline, Donna Staley. *Olga Samaroff: An American Virtuoso on the World Stage.* College Station, Texas: Texas A and M University Press, 1996.

Kolodin, Irving. *The Metropolitan Opera 1883–1966.* 4th ed. New York: Alfred A. Knopf, 1966.

Krehbiel, Henry Edward. *The Philharmonic Society of New York: A Memorial.* New York and London: Novello, Ewer and Co., 1892.

Krueger, Karl. *The Musical Heritage of the United States.* New York: Society for the Preservation of the American Musical Heritage, 1973.

Ladd, George Trumbull. *Why Women Cannot Compose Music.* New Haven, Connecticut: Yale Publishing Association, 1917.

Lahee, Henry Charles. *Annals of Music in America.* Boston: Marshall Jones Co., 1922.

————. *Famous Pianists in America.* Boston: L. C. Page and Co., 1901.

————. *Famous Violinists in America.* Boston: L. C. Page and Co., 1899.

————. *The Organ and Its Masters.* Boston: L. C. Page and Co., 1903.

Lang, Paul Henry, ed. *One Hundred Years of Music in America.* New York: Grosset and Dunlap, 1961.

Le Page, Jane Weiner. *Women Composers, Conductors, and Musicians of the Twentieth Century.* 3 vols. Metuchen, New Jersey: Scarecrow Press, 1980–1986.

Locke, Ralph P., and Cyrilla Barr. *Cultivating Music in America: Women Patrons and Activists since 1860.* Berkeley: University of California Press, 1997.

Loesser, A. *Men, Women, and Pianos.* New York: Simon and Schuster, 1954.

Lowens, Irving. *Music and Musicians in Early America.* New York: W. W. Norton, 1964.

MacBridge, Jessie, and Dorothy DeMuth Watson. "American Women Composers Hold Festival in Washington." *Musical America,* vol. 52, no. 9, May 10, 1932, pp. 20, 40.

MacDonald, Margaret I., ed. *The Greatest Battles Ever Fought Are the Silent Ones Fought by Women.* Self published, March 17, 1918.

McPartland, Marian. *All in Good Time.* New York: Oxford University Press, 1981.

Mangler, Joyce Ellen. *Rhode Island Music and Musicians 1733–1850.* Detroit: Information Service, 1965.

"Margaret Hillis." *Panpipes,* vol. 68, no. 4, May 1976, p. 22.

Mathews, W. S. B. *A Hundred Years of Music in America.* Chicago: G. L. Howe, 1889. Reprint. New York: AMS Press.

————. "Personal Glimpses of Teresa Carreño." *Music,* vol. 11, 1896, pp. 142ff.

McCarthy, Margaret William. *Amy Fay: America's Notable Woman of Music.* Warren, Michigan: Harmonie Park Press, 1995.

McCusker, Honor. *Fifty Years of Music in Boston.* Boston: Trustees of the Public Library, 1938.

McKay, David P., and Richard Crawford. *William Billings of Boston.* Princeton, New Jersey: Princeton University Press, 1975.

Menuhin, Yehudi. *Unfinished Journey.* New York: Alfred A. Knopf, 1977.

Merrill, E. Lindsey. "Mrs. H. H. A. Beach: Her Life and Music." Ph.D. dissertation, University of Rochester Eastman School of Music, 1963.

Milinowski, Marta. *Teresa Carreño, "By the Grace of God."* New Haven: Yale University Press, 1940.

Möller, Heinrich. "Can Women Compose?" *Musical Observer,* vol. 15, nos. 5 and 6, May and June 1910, pp. 9–10, 11–12.

Moore, John W. *Complete Encyclopaedia of Music.* Boston: Oliver Ditson Co., 1876.

Morin, Raymond. *The Worcester Music Festival, Its Background and History 1858–1946.* Worcester, Massachusetts: Worcester County Music Association, 1946.

Morini, Erica. "Women as Musicians." *Who Is Who in Music,* Chicago, 1940–41, pp. 76–77.

Mueller, John H. *The American Symphony Orchestra.* Bloomington: Indiana University Press, 1951.

Mumma, Gordon. "Live Electronic Music." In *The Development and Practice of Electronic Music.* Edited by Jon H. Appleton and Ronald C. Perera. Englewood Cliffs, New Jersey: Prentice-Hall, 1975.

The Musical Woman: An International Perspective, 3 vols. Judith Lang Zaimont, Catherine Overhauser, Jane Gottlieb, and Michael J. Rogan, eds. Westport, Connecticut: Greenwood Press, 1984, 1987, 1991.

Naylor, Blanche. *The Anthology of the Fadettes.* Boston: n.p., 194?.

Neuls-Bates, Carol. "Sources and Resources for Women's Studies in American Music: A Report." *Notes,* vol. 35, no. 2, December 1978.

Nicholson, Jim. *Billie Holiday.* London: Victor Gollancz, 1995.

Norton/Grove Dictionary of Women Composers. Julie Anne Sadie and Rhian Samuel, eds. New York: W. W. Norton and Co., 1995.

Ochse, Orpha. *The History of the Organ in the United States.* Bloomington: Indiana University Press, 1975.

Odell, George C. D. *Annals of the New York Stage.* 5 vols. New York: Columbia University Press, 1931.

Oliveiros, Pauline, "And Don't Call Them 'Lady' Composers." *New York Times,* May 13, 1970.

Opera News, February 14, 1976, p. 14.

"Opinions of Some New York Leaders on Women as Orchestral Players." *Musical Standard,* vol. 21, no. 535, April 2, 1904, pp. 217–18.

Osburn, Mary Hubbell. *Ohio Composers and Musical Authors.* Self published, 1942.

Otis, Philo Adams. *The Chicago Symphony Orchestra: Its Organization, Growth, and Development 1891–1924.* Chicago: Clayton F. Summy, 1924.

Paige, Paul Eric. "Musical Organizations in Boston: 1830–1850." Ph.D. dissertation, Boston University, 1967.

Paige, Raymond. "Why Not Women in Orchestras?" *Etude Music Magazine,* January 1952, pp. 14–15.

Parker, John Rowe. *Musical Biography, Or Sketches of the Lives and Writings of Eminent Musical Characters.* Boston: Stone and Fovell, 1824.

Patterson, Lindsay, ed. *The Negro in Music and Art (International Library of Negro Life and History).* New York: Publishers Company, 1967.

Pendle, Karin, ed., *Women and Music: A History.* Bloomington: Indiana University Press, 1991.

Penny, Virginia. *The Employments of Women: A Cyclopaedia of Woman's Work.* Boston: Walker, Wise and Co., 1863.

Perle, George. "The Music of Miriam Gideon." *American Composers Alliance Bulletin,* vol. 7, no. 4, 1958.

Petrides, Frederique. "Women in Orchestras." *Etude Music Magazine,* vol. 16, no. 7, July 1938, pp. 429ff.

Petteys, M. Leslie. "Julie Rivé-King, American Pianist." D.M.A. thesis, University of Missouri, Kansas City, 1987.

Phillips, Karen. "Women Musicians Offer Advice." *Music Journal,* vol. 32, no. 3, March 1974, pp. 18ff.

Pincherle, Marc. *The World of the Virtuoso.* Translated by Lucile H. Brockway. New York: W. W. Norton, 1963.

Plackson, Sally. *American Women in Jazz, 1900 to the Present.* New York: Seaview Books, 1982.

Powell, Maud. "The Violinist." *Delineator,* October 1911, p. 274.

Reis, Claire. *Composers in America: Biographical Sketches of Living Composers with a Record of Their Works, 1912–1937.* 1st ed., 1938. Rev. ed. New York: Macmillan, 1947.

Rich, Alan. *Careers and Opportunities in Music.* New York: E. P. Dutton and Co., 1964.

Riegger, Wallingford. "The Music of Vivian Fine." *American Composers Alliance Bulletin,* vol. 8, no. 1, 1958.

Ritter, Fanny Raymond. *Lyre, Pen, and Pencil: Essays, Studies, Sketches.* Edited by Millie W. Carpenter. New York: Edward Schuberth and Co., 1891.

Ritter, Frédéric Louis. *Music in America.* Rev. ed. New York: Charles Scribner's Sons., 1890.

Rivé, Caroline. *Madame Rivé's System of Sight Singing, based upon Rodolphe's solfeggi.* Cincinnati: John Church and Co., 187?.

Roach, Hildred. *Black American Music: Past and Present.* Boston: Crescendo Publishing Company, 1973.

Rogers, Clara Kathleen. *Clara Kathleen Rogers, The Story of Two Lives: Home, Friends, and Travel.* Norwood, Massachusetts: Plimpton Press, 1932.

Rosenberg, Deena, and Bernard Rosenberg. *The Music Makers.* New York: Columbia University Press, 1979.

Ryan, Thomas. *Recollections of an Old Musician.* New York: E. P. Dutton, 1899.

Sablosky, Irving L. *American Music.* Chicago and London: University of Chicago Press, 1969.

Saenger, Gustav. "Maud Powell." *Musical Observer,* vol. 8, no. 4, August 1913.

"Salute to an American Woman Composer [Julia Smith]." *Music Clubs Magazine,* vol. 49, no. 2, Winter 1969–70, p. 8.

Sand, Barbara Lourie. *Teaching Genius: Dorothy DeLay and the Making of a Musician.* Portland, Oregon: Amadeus Press, 2000.

Samaroff Stokowski, Olga. *An American Musician's Story.* New York: W. W. Norton, 1939.

Sargeant, Winthrop. *Geniuses, Goddesses, and People.* New York: E. P. Dutton, 1949.

Sax, Alphonse, Jr. *Gymnastique des Poumons: La Musique Instrumentale au point de vue de l'Hygiène et la Création des Orchestres féminins.* Paris: n.p., 1865.

Scheibert, Beverly. "Equal Opportunities in Church Hiring." *Diapason,* August 1976, p. 2.

Schwartz, Elliott. *Electronic Music: A Listener's Guide.* New York: Praeger Publishers, 1973.

Scruggs, Leigh K. "Creative Women in Music." *Music Clubs Magazine,* vol. 55, no. 2, Winter 1975–76, pp. 8–9.

Seabury, Deborah. "La Maestra." *Opera News,* February 14, 1976.

Searle, Humphrey, and Robert Laton. *Twentieth Century Composers.* Vol. 3, *Britain, Scandinavia, and the Netherlands.* New York: Holt, Rinehart and Winston, 1972.

Seeger, Charles. "Ruth Crawford." In *American Composers on American Music.* Edited by Henry Cowell. 1933; renewed 1961. Reprint. New York: Frederick Ungar Publishing Co., 1961.

Shaffer, Karen A., and Neva Garner Greenwood. *Maud Powell: Pioneer American Violinist.* Arlington, Virginia: The Maud Powell Foundation and Ames: Iowa State University Press, 1988.

Shanet, Howard. *Philharmonic: A History of New York's Orchestra.* New York: Doubleday and Co., 1975.

Slenczynska, Ruth, and Louis Biancolli. *Forbidden Childhood.* New York: Doubleday and Co., 1957.

Smith, Catherine Parsons, and Cynthia S. Richardson. *Mary Carr Moore, American Composer.* Ann Arbor: University of Michigan Press, 1987.

Smith, Eva Munson, ed. *Woman in Sacred Song.* Boston: D. Lothrop and Co., 1885.

Smith, Geoff, and Nicola Walker Smith. *New Voices: American Composers Talk about Their Music.* Portland, Oregon: Amadeus Press, 1995.

Smith, Julia. *Aaron Copland.* New York: E. P. Dutton, 1955.

Smith, Leona May. "Is There a Career for Women Musicians?" *Metronome,* January 1938, p. 48.

Smyth, Ethel. *Female Pipings in Eden.* London: Peter Davies, Ltd., 1933.

Sonneck, Oscar George Theodore. *A Bibliography of Early Secular American*

Music. Revised by William Treat Upton. Washington, D.C.: Library of Congress, 1945. Reprint. New York: Da Capo Press, 1964.

————. *Early Concert-Life in America, 1731–1800.* Leipzig: Breitkopf and Härtel, 1907. Reprint. Musurgia Publishers, 1949.

————. *Early Opera in America.* New York: G. Schirmer, 1915.

Southern, Eileen. *The Music of Black Americans: A History,* 1st ed. 1971. 3rd ed. New York: W. W. Norton, 1997.

————. *Readings in Black American Music.* New York: W. W. Norton, 1971.

Starr, Susan. "The Prejudice Against Women." *Music Journal,* vol. 32, no. 3, March 1974, pp. 14ff.

Stewart, Nancy. "The Solo Piano Music of Marion Bauer." Ph.D. dissertation, University of Cincinnati, 1990.

Stoddard, Hope. *Symphony Conductors of the United States of America.* New York: Thomas Y. Crowell Co., 1957.

————. "Fine Musicianship Knows No Sex." *Independent Woman,* November 1947.

Stoeving, Paul. *The Violin: Its Famous Makers and Players.* Boston: Oliver Ditson Co., 1928.

Sutro, Florence. *Women in Music and Law.* New York: Authors' Publishing Company, 1895.

Swados, Elizabeth. *Listening Out Loud: Becoming a Composer.* New York: Harper and Row, 1988.

Talalay, Kathryn. *Composition in Black and White: The Life of Philippa Schuyler.* New York: Oxford University Press, 1995.

Taylor, Frank, and Gerald Cook. *Alberta Hunter: A Celebration in Blues.* New York: McGraw-Hill, 1987.

Taylor, Vivian, ed. *Art Songs and Spirituals by African-American Women Composers.* Bryn Mawr, Pennsylvania: Hildegard Publishing Company, 1995.

Thomas, Theodore. *A Musical Autobiography.* 2 vols. Edited by George P. Upton. Chicago: A. C. McClurg and Co., 1905. Reprint of vol. 1. New York: Da Capo Press, 1964.

Thomson, Virgil. *American Music Since 1910.* New York: Holt, Rinehart and Winston, 1971.

Tick, Judith. *American Women Composers before 1870.* Ann Arbor: UMI Research Press, 1983.

————. *Ruth Crawford Seeger: A Composer's Search for American Music.* New York: Oxford University Press, 1997.

————. "Women as Professional Musicians in the United States, 1870–1900." *Yearbook for Inter-American Research in Music,* vol. 9, 1973, pp. 95–133.

————. "Why Have There Been No Great Women Composers, or Notes on the Score of Sexual Aesthetics?" *International Musician,* vol. 74, no. 1, July 1975, p. 6.

Towers, John. *Woman in Music.* Winchester, Virginia: 1897.

Trotter, James M. *Music and Some Highly Musical People.* Boston: Lee and Shepard, 1878. Reprint. Johnson Reprint Corp., 1968.

Tucker, Sherrie, "Female Big Bands, Male Mass Audiences: Gendered Performances in a Theater of War." *Women in Music,* vol. 2, 1998, pp. 64–89.

Tuthill, Burnet C. "Mrs. H. H. A. Beach." *Musical Quarterly,* July 1940, pp. 297–310.

Upton, George P. *Musical Memories 1850–1900.* Chicago: A. C. McClury and Co., 1908.

———. *Woman in Music.* 6th ed. Chicago: n.p., 1899.

Upton, William T. *Art-Song in America.* Boston: Oliver Ditson Co., 1930.

Urso, Camilla. *Violin-Playing and the Paris Conservatory.* Vol. 1 of *The Music of the Modern World.* Edited by Anton Seidl. New York: D. Appleton and Co., 1895.

Van der Straeten, E. *The History of the Violin.* 2 vols. London: Cassell and Co., Ltd., 1933.

Van de Vate, Nancy. "Notes from a Bearded Lady: The American Woman Composer." *International Musician,* vol. 74, no. 1, July 1975.

———. "The American Woman Composer: Some Sour Notes." *High Fidelity/Musical America,* vol. 25, no. 6, June 1975, pp. MA-18–19.

———. "Every Good Boy (Composer) Does Fine." *Symphony News,* December 1973/January 1974.

Vinton, John, ed. *Dictionary of Contemporary Music.* New York: E. P. Dutton and Co., 1974.

Walker, Greta. *Women Today: Ten Profiles.* New York: Hawthorn Books, 1975.

Walker-Hill, Helen, ed. *Black Women Composers: A Century of Piano Music.* Bryn Mawr, Pennsylvania: Hildegard Publishing Company, 1992.

Wallace, Robert K. *A Century of Music-Making: The Lives of Josef and Rosina Lhévinne.* Bloomington: Indiana University Press, 1976.

Ward, John Owen. *Careers in Music.* New York: Henry Z. Walck, 1968.

Wier, Albert E. *The Piano: Its History, Makers, Players, and Music.* New York: Longmans, Green and Co., 1941.

Willhartitz, Adolf. *Some Facts About Woman in Music.* Los Angeles: Out West Co., 1902.

Williams, Amedee Daryl. *Lillian Fuchs, First Lady of the Viola.* Lewiston, New York: Edwin Mellen Press, 1994.

Winn, Edith L. "Maud Powell as I Knew Her." *Musical Observer* vol. 19, no. 3, March 1920, pp. 58–59.

Wolff, Konrad. "Dika Newlin." *American Composers Alliance Bulletin,* vol. 10, no. 4, December 1962.

Wolverton, Byron Adams. "Keyboard Music and Musicians in the Colonies and United States of America Before 1830." Ph.D. dissertation, Indiana University, 1966.

Yuhasz, Sister Marie Joy, O.P. "Black Composers and Their Piano Music." *American Music Teacher,* vol. 19, no. 4, February/March 1970, pp. 24–26.

INDEX

Boldface is used for the pages containing an individual's principal biographical information.